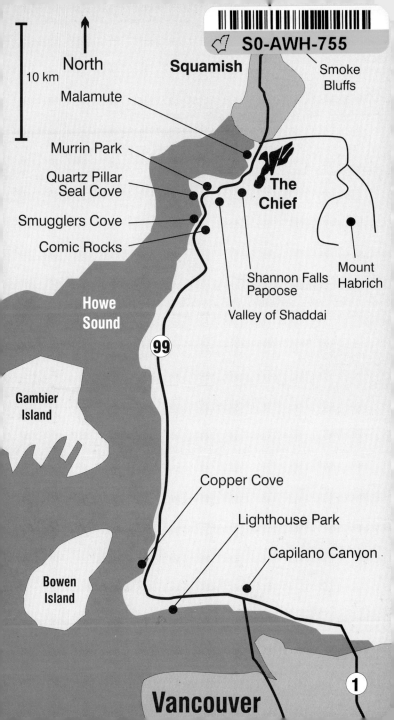

North

10 km

Squamish

Smoke Bluffs

Malamute

Murrin Park

Quartz Pillar
Seal Cove

Smugglers Cove

Comic Rocks

The Chief

Shannon Falls
Papoose

Valley of Shaddai

Mount Habrich

Howe Sound

99

Gambier Island

Copper Cove

Lighthouse Park

Capilano Canyon

Bowen Island

Vancouver

1

THE CLIMBERS
GUIDE TO
SQUAMISH

Kevin McLane

1999
Elaho Publishing Corporation

The Climbers Guide To Squamish

Original edition June 1999; this revised edition March 2001.

© Kevin McLane 2001

ISBN 0-9682472-1-0

Elaho Publishing Corporation, Squamish BC.
Printed in Canada by Kromar Printing Ltd, Winnipeg, Manitoba.

Front: Joe Turley and Marc Bombois on *Sunblessed*
Back: John Howe on *Unfinished Symphony.*
Kai Hirvonen on *Tantalus Crack*. **Photo:** Richard Wheater
Josh Korman on *Burning Down The Couch*

All uncredited photos, graphics and book design by Kevin McLane

Canadian Cataloguing in Publication Data

McLane, Kevin, date-
  The Climbers Guide To Squamish
  Previous edition has title: The Rockclimbers Guide to Squamish
  Includes index.
  1. Rock climbing--British Columbia--Squamish Region--Guidebooks.
  2. Squamish Region (B.C.)--Guidebooks. I. Title II
  Title: The Rockclimbers Guide to Squamish
  GV199.44.C22B7463 1999   796.5'223'0971131   C99-910280-X

The publisher wishes to acknowledge the support of the BC Mountaineering Club toward publication of this guidebook.

§

This guide is dedicated to all those who come to Squamish in search of stone, adventure and discovery.

§

6

Contents

Contents

ADVERTISERS

Introduction

It is seven years since the last edition of the climbers guide to Squamish was published in 1992, and much has changed in that time. There are many more climbs and far more climbers, spreading over a wider range of territory, and a rockclimbing community that is thriving and vibrating with energy. This is especially noticeable in Squamish itself, now with upwards of 300-500 residents who climb; some for the fun of it, and those who live for nothing else.

The previous edition of the guide listed about 680 climbs in the area covered by this one–North Vancouver to Squamish–this guide holds 1,250. Not all are new climbs, over 100 were culled from previous editions going back to Glenn Woodsworths 1964 guide, some of which had never been reported, but this guide is indeed an attempt to give a comprehensive listing of all the energy and development that has gone into rockclimbing at Squamish in more than four decades. It is quite a collection of human endeavour. Climbs north of Squamish, through the Cheakamus Canyon and Whistler to Pemberton, have not been included as that area has more than enough climbs to merit a guide of its own.

So what's new?
In 1995, after years of lobbying, the Chief became Stawamus Chief Provincial Park–a class A park–and became protected from commercial and industrial development. BC Parks is the government agency that now controls the Chief, and a sense of order and good management has replaced the previous free-for-all attitudes of both climbers and wannabe developers. However, the Smoke Bluffs remain a municipal and political jungle. Hopefully, by the time of the next edition of this guide, it too will have received long-needed protection as a civic park.

Climbing at Squamish has broadened its attraction considerably in the last decade and is no longer the preserve of those willing to stick their necks out every time they step on the rock. Sport climbing really got going at Squamish shortly after the last guide was published, and has developed great appeal. It is well-suited to those who want to pursue technical difficulty in a low-risk setting and novices who want to simply enjoy rockclimbing without the need to grapple with the esoteric joys of placing gear. That covers pretty well everybody at one time or another. The advent of climbing gyms has fuelled this phenomenon, and climbing is richer and more diverse as a result.

At the opposite end of the risk spectrum, and which is probably not a coincidence, there has been a remarkable renaissance in aid climbing. Scarcely a week goes by without several parties up on the walls of the Grand, whatever the weather or season, a rare sight since the days of the 1970s. Unlike sport climbing, which appeals to a wide cross-section of people, modern aid climbing is driven by a new generation of young climbers who enjoy pushing limits in wild places, and for whom risk is one of the attractions. But there is nothing new about that, it is one of the oldest traditions of climbing.

The boulders that are scattered and hidden in the forest below the Chief have become the focus of great attention. Several hundred problems have been developed over the last three years, largely as a result of the dedication of a small group of Victoria-based climbers. The problems all have names, grades and tales, as any other climb, and hopefully will soon be collected together in the form of a guide. Unfortunately they are not included here—it is too much for this guidebook. The exploration of all the bouldering potential below the Chief is yet another indication of how the culture of rockclimbing is diversifying.

Although many climbers have committed great amounts of time and energy to developing new climbs in the last seven years, two climbers in particular—Glenn Payan and Jeff Thomson—have made a remarkable contribution, with well over 150 new climbs to their credit, opening up entirely new areas such as the Valley of Shaddai, the Upper Malamute, and Seal Cove. Andrew Boyd made a number of fine ascents in 1997 and 1998, including the first free ascent of The Opal, proving that the art of hard gear leads is far from disappearing. And as ever, Robin Barley continues to scope and climb new routes at an astonishing rate. And now, in the spring of 1999, Uncle Bens on the Grand is undergoing a sustained effort to climb it free by Jim and Jola Sandford. History in the making.

It is now 41 years since the first rockclimb was established at Squamish, *Peasants Route*, by Les McDonald and Jim Baldwin, a few months before the highway from Vancouver was completed. Since then, the scale of the enterprise has echoed around the world. Squamish is now one of the planet's finest granite rockclimbing areas, evident every year with the number of happy Europeans and international visitors, for whom 'Squamish' is synonomous with superb climbs, excellence and potential.

Kevin McLane

May 1999

10 **Acknowledgements**

I wish to give deep thanks for the effort and encouragement so many people have given toward successful completion of this guide. Without such support, it would not be possible. My very special thanks to Glenn Payan for his wicked editing, and Colin Moorhead, Jeff Thomson, Robin Barley, Luc Mailloux and Sean Easton for their enthusiasm and suggestions.

For general feedback and corrections, my thanks to Perry Beckham, Andrew Boyd, Will Dorling, David Harris, Dean Hart, Jack Fieldhouse, Greg Foweraker, Hamish Fraser, John Howe, Sig Isaac, Matt Maddaloni, Peter Michaux, Brian Pegg, Anders Ourom, Jim Sandford and Richard Wheater, and to Ron Enns for sharp editing.

My thanks Aaron Black, Jia Condon, Fred Beckey, Jack Fieldhouse, David Harris, Angela Muellers, Rich Prohaska and Richard Wheater for generous use of their excellent photographs, and again to Angela Muellers for her expertise helping with crag drawings. Special recognition is due to Jim Campbell, whose detailed and exhaustive topos from his 1985 guide continued to used by many climbers long after the 1992 guide was published.

And finally, a sincere thank you to my sons Barry and Tony for their patient assistance with many things.

Thanks also to:

Ron and Lisa Clements	Marc Gandy	Jean McRae
Chris Atkinson	Chris Geisler	Peder Ourom
Fred Beckey	Brian Goldstone	Howie Richardson
Tom Bell, BC Parks	Ron Goldstone	Janet Roddan
Marc Bombois	Vicky Haberl, BC Parks	Rolf Rybak
Russ Booth	Kai Hirvonen	Jola Sandford
Marc Bourdon	Dave Jones	Brandin Schultz, BC Parks
Drew Brayshaw	Tyler Jordan	Jim Sinclair
Tom Clark	Damien Kelly	Graeme Taylor
Jason Camp	Bill Kipper	Chris Trautmann
Anthony Chahal	Larry Klein	MEC climbing staff
Rob Cocquyt	Tami Knight	Joe Turley
John Crooks, BCFS	Bruce McDonald	Alistair Veitch
Vicky Earle	Gary McFarlane	Glenn Woodsworth
Jim Firstbrook	Don McPherson	. . . apologies to anyone missed

Bibliography Of Past Squamish Guides

Jim Baldwin	A Climber's Guide To The Squamish Chief	1962
Dick Culbert	A Climber's Guide To The Coastal Ranges of BC *(Partial)*	1964
Glenn Woodsworth	A Climber's Guide To The Squamish Chief	1967
Dick Culbert	Alpine Guide To Southwestern BC *(Partial)*	1974
Gordie Smaill	Squamish Chief Guide	1975
Anders Ourom	A Climber's Guide To The Squamish Chief	1980
Kevin McLane	Squamish - The New Freeclimbs	1984
Jim Campbell	Rock Climbs of The Little Smoke Bluffs	1984
Jim Campbell	Squamish Rockclimbs	1985
Kevin McLane	The Rockclimbers Guide To Squamish	1992
Marc Bourdon / Scott Tasaka	Sport Climbing in Squamish *(Partial)*	1998

Squamish is located on the southwest coast of British Columbia, Canada, about 60km north of the city of Vancouver. The rugged mountainous coastline of British Columbia is one of the world's great scenic wonders, a land of deep inlets and vast dense forests of tall douglas fir, cedar and hemlock. High mountain ranges and vast icefields tumble from the interior into the ocean. The dense forest landscape and the corresponding lush undergrowth are a hallmark of almost all the crags in this guide. While much of the United States scorches in summer heat, Squamish is green and pleasant.

The population of Squamish is around 16,000 and growing. Tourism, city commuters and some heavy industry are the mainstays of the local economy. This is the centre of a world-class playground for adventure sports: rockclimbing, mountainbiking, alpine hiking, backcountry skiing, windsurfing, mountaineering and whitewater rafting are all major. Estimates of the number of Squamish residents who climb are between 300 and 500 depending on the season, and rising fast.

The Highway from Vancouver to Squamish and Whistler is legendary for heavy traffic with travellers heading for the playgrounds north of the city. Be prepared for slow driving at busy periods.

If you arrrive at Vancouver International Airport. Squamish is an hour and a half to the north by bus or rented car. Bus travellers can take the airport shuttle bus to Pacific Central Station at Main and Terminal in downtown Vancouver (604) 662-8051. Look for the Pemberton or Whistler bus, which runs several times a day.

Approaching Vancouver from the east. Stay on Highway 1 to Horseshoe Bay then continue along Highway 99 to Squamish. It is about a one hour drive from downtown Vancouver.

Approaching Squamish from the north or the Rockies. Exit the Trans Canada #1 at Cache Creek, head north on 97 for 12km to a junction with Highway 99. This is a scenic mountain route to Squamish through Lillooet, Pemberton, and Whistler enroute.

Approaching Vancouver from Interstate 5. Head north from Bellingham directly to the Trans-Canada Highway #1, east of Vancouver.

A few minutes spent studying these pages will help make it easier to understand how best to use this guide, and the meanings of the various symbols and abbreviations used throughout.

♦ **To find a crag.** Use the Table of Contents.

♦ **To find a climb.** Use the Index, which starts on page 434.

♦ **Right** and **left** assume the climber to be facing the rock.

♦ **Pitch lengths** generally refer to the length of the climbing rather than the amount of rope required, although in many cases, single pitch climbs which are indicated as between 25m and 30m refer to the amount rope required for lowering.

♦ **Topos.** In most cases, a photograph is used as the base for a topo. Where decent crag photos are not possible, hand-drawings are used. In the case of multi-pitch climbs of 5 pitches or more, hand-drawn topos of the route are given, as well as a photo-topo for additional clarity.

♦ **Rating stars** indicate the relative quality of the climbs.

   *   Worth doing   **   A quality climb   *** A stellar climb
   ●   A once-clean route which has badly overgrown. This is not an exact science, as conditions change every season.
   ☺   A black-spot route which offers good climbing—worth re-cleaning. It is an estimate only, other climbs may be equally deserving.

♦ **Grading.** The following designations adjacent to the name of the climb are used in addition to the standard YDS free grade.

11c (10a+2pa)	Indicates that if 2 points of fixed aid are used, the free grade will drop several letters.
11c (10a)	Indicates that the first pitch or two are worth climbing in their own right, at a much easier grade.
#7	The number of bolts on a sport route.
#	An all-fixed climb which is too runout to be called sport.
<u>299</u>	The page number of a topo of the climb.
x	Indicates there is no topo of that climb.
SPORT	A climb which is all-fixed and has no big run-outs.
SPORT+	A sport climb which requires a few pieces of gear.
(2p.)	Parentheses around a climb's length indicates that climbing another route to reach its start is required.

♦   **Stuff to read..** The following pages are suggested reading if you are unfamiliar with local ways.

♦   **Gear lists.** The gear lists as given for the longer routes are a suggestion only. Some climbers will be comfortable with less, some will want more. Sizes of camming devices are shown in inches, rather than brand names, and they are referred to as a CU, for Cam Unit (or CD).

Abbreviations

m	metres
km	Kilometres
FP	Fixed pin
CU	Spring-Loaded Cam Device
TR	Point of aid
pa	Top-rope climb (not led)
var.	Variation
RPs	Small brass wires

First Ascent Credits

FA	First Ascent
FFA	First Free Ascent
FRA	First Recorded ascent
FCA	First Continous Ascent
2p	Number of pitches
(alts)	Alternate pitches led
c.	Approximate date
p1	specific pitch

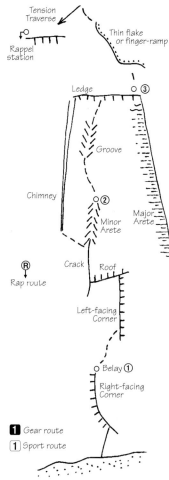

♦ **Camping.** There are several campgrounds in the valley. The best one for climbers is the BC Parks campground at the Chief, with 60 walk-in sites at $8.00 (Canadian) per night per site. Another good one is the Municipal campground at Brennan Park Leisure Centre, a kilometre north of the Smoke Bluffs on Loggers Lane. Both sites are first-come first-served. BC Parks also operates a major drive-in site at Alice Lake Provincial Park, 10km north of Squamish, usually desperately full in high summer. Several other private campgrounds exist; check with the Tourism Information Centre (604) 892-9244.

♦ **Groceries.** There are two large supermarkets in Squamish town centre: Save-On Foods in the Chieftain Centre; and IGA Marketplace in Squamish Station Mall. Both have good vegetarian supplies, as does Health Food Heaven beside Starbucks.

♦ **Restaurants.** Squamish is full of them, but some are especially popular with climbers. For evenings on the main street in the Town Centre, try: Yianni's (Greek); Coyote Cantina (all sorts); and the Indian Hut (as in East Indian); they all offer excellent food. The Red Heather Grill at the Brewpub is more upmarket, but offers some of the best food in Squamish. The Mountain Burger House (24hrs) and the Loaves and Fishes on Cleveland Ave are good for old-style breakfasts and burgers. Taco Bell and Wendy's on the Highway are the best fast-food choices for vegetarians.

♦ **Pubs.** There are several pubs in Squamish, but only one has caught the interest of climbers: the Howe Sound Brewpub at the south end of Cleveland Ave. Deservedly so: they sell a range of excellent natural beers from their own microbrewery, including the legendary Baldwin & Cooper Ale (the first ascentionists of the Grand). The place is hugely popular with mountainbikers too, and the grub is excellent.

♦ **Lattes and Goodies.** Three places are popular with climbers: Starbucks in Squamish Station Mall, a popular gathering place for morning where-shall-we-go sessions in the sun; Xanthines on Cleveland Ave, with a casual sit-down-and-relax atmosphere, and the Sunflower Bakery on the next block of Cleveland Ave: great baked goods and a long-time favourite of climbers.

♦ **The Aquatic Centre.** The municipal pool is well worth checking out. Great for showers (only $1), the hot tub and a large modern swimming pool ($3.25). It's at Brennan Park Leisure Centre on Loggers Lane, a kilometre north of the Smoke Bluff Parking Centre and within walking distance of the Smoke Bluffs.

♦ **Climbing Gear.** There are several climbing stores in Squamish. Climb On on beside Save On Foods, has all you need for cragging, and the local new route book is kept there. Valhalla Pure beside IGA in Squamish Station mall operates a full-featured climbing store and Vertical Reality on Second Ave offers a range of services.

♦ **The Climbing Gym.** Squamish has gone from no gyms to at least two in two years. Howe Sound Secondary School, Brackendale Junior High both have full-featured walls, although it is uncertain if they are open to the public yet. And the bouldering cave at Climb On has gone from a wee pit to a large cavern. Great for rainy days.

♦ **Bank Machines.** There are ATMs at the 4 banking institutions in Squamish Town Centre, and at both the major supermarkets.

♦ **Tourism Information Centre.** The Tourism Information Centre is at the south end of Cleveland Ave. Easy to find, on the Chief side of the street. Call (604) 892-9244. They are a good source of local information on hotels, motels, private campgrounds and some excellent Bed and Breakfast locations.

♦ **Post Office.** On Cleveland Ave, Chief side.

♦ **The Public Library.** The excellent public library is well worth visiting on rest days, or to check your e-mail. A nice place to while some time away in pursuit of study or quiet reading. It's on Second Ave in the Town Centre, three blocks south of Chieftain Centre.

♦ **Guiding Services.** There are three local operators: Slipstream 800-616-1325, Squamish Rock Guides (604) 892-2086 and Cloudraker (604) 892-6384. All provide good services.

♦ **Mountainbiking.** Squamish is the major centre for mountainbiking in British Columbia, so if you can, bring your bike along and head for the trails: great for rained-out days. Squamish is also the home of one of the world's great mountainbike races, the legendary 67km Test of Mettle which passes through the Smoke Bluffs.

♦ **Shoe Repair.** Newport Cobbler on Second Ave does an ace job of rock shoe repairs. Quick turnaround for road-trippers.

♦ **Hiking.** For a peaceful easy walk of a half-hour or more, head for the Squamish River estuary. An excellent map and brochure is available at the nearby Howe Sound Brewpub.

♦ **Squamish Hostel.** The most economic place to stay in town for those with little or no budget is the Squamish Hostel on Buckley Avenue. Run by climbers, full of climbers.

The grading system used in this guide is the decimal system, as used across North America. Technical rockclimbs are graded on a numerical scale from the easiest at 5.0, through to 5.14. Grades from 5.10 ('five-ten') upward are further subdivided into a, b, c, and d. In general, grades are quite consistent on the more popular and older routes, but this is less true with newer climbs, where a letter-grade off may occur. The stated grades should always be used as a guide to the difficulty, not a definitive statement. They can be wrong... The 5th class prefix has been dropped to avoid repetition.

For fledgelings who have little idea what the art of technical grades and the finer points of ascent style are all about, rest assured you are in good company. Nominally, the **5.** prefix ('fifth class') refers to technical rockclimbing requiring ropes and protection equipment. **4.** ('4th class') refers to climbing that requires only a rope and belay stations. **3.** ('third class') indicates that a rope is not needed, typically called 'soloing'. Grades **2.** and **1.** are never used. Most novices gain their introduction to the rock in the **5.6-5.8** grades. At **5.9**, you're getting there, and **5.10** is the happy level that most weekend warriors are able to lead: the doorway to the great climbs of Squamish. To be able to climb **5.11** will get you onto a vast number of stellar Squamish routes: and is an ideal level to achieve, but requires training for most people. **5.12** requires a lot of time at the crag and training. **5.13** is the highest grade in this guide, and demands great talent as well as dedication. Most climbers will be able to lead 2-4 letter grades higher on sport routes than on gear routes. For aid grades, see page 318.

▄▄▄ VALID LEAD ASCENT STYLES   ▄▄▄

♦   **On-Sight.** No falls your first time ever on a route, and no prior hint of how to make moves, solve cruxes, or protection beta: climbing at its very finest. In-situ draws are okay on sport routes, but pre-placing on gear routes (uncommon) is considered On-Sight with ppg.

♦   **Redpoint.** Sending a worked, or previously climbed route or pitch with no falls. If you fall, you must pull your rope and start the climb again, although it is okay to leave protection gear, or draws placed on lead insitu. Pre-placed draws on sport routes are acceptable, but not pieces on gear routes. The redpoint evolved from the yo-yo in the mid-1980s, which is an ascent with falls where the rope is not pulled. Individual pitches on a multi-pitch climb can be redpointed.

♦   **Flash.** No falls your first time ever on a route, but you already have inside knowledge of moves, cruxes or protection beta. A beta flash is one where someone literally talks you up move by move.

Protection equipment required for this area covers everything from offwidth cracks to bolted sport climbs, with every conceivable type of climb in between. The standard Squamish rack is a range of small to medium size wire nuts and camming devices from ½″ to 3″, some smaller RP-style wires, a dozen quick-draws, and a few standard tape slings. Stickclips are not commonly used in the Squamish area, but if you're determined, you could make one work. On most climbs you can expect to meet some fixed gear. Fifty metre ropes are standard, but 55 metre and 60 metre ropes are helpful for lowering off, especially on sport routes. Double ropes will sometimes offer more security, can help reduce rope drag and improve marginal protection. Rest assured, however, you can have a great time with only a dozen quickdraws, especially if combined with climbing in the Whistler area north of Squamish.

When assessing the gear required to get up and down a climb, it is essential to apply a large dose of common sense. Some climbers require more protection than others in order to be comfortable. Owning a rack of expensive gear is no substitute for understanding the rock and experience. **Competence at assessing and placing protection, setting up belays and good rope handling, are fundamental and life preserving skills for the climber and should never be underestimated.** *Caveat emptor.*

International Grading Systems Compared

Yosemite	French	German	British		Australian
5.9	5c	6	5a		18
5.10a	6a	6+		E1	19
5.10b	6a+	7-	5b	E2	20
5.10c	6b	7			20
5.10d	6b+	7	5c	E3	
5.11a	6c	7+			21
5.11b			6a	E4	22
5.11c	6c+	8-			
5.11d	7a	8		E5	23
5.12a	7a+	8+	6b		24
5.12b	7b	9-		E6	25
5.12c	7b+	9			26
5.12d	7c		6c	E7	27
5.13a	7c+	9+			27
5.13b	8a	10-	7a		28
5.13c	8a+	10		E8	29

Accreditation to the crags and the opportunity to climb is no longer a simple matter. Private lands, user fees, liability concerns, environmental impacts, other users, and management of public land and parks are only some of the issues which affect climbers today. The Climbers Access Society of B.C. is the only group working to help resolve climbers' access issues throughout British Columbia, so its efforts affect all climbers who visit the crags in this province. CASBC was founded in 1995 and has several hundred members, including most climbing-related businesses and clubs in BC.

Access to the crags is becoming an issue almost everywhere in one form or another, and the impacts more pressing once we get there. This is a major trend which will grow, not recede. As climbing becomes mainstream and land managers take notice, our impact brings reaction: not always negative, but almost always discussion is required, action is needed, letters must be written, plans hatched. Someone does this, and if you are not a member of the Access Society, taking out a membership is one simple way of being proactive in your own interests, and directly helping that volunteer.

PLEASE BE AN ADVOCATE FOR YOUR SPORT, JOIN THE ACCESS SOCIETY.

CASBC works with governments, landowners, climbers, and other parties to resolve access issues; supports the work of local climbers' groups; educates about access issues where needed; helps build facilities; and has regular contact with other climbers' access groups across North America. In Squamish, CASBC helped develop the management plan for Stawamus Chief Provincial Park, and in the Smoke Bluffs they worked with the Municipality of Squamish to expand the parking centre in 1996, build new toilets and finalise a code of conduct with local residents.

The future of climbing in many of our most popular climbing areas depends on working effectively with land managers and resolving issues in a timely fashion. **Please join the Access Society**, the cost is only $20 per year, about one-third the cost of a Camalot or Friend, and less than the cost of this guide. Students are only $10, families $30, and businesses and clubs, $50. Take a positive step toward helping yourself on the crags. Being a member also means you'll get a regular, informative newsletter, and be kept up to date with events.

The Climbers Access Society of BC

Box 72013 - 4479 West 10th, Vancouver, BC V6R 4P2. (604) 228-1798

The crags in this guide cover a wide range of territory in a corridor about 70 kilometres long, centred on Highway 99 from Vancouver to north of Squamish. The vast majority of climbs are on public lands. Whatever the jurisdiction, always remember that someone, somewhere owns the land and has responsibility for caring for it. That task is made easier by users minimising erosion, observing posted signage, leaving no garbage and respecting other users. Listed below are the primary bodies that control access to the crags.

The District of Squamish.   Controls about 35% of the climbs, almost entirely in the Smoke Bluffs. Also the Art Gallery which is presently closed to the public, and some of the Murrin Park area. The District of Squamish does not have a rockclimbing or outdoor recreation management plan.

BC Parks.   Controls about 50% of the climbs, and with climbers, developed a rockclimbing vision strategy in 1999. An agency of the provincial government, BC Parks is responsible for management of park areas in British Columbia, protecting the natural environment and providing recreational opportunities. Stawamus Chief, Shannon Falls, and Murrin Provincial Parks all fall under their jurisdiction.

The BC Forest Service.   Controls about 5% of the climbs, and has had little to do with climbers. So far. An agency of the provincial government, they are responsible for integrated managment of logging, conservation and recreation on public forest lands. The only crags of significance that fall under their jurisdiction are Fluffy Kitten wall in the Stawamus River valley and the climbs on the west side of Mount Habrich. Others include the vast undeveloped resources of granite on the west side of the Squamish River. The Forest Service is mandated to provide many opportunities for outdoor recreation. Where competing uses exist, the Forest Service may develop a management plan to integrate activities and conservation.

Crown Corporations.   A Crown Corporation is a company that is established by the provincial government. The only one that controls crags in this guide is believed to be BC Rail, at the Lower Malamute. Much of the Upper Malamute is private land, and together they comprise 8% of all the climbs.

Undeveloped Private Land.   Some of the minor crags listed may fall on private land with no habitation or commercial activity, and where the public has been unrestricted from visiting, such as Smugglers Cove, Crumpit Woods and Mamquam Blind Channel. These situations may change, so please observe any posted signage.

Climate on the southwest coast of BC is characterised by warm wet winters and dry summers, although the weather can be very changeable, especially during the Spring and Fall.

The climbing season is virtually year-round on the south facing cliffs, and even in winter when the rain stops, local climbers are on the rock. When it freezes, out come the ice tools. For visitors, the effective season runs from early April to October. Rainfall averages very close to 2000mm per year, which is quite a lot.

Spring. Winter usually relents sometime in late February to mid-March, and climbers are out in force from this point on whenever the rock is dry. Expect very changeable weather, from cold rain to 30° days. Long dry spells do not occur every year, but they can dig in for weeks at a time and are usually followed by a dampish summer. Some climbs have lingering wet streaks that will either make them a little harder or not possible: *Snake, Black Water/Baraka/DOA* at the Pet, the first pitch of *University Wall, Angel's Crest, Rock On* and more. A little patience is required with the weather, but as a bonus, the mountains look inspiring loaded with spring snow. You'll find quite a difference most of the time between valley crags like the Bluffs and Pet Wall–warm and pleasant–and the high walls of the Chief or the Upper Malamute, where it can be surprisingly cold in the wind. The Smoke Bluffs are especially popular at this time of year, mostly because of their sunny aspect and quick-drying climbs. One way or another, there is lot of climbing going on every spring.

Summer. Between early July and late September there are almost always extended dry sunny periods and temperatures often hover above 30° for days at a time. This is prime time for Euros and long-distance roadtrippers. Rain tends to be forgotten. The long climbs on the Chief and Mount Habrich see many ascents. However, rain can dampen the crags at any time if a high-pressure system is not resident. Thunderstorms will drench the crags, but they are usually dry again the following day.

Fall. Much the same as summer, except with cooler temperatures and more rain. Typically, the summer ends when the last high-pressure system breaks up and the first fall storm arrives, anytime from late September to late October. Between storms however, there is still enough heat in the rock to dry it out quite quickly.

Winter. Yes it rains and storms lot, it but keeps the land green. Living in Squamish allows stepping out onto the rock whenever the sun shines and the rain stops. Which it always does eventually.

The region covered by this guidebook is a land with a fascinating geological history. In the time when the dinosaurs roamed the Earth 94 million years ago, the Chief was formed as a huge blob of molten magma some 25kms below the surface, a by-product of the colossal forces of subduction of oceanic plates sliding underneath the North American plate. The magma, less dense than the surrounding rock, rose through the crust until it completely solidified about 10 km below the surface. During this period of about a million years, the stresses of variable cooling caused continual fracturing into which adjacent, hotter magma quickly flowed and was suddenly subject to rapid cooling, forming the sinuous aplite dykes which are so endearing to climbers.

Little by little, the earth above was eroded under the force of wind, weather and earthquake, and the land carried into the sea by the rivers. Some tens of millions of years ago, the Black Dyke was formed by an injection of basaltic magma into a great crack in the now-solid granite. By the time the last ice age began to cover most of Canada, the Chief had reached the surface and it was during this period that the grinding glaciers created the familiar shape we know today. The gullies became deeper, and the great walls were sheared off, leaving in their wake the tumble of massive boulders at the base. The four gullies that create such dramatic cleavage through the Chief are zones where the rock became intensely fractured and chemically different, most likely long before the Chief reached the surface. Being much less resistant to weathering than the surrounding granite, water and ice eroded them into the great chasms of today.

It was probably about 9,000 years ago that the retreating ice revealed the Chief, a shining dome of white granite rising above a sea of ice. The centuries rolled on, the glaciers receded to the high country, and the shape of the land as we know it today was in place. A tundra-like ecosystem would have existed, and the first vegetation to return would have been hardy lichens. As they broke down and merged with rock dust, the first soils emerged creating a fertile environment for more advanced plant life. Insects returned from the warmer southern latitudes, followed by small rodents. The first trees to return were pines and spruces, which would have covered the landscape within a few hundred years of the ice receding. The Chief would have presided over a great fjord which stretched far up the valley. For much of the last 9,000 years, the Chief was very likely a barren dome of rock with few trees: an immaculate stone wonderland. It must have been quite a sight.

♦   🐦 **Falcons.** If you wish to climb a route with a 🐦 symbol noted in the guide, check first with BC Parks (604) 898-3678 to see if it is closed due to nesting peregrines. Other climbs not noted may also be affected. Be aware of all nesting birds, and stay well clear.

♦   **Toilets.** Please use them. In the Bluffs parking centre, in front of Krack Rock, the Apron, Bulletheads campground and the parking lot on Highway 99.

♦   **Belay Trees.** Try to avoid belaying off trees in high-use areas. While you may not have much choice about it at the time, encourage the use of bolt stations in high-use areas to avoid tree damage.

♦   **Fixed Gear.** Fixed gear is on a climb for good reason–the first ascentionist put it there. Please do not remove any.

♦   **Dogs.** Keep your dog on a leash and under your control.

♦   **Smoking.** If you smoke at the crags, pack your butts out. It is surprising how many smokers throw their butts away like garbage.

♦   **Boomboxes.** Please don't take boomboxes to the crag or up on the walls. You are sure to annoy someone. Take a walkman.

♦   **In-Situ Quickdraws.** If a climb has quickdraws in place, do not remove them–they belong to someone else. Climbing the route and using them is okay. If you equip a route like this, be expeditious and remove them as soon as possible–patience has its limits.

♦   **No-Trace Bivouacs.** If you are up on a wall and need to pull a bivi, leave your site or ledge with no trace of your presence. This includes hauling your own garbage and human waste.

♦   **Throwing Haulbags.** No, not any more. Those days are gone. Someone might think it is a body, and you will have the Cliff Rescue Group after you. Besides, you might hit someone.

♦   **Registration.** Compulsory registration is not required for any of the climbs in this guide. But if you are planning a bivi on a route, avoid a situation where your vehicle is parked suggestive of someone late or overdue. Tell friends, leave a note on the windshield.

♦   **Respond If Hailed.** If you are bivouaced, warm and snug and the RCMP start bellowing up from below asking if you are okay: respond! Someone, often Squamish residents with good intentions, will have reported you as 'stuck'. Don't ignore appeals, you are simply wasting others' time. Shout back–they'll hear you...

♦   **Stay On The Trails.** Always try to stay on the trail to minimise erosion, and be gentle with tree roots. Areas of special concern are the numerous trails in the Grand Wall Boulders and Smoke Bluffs.

♦ **Large Groups.** If you operate a commercial guiding business or travel in a large group, please minimise your impact–try to avoid monopolising popular crags and routes.

♦ **Nailing on free climbs.** Incredibly, thoughtless climbers still nail established free cracks–it happens several times a year. Leave the hammer behind or stay away. A more problematic situation lies on routes like *Genius Loci/Ten Years After*, which share sections. Always minimise your impact, don't use pins in such places, and hook carefully to avoid breaking holds. Respect the rock and other climbers. Try harder...

♦ **Excessive Top-Roping Polishes.** Excessive top-roping on popular climbs polishes the rock–an irreversible process–look at *Flying Circus*. This damage can be reduced by avoiding excessive top-rope sessions on such climbs until your skill is up to climbing them without falls. Please exercise restraint and have fun flailing on easier, less-travelled routes. **It is the pressure of climbers flailing above their ability level that does most damage to the rock.**

♦ **Don't hog climbs.** Top-roping can also be a contenious issue when people camp out excessively on popular routes in busy areas: doing laps; inviting passing friends along; whiling the day away slowly; climbing in large groups; all ongoing while others who wait in hope nearby–perhaps distant visitors–give up and leave while others hog the routes. This is a problem that scarcely existed ten years ago. Courtesy and understanding will go a long way toward resolving situations as they develop. Top-roping is perfectly acceptable of course, but a dominant ethic in climbing is that leading is how it's done, unless a climb has never been led. All that being said, there are no laws against top-roping, it is fun, low-risk and sociable and for most people, an essential part of learning how to climb. If all else fails, ask the offending party if they have read this page...

♦ **Thieves.** Protect yourself. Lock it. Stash it. Everywhere.

♦ **Nearby Residences.** This is a problem unique to Burgers and Fries and Neat And Cool in the Smoke Bluffs. A number of houses were built in the mid-1990s and two in 1998, right by the already heavily used public crags and some of the new residents don't seem amused at being in such a public place. Please keep noise down, **always be courteous, and do not bother the residents.** If you get hurt, it is less than a kilometre to crawl or limp to the emergency room at the hospital. Try to climb elsewhere in the early mornings and evenings. And always know that you are entitled to be there; the climbs and access to them is public land.

Climbing is a game which exists without written rules, but with a set of conventions based on fair play and trust that have evolved over the last century. At Squamish, how you climb a new route is pretty much your own business provided you don't spoil the game for others and accurately report how you did it. Rappel inspection, cleaning, and placing fixed pro if required prior to a first ascent and ground-up on-sight leading are all accepted practices. There are few things more satisfying in climbing than putting up a new route. It is a contribution to the game that thousands of people may enjoy long after you are dead, and a personal statement from you that other climbers will appreciate. You will need excellent rope-skills, plenty of energy, a willingness to work hard, and often alone. Remember you are making a permanent alteration to the natural environment and people will be looking at your work, with your name on it, 100 years from now: make it good. Although climbers who do new routes regularly can be particularly hard-nosed individuals and listen to no-one except peer pressure, it is a good idea to take the advice below to heart. It is a summary of the knowledge and experience of many career climbers.

♦   **Mark your project.** Use a ribbon or a sign to alert others that a project is in progress. Get on with the job and finish it. Many climbers dislike someone plastering a crag with projects that drag on and on. But if someone is diligently working away trying to raise their standard to a difficult route, be patient and encourage them.

♦   **Bolts.** Place them with care as to the best sites. Get advice from experienced climbers if necessary; everyone loves to say how it should be done. Use only 3/8″ stainless steel bolts and try to balance these often conflicting aims when drilling:

* Place bolts as directly above each other as possible to minimise rope drag.
* Try to place bolts where the draws will not let the rope slip over a sharp edge.
* Arrange bolts where they can be reasonably clipped, no huge stretches.
* Try not to place bolts immediately beside a hand- or foothold.
* Arrange bolts on a solid piece of even rock: no hollow flakes thank you.

♦   **Gear.** Use natural gear wherever possible, it is has less impact on the rock and is cheaper anyway. If you need to place a bolt, keep it well away from good natural placements.

♦   **So Exactly What Is Free?** A new pitch or FFA is considered free *only* if it is climbed as a Redpoint, On-Sight or Flash. A multi-pitch climb must be climbed with no falls or rests, or aid of any kind whatsoever, to be declared 'continuously free'. Be honest about your effort and define it accurately, noting any aid points used.

◆ **Think Twice.** Many well-intentioned climbers have developed so-so routes in places that are off the beaten track. As a result, their climbs have not proven popular and were reclaimed by the jungle. There is nothing wrong with that unless a forest of high stumps was left behind. So carefully consider the impact on the environment your climb will have, and balance that against the value of the climb to others. And only you can know if your effort is worth the time.

◆ **$$ Cost.** Equipping new climbs, especially multi-pitch or sport routes, can be an expensive proposition. For example, Robin Barley has spent on average $1,000 a year for 10 years on bolts, hangers, drills, bits, and batteries on his travels around BC, and many other climbers spend several hundred dollars a year. A 25m sport route usually costs at least $50, so do it right.

◆ **Building Stations.** At stations, choose the best anchor setup for the particular situation: rap hangers, rings or chains if people will be descending; gear only or regular hangers on a multi-pitch or in a little-travelled area. Rap hangers and custom devices are fast and convenient, especially if the climb is in a high-use area, however, rap hangers can cause the rope to suffer kinking. Chains attached to bolts by means of quicklinks are arguably the best in most situations, but are more obtrusive. Use only 3/8″ size galvanised chain link, and nothing less than 5/16″ quicklinks. Adding large quicklinks at the lower end of the chain can be very useful for lowering, as they allow the bight of the rope to be threaded, and tied back into your harness *before* you untie the end. If the belay is hanging, a third bolt is useful for clipping while rigging the rappel. In little-climbed areas, trees are often used. If you do so, please use *two* rap rings on the webbing.

◆ **Don't chip.** This is seriously uncool. It is illegal in provincial parks and highly contentious everywhere. If you need to chip to bring the difficulty down to your level, your ego, your desire, or both are probably out of control. Excessive desire and ego are the fast track to bad karma. All that said, there is a very grey area between needed removal of decomposed or loose rock, and hard-core chiselling for holds where none exist. Life can be difficult...

◆ **Grade Carefully.** Be cautious about assessing the grade of your route for on-sight leaders. If your experience is limited, it's wise to be humble and ask more experienced climbers for input.

◆ **Squeezing.** Don't bother. Another route squeezed in tight between two good ones is not an asset. If a crag gets gridded with bolts the individual climbs lose appeal.

◆ **Trails.** If you open a new crag, you'll end up with a trail to it. Consider it part of the task and build it properly.

Climbing is an almost unique recreational activity in that it involves direct body contact with the earth, unlike mountainbiking, kayaking, and a host of other popular adventure sports where hardware and equipment provide an interface. In fact, the solo climber needs only a pair of shoes, and even they are optional. So it is no surprise that climbers and mountaineers in general are staunch environmentalists. But on the west coast of Canada, we live in one of the world's most fertile ecosystems where the warm, wet pacific climate has created great forests of fir, cedar and hemlock that surround the crags. For climbers, there is a need to balance this with the demand for a quality recreational experience on clean stone, yet create minimal intrusion on the environment. Thus 'scrubbing', 'gardening' and 'cleaning' to remove lichen, moss, salal, dirt and small trees has evolved. The underlying objective is simple: to create a quality rockclimbing experience in a stone environment where technical skill can flourish.

The highway to Squamish opened in 1958 and for over a decade and a half climbers sought natural lines, cheerfully climbing in the vegetation and the dirt-filled cracks, but valued more the wide expanses of open rock of the Apron and the few naturally clean cracks such as those on the Grand Wall and Yosemite Pinnacle. That era drew to a close in 1974 when Robin Barley began a new epoch by rappelling down *St Vitus' Dance* to pull copious amounts of moss, salal, small trees and lichen, producing the first cleaned route.

The climbers of 1974 thought Barley was mad, so it took a while for this time-consuming top-down approach to become accepted. Not because of any concern for the vegetation, it was more a case of "Why bother? Go climb elsewhere". But by the end of the 1970s, almost all the active first-ascentionists and leading climbers were getting in on it because of the higher quality and difficulty of the climbs being opened up. So began a golden era of climbing first ascents that have become the classic climbs of today: *Seasoned In The Sun, Rock On, Birds Of Prey, Angel's Crest,* Petrifying Wall, and scores of Smoke Bluff gems are only a few examples. Other climbs that were basically dirt-filled lines of bush, like *Diedre, Snake* and *Exasperator*, became clean because they were nonetheless superb natural lines, and the passage of thousands of climbers gradually eroded the vegetation. By the 1980s, a free-for-all had opened up. A wire brush, a small saw, jumars and an old ice-axe for raking the cracks was all that was required to get your own three-star classic.

Climbers who have entered the sport since the early 1990s often seem unaware that most of the clean classic climbs of today came into being because someone removed moss, dirt and salal and trees, and it is only regular traffic that keeps them clean today. Until 1984, a tree move was once at the crux of *Exasperator* and I bet that few climbers would care to see it back; *Clean Crack* sported a large cedar tree until I removed it in 1983, after Anders Ourom had previously reamed out the upper crack; *High Mountain Woody* was a wall of trees and salal until Glenn Payan put 100 hours of work into that single pitch; Dave Jones spent 24 days working on the Ronins Corner area of the Smoke Bluffs. And countless other such efforts had been made. First ascentionists earn respect because their efforts are at the heart of the climbing culture and they provide the routes that thousands of other climbers seek. There are hundreds of quality routes yet to be climbed here and absorb the pressure from ever-increasing numbers of visitors seeking a quality experience on Squamish stone.

Up in the subalpine, the heightened sense of adventure makes greenery on a climb more acceptable. But in a valley bottom setting the demand for technical rock climbs, which includes all of the climbs in this guide except Mt Habrich, brings with it a demand for clean routes, so the crags in this guide are best considered 'recreational parks', and sensitively maintained as such. A climb after all, is just a vertical recreational trail for lateral thinkers in a fast-changing society. And as rockclimbing becomes a mainstream sport, perhaps the definition of 'trail' on the west coast needs to be redefined.

There is a strong sentiment among longtime first-ascentionists to be diligent about putting in the time and effort to create a clean stone environment with minimal vegetation removal. If a potential lone climb requires removing a thick swath of moss or salal, or is of marginal quality, it's worth asking if it is really worth the effort. Unless it is climbed regularly, the greenery will be back. Success is more likely if it is a decent climb and nearby climbs completed too. Trees on climbs, especially short ones, or close by at the base are often troublesome: they can cause greasy rock; cracks and holds get plugged by falling leaves and needles; climbers have broken bones hitting them; unstable and dead trees can render a climb unsafe. On existing climbs, trees continue to grow and encroach on the rock. Opinion varies as to how much trees affect the aesthetic experience. What may be a welcome oasis of greenery on a long climb can be a hassle on a short one. Nobody likes stumps, so if you remove a tree from a climb, be willing to pull the roots too. Consider trimming or removing adjacent trees that may result in falling leaves piling up on the climb, or branches encroaching.

Old ¼" bolts, belays and rappel stations rot; good but overgrown climbs sit unloved. There are many such situations at Squamish, and a widespread interest in addressing these issues is developing, to replace unsafe protection bolts and rusty pins, replace and improve belay and rappel stations. Some climbs that were reclaimed by the bush over the years are good, but at the time of the first ascent, usually in the 1980s, not enough climbers were around to keep them free of re-growing moss. Re-cleaning such climbs will increase the number of quality routes, and encourage exploration on less-travelled routes.

A couple dozen climbs have already been refitted with new hardware, including *Snake, Grand Wall, Diedre, The Calling, The Great Game, Hungry Wolf, Grandaddy* and *Cruel Shoes*, and many climbers have changed a bolt here and there on other climbs. This work to re-fit unsafe gear has invariably been done by climbers from their own resources. Some stores keep Manky Bolt Fund boxes, and the MEC has made a stellar contribution over many years.

It is almost always best to replace old pins with stainless bolts; fewer clips better arranged are often possible. Old ¼"bolts usually rip out well with a hammer and a carpenter's nail-puller. The same hole enlarged can be used if it is in the best place. Whatever you may choose to do, always keep in mind the historical character of the route and try to retain the spirit of the first ascent.

Retrobolting in a manner that gives a climb a different character is an activity that can be fraught with confrontation, and arouse plenty of bad feeling, especially if the climb's character is well-known and liked, or the first ascentionist disagrees with the action taken. Adding more bolts or eliminating gear placements is not for the faint-hearted, as someone, somewhere will disagree with your action, perhaps to the point of removing your work. Almost all leading climbers have their own, often strong opinion on this matter, but when pressed, will usually acknowledge that some routes could be exceptions to their principles: not a simple matter. All this is both distressing yet interesting too–a clash of well-intentioned values.

There is a fine line of judgement between a thoughtful job of removing and replacing rotten protection bolts and pins, as distinct from adding bolts that significantly change the character of the climb from what it was. Climbers in general applaud R and R efforts, but many will not care much to see the character of the climb, as it affects their experience, significantly altered. Unless it means they can now do the climb and could not before...

Peregrine falcons live on the Chief for about half the year, and usually nest in a different site in the southern walls each season. Less commonly, they may nest in other sites north of the Dihedrals. BC Parks may place restrictions on climbing certain routes or pitches during nesting season, as disturbance could set back the likelyhood of success for the fledgelings. Route and pitch-specific closures will be announced each spring. Prior to such announcement, assume that all long climbs in the Dihedrals area noted with a 🗡 symbol, from *Negro Lesbian* to *Freeway* inclusive are closed March 15th until route and pitch-specific closures are announced. **Closures will be in effect until July 31st each year**. Please contact BC Parks at (604) 898-3678, or check the notice boards in the campground and the Apron parking lot, or www.elaho.ca for up to date information.

There are no recollections among climbers of falcons being on the Chief before the mid-1980s, but since their return, they have most commonly nested in the upper regions of the Dihedrals. It is in the early period of nesting when falcons become most annoyed by interference. Once the eggs are hatched, they seem much less perturbed. They are territorial, rarely nesting closer than 1-2km from another pair, which suggests there may be only one pair on the Chief. Their average lifespan is 10-12 years and they mate for life. Albert and Elsie (hey, everything on the Chief gets a name...) are a known subspecies; *Falco peregrinus freeway*, although biologists use Falco peregrinus anatum for some reason.

Peregrines are a common sight from March to September, flying, tumbling and diving around the Chief and the Malamute, and are a pleasure to watch from the walls. A number of climbers report seeing peregrines flash past down the walls in high-speed dives and seconds later, hit their hapless prey in a cloud of feathers far below. Albert and Elsie seem to have a lot of fun, and the sound of their high-pitched twittering travels a long way. Like the raven, they are a valued part of the culture of the Chief, and such fearless hunters that even the eagles avoid them. They cruise along the walls, checking out whose doing what, who may be pulling on gear when they aren't supposed to, and all in all, quite unaffected by climbers' activities.

Observation from numerous climbers suggests that more than one pair of falcons may be active in the area–perhaps the population is increasing. One thing for sure, peregrines flying around the cliffs, or preening themselves on a ledge seem not the least bit afraid of climbers. Relations are good, let's keep them that way.

Risk and climbing go together, but always tagging along unseen is the ever-present potential of a dreaded rescue, and the number of call-out incidents is rising annually. Squamish has a volunteer Cliff Rescue Group of about 20 local climbers that is one of the best in North America, operating as an arm of the Squamish Emergency Program, a regional organisation of the Provincial Emergency Program. Operational and rescue funding comes from several sources, but it is the provincial government who pays the big bills.

From the days of the first climbers at the end of the 1950s to the mid 1980s, there were very few accidents on the crags. Climbers were highly resourceful and motivated individuals seeking adventure on the stone, self-reliant and well versed in staying alive. Technique was learned from a friend, by just doing it, and above all by starting with modest ambition. When an accident did occur, climbers were simply carried out by their partners. On *Negro Lesbian*, a huge fall and broken limb ended in self-rescue; a similar incident on *Uncle Ben's* brought rescue from nearby climbers on Dance Platform.

By the end of the 1980s, the number of climbers was rising steadily, part of the continent-wide move toward outdoor adventure activities, and as the frequency of accidents began to rise, a local volunteer rescue group of climbers was formed. They were called out perhaps three or four times a year.

In the early 1990s, an exponential increase in the number of climbers began, driven by the ever-rising attraction of adventure sports and in the case of climbing, also fuelled by the advent of sport climbing and indoor gym-induced climbers. The first climbing gym opened in Vancouver in 1992 and within a couple of years, the phenomenon of a large wave of people heading for the crags at Squamish was well underway. Armed with some basic technical skill and fitness, and a heady mix of expectations, excitement, fear and naivety, most were focussed on climbing as a sport rather than an adventure. A lack of awareness of how to protect their well-being on real stone, but with expectations of quick progress, has led to an entire industry of guides conducting courses in basic rock technique, leading, rope skills and more. There are few novice climbers today who have not benefitted from this process. As with any wide range of people, most are able to apply a large dose of common sense to what is a risky business, some learn the hard way, and others would have fit in comfortably with the wild ways of thirty years ago.

In 1998, the Cliff Rescue Group was called out to assist climbers on approximately 12 occasions, and over 35 times to rescue hikers on the Backside trail. The Fire and Ambulance services also responded to a couple of incidents in drive-to places: the Smoke Bluffs and Murrin Park. Most climbing accidents are in the Bluffs, and follow a trend of inexperienced climbers sustaining broken limbs in long leader falls, even grounders, on climbs that are well-protected and 5.10 or easier. Many are a result of ambition being well ahead of skill.

Rescues are a public service in British Columbia for all outdoor users: snowmobilers, hunters, climbers, skiers, sailors and more. But judging from the way in which costs are spiralling upward, it is doubtful that this can remain the case. With climbing, rescue costs are rising more rapidly than call-out frequency because of the disproportionately high price tag of major rescues.

The sight of helmets at the crags is no longer unusual, the result of a more risk-aware attitude, although serious head injuries from leader falls are rare. The higher risk situations include inexperienced leaders pushing their limits too hard on gear routes, falls on broken terrain such as *Angel's Crest*, stonefall in the major gullies, and sad to say, even stonefall down the Grand Wall thrown by thoughtless hikers at the top: yes, really.

Rescues on the Chief are far less common than the Smoke Bluffs –one or two per year–but invariably involve experienced climbers and can be spectacular and complex to resolve: an example being two major helicopter rescues on *Angel's Crest* after serious falls. On a lighter note, a lone 'climber' hiked up the Grand Wall trail to the base of *U Wall*, started up the first pitch of *Wall of Attrition* then got stuck. Turns out he was a hiker who thought he was on the Backside Trail (honest!). There has been only one climber fatality–in 1991 on the Pan Wall–when a worn fixed rope broke over an edge under the strain of jumaring. In fact, all rescues at Squamish have been caused by self-induced human error.

And there have been numerous close shaves. One climber rapped off the end of his rope in 1998 on the last, diagonal rappel off *Cruel Shoes* and tumbled down to the trail. He is one of the most experienced dudes around, but nonetheless he has done it not once– but twice–and walked away. Another climber fell off the second pitch of *Tantalus Wall* in 1973 when a tree branch broke and he fell 50m to the trail, scorching two new ropes and walked away. I know him well: it was me.

Serious injuries and deaths happen when inevitable mistakes collide with bad luck. Some climbers are fortunate, others die for the same error. Take care.

West Vancouver

Lighthouse Park has a pleasant collection of short climbs in a sunny sea-cliff atmosphere. Copper Cove at Horseshoe Bay offers an escape from the city to a dozen harder climbs.

Britannia

Activity in the Britannia area, 12km south of Squamish is increasing, with climbs generally 5.9 to 5.11. The sea cliffs of Seal Cove and the Quartz Pillar are both located here: well worth a visit.

Valley of Shaddai

This is a deep wooded valley east of Murrin Park. with 8 crags offering 30-plus sport and gear climbs, 5.9 to 5.11.

Murrin Park

This complex area of 24 single-pitch crags, about 8 kilometres south of the Chief has something to offer every climber: quick access, quality climbs and about 180 routes: sport climbs; cracks; and mixed face routes abound. For 5.10s, check Up Among The Firs and the crags above the parking lot. Petrifying Wall is the major crag of the area, with a couple dozen stellar sport routes from 5.11 to 5.13, and several equally stellar gear routes. Up Among the Firs offers many fine 5.10s, with great views too. Nightmare Rock hosts one of the best collection of hard cracks at Squamish, 5.11 and up.

Shannon Falls-Papoose

A kilometre south of the Chief, and with a short approach, these large cliffs offer climbs that have a wide range of characteristics: multi-pitch friction; moderate cracks; a collection of stellar one- and two-pitch 5.11s on Gobsmacking Wall, and a few excellent multi-pitch 5.10s. In all, over 40 climbs.

The Malamute

There are now 100 climbs here, divided into separate Upper and Lower areas. The upper cliffs, which are heavily laced with sport routes, are accessed directly from the highway by the Chief. The Lower Malamute has stellar crack climbs and several fine multi-pitch routes, some of which link into the Upper Malamute.

Mount Habrich

A 1700m alpine peak south-east of Squamish with 16 climbs up to 9 pitches on its west and east sides, some of which are exceptionally good.

The Chief
The Chief is the centrepiece of the guide, and the 400 climbs encompass half of all the climbing in this guide, with close to 100 multi-pitch climbs up to 17 pitches, magnificent cracks, superb aid walls, and nerve-tingling friction climbs. See the map on page 162.

Chief – The Bulletheads
A rambling collection of tiered cliffs above the campground that offer an escape from the more crowded places.

Chief – The Dihedrals-Tantalus
Long corners, cracks, and the mighty *Freeway* and T*antalus Wall.*

Chief – The Grand Wall
The spiritual home of Squamish climbing. Long freeclimbs, tremendous cracks and 40 climbs of one to six pitches scattered along the base, and many developing short climbs above Bellygood.

Chief – The Apron
The great sweep of granite that cascades down to the highway, the Apron is home to over 60 routes, including well over 20 that are 5 pitches or more in length.

Chief – The North Walls
Although there are only a couple dozen freeclimbs here, with few exceptions, they are for heavy-hitters only–multi-pitch climbs of 5.11 and up.

Chief – The Squaw
The crag of choice for a wide selection of 5.10 multi-pitch climbs.

Chief – The Backside
Less travelled than it deserves, the 50 or so climbs here offer quality climbing up to 3 pitches long, far removed from the hustle of the valley. Mostly 5.10–5.11.

Smoke Bluffs
With 400 single-pitch climbs on more than 40 crags, close to the town centre, a sunny aspect and quick-drying rock, the Smoke Bluffs is by far the most heavily-used area in the guide. Difficulty ranges from low-fifth-class to hard 5.12, there are excellent teaching cliffs, good cracks and face climbs, and you'll never be alone. Unless it is raining. Really hard, that is. See the map on page 342.

Multi-Pitch

Banana Peel	Friction	8	7p	Chief - Apron
Clean Corner	Corner	8	(2p)	Chief - Dihedrals
Diedre	Corner/friction	8	7p	Chief - Apron
Sparrow	Friction	9	7p	Chief - Apron
A Cream of White Mice	Face	9	4p	Chief - Bulletheads
Jungle Warfare	Crack	9	5p	Chief - Squaw
Snake	Corner/friction	9	7p	Chief - Apron
St Vitus Dance	Crack	9	4p	Chief - Apron
Dream of White Kittens	Face	10a	2p	Habrich East
Papoose One	Face	10a	6p	Papoose
Rock On	Corner/layback	10a	5p	South Gully
Smoke Bluff Connection	Crack/face	10a	4p	Bluffs
Solar System	Corner/face	10a	7p	Habrich West
The Angels Crest	Mixed	10a	13p	Chief - Sheriffs Badge
Avalon Connection	Mixed	10b	3p	Valley of Shaddai
Birds of Prey	Crack/face	10b	5p	Chief - Squaw
Centrefold	Face	10b	3p	Papoose
Sunblessed	Crack/face	10b	3p	Chief - Solarium
Baseline Direct	Friction	10c	3p	Chief - Apron
Dancing with.....Idiot	Crack/face	10c	3p	Chief - Solarium
Enlightened	Face/crack	10c	3p	Chief - Backside
Godforsaken Land	Mixed	10c	5p	Chief - Squaw
Life On Earth	Face	10c	6p	Habrich West
Milk Run	Corner	10c	4p	Chief - Tantalus Wall
Mirkwood Forest	Face	10c	2p	Malamute Lower
Pan Tease Lower	Mixed	10c	(5p)	Chief - Above Apron
Squamish Buttress	Crack/mixed	10c	(7p)	Chief - Above Apron
The Climbers.....Crazy	Friction	10c	6p	Chief - Apron
Wonderful.....Tiggers	Corner/face	10c	7p	Habrich East
Borderline	Crack	10d	4p	Chief - Sheriffs Badge
Cruel Shoes	Face	10d	6p	Chief - Grand Wall Base
Pipeline	Offwidth	10d	5p	Chief - Squaw
Checkmate	Face/cracks	10d	7p	Chief - Squaw
The Great Game	Cracks	10d	4p	Chief - Squaw
The Shortest Straw	Mixed	10d	3p	Chief - Bulletheads
Whirlwind	Corner/friction	10d	7p	Chief - Apron

Multi-Pitch

Bloodlust Direct	Friction	11a ... 6p	Chief - Apron
Grand Wall	Corner/face	11a ... 16p	Chief - Grand Wall
Local Boys Do Good	Face / friction	11a ... 3p	Shannon Falls
Movin to Montana	Face	11a ... 4p	Chief - Grand Wall Base
Scatterbrain	Crack	11a ... 2p	Chief - Backside
Frayed Ends.....Sanity	MIxed/face	11a - 12c 6p	Chief - Squaw
Dancing in the Light	Friction	11b .. 6p	Chief - Apron
Overly Hanging Out	Corner/mixed	11b .. 3p	Malamute Lower
Teetering on the Brink	Friction	11b .. 6p	Chief - Apron
Unfinished Symphony	Corner/friction	11b .. 8p	Chief - Apron
Wall of Attrition	Crack/mixed	11b .. 7p	Chief - Grand Wall
Tantalus Wall	Face crack	11b/c 8p	Chief - Tantalus Wall
Alaska Highway	Corner	11c ... 5p	Chief - Zodiac
Into The Void	Crack	11c ... 2p	Chief - Bulletheads
Hot Rod	Crack	11c ... 3p	SChief - heriffs Badge
Java Jive	Face	11c ... 2p	Chief - Grand Wall Base
Magic Carpet Ride	Friction	11c ... 4p	Shannon
The Big Scoop	Crack	11c ... (2p)	Chief - Sheriffs Badge
The Clearing	Mixed	11c ... 4p	Malamute Lower
Freeway	Mixed	11c/d 12p	Chief - Dihedrals
Cerebrus	Face/crack	11d .. 3p	Chief - Tantalus Wall
Deadend Dihedral	Corner	12a ... 3p	Chief - Dihedrals
Dream On	Friction	12a ... 7p	Chief - Apron
Northern Lights	Corner	12a ... 12p	Chief - Zodiac
The Calling	Corner	12a ... 7p	Chief - Zodiac
University Wall	Corner/face	12a ... 8p	Chief - Grand Wall
Visionquest	Corner	12a ... 3p	Chief - Zodiac
Voodoo Amour	Friction/crack	12a ... (3p)	Chief - Apron
The Daily Planet	Corner	12b .. 4p	Chief - Sheriffs Badge
War of the Raptors	Face	12c ... 4p	Chief - Grand Wall Base
The Opal	Corner/face	12c/d 6p	Chief - Above Apron
The Shadow	Corner/stem	12d .. 7p	Chief - Grand Wall

Crack Pitches — Finger to Fist

These climbs are mostly single-pitch routes, with a few excepted pitches on longer climbs. The long multi-pitch routes are in general, loaded with quality cracks.

Pauls Crack	Finger	10a	F	Malamute Upper
Slap and Tickle	Finger	10b	F	Malamute Upper
Partners in Crime	Finger	11a	F	Penny Lane
Clean Crack	Finger	11b	F	Malamute Lower
Crime of the Century	Finger	11b	F	Penny Lane
Sentry Box	Finger	12a	F	Nightmare Rock
Vital Transformation	Finger	12c	F	White Cliff
Penny Lane	Finger-hand	9	F	Penny Lane
Eagles Domain	Finger-hand	8	F	Squaw
Slot Machine	Finger-hand	8	F	Bulletheads
High Mountain Woody	Finger-hand	9	F	Malamute Upper
Sunblessed (pitch 2)	Finger-hand	10a	F	Solarium
The Zip	Finger-hand	10a	F	The Zip
A Little Testis	Finger-hand	10b	C	Up Among Firs
Arrowroot	Finger-hand	10b	F	Dihedrals
Seasoned in the Sun	Finger-hand	10b	F	Grand Wall Base
Split Pillar	Finger-hand	10b	C	Grand Wall
Exasperator (pitch 2)	Finger-hand	10c	F	Grand Wall Base
Just Blessed	Finger-hand	10c	F	Up Among Firs
Perspective	Finger-hand	11a	G	Nightmare Rock
Shaved Bum	Finger-hand	11c	G	Above Bellygood
Claim Jumper	Finger-hand	12a	F	Nightmare Rock
Flight of the Challenger	Finger-hand	12c	G	Petrifying Wall
Caboose	Finger-layback	10b	C	Malamute Lower
Crescent Crack	Finger-layback	10d	C	Malamute Lower
Apron Strings	Finger-layback	10b	C	Grand Wall Base
Ron Zalko Workout	Finger-layback	12a	C	Zodiac Upper
Deadend Dihedral (pitch 1)	Finger-layback	11a	C	Dihedrals
Pixie Corner	Finger-stem	8	C	Pixie Corner
Rutabaga	Finger-hand-stem	11a	C	Dihedrals
Laughing Crack	Finger-thinhand	7	F	Smoke Bluff Wall
Exasperator (pitch 1)	Finger-thinhand	10a	F	Grand Wall Base

Crack Pitches — Finger to Fist

Mushroom	Thinhand	9	F	Papoose
Hot Cherry Bendover	Thinhand	11b	F	Burgers Fries South
The Left Side	Thinhand	12a	F	Grand Wall
Cat Crack	Thinhand-hand	6	F	Neat and Cool
Octopus Garden	Thinhand-hand	7	F	Octopus Garden
Orifice Fish	Thinhand-hand	9	F	Spilt Beaver
Hand Jive	Thinhand-hand	10b	F	Malamute Lower
Cruising to Infinity	Thinhand-hand	10c	F	Above and Beyond
Golden Throat Charmer	Thinhand-hand	12b	F	Grand Wall Base
Astrologger	Thanhand-stem	11b	G	Zodiac Base
Quarryman	Hand-layback	8	C-F	Penny Lane
The Reacharound	Hand-layback	9	C	Lakeside
World's...Milkman	Hand-layback	9	F	Milkmans Wall
Talking Holds	Hand-layback	10a	F	Boulder Gully
Mercy Street	Hand-Layback	10b	C	South Gully
Talking Crack	Hand	7	F	Ravens Castle
Klahanie Crack	Hand	7	F	Shannon Falls
Cardu Crack	Hand	8	F	Shannon Falls
Blazing Saddles	Hand	10b	F	Sheriffs Badge
High Plains Drifter	Hand	11a	F	Sheriffs Badge
The Promised Land	Hand	11b	F	Promised Land
A Pitch in Time	Hand-fist	10b	F	Bulletheads
Bop till You Drop	Hand-fist	10b	C	Cirque Uncrackables
Elephantiasis	Hand-fist	10c	F	Ronins Corner
Vector (pitch 1)	Hand-fist-offwidth	9	F	Apron
Grandaddy Overhang	Undercling	11c	C	Nightmare Rock
Big Daddy Overhang	Undercling/finger	12b	C	Nightmare Rock
The Underfling	Undercling-hand	12d	U	Grand Wall
Pipe Dream	Fist	8	4-5"	Octopus Garden
Root Canal	Fist	8	4-5"	Octopus Garden
Split Beaver	Fist	10b	4"	Split Beaver
The Grip ...Kaffir Dog	Fist-offwidth	11a	4-6"	White Cliff

F = Face crack   C = Corner-crack   G = Groove   U = Undercling

Mixed Climbs

The single-pitch climbs listed here require a wide variety of climbing types, skills and techniques, as well as savvy at placing gear in some cases. In general, they are steep gear routes.

Garfield	7	Comic Rocks
Stephanies Tears	9	Malamute Upper
Heavenly Ladder	9	Split Beaver
Cold Comfort	9	Boulder Gully
Old Age	9	Smoke Bluff Wall
Man of Leisure	10a	Gobsmacking Wall
The Shaman (pitch 1)	10a	The Shaman
Neat and Cool	10a	Neat and Cool
Centre Street	10b	Crag X
Even Steven	10c	Petrifying Wall
Peanuts	10c	Comic Rocks
Strol On	10c	Boulder Gully
Backwoods Beebop	10d	White Cliff
Chasing Rainbows	10d	Malamute Lower
Little Feat	10d	Pixie Corner
Frail Scales	11a	Jalap Bluff
Silly Putty	11a	Auntie Gravity
Token Brits	11a	Black Zawn
Perfidious Albion	10d	Black Zawn
Black Flag	10d	Black Zawn
Hungry Wolf	11b	Gobsmacking Wall
Never Say Never	11b	Gobsmacking Wall
Smell of Fat Chick	11b	Above The Lake
Turbocharger	11b	Boulder Gully
Dead on Arrival	11c	Petrifying Wall
El Indio	11c	Milkmans Wall
Hellfire Wall	11c	Jalap Bluff
Horrors of Ivan	11c	Milkmans Wall
Hunters Moon	11d	Gobsmacking Wall
Take No Prisoners	11d	Petrifying Wall
Future Shock	12a	White Cliff

Offwidths and Chimneys

March of K...Utensils	Offwidth-Layback	9	5"	Cirque Uncrackables
Tantalus Wall (pitch 2)	Offwidth Face	10a	4½"	Tantalus Wall
Berrycup (pitch 2)	Offwidth Face	10a	5"	Malamute Lower
Boogie till You Puke	Offwidth Face	10c	6-7"	Cirque Uncrackables
Fissure Flavelle (pitch 2)	Offwidth Face	10c	5"	Above and Beyond
Angels Crest (p. 8 var.)	Offwidth Face	10b	7"	Sheriffs Badge
Hypertension	Offwidth Face	11a	5"	Nightmare Rock
Pipeline (pitch 4-5)	Offwidth Corner	10d	8-9"	Squaw
The Scimitar	Offwidth Corner	11b	8-9"	Cirque Uncrackables
Wild Turkey	Chimney-Hand-fist	10d		Bulletheads
Sunshine Chimey Centre	Chimney	8		Bulletheads
Kneewrecker (pitch 5)	Chimney	10a		Grand Wall Base
Tall Skinny People	Chimney	10c		Zodiac
Brunser Overhang	Chimney	11a		Brunser

Combination Climbs

The climbs listed here are little-known, or interesting combinations of more than one climb, and offer either easier or higher quality climbing.

Borderline—Blazing Saddles	10b	4p	Sheriffs Badge
Baseline Direct—Vector (or Evergreen State)	10c	5p	Apron
The Bottom Line—Diedre	9	9p	Apron
Dream On—Unfinished Symphony	11b	7p	Apron
Dream On—Anxiety State	10d	7p	Apron
Sunblessed—Mere Mortals	10a	3p	Solarium
Cruel Shoes—Grand Wall—Roman Chimneys	11a	16p	Grand Wall
The Great Game—Godforsaken Land	10c	4p	Squaw
Godforsaken Land—The Great Game	10d	4p	Squaw
Pan Tease—Squamish Buttress	10c	12p	Apron
Rock On—Squamish Buttress	10c	12p	Apron
Baseline Direct/Vector—Squamish Buttress	10c	12p	Apron
Grand Wall to Bellygood—Upper Black Dyke	11a	16p	Grand Wall

Friction Climbs

A Question of Balance	8	2p	Chief - Apron Upper
Pig Dogs on Parade	8	2p	Chief - Apron Upper
Banana Peel	8	7p	Chief - Apron
Slab Alley	9	6p	Chief - Apron
Sparrow	9	7p	Chief - Apron
Dancing with Pigs	10a	2p	Chief - Apron Upper
Lost Horizon	10b	45m	Seal Cove .... SPORT+
Sea of Diamonds	10b	2p	Seal Cove .... SPORT+
Baseline Direct	10c	3p	Chief - Apron North
Climbers... Crazy	10c	6p	Chief - Apron North
White Lightning	10c	8p	Chief - Apron
Whirlwind	10d	7p	Chief - Apron North
Local Boys Do Good p2, p3	11a	4p	Shannon Falls
That Dog Don't Hunt	11a	2p	Chief - Apron
Dancing in the Light	11b	6p	Chief - Apron
Local Heroes	11c	28m	Shannon Falls
Magic Carpet Ride	11c	4p	Shannon Falls
Not Your Normal Nightmare	11c	4p	Shannon Falls
Dream On	12a	7p	Chief - Apron

No Crowds Here

These routes are rarely climbed, but offer an adventurous flavour, on rock and bush. The grades are not an exact science here...

North Gully	4th	full height of the Chief	
North-North Gully	4th	full height of the Chief	
Caramba Crags	8	full height of the Chief	
South Gully	8	full height of the Chief	
Sunshine Chimneys	8	2p	Chief - Bulletheads
Amazon Slabs	9	full height of the Chief	
Echelon	9	full height of the Chief	
North-North Arete	9	6p	
Petgill Wall	9	7p	Petgill Wall
Koyaanisqatsi	10c	5p	Chief - South Gully
Right Wing	10c	6p	Chief - Squaw
Capilano Classic	11a	2p	Capilano Canyon
Snakes and Ladders	11a	3p	Stony Creek Wall

Sport Climbs

Coyote	11a	Chief - Grand Wall Base	SPORT
Eurasian Eyes	13a	Chief - Bulletheads	SPORT+
Flight of the Fledgelings	.7	Chief - Raven's Castle .	SPORT
Joe's Dyke	.7	Chief - Raven's Castle .	SPORT
The Archer's Arrows	.7	Chief - Raven's Castle .	SPORT
That Dog Don't Hunt	11a	Chief - Apron	SPORT
Gold Medal Ribbon	11a	Chief - Skyline Slab	SPORT
The Trimark Years	11b	Chief - Penthouse	SPORT
High Society	11c	Chief - The Penthouse	SPORT+
Now With Wings	11c	Chief - The Penthouse	SPORT+
Archives	12d	Chief - Grand Wall Boulders	SPORT
Permanent Waves	13c	Chief - Grand Wall Boulders	SPORT
Technical Ecstacy	13b	Chief - Grand Wall Boulders	SPORT
Baraka	12b	Murrin - Petrifying Wall	SPORT+
Black Water	12a	Murrin - Petrifying Wall	SPORT
Burning Down The Couch	11d	Murrin - Petrifying Wall	SPORT
Elastic Man	11a-c	Murrin - Petrifying Wall	SPORT+
Exploding Syringe	12c	Murrin - Petrifying Wall	SPORT
Lost Highway	13c	Murrin - Petrifying Wall	SPORT
No Name Road	11b	Murrin - Petrifying Wall	SPORT
Pleasant Pheasant	11a	Murrin - Petrifying Wall	SPORT
Jeff and the Giant Reach	11c	Murrin - Shaman	SPORT
Presto	13a	Murrin - Presto	SPORT
The Flingus Cling	12b	Murrin - Petrifying Wall	SPORT
Totally Clips	10b	Murrin - Up Among The Firs	SPORT
Silver Surfer	11b	Quartz Pillar	SPORT+
Lost Horizon	10b	Seal Cove	SPORT+
Sole Mate	10b	Seal Cove	SPORT+
Swept Away	9	Seal Cove	SPORT+
Cliptomaniac	12d	Valley of Shaddai	SPORT
Dream's Descent	10d	Valley of Shaddai	SPORT+
Famous Last Moves	11b	Valley of Shaddai	SPORT+
Man of Leisure	10a	Gobsmacking Wall	SPORT+
Evaporation	11a	Bluffs - Crystal Wall	SPORT+.
Fatty Bolger	11a	Bluffs - Blind Channel .	SPORT
Gaia	12b	Bluffs - Zip	SPORT
The Leading Edge	11a	Bluffs - Blind Channel .	SPORT
Triage Arete	10a	Bluffs - Boulder Gully ..	SPORT

Face Climbs

These climbs offer predominately less-than-vertical face climbing.

Joes Dyke	7 .... 2p	Chief - Ravens Castle
Merci Me	8 .... 2p	Chief - Grand Wall
Dream of White Kittens	10a 2p	Habrich East
Upper Black Dyke	10a 4p	Chief - Grand Wall
Survival of the Flatus	10b 2p	Malamute Lower
Cruel Shoes	10d 6p	Chief - Grand Wall
Aged in Oak	11a 2p	Chief - Grand Wall
Ghostdancing	11b 3p	Chief - Grand Wall
Never were Warriors	11b 5p	Chief - Grand Wall
Los Zapatos	11b .... 50m ...	Chief - Grand Wall
Sunday Whites	11c .... (40m)	Chief - Grand Wall
Genius Loci	12b .... 5p.	Chief - Grand Wall
The Opal (p3-p6)	12d .... 6p.	Chief - South Gully

A Few Suggested First-Lead Gear Routes

These single-pitch climbs all offer excellent natural protection.

Fern Gully	4	Smoke Bluffs - Fern Gully
Cat Crack	6	Smoke Bluffs - Neat and Cool
Magical Child	6	Smoke Bluffs - Ronins Corner
People Of Size	6	Smoke Bluffs - Pink Cliff
Corner Crack	7	Smoke Bluffs - Neat and Cool
Laughing Crack	7	Smoke Bluffs - Smoke Bluff Wall
Octopus Garden	7	Smoke Bluffs - Octopus Garden
Sparkletoast	7	Smoke Bluffs - One Toque Wall
Easter Island	8	Smoke Bluffs - Crag X
Pixie Corner	8	Smoke Bluffs - Pixie Corner
Slot Machine (2p)	8	Chief - Bulletheads
Up From The Bog	8	Murrin - Bog Wall
Quarryman	8	Smoke Bluffs - Penny Lane
Cold Comfort	9	Smoke Bluffs - Boulder Gully
Lybia Sucks	9	Smoke Bluffs - Burgers and Fries
Movin On Over	9	Smoke Bluffs - Burgers and Fries

Places where top-ropes are easy to set up, and the climbs moderate, are in demand. At the crags listed, it is possible to walk to the top and arrange ropes with a minimum amount of difficulty. Keep in mind that if you need to top-rope because you are unable to lead, then setting the top-rope, unroped at the top of the crag, could be the most hazardous thing you do all day.

Murrin - Sugarloaf	Murrin - Bog Wall
Upper Malamute - The Terraces	Murrin - Up Among The Firs South
Upper Malamute - Jacobs Wall	Upper Malamute - Highest Tier
Smoke Bluffs - Jug Slab	Smoke Bluffs - Bughouse Heights
Smoke Bluffs - Krack Rock	Smoke Bluffs - Fern Gully
Smoke Bluffs - Fatty Bolger	Smoke Bluffs - One Toque
Smoke Bluffs - Neat and Cool	Smoke Bluffs - Burgers Fries
Smoke Bluffs - Call It A Day	Smoke Bluffs - Alexis
Smoke Bluffs - Octopus Garden	Smoke Bluffs - Ronins Corner

First-Pitch Specials

These routes all offer substantially easier climbing on their first pitch or so, and which can be overlooked as a source of quality climbing.

Local Boys Do Good	10b .. pitch 1 — 11a beyond. ...	Shannon Falls
Fungus Razor	10d .. pitch 1 — 12b beyond	Malamute Lower
Grey Matter	11a .. pitch 1 — 11d beyond	Chief - Grand Wall
Deadend Dihedral	11a .. pitch 1 — 12a beyond	Chief - Dihedrals
Java Jive	10c .. pitch 1 — 11c beyond	Chief - Grand Wall
The Opal	12a .. pitch 1-2 — 12d beyond .	Chief South Gully
Frayed Ends of Sanity	11a .. pitch 1-5 — 12c beyond .	Chief - Squaw

Some Short Aid Climbs

The following areas offer a number of short aid routes for rainy-day fun, or practise for bigger things.

Leviticus

Jalap Bluff

Zombie Roof area of the Smoke Bluff Wall

Rurp Riot in the Kacademon Caves

Angel's Crest Trailside

Iconoclast at the base of the Grand Wall

When the last guide was published in 1992, 'sport-climbing' was an expression almost unknown at Squamish, the land of cracks and bold friction. That has all changed with a major growth in the number of climbs with generous amounts of all-fixed protection requiring quickdraws only. This is a world-wide phenomenon, and Squamish is no different.

Personal motivation for climbing has broadened and shifted with the vast increase in climbers during the last 10 years or so. The appeal of adventure is high for many climbers, but the changing demographic mix has brought a demand for quick-fix, low-stress rocktime too. Well-protected, all-fixed routes fill that need.

A few trends are evident: the athletic pursuit of difficulty for which sport climbs are well suited appeals to many; and sport routes make it relatively low-risk to lift your skill in the physical realm as high as possible. Then there is the declining potential for unclimbed gear routes within a ten minute walk of the car in this region. Given the amount of unclimbed rock that is close to hand with limited or no natural protection, it is no surprise that ambitious climbers armed with a Hilti drill are quick to take advantage. Finally, there is a high demand for low-risk, quickdraw-only climbs from novice climbers, an outcome of so many people gaining their first taste of 'rock' in a gym. And not surprisingly, there are few experienced climbers who do not enjoy the lower-stress situations of sport climbs.

While compiling this guide, I asked numerous climbers how they defined a sport climb. The answers were surprisingly varied. The only common factor was 'quickdraws only'; opinion on the length of acceptable run-outs and steepness varied widely. As used for the purposes of this guide, the designation **SPORT** indicates climbs which are all-fixed, with enough protection to place them at the low end of the risk spectrum. Climbs like *Mercy Me*, *The Shaman* and those on the Apron are not included, as the bolts are too sparse and the length of the runouts too long to call them low-risk climbs. **SPORT**+ is an indication of climbs which have protection that is mostly fixed, but still require the use of a small amount of gear in addition to the listed number of quickdraws; usually one to three pieces. Please keep in mind that many of these routes are new and have had few if any repeat ascents.

In all, about 14% of the climbs–7% of all the pitches–fall into the **SPORT** and **SPORT**+ categories. 80% of them are 5.10d and up.

David's	.6	#2	Bluffs - Blind Channel	SPORT+	12m
Hamish's	.6	#3	Bluffs - Blind Channel	SPORT	14m
Stepladder	.7	#4	Bluffs - Blind Channel	SPORT	12m
Moominland	.9	#4	Bluffs - Blind Channel	SPORT	14m
Bumper *	11c	#5	Bluffs - Blind Channel	SPORT+	23m
Fatty Bolger **	11a	#6	Bluffs - Blind Channel	SPORT	35m
The Leading Edge **	11a	#6	Bluffs - Blind Channel	SPORT	24m
Crag Rat *	10a	#4	Bluffs - Boulder Gully	SPORT	18m
Triage Arete **	10a	#4	Bluffs - Boulder Gully	SPORT	22m
Don't Believe The Hype	11a	#4	Bluffs - Boulder Gully	SPORT	18m
Digital Dexterity	12c	#	Bluffs - Pixie Corner	SPORT	18m
Evaporation **	11a	#7	Bluffs - Crystal Wall	SPORT+	2p.
Fidget With Your Digits	10b	#2	Bluffs - Pink Cliff	SPORT	15m
Father and Son **	11a	#6	Bluffs - Ronins	SPORT+	30m
Eggrolls Dude!	12a	#8	Bluffs - Ronins	SPORT	30m
High Boltage Line *	10a	#5	Bluffs - Burgers & Fries	SPORT	15m
French Leave *	10b	#3	Bluffs - Burgers & Fries	SPORT+	15m
Resoler *	11c	#7	Bluffs - Smoke Bluff Wall	SPORT+	24m
Jacob's Ladder	12b	#4	Bluffs - Smoke Bluff Wall	SPORT	15m
Savage Amusement *	13b	#6	Bluffs - Smoke Bluff Wall	SPORT+	20m
Through The Never	13c	#6	Bluffs - Smoke Bluff Wall	SPORT	15m
Twin Peaks Of Kilmanjaro *	10c	#6	Bluffs - Bughouse Heights	SPORT	16m
Sudden Impact **	11a	#7	Bluffs - Bughouse Heights	SPORT	18m
Shakey The Moyle	11c	#3	Bluffs - Penny Lane	SPORT	(10m)
Old Maid *	10a	#4	Bluffs - Nubile Woman	SPORT	20m
Tools Of Moss Destruction *	11b	#5	Bluffs - Fern Gully	SPORT+	22m
Bolt It And They Will Come	10c	#5	Bluffs - Pink Cliff	SPORT	18m
Gaia **	12b	#7	Bluffs - Zip	SPORT	25m
Coyote	11a	#7	Chief - Grand Wall Base	SPORT	50m
Grey Matter **	11a / 11d	#7	Chief - Grand Wall Base	SPORT	2p.
The First Course **	11a	#8	Chief - Grand Wall Base	SPORT (p1)	2p.
Panic *	10a	#6	Chief - Grand Wall Boulders	SPORT	18m
Button *	10d	#4	Chief - Grand Wall Boulders	SPORT	10m
Archives *	12d	#8	Chief - Grand Wall Boulders	SPORT	15m
Force Of Habit	12d	#5	Chief - Grand Wall Boulders	SPORT	8m
Animal Magnetism	13a	#3	Chief - Grand Wall Boulders	SPORT	7m
Natural Reflex *	13a	#9	Chief - Grand Wall Boulders	SPORT	18m
Neurotica	13b	#4	Chief - Grand Wall Boulders	SPORT	8m
Technical Ecstacy *	13b	#8	Chief - Grand Wall Boulders	SPORT	15m
Young Blood *	13b	#5	Chief - Grand Wall Boulders	SPORT	10m
Creepshow *	13b-c	#10	Chief - Grand Wall Boulders	SPORT	15m
Permanent Waves **	13c	#10	Chief - Grand Wall Boulders	SPORT	18m
Bravado *	13d	#8	Chief - Grand Wall Boulders	SPORT	15m
That Dog Don't Hunt	11a	#9	Chief - Apron	SPORT	(2p.)
The Black Streaker *	11a	#8?	Chief - Apron	SPORT	(2p.)
There Goes The Neighbourhood *	11b	#6	Chief - Bulletheads	SPORT	25m
Eurasian Eyes ***	13a	#5	Chief - Bulletheads	SPORT+	25m
Another Imperfection *	10c	#6	Chief - Solarium	SPORT	30m
Dafter By The Day *	11a	#8	Chief - Solarium	SPORT	30m
Dimmer Still *	11a+1pa	#7	Chief - Solarium	SPORT+	35m
Message From The Stars ***	11c	#10?	Chief - Solarium	SPORT+	3p.
Kashmir *	11c	#10	Chief - Squamish Buttress	SPORT	(28m)
Anxiety **	12a	#9	Chief - Squaw	SPORT	25m
Frayed Ends of Sanity ***	12c	#7	Chief - Squaw (p3, rap-in)	SPORT	(3p.)
The Flight of the Fledgelings **	.7	#5	Chief - Raven's Castle	SPORT	2p.
Joe's Dyke ***	.7	#6	Chief - Raven's Castle	SPORT	2p.
The Archer's Arrows ***	.8	#3	Chief - Raven's Castle	SPORT	2p.

Slesse's 500 **	.9	#6	Chief - Raven's Castle	SPORT	2p.
The Bow *	.9	#3	Chief - Raven's Castle	SPORT	2p.
Gold Medal Ribbon **	11a	#9	Chief - Skyline Slab	SPORT	30m
Bad Religion **	10d	#10	Chief - The Penthouse	SPORT+	40m
The Trimark Years **	11b	#10	Chief - The Penthouse	SPORT	40m
High Society ***	11c	#9	Chief - The Penthouse	SPORT+	30m
Now With Wings ***	11c	#8	Chief - The Penthouse	SPORT+	30m
Hit The Ground And Mean It	.6	#3	Valley of Shaddai	SPORT	10m
Japhia **	10a	#6	Valley of Shaddai	SPORT+	1-2p.
Necessary Dorsal Muscles	10b	#3	Valley of Shaddai	SPORT	7m
Gym Dandy **	10c	#7	Valley of Shaddai	SPORT	18m
Dream's Descent ***	10d	#8	Valley of Shaddai	SPORT+	20m
Dovey *	11a	#3	Valley of Shaddai	SPORT+	12m
I Don't Need This	11a	#5	Valley of Shaddai	SPORT	12m
Famous Last Moves ***	11b	#7	Valley of Shaddai	SPORT+	24m
Cliptomaniac ***	12d	#14	Valley of Shaddai	SPORT	32m
Rosebud **	.8	#3	Malamute Upper	SPORT	18m
Curly	.9	#4	Malamute Upper	SPORT	8m
Larry *	.9	#5	Malamute Upper	SPORT	18m
Franz's Son	.9	#2	Malamute Upper	SPORT	10m
Pacing The Cage *	10a	#5	Malamute Upper	SPORT	12m
Sparky **	10b	#5	Malamute Upper	SPORT	18m
Stone Cold *	10b	#7	Malamute Upper	SPORT	22m
The Shallow End *	10b	#4	Malamute Upper	SPORT	10m
Consolation *	10c	#5	Malamute Upper	SPORT	20m
Train Boy *	10c	#5	Malamute Upper	SPORT	18m
Besot and Flushed **	10d	#4	Malamute Upper	SPORT+	35m
NPCC	10d	#2	Malamute Upper	SPORT	10m
Whip Cream Boy *	10d	#5	Malamute Upper	SPORT	18m
Featureless Face *	11a	#4	Malamute Upper	SPORT	12m
Neighbourhood Bully **	11a	#5	Malamute Upper	SPORT+	25m
Pooshwityorrfout *	11a	#6	Malamute Upper	SPORT	20m
Remembrance Day *	11c	#3	Malamute Upper	SPORT	10m
Shockload *	11c	#4	Malamute Upper	SPORT	10m
Arm Yourself *	12b	#6	Malamute Upper	SPORT	18m
Just A Little Pull	10d+1pa	#5	Malamute Lower	SPORT+	20m
Trainspotting	10d+1pa	#4	Malamute Lower	SPORT	20m
To Gliby Grab	11a	#4	Malamute Lower	SPORT+	15m
Will Power	11a	#6	Malamute Lower	SPORT+	25m
Invertigo	11c	#4	Malamute Lower	SPORT+	20m
Last Train To Hicksville **	12b	#6	Malamute Lower	SPORT	20m
Fly By Night *	11a	#4	Murrin - Above The Lake	SPORT	10m
Labyrinth *	11c+1pa	#7	Murrin - Above The Lake	SPORT	15m
A Show Of Hands	11d	#4	Murrin - Above The Lake	SPORT	26m
No More Tears **	11d	#10	Murrin - Above The Lake	SPORT	28m
Poltergeist 2 *	11d	#11	Murrin - Above The Lake	SPORT	2p.
Under Pressure *	11d	#6	Murrin - Above The Lake	SPORT	15m
Surveillance *	12b	#4	Murrin - Above The Lake	SPORT	10m
Chok'in A Grogan	.8	#4	Murrin - Up Among The Firs	SPORT	20m
Collet A Day	.8	#3	Murrin - Up Among The Firs	SPORT+	18m
Totally Clips **	10b	#10	Murrin - Up Among The Firs	SPORT	25m
Wallow Up To The Trough *	10b	#5	Murrin - Up Among The Firs	SPORT	18m
Poster Boy ***	10d	#7	Murrin - Up Among The Firs	SPORT+	27m
Seam's Dubious	10d	#6	Murrin - Up Among The Firs	SPORT	20m
The Nose *	10d	# 7	Murrin - Up Among The Firs	SPORT	45m
Usual Panic *	10d	#4	Murrin - Up Among The Firs	SPORT+	30m
Jacquester *	11d	#10	Murrin - Up Among The Firs	SPORT	30m

Zoë ******	10a	#7	Murrin - Zoe	SPORT	25m
Jeff and the Giant Reach *******	11c	#8	Murrin - Zoe	SPORT	25m
Breathe ******	12b	#6	Murrin - Zoe	SPORT	21m
Beat The Clock *****	11d	#3	Murrin - Xodus Wall	SPORT	10m
Betazoid *****	12b	#3	Murrin - Xodus Wall	SPORT	10m
Hand Over Fist	12b	#4	Murrin - Lakeside	SPORT	10m
Pleasant Pheasant *******	11a	#7	Murrin - Petrifying Wall	SPORT	22m
Elastic Man ******	11a-c	#5	Murrin - Petrifying Wall	SPORT+	22m
No Name Road *******	11b	#10	Murrin - Petrifying Wall	SPORT	45m
Czech It Out *****	11c	#3	Murrin - Petrifying Wall	SPORT	15m
If Only I Was Taller *****	11c	#3	Murrin - Petrifying Wall	SPORT+	15m
Air BC Direct	11d	#5	Murrin - Petrifying Wall	SPORT+	50m
Burning Down The Couch *******	11d	#10	Murrin - Petrifying Wall	SPORT	40m
Through Pastures Green *****	11d	#10	Murrin - Petrifying Wall	SPORT	40m
Black Water *******	12a	#11	Murrin - Petrifying Wall	SPORT	35m
Mr Fun *****	12a	#10	Murrin - Petrifying Wall	SPORT	40m
Baraka *******	12b	#8	Murrin - Petrifying Wall	SPORT+	35m
The Flingus Cling *******	12b	#6	Murrin - Petrifying Wall	SPORT	18m
Youth Gone Wild	12b	#4	Murrin - Petrifying Wall	SPORT+	12m
Fantastic Exploding Syringe *******	12c	#9	Murrin - Petrifying Wall	SPORT	35m
Animal ******	12c	#4	Murrin - Petrifying Wall	SPORT	16m
Panacea ******	12c	#5	Murrin - Petrifying Wall	SPORT	20m
Pigs on the Wing ******	12c	#13	Murrin - Petrifying Wall	SPORT	45m
Alistair's Route *****	12d	#5	Murrin - Petrifying Wall	SPORT	15m
Mata Hari *******	12d	#4	Murrin - Petrifying Wall	SPORT	22m
Rocket *******	12d	#4	Murrin - Petrifying Wall	SPORT	18m
Second Nature *****	12d	#5	Murrin - Petrifying Wall	SPORT+	30m
Animal Instinct ******	13a	#4	Murrin - Petrifying Wall	SPORT	16m
Caress Of Steel *****	13b	#4	Murrin - Petrifying Wall	SPORT	10m
Run For Cover ******	13b	#11	Murrin - Petrifying Wall	SPORT	40m
Lost Highway *******	13c	#6	Murrin - Petrifying Wall	SPORT	20m
The Pass ******	13a	#4	Murrin - Milkmans Wall	SPORT	15m
Thriller Off The Void ******	11b	#3	Murrin - Sugarloaf	SPORT+	20m
Wabbit Handcuffs	12c	#4	Murrin - Milkmans North	SPORT	7m
Infinite Decibels *****	12d	#6	Murrin - Leviticus	SPORT	15m
Vultures Circling *****	13b	#5	Murrin - Leviticus	SPORT	18m
Presto *******	13a	#5	Murrin - Presto	SPORT	25m
Jack In The Box *****	10c	#13	Quartz Pillar	SPORT	40m
Slopers ******	10c	#9	Quartz Pillar	SPORT	25m
Pulling Mussels ******	10d	#6	Quartz Pillar	SPORT+	23m
Silver Surfer ******	11b	#8	Quartz Pillar	SPORT+	35m
Swept Away ******	.9	#7	Seal Cove	SPORT+	2p.
Sea of Diamonds ******	10a	#4	Seal Cove	SPORT+	2p.
Lost Horizon *******	10b	#8	Seal Cove	SPORT+	45m
Sole Mate ******	10b	#7	Seal Cove	SPORT+	2p.
Local Boys Do Good *******	11a	#6	Shannon Falls (p1, p2)	SPORT	4p.
Local Heroes ******	11c	#5	Shannon Falls	SPORT	28m
Sexual Frustration	10b	#4	Smugglers Cove	SPORT	18m
The Whore	10b	#4	Smugglers Cove	SPORT	18m
Southern Man	11b	#4	Smugglers Cove	SPORT	15m
Price is Right	10a	#4	Alice Lake	SPORT	12m
Escape is at Hand	11a	#6	Alice Lake	SPORT	15m
Yellowjackets Glee ******	10c	#6	Copper Cove	SPORT	22m
The Amazing Fantini ******	12a	#9	Copper Cove	SPORT+	25m
Solitary Confinement	11a	#12	Crumpit Woods	SPORT	30m
The Schmoo *****	10b	#4	Dynamite Alley	SPORT	16m
Man of Leisure *******	10a	#7	Gobsmacking Wall	SPORT+	42m

If an accident should occur and help is needed, phone 911. This will alert the police who will initiate emergency rescue services. Hospital facilities are located at Squamish General Hospital, adjacent to the Smoke Bluffs. For the Lighthouse Park, Capilano Canyon and Copper Cove climbing areas, the closest medical facility is at Lions Gate Hospital, 231 East 15th Street, North Vancouver. Around Britannia, take your chance—north or south.

Emergency	911
Police (RCMP) non-emergency	(604) 898-9611
Squamish Tourism Information	(604) 892-9244
Bus Service (in Vancouver)	(604) 662-8051
Bus Service (in Squamish)	(604) 898-3914
BC Forest Service	(604) 898-2100
Fax number	(604) 898-2191
District of Squamish	(604) 892-5217
Fax number	(604) 892-1083
BC Parks	(604) 898-3678
Fax number	(604) 898-4171
Squamish General Hospital	(604) 892-5211
Local Internet Service Provider	www.mountain-inter.net
	(a useful local information resource)
Squamish road conditions and weather	(604) 892-3050
	(a service of Mountain FM radio)
Environment Canada Weather Forecasts	http://weather.ec.gc.ca/current.html
Squamish Weather Site...	http://www.weatheroffice.com/scripts/generator.pl?Squamish_WSK
Elaho Publishing Corporation	www.elaho.ca

Reporting New Routes

There are a number of ways you can report a new route or significant changes to existing ones. Providing accurate information will help ensure your climb gets posted on our website **www.elaho.ca** New routes books are kept at two locations:

♦ in Squamish at the **Climb On** store on Cleveland Avenue;
♦ in Vancouver at the **Mountain Equipment Co-op**;
♦ Send info. by fax to Kevin McLane/Elaho at (604) 892-3609.
♦ Or by e-mail to **stone@elaho.ca**

When listing your climb, try to follow the format in this guide: the grade of each pitch; the number of fixed protection points if any; the full credits of who led and followed; the gear used; the date it was done; whether you consider it to be a sport route; and above all, describe accurately where it is, or your effort will be wasted. Please make that clear, and draw a topo of the climb if you can.

Capilano Canyon

Capilano Canyon is a densely wooded gorge where the Capilano River winds its way down from the mountains north of Vancouver to Burrard Inlet. There are two climbs of unique character in this guide. Although there is some loose rock, the hard pitches are solid and well protected in an exhilarating position above the river.

Getting there... From the Trans Canada Highway, turn north on exit 14 up Capilano Road. After 1.7km, go left onto Fish Hatchery Road, park after 200m on the left. Walk 100m or so into the forest to the rim of the canyon. Scramble down to the river 200m to the north, then back downstream. Otherwise, make 2 double rope rappels down *Hydro Power*. Helmets recommended.

The Capilano Classic * 11a 4p
Robin Barley Nick Barley (Alts) Aug 1990
Climb the blunt rib easily to an alcove where the cliff steepens (.8). Belay, or traverse right past blocks and up a steep wall in an exposed position to a good ledge (10c). Back left and through bulges to gain a steep ramp. Superb climbing (11a). From the left end of the narrow belay ledge above, climb a crack (10b) finishing up tree roots.

Hydro Power * 11c 2p.
Simon Parsons Robin Barley (Alts) May '92
Just right of *The Classic*. A strenuous pitch of steep face climbing, mostly bolt protected with a few medium nuts. (11c). Easier-angled climbing past 2 bolts. A bit mossy (10b).

*Have you read
Conservation and
Courtesy? Page 22.*

THE CAPILANO CANYON

Rappel from here
for both routes

Loose

10b
10b
11a
10c   11c
2
1

Original
Start

Scramble in
at low water   **1**

| 1. Capilano Classic | 11a |
| 2. Hydro Power | 11c |

Lighthouse Park

The granite sea-cliffs at Juniper Point in West Vancouver's Lighthouse Park have long been popular with Vancouver climbers. The rock is delightfully rough and generously endowed with jugs, and with an approach through a magnificent old growth forest this area is a fine place to spend a summer evening or enjoy winter sunshine. The coastline is rugged and holds plenty of small surprises, so adventurous climbers can have fun exploring, traversing at sea level to the east and the west. Of particular note is a small zawn just west of the lighthouse. West of the park, private property will be encountered. Lighthouse Park suffers severely from overcrowding, so please act with patience and respect for all other users.

This park is very popular with the public as well as climbers, so being courteous and having minimal environmental impact are important.

Getting there...   This applies to approaches both from Squamish and Vancouver. Turn off Highway 1, 3km east of Horseshoe Bay at exit #4. Then turn left onto Caulfeild Drive beside the shopping mall, and drive steeply down for 700m to Willow Creek Rd. Go sharp left here for 500m to Keith Road, then left again for 500m to Marine Drive. Turn right (west) and proceed for 1.7km to the park sign on the crest of a hill, then left down Beacon Lane into the parking lot.

Take the wide trail that leaves the lower end of the parking lot on the right, behind a gate marked 'Fire Road'. Turn right after 100m, and 100m further go left at a fork, arriving within a few minutes at the top of the crag. The seaward side of the main crag can be accessed down ledges on the left or down a gully on the right, followed by some scrambling back down left to the top of a narrow cleft above the water. The climbs are described from west to east. Top-roping is popular, with anchors available for most climbs.

Ancient Mariner	.6	15m

Start in the bottom of the cleft. Steeply up to an easier finish.

Arbutus Tree	.9	15m

5m further right, climb the wall, keeping left to an overhang finish. Easier if the wall is climbed on the right.

Double Overhang Bypass	10c	15m

Climb the overhang on the left.

Double Overhang	10b	15m

An old classic. Climb the overhang at its right side.

Dolphin   .8   20m
Good. Steeply up a corner, pull past an overhang, then easy.

Two top-rope climbs take the wall above the mid-height overhang on Dolphin—5.11c (Orca - left-hand) and 5.10d (Starfish - right-hand), starting up the wall above the initial corner.

Big Pin   .8   10m
Takes the dyke on fine rough holds.

Coho   10a   10m
The wall on the right is taken up its steepest part behind a tree.

Jugs Away   .7   7m
The right edge offers a short steep climb.

Arbutus Alley is a 10m wall in the trees 50m north of the main crag, rising from a shallow gully facing the sea.

Cauliflower   10c   x   10m
Seamed cracks just left of the tree.

Arbutus One   10c   x   10m
Start as for *Cauliflower*, but go up right along a vague line.

Arbutus Two   10a   x   10m
Just right of the tree a mantel leads to steep climbing.

5m down from Arbutus Two is a top-rope face climb at 5.11a.

LIGHTHOUSE PARK

1. Ancient Mariner 6	5. Big Pin 8
2. Arbutus Tree 9	6. Coho 10a
3. Double Overhang ..10b/c	7. Jugs Away 7
4. Dolphin 8	TR. Left=11c Right=10d

Copper Cove

Surprisingly close to Horseshoe Bay but visible only from the seaward side, this 30m high west-facing seacliff is composed mainly of good granite with some queer black rock and basalt intrusions. The climbs are not tidal but the approach is, and the return trip can reach epic proportions if a high tide catches you unaware: epic, as in 5th-class climbing unroped with a pack, half-submerged in the deep dark water, spray lashing the rock overhead. I'm not making this up, it happened to me in the company of the redoubtable Barley and his two labradors Snot and Grot (they have otherwise unpronounceable names) who were cast into the frothy swell to fend for themselves. Much hulabaloo followed, but they made it. Beware the innocent passage of ferries too, as a minute or so after their passing the wash will sweep onto the crag, and when two ferries pass each other, it reaches tsunami-like proportions. If you value your innocent new girl/boyfriend who wants only to be your belay slave, better pay attention.

Getting there... Exit Highway 99 into Horseshoe Bay and follow signs for Whytecliff Park. Look for Copper Cove Road on the right, 1.3km from the highway. Turn and park near the bottom. Space is limited, so do not park in any way that interferes with local residents. A walkway leads down to the public beach. Head north along the intertidal zone. 10 minutes to the crag. Along the way are some very short overhanging zawns with bolted routes.

Climbs and gear... Wires and cams ½"–2", draws and a 50m rope.

Yellowjackets Glee ** 10c #6 **SPORT** 22m
Robin Barley John Fantini August 1997
A surprisingly good climb up the gray pillar at the right end of the crag, the crux being a long reach off a peculiar wafer at mid-height.

Tennis Anyone? 10b 20m
Robin Barley Judy Komori July 1998
Climb off the lawn into a shallow corner system, finishing diagonally left.

Guttersnipe * 10b 20m
Robin Barley Nick Barley August 1997
Climb over the right side of the roof on amazing jugs. Nice face climbing above.

Roof Tiles .9 25m
Robin Barley Judy Komori June 1997
Immediately left of the roof, climb a narrow basalt dyke for 7m past a spike to a bolt. Go diagonally right up a tiled ramp. Protection is a challenge but improves higher up toward the chains.

Neo Classical ** 10b 25m
Robin Barley Doug Jamieson July 1997
A fine climb starting up the basalt dyke and continuing up good granite.

The Friability Factor * 10b 30m
Robin Barley Judy Komori June 1998
Starting from a ledge 5m above the sea, step right and climb over flakes up a bulging white wall. An easy middle section and a steeper finish.

Dark Vein * .9 30m
Robin Barley Doug Jamieson July 1997
From the same ledge, follow a narrow basalt dyke upwards over a couple of turf ledges to cleaner rock above.

The Oddity 11a 30m
John Fantini Robin Barley August 1997
Approach a black intrusion from the left, a bit thin at first. Then climb it.

Shamefaced 11a A0 25m
Robin Barley July 1998
The lower walls give fingery, flakey climbing on sharp edges with a better finish. Climbed only with many rests on bolts so far...

The Amazing Fantini ** 12a #9 **SPORT**+ 25m
John Fantini Robin Barley July 1997
Similar to the previous route. John Fantini is still climbing 5.12 at 55 years of age—not bad for an Aussie. Take a couple pieces ½-1".

Pussyfooting .8 18m
Robin Barley Judy Komori August 1997
Easy-angled face climbing with fiddly but adequate protection.

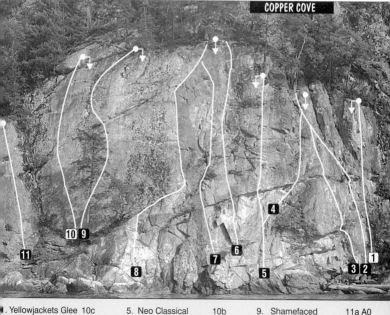

COPPER COVE

1. Yellowjackets Glee	10c	5. Neo Classical	10b	9. Shamefaced	11a A0
2. Tennis Anyone?	10b	6. The Friability Factor	10b	10. The Amazing Fantini	12a
3. Guttersnipe	10b	7. Dark Vein	.9	11. Pussyfooting	.8
4. Roof Tiles	.9	8. The Oddity	11a		

Comic Rocks

This interesting crag south of Britannia Beach offers a number of fine climbs, generally of a half-pitch in length in a pleasant environment. They are in three groups: a short slab by the highway; the main crag; and a pair of small buttresses 100m beyond. This place is surprisingly quiet considering the quality of the climbs, so if you need respite from the crowds further north try climbing here.

Getting there...   From the south, a wide shoulder leads into a spacious parking area 30km north of Horseshoe Bay, 12km south of the Chief (3km north of the Furry Creek intersection). The open top of the southeast-facing crag can be seen poking above the trees 100m to the east. A wide trail below the cliffs gives a pleasant approach.

Climbs and gear...   There is a variable collection of routes here, generally following natural lines. Most are surprisingly good, offering plenty of variety. Recommended are *Peanuts, Popeye, Desperate Dan* (5.10s) and *Garfield*, one of the best 5.7s in the guide. Most routes require crack gear, generally small to mid-size, but throw a couple of 2½" – 3" cams in the bag too. *Li'l Abner* will need a larger piece. A descent trail heads around to the west and allows use of a single 50m rope.

> *Two climbs are on a small south-facing cliff, 35m north of the entrance gate to Comic Rocks. Faith, 5.9 climbs the left edge of the slab past a bolt, and Hope, 5.6 climbs the obvious crack up the centre of the slab.*

Biffo The Bear   10b   20m
Bob Milward Jim Campbell June 1983
A groove and corner line, with a roof at mid-height at the far left of the crag.

Popeye *   10d   20m
Jim Campbell Bob Milward (1pa) June 1983   FFA Dean Hart Randy Atkinson
A deceptively sustained pump up an obvious crackline slanting right to left.

Dennis The Menace   .9   23m
Jim Campbell Bob Milward June 1983
Climb a square corner to a roof, then go left to finish. An entertaining crux.

Peanuts **   10c   45m
Carl Austrom and others 1978   FFA: R.Milward J.Campbell Aug 1983
A fine climb up a tricky groove with only modest protection and an exciting traverse. Belay, or continue up easy block overhangs.

Vargas Girl *   12b   20m
Carl Austrom and others (aid, previously Spiderman) c1978   FFA Keith Reid 1986
The smooth wall right of *Peanuts*. Climb left past a bolt and a flake crack. Pull through the bulge to an easy hand crack. Left to belay bolts.

Garfield ★★★ .7 40m
Bob Milward Jim Campbell June 1983

Excellent climbing in fine situations. Start 15m right of *Vargas Girl*, at the base of a high smooth slab. Hand traverse the prominent flake sweeping leftwards across the wall and up a fine handcrack and blocky overhangs above.

Broom Hilda ● .8 40m
Bob Milward Jim Campbell Aug 1983

Start as for *Garfield*, but take the slabby wall above, left of the dark chimney and the burnt cedar snag. Traverse out left to finish.

Clean And Free 11a x 10m
Jim Campbell Bob Milward Aug 1983   FFA: G.Barber J.Fredericks June 1988

The short steep crack 8m right of *Garfield*.

Li'l Abner ● 11a x 15m
Bob Milward Jim Campbell Aug. 1983

A wide crack 15m right of *Clean And Free*. Was good once.

■ *The next three climbs are on twin buttresses, 100m further easdt*

Desperate Dan ★ 10d x 15m
Bob Milward Jim Campbell John Howe. Aug 1983   FFA: Bob Milward Aug. 1983

The prominent crescent shaped flake on the left buttress. Gain it from the right. Deceptively strenuous and technical.

Rocky And His Friends .8 x 15m
John Howe Bob Milward Jim Campbell Aug.1983

The hand crack in the back of the recess between the buttresses. Overgrown.

Rufus ★ 11c x 20m
Jim Campbell Bob Milward Aug 1983   FFA: Dave Lane Perry Beckham May 1984

A roof flake on the right-hand buttress that offers a fine handjamming problem. Start on the right, swing into the crack and go. Finish up the headwall crack.

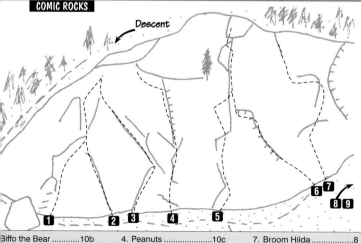

COMIC ROCKS

Descent

Smuggler's Cove

These quiet seacliffs overlooking Howe Sound are located on a headland a short walk south of Britannia Beach.

Getting there...   Park at the south end of the flat section of highway, about a kilometre south of Britannia Beach. Cross the tracks and take a wide trail that leads southward along the shoreline. Within a few minutes, a pleasant cove is reached. Walk south 100m through a grassy glade on the shorefront toward a promontory that juts out into Howe Sound. Take a steep trail that climbs along its north side, then drops to the base of a west-facing cliff and the first route.

Access...   The crags and the approach may lie in part on undeveloped private land, so if you visit this area, please proceed with respect and observe any signage that may be posted. The climbs are included in this guide as a matter of historical record.

> *The first apparent climb, with 2 bolts above a 2m block, is about 15m from the south end of the west face, just left of a prominent unclimbed finger-crack. Nothing is known about it.*

Guinness Pillar	11a		x		15m

Nick Jones 1994
A curving, open groove just left of the southern end of the west-facing crag. Move out right at the top to a ledge belay.

Southern Man	11b	#4	x	*SPORT*	15m

Nick Jones 1994
Just right of *Guinness Pillar*, climb over a steep bulge to gain a thin crackline. Move left onto the ramp to join *Guinness Pillar*.

> *The next two climbs are on the south face, starting by a prominent fir tree, 10m right of Southern Man.*

The Whore	10b	#4	x	*SPORT*	18m

Nick Jones 1994
Move left from the tree to reach the lefthand bolt line.

Sexual Frustration	10b	#4	x	*SPORT*	18m

Paul Elson 1994
Go straight up from the tree.

> *The trail continues for another 50m below the 40m high south face and becomes a very exposed and increasingly difficult scramble. Below Southern Man, the ground drops off steeply into the water 30 metres below. There is believed to be a climb (5.10 ?) from the waterline on the east face of a tower in a narrow zawn. Bolts are on top.*

Dynamite Alley

This is the large canyon-like rock cut on the highway north of Britannia Beach, 1km south of Browning Lake at Murrin Park. Park at the large paved turnout on the southbound lane of the highway, or a smaller gravel pull-out on the north side. The climbs are in two places, both on the east side of the highway: a slab facing northwest that lies down in a hole below the highway and a steeper, south-facing cliff at the south end of the rock cut.

The climbs on the slab start at the lowest point and diverge above an obvious flake 7m up. The slab is overgrown at present. Scramble down to the base, and you'll realise the climbs are much longer than they appear. Top-roping should be easy to arrange.

The Resurrection Factor ● ☺ 10d   x   30m
S.St Louis   M.Davis   1987
From the top of the flake, move up, then left to a vague crackline.

Enoch Walked ● ☺   10c   x   30m
S.St Louis   W.Dyck   1987
Everyone else climbs. Go straight up from the top of the flake.

First Commandment ● ☺   10c   x   30m
S.St Louis   M.Davis   1987
Follows the right hand line up to an easier crack.

The next two climbs are on the wall above the Squamish sign.

The Schmoo   *   10b   #4   **SPORT**   16m
Tim Holwill   Bill Noble   Nick Jones   Aug 1992
A pleasant face climb on the wall just right of the crack of *Welcome To Squamish*. Pull well off the road. A quick tick.

Welcome To Squamish * 11a   15m
Geoff Creighton   Philip van Wassenaer   June 1986
Climb the obvious parallel cracks on the south-facing wall behind the Welcome To Squamish sign. Start from a big tree stump. Crux at half height.

Seal Cove

This is a delightful west-facing seacliff in a small secluded bay between Britannia Beach and Murrin Park. There is an astonishingly short approach. If you are quick the base is only 4 minutes from the highway. Well worth a visit and well named, given the number of seals that pop up to see what's going on. The main crag is a steep, smooth slab with a friendly ambience dropping straight into the water. An adjacent rocky beach gives a good view of the climbs. There are two trails to the crag, to the base and to the top. Access from the top to the base is possible only by a 25m rappel off a tree at the north end of the crag.

Getting there...   To the base. Park at the large turnout on the south-bound lane of Highway 99, south of Dynamite Alley at the upper end of the long straight section of road north of Britannia Beach. If driving north, it is also possible to park in a gravel turnout on the east side. Walk north through Dynamite Alley to the trailhead on the left, just where hydro lines are overhead. Drop steeply over talus into the forest below. The railway tracks just above Seal Cove are reached in 5-6 minutes from the highway. Head down to the rocky beach.

Getting there...   To the top. A trail to the top of the crag starts just north of the parking. Walk north to the first rocks of Dynamite Alley and head left down talus onto the trail. The top of the crag is reached in a few minutes. There is a 25m rappel station off a tree at the north end.

Climbs and gear...   The climbs are either fully bolted or require a minimal number of medium-size CDs and wires, as does *The Seal Cove Traverse.*

Lost Horizon ******   10b   #8   **SPORT**+   45m
Glenn Payan Jeff Thomson April 1997
A fine climb up the most left-hand route, starting from the rocks at the base. Perhaps the best route on the crag, with a couple pieces of gear to 1½".

A Future and a Hope *****   .9   48m
Glenn Payan Jeff Thomson Shannon Price Jack Fieldhouse July 1998
Traverse in to the start just above the waterline. Climb a good finger-crack up right of the tree ledge, then left and back right to a tree belay.

The Seal Cove Traverse ****** .8 - 11a   50-120m
Jeff Thomson Jack Fieldhouse Glenn Payan Kevin McLane Shannon Price Oct 1998
Full Traverse: *Jack Fieldhouse, solo Oct 1998.*
This exciting crackline traverse above the water is the means of reaching the start of the next three climbs, creating a first pitch for each. The difficulty gets up to 5.9 toward the end. Take a few ½"-2" CDs, and draws. It is also possible to continue traversing beyond *Swept Away* to the next cove, at 5.11a.

Sole Mate **   10b   #7   **SPORT**+   2p.

Jeff Thomson   Glenn Payan   Shannon Price   Jack Fieldhouse   July 1998

Take the *Seal Cove Traverse* to the first belay (.8). Tricky to the first bolt [potential for falling in the drink at high tide!], then easier (10b).

Sea of Diamonds **   10a   #4   **SPORT**+   2p.

Jeff Thomson   Glenn Payan   Jack Fieldhouse   Shannon Price   October 1998

Take the *Seal Cove Traverse* to the second belay (.8). Climb straight up (10a).

Swept Away *   .9   #7   **SPORT**+   2p.

Jeff Thomson   Kevin McLane   Jack Fieldhouse   Glenn Payan   Shannon Price   October 1998

Take the *Seal Cove Traverse* to the third belay, 45m (.9). Climb up past 7 bolts, finishing with a short traverse to the right (.9).

> *South of the previous climbs are two more, both starting from the water's edge. From the top of Sole Mate or A Future... scramble up to the next ledge above. Head south to a rock promontory, then for Beware The Tides of March, go right and scramble down to the water's edge. For Tsunami Laugh, go left down a gully to the east.*

Beware The Tides of March   *   11a   #7   x   **SPORT**+   25m

Glenn Payan   Jeff Thomson   October 1998

A friction slab rising from the small terrace. Take a couple of CDs to 1.5″.

Tsunami Laugh   10d   x   15m

Glenn Payan   Jeff Thomson   October 1998

A short corner and thin finger crack on a clean wall facing south down Howe Sound. Take small wires and mid-size CDs.

SEAL COVE

1. Lost Horizon 10b
2. Seal Cove Traverse...8-11a
3. Future and a Hope...........9
4. Sole Mate...................10b
5. Sea of Diamonds 10a
6. Swept Away 9

The Quartz Pillar

A fine sea-cliff between Britannia Beach and Murrin Park in a scenic position facing south down Howe Sound. The climbs are excellent and well worth a visit, and can be combined with a visit to Seal Cove. Climbing at this crag and Seal Cove is a startling, and for most people, very unexpected contrast to the rest of Squamish.

Getting there...   Park and take the trail down to Seal Cove. The Quartz Pillar is a 13-minute walk west of Seal Cove. At that point, just before the rail tracks enter a tunnel, the cliff can easily be seen 70m down to the left, an enticing buttress rising from a perfect terrace.

Access...   Take care to listen for trains if you are walking on the tracks.

Climbs and gear...   Two 50m ropes if you want to rap off, otherwise walk and scramble off the back. A medium rack to 3″ and 10 draws.

Silver Surfer ******   11b   #8   **SPORT+**   35m
Nick Jones   June 1992
A fine climb, deceptively difficult and sustained. A few small CDs and wires are optional. Rappel or scramble off the back.

Howe Unsound ******   11a   35m
Nick Jones   June 1992
Tread lightly up the left side of the unbelievably thin flake and then past a bolt on the wall above. Finish up the arete. Take a full rack to 2″.

Free Willy *****   .8   24m
Glenn Payan Jeff Thomson June 1997
The buttress right of *Howe Unsound*. 3 bolts, gear to 2″.

Pulling Mussels ******   10d   #6   **SPORT+**   23m
Glenn Payan Jeff Thomson June 1997
Start up a short crack right of *Free Willy*, then face climb past bolts to a horizontal crack. Traverse right then up past more bolts (cruxy) to a small patch of dark rock. Gear to 3″. Traverse back to *Free Willy*.

▪▪▪▪ SLOPERS   ▬▬▬▬▬▬

This is the wall by the tracks, 50m before the Quartz Pillar.

Slopers ******   10c   #9   *x*   **SPORT**   25m
Glenn Payan Jeff Thomson Jack Fieldhouse Kevin McLane Jan 1 1999   var: Jack Fieldhouse
A face climb up the centre of the wall. This climb is unique in the guide for being so perversely endowed with small, square wickedly sloping holds. Start on the right. The station at 25m keeps the grade to 10c, otherwise traverse out left to finish *(Holy Devoted —*11a #3). A harder variation starts directly below the main line of bolts and also finishes direct (11c).

Jack-In-The-Box *****   10c   #13   *x*   **SPORT**   38m
Jeff Thomson Jack Fieldhouse Jan 1999
Start as for *Slopers* then move out right to go directly up the impressive wall above to a cruxy finish. Walk off to the south.

THE QUARTZ PILLAR

Seal Cove
Slopers (50m)

1
2
3
4

QUARTZ PILLAR

1. Silver Surfer..............11b
2. Howe Unsound 11a
3. Free Willy.....................8
4. Pulling Mussels.........10d

1
2
3
4

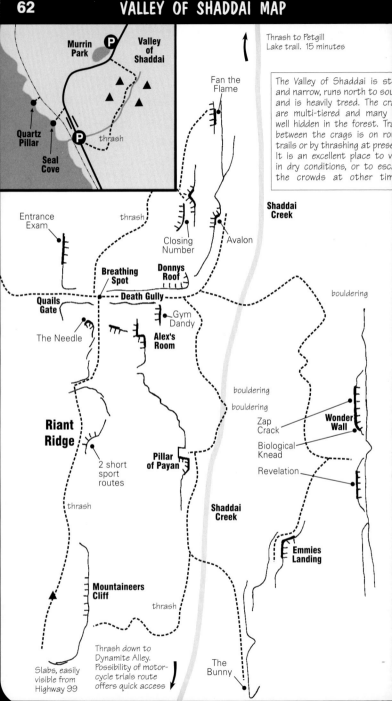

Murrin Park

Valley of Shaddai

Quartz Pillar

Seal Cove

thrash

Thrash to Petgill
Lake trail. 15 minutes

The Valley of Shaddai is st...
and narrow, runs north to sou...
and is heavily treed. The cra...
are multi-tiered and many...
well hidden in the forest. Tra...
between the crags is on ro...
trails or by thrashing at prese...
It is an excellent place to v...
in dry conditions, or to esc...
the crowds at other tim...

Fan the Flame

Shaddai Creek

Entrance Exam

thrash

Closing Number

Avalon

Breathing Spot

Donnys Roof

Quails Gate

Death Gully

bouldering

The Needle

Gym Dandy

Alex's Room

Riant Ridge

bouldering

bouldering

Zap Crack

Wonder Wall

2 short sport routes

Biological Knead

Pillar of Payan

Revelation

thrash

Shaddai Creek

Emmies Landing

Mountaineers Cliff

thrash

Slabs, easily visible from Highway 99

Thrash down to Dynamite Alley. Possibility of motor-cycle trials route offers quick access

The Bunny

THE VALLEY OF SHADDAI

This is a deep valley running north-south for two kilometres, east of and parallel to Highway 99 as it passes through Murrin Park. The southern end can be seen when descending northward on Highway 99 down to Britannia Beach, noted by a mass of rounded crags that offer promise. Although an approach is possible from that direction, as is an approach from the trail to Petgill Lake, both are thrashes (for now, at least) and unlikely to offer better access than the approach described, directly from the parking lot at Murrin Park.

The valley itself is deep and heavily wooded, and little sunlight filters into the bottom, although the crags poke above the trees. It has never been logged, so there is natural ambience of coastal rainforest. Despite the proximity to the highway, there is a surprisingly remote and adventurous feel to the place. Many trails are not yet well defined and some routes require bushwhacking to reach. There are steep banks and gullies with long dropoffs. Loose rock on the tops of some cliffs and on ledges can be precarious. Most routes have had few if any repeat ascents.

Getting there...   From the Murrin Park parking lot, walk back down the highway underneath Browning Bluff, opposite the lake. Thirty metres south of the crag, head steeply uphill on a rough trail under the hydro lines. This is also the approach for the routes at Above-The-Lake. Above the hydro lines, the going gets easier in open timber. Follow the trail up rightward, and within 15 minutes of leaving the highway you'll arrive at the Quail's Gate, a queer pass-like feature between small bluffs. In another 100m you'll reach the Breathing Spot at the top of Death Gully on Riant Ridge. The ridge stretches to your left and right offering a pleasant hike in its own right, and the climbs are open to the sky. Death Gully lies ahead, a steep descent down to the valley bottom, assisted by a fixed line. Despite the name, it is not dangerous, but on the return trip, searing lungs and burning quads will have visions of death providing a blissful release.

Climbs and gear...   There are about 30 climbs in all, offering a good variety with an emphasis on 5.10 and up. Most routes are single pitch but a few require two ropes to get down. Take plenty of draws, and a full granite crack-rack up to 3½″ for longer routes. There are some sport climbs, and if you are having a quickdraw-only day at 5.11 or above, it is possible to climb at Above-The-Lake enroute. Recommended crags are the Pillar of Payan (mid-10 and up), Donny's Roof (hard-10 and up), Emmie's Landing (one mid-11). The *Avalon Connection* (low-10), and *Gym Dandy* (10c) are good climbs too.

TRAIL TO VALLEY OF SHADDAI

← **Riant Ridge** →

15 mins to the top.

Above-The-Lake
(Crags hidden in the trees)

POLTERGEIST

NO MORE TEARS

SMELL OF FAT CHICK

Browning Bluff

Highway 99

The view from Browning Lake at Murrin Park

Expandos... One of the defining trademarks of many Squamish aid routes is the ubiquitous expanding flake. Sometimes encompassing entire corner systems as on Ten Years After, or great arches as on Humpty Dumpty. As you cheerfully nail away on what appear to be A1 placements, you wonder what all the gentle tinkling below is—everything falling out. There have been many huge falls as a result. But the technical advances of tiny camming devices have taken a good chunk of the bite and fear away, and today's climbers can safely shudder at the prospect of the great Daryl Hatten and Eric Weinstein actually driving pin stacks into all the creaking expandos on Up From The Skies.

Riant Ridge Routes

Riant Ridge is the high wooded ridge that runs parallel to Highway 99 east of Murrin Park, and which is bisected by the trail into the Valley of Shaddai at Quail's Gate and the Breathing Spot. The ridge crest is a pleasant hike through salal and small open timber, weaving around small domes and over bedrock slabs; a nice hike in its own right with good views down Howe Sound and Britannia, and with unusual views of the upper crags in Murrin Park. At present, there are five climbs in 3 groups on those bluffs.

Getting there...   Just before entering Quail's Gate from the west, go north along a broken cliff that forms the northern escarpment of the ridge. The finger-crack of *Entrance Exam* is reached after 35m. There are two short (really short) climbs within a stone's throw southwest of the Breathing Spot. Step up the short bluff on the south side and continue 30m through the salal. Below the left side of the crest, look for an obelisk-like 3m block, laying flat and pointing east into the valley. *Necessary Dorsal* is 8m past the block, facing north down in a gully-like hole. *The Needle* can also be seen to the right, an obvious short flake crack that ends in a 'summit'.

Entrance Exam ******　　　11d　(11a+1pa)　*x*　　　　　　　30m
Glenn Payan Jeff Thomson July 98　　FFA Jack Fieldhouse Aug 98
A bolt by the initial seam can be used for aid, or crank through to the fine crack that awaits.

Necessary Dorsal Muscles　10b　#3　　*x*　　**SPORT**　7m
Glenn Payan Jeff Thomson Sept 98
A very short overhanging dyke.

The Needle　　　　10a　　　　*x*　　　　　　8m
Jack Fieldhouse Aug 98
Located directly 25m west of *Necessary Dorsal...* on the ridge crest.

Less than 5 minutes south along the ridge, a narrow trench-like gully bisects the ridge. Drop down into it and scramble easily out the other side. 40m beyond, the top of a small south-facing outcrop of rock is reached, with good views to the east and south. Look for bolt stations. Below you are two short, somewhat scruffy routes. Scramble down a short chimney-gully on the right (looking down).

Hit The Ground And Mean It　　.6　#3　*x*　　**SPORT**　10m
Glenn Payan September 97
Climb the dyke. Anchor bolts on top.

I Don't Need This ●　　11a　#5　　*x*　　**SPORT**　12m
Glenn Payan, Jeff Thomson March 98
Start up the dyke to the second bolt then make an awkward traverse to the right and up past bolts and slightly better climbing.

Alex's Room

This name refers to a collection of small crags on the east side of Riant Ridge, immediately south of Death Gully. Most of the climbs are enjoyable, the best being *Gym Dandy* (10c) and *Keep The Faith* (10a). Walking up or down to the valley bottom via these routes is an alternative to Death Gully.

Getting there...   **From Riant Ridge**, approach as for the *Needle* on the Ridge, and head down the gully past *Necessary Dorsal Muscles.* Just below the gully is the top of the climbs by *Keep The Faith* (10a). Walk around to the left (looking down) and scramble easily to the base. An enticing wall, bounded on the left by a buttress, sports the north facing finger and hand crack of *Keep The Faith.* From here, angle down northeastward for 40m to a steep east facing crag with a black water streak on its north end, beyond which is Death Gully.

Getting there...   **From the creek**, walk up past Donny's Roof, then go left to *Gym Dandy* and up from there.

Scheherazade .9 x 8m
Glenn Payan July 98
A flake climb facing east 15m north of *Keep The Faith*.

Keep The Faith   ** 10a 10m
Glenn Payan Aug 98
The obvious crack. Start on the right in the easier flake. Good fun.

A Maze Of Grace   * 10b 12m
Glenn Payan Jeff Thomson Aug 98
Start as for *Keep The Faith* but keep low and traverse left around the buttress on small ledges, clipping a bolt right on the buttress edge. Finish up a juggy dyke on the east side.

Muck 11a 10m
Jeff Thomson Glenn Payan Aug 98
Climb the difficult flaring crack just left of the start of *Keep The Faith*, then follow that route until a high traverse left on jugs to a bolt near the buttress is possible. Pull left around the buttress to the top.

Dovey   * 11a   #3 **SPORT**+   12m
Jeff Thomson Glenn Payan July 98
Climbs the left side of the prow. Start 3m left of *Muck*, pull the roof and climb past 3 bolts to join the jug haul finish of *A Maze Of Grace*.

Shaddai is an arabic word which means 'strength'.

The next climb is obscurely tucked away south of Dovey. Walk south for 25m, until a step down to a lower ledge is necessary. Ahead is a broken gully-like zone. Barking At The Ants is on the opposite side, on a wall facing east.

Barking At The Ants   10c   x   15m
Glenn Payan   Jeff Thomson   Aug 98

Start in a deep, short corner facing into the gully. Climb up and around the corner to a crack in a face. When the crack thins to a seam make full use of holds on the right, passing a bolt, then move back into the crack.

The next two climbs are on an east-facing cliff halfway up the valley side, just 30m or so from Death Gully, and below Keep The Faith. There are 2 routes on this 20m long crag, which is dark and wet at the north end, dryer at the south.

Gym Dandy **   10c   #7   x   **SPORT**   18m
Glenn Payan Jeff Thomson   Aug 98

The left hand route. Excellent. Easily found by the line of bolts. A juggy entrance from the right by-passes the more difficult 5.11a undercling start and lowers the grade a bit, though the sting in the tail is still unavoidable.

Pitch Black ●   10c   x   15m
Glenn Payan Jeff Thomson   Aug 98

10m right of *Gym Dandy*, start up a crack in a dark, fuzzy face, then up past two bolts. Move right into a hand crack then up. Awkward.

The Needle, 5.10a. Climber Jack Fieldhouse
Photo Fieldhouse Collection

ALEX'S ROOM

1. Keep the Faith 10a
2. A Maze of Grace 10b
3. Muck...........................11a
4. Dovey 11a

Donny's Roof

This crag is a large buttress with south and east faces located at the bottom of Death Gully. It sports three fine routes and is easily identified by a large hole-like roof midway up the gloomy south face.

Getting there... Hike down Death Gully. The crag is unmistakeable on the left side (looking down) near the valley bottom. Alternatively, walk down via *Keep The Faith* and *Gym Dandy*. It is also possible to reach the top of the crag by devious scrambling and an exposed ledge traverse that leaves the gully two-thirds of the way down.

Desperate Echo **   11a   *x*   18m
Glenn Payan Jeff Thomson (1pa) August 98   FFA Jack Fieldhouse August 1998
If you like slightly overhanging, flaring offwidths, you'll love this slug-fest. Start under the left edge of the roof and climb it on the left past 2 bolts. Then the fun begins. Climb the ever widening crack. Gear to 4".

Follow the crag down to the base. There are two impressive climbs here, mostly bolt-protected, which face east into the valley bottom.

Famous Last Moves ***   11b 24m
                #7   **SPORT+**
Glenn Payan Jeff Thomson June 98
FFA Jeff Thomson Glenn Payan June 98
Climb the steep right facing open book. Pass a small roof up high, then move up and right to a easier slab finish, which some climbers oddly enough find to be the crux. Take two CDs to 1".

Dream's Descent ***   10d 20m
                #8   **SPORT+**
Glenn Payan Jeff Thomson Aug 98
Clip the first bolt of *Famous...* and go up to the flake crack at 8m. Step around left into the corner on the left and up to the first roof. Step back right out of the corner to pass the roof then trend left, following bolts, above the roof and up an exposed buttress. Finish back right to the anchors. Take a 1" CD.

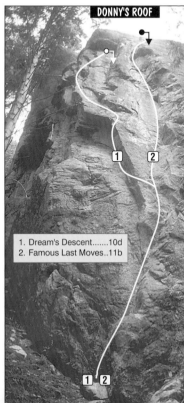

DONNY'S ROOF

1. Dream's Descent.......10d
2. Famous Last Moves..11b

Avalon Connection

This crag encompasses the cliffs, ramps and forested ledges on the east facing crags north of Donny's Roof. The climbs are especially attractive as a tiered linkage–the *Avalon Connection*– offering a fine moderate climb of four pitches. It is well worth hiking into the valley just for it alone, and as a way back home it is an alternative to struggling up Death Gully. The top of *Closing Number* deposits you near Riant Ridge, north of the top of the Breathing Spot. Wander north, then back south to reach the main trail.

Getting there... Hike down Death Gully to the base of Donny's Roof, then north for 40m to *Avalon,* a series of left-facing flakes and small roofs. *Pyrix* is above. *Closing Number* can be reached via *Avalon-Pyrix,* or by scrambling up a ramp right of the base of Donny's Roof.

Avalon   **   10b   25m
Glenn Payan Jeff thomson Sept 98
Climb the flake to a ledge then up a short corner keeping left to finish on a large ledge: excellent. Belay, rappel, or continue up *Pyrix* in one full pitch.

Pyrix   **   10a   18m
Glenn Payan Jeff Thomson Sept 98
A splendid finger crack up a exposed buttress to a wonderful belay.

Closing Number   **   10a   20m
Glenn Payan Jeff Thomson Sept 98
Start in a short flaring corner and hand traverse the spectacular incut crack.

Fan The Flame   **   10c   18m
Glenn Payan Sept 98
A stellar little crack in a great position.

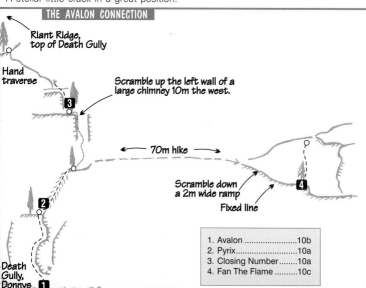

THE AVALON CONNECTION

Riant Ridge,
top of Death Gully

Hand traverse

Scramble up the left wall of a
large chimney 10m the west.

3

← 70m hike →

Scramble down
a 2m wide ramp

Fixed line

4

2

Death
Gully,
Donnys   **1**

1. Avalon	10b
2. Pyrix	10a
3. Closing Number	10a
4. Fan The Flame	10c

Pillar Of Payan

This striking buttress offers a couple of the best climbs in the valley. It has the appearance of a pillar, bordered on the north by a large, impressive chasm. The smooth north face of the pillar holds the superb crack of *Just Blessed.*

Getting there... Hike down Death Gully to Donny's Roof, then follow the trail heading south along the sidehill above the creek. After 100m or so it descends to the creek. Another 40m, and the pillar can be seen facing north, just up the hill. Take two ropes to get down.

Just Blessed ★★★ 10c   35m
Glenn Payan Jeff Thomson John Thompson Aug 97
Amazing finger and hand jams, as well as superb edges and stances lead up the steep cracks in the smooth north face.

Cliptomaniac ★★★   12d   #14   **SPORT**   35m
Glenn Payan Jeff Thomson Aug 98 (many pa)   FFA Jack Fieldhouse July 98
The long, steep arete left of *Just Blessed.* Occasional forays onto the left wall at the blocks and at the second last bolt were used on the FFA. Following the original route directly up the right side of the arete would be harder.

The following two routes start in a bay at the foot of an obvious left-facing chimney-corner around to the left of the pillar.

World's Apart ★ 10b × 15m
Glenn Payan Jeff Thomson July 98
Climb the steep hand crack leading up the narrow south face of the pillar to a ledge and anchors. Creative stemming into the chimney to the left helps.

Heart In Flames ★★ 10c × 25m
Glenn Payan Jeff Thomson Aug 98
Climb the left angling crack on the wall just south of the pillar. More difficult than it appears but very satisfying. Until the scary finish, anyway.

Have you joined the Climbers Access Society yet?

PILLAR OF PAYAN

1. Cliptomaniac....12d
2. Just Blessed 10c

The Man of No Leisure, 5.10a
Climber Glenn Payan. Photo: Payan collection

Wonder Wall

Though this crag is a healthy 45-minute hike from the Murrin parking lot, it is the showpiece cliff of the Valley of Shaddai. It rises to 65m in spots over its 200 m length. It is steep and offers little in the way of easy routes though the new route potential at the higher levels is outstanding. It is a wonderful and remote crag.

Getting there... Hike down Death Gully to Donny's Roof, then down to cross the creek. Pick up a flagged trail and hike up the far slope trending north-east. Follow the flagged trail as it heads back south for 200 m until the wall comes into view to the east. Walk directly to the cliff. A wide but fairly shallow chimney here marks the approximate centre of the crag and offers a good reference point.

Zap Crack **   10d+8pa   18m
Glenn Payan April 97
This immaculate finger crack is 25m north of the large chimney, on a golden over-hanging wall. A major FFA prize is waiting here. Scramble off to the south.

Biological Knead **   10d   45m
Glenn Payan Jeff Thomson Sept 98
Excellent steep finger and hand crack 10m left of the chimney. Gear to 3½".

Revelation **   11c   20m
Glenn Payan Jeff Thomson Aug 97 FFA Jeff Thomson Glenn Payan Sept 98
A steep finger crack, with a hard start located 15m right of the chimney. Scramble up to the base from the north below the wide chimney. Pro: bolt and gear to 2.5".

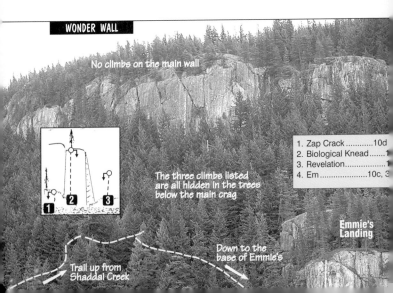

WONDER WALL

No climbs on the main wall

The three climbs listed are all hidden in the trees below the main crag

1. Zap Crack 10d
2. Biological Knead 1
3. Revelation 1
4. Em 10c, 3

Emmie's Landing

Trail up from Shaddai Creek

Down to the base of Emmie's

Emmie's Landing

This is the large, prominent west facing crag located below Wonder Wall and south east from Pillar of Payan. *Em* is one of the gems of the Valley.

Getting there... Hike down Death Gully to Donny's Roof, then take the trail for Wonder Wall. Just where it rounds the final corner and Wonder Wall comes into view, begin a gradual south-west descent through open forest. After 70m a large west facing crag is reached. Walk around on an exposed ledge to the base of a stunning, slightly overhanging right facing corner.

Em **   10c+3pa   35m

Glenn Payan   Sept 97 (has been freed at 11b by Jeff Thomson on TR)

Climb the corner with 3 aid points (crux). Pass the roof on the right and climb a finger crack past a bonsai tree and a hollow flake, to the top. Walk off south then back north. Gear to 3½".

> *For the next climb, walk south 50m from the Pillar of Payan then cross the creek. Climb up to the base of Emmie's Landing then walk south 50m, crossing a small boulderfield en route. 40m beyond is a short, well scrubbed crack.*

The Bunny *   .9   x   15m

Glenn Payan Sept 98

Located at the far south end of this large crag. Boulder start. The bunny awaits at the top offering a fine jam between its ears. Gear to 2".

Mountaineer's Cliff

This is a large east-facing cliff rising out of the south end of the valley, clearly visible from Highway 99 south of Britannia.

Getting there... The best approach is to walk along Riant Ridge to the top of the cliff. Ten minutes or so after leaving the top of Death Gully, you end up on bedrock along the top of the cliff. Continue, wandering down slabs on the south end of the cliff, some scrambling, until it is possible to follow the base back north (lots of salal) for 60m. A 4m scramble gains the base of a prominent clean slab-buttress, the first route. *Japhia* can also be reached from the Pillar of Payan.

Japhia   ✸✸   10a   #6   x   **SPORT**+   1-2p.
Glenn Payan Jeff Thomson June 98
Follow bolts up the clean slab-buttress to a tree ledge at 28m. Rappel off or traverse north, wandering up dirty, blocky 4th class rock. Take one 1" CD.

Maiden Voyage   10a   x   45m
Glenn Payan Paul Starr Aug 97
Scramble up to a ledge and belay bolt 10m right and above the start of *Japhia*. Climb small quartz intrusions then up more 'alpine' rock to the top.

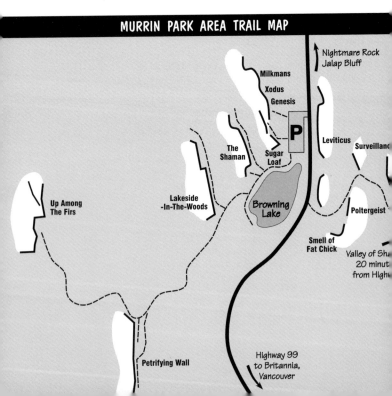

MURRIN PARK AREA TRAIL MAP

MURRIN PARK

Murrin Provincial Park is a small picnic and fishing area beside Highway 99, centred on Browning Lake between Squamish and Britannia Beach, and managed by BC Parks. The climbing is remarkably varied, from the short friendly routes on Sugarloaf to modern hard climbs at Petrifying Wall, the great cracks of Nightmare Rock and the wealth of interesting climbs over the hill in the Valley of Shaddai: in all, about 250 routes to satisfy all tastes. Murrin Park captures one of the great appeals of Squamish climbing: variety and diversity on superb rock. Hence, it is one popular place, great for getting onto the rock quickly, but expect lineups and many climbers at the better crags. BC Parks expanded the parking lot considerably in 1994, but it already overflows at peak times, and the Valley of Shaddai and this guide will increase the load further. Get there early on busy summer days.

Getting there...   Easy. Murrin Park is 2km north of Britannia Beach, and 6km south of the Chief. Park in the large lot by the highway.

The Climbs...   The crags near the parking lot–Sugarloaf, Block and Tackle, Brunser, Xodus and The Shaman–continue to remain terminally popular. Petrifying Wall holds its appeal as ever with over 40 mostly superb hard climbs, and is the pre-eminent sport-climbing crag in this guide for 5.11s to 5.13s. Up Among The Firs is a new crag, offering a good number of 5.9–5.10 climbs in a fine scenic setting high above Pet Wall. The trail to the crag passes many huge fir trees, and demonstrates the potential of the Murrin Park area for short enjoyable hikes. Leviticus has been lifted out of its identity as a lacklustre wall of short, forgotten aid routes by Andrew Boyd, who freed some of the most startling lines.

The crags are described in a counterclockwise direction, starting with the crags immediately adjacent to the parking lot on the west side, then south to Petrifying Wall, over to Shaddai and back north along the highway to Nightmare Rock. Between the parking lot and the lake is a popular bouldering wall and meeting place.

Murrin Park is a good place to head for on hot summer afternoons, but a place to avoid in cold windy weather.

MURRIN PARK NORTHERN AREA

The Shaman

Sugarloaf - Brunser
Xodus - Milkmans

Nightmare Roc

Petrifying Wall
Up Among the Firs

Parking
Lot

See map, page 74

MURRIN PARK CRAGS - SOUTHERN AREA

Up Among the Firs

Lost in Obscu

Lakeside-In-
the-Woods

Petrifying
Wall

The Sl

Dam Hydro lines

Browning Lake

The Bog Wall

A small but heavily used cliff at the edge of the parking lot. Despite its present demise as a top-rope jungle, the climbs are good if you can get on them. Climbs are obvious and listed from left to right. The crag gets its name from the swamp that existed at the base until about 1990.

Getting there...   It's smack at the edge of the parking lot.

Focus 10 .7   8m
Unknown
The left-hand, offwidth crack.

Holy Grail * 10a   18m
Dave Jones Dale Caldwell June 1990
A face climb just left of the two most prominent cracks.

Up from the Bog ** .8   18m
Unknown   FFA Kevin McLane Andreas Maurer 1975 (possibly earlier)
The left-hand of the two main cracks, up the centre of the crag.

Fathers And Sons * 11a   18m
S.Hutchinson D.Hutchinson July 1990
A face climb between the two cracklines.

Veils of Illusion *.9   18m
Dave Jones Tim Ryan May 1990
The second crackline from the right.

Black Butterfly * .9   15m
Dave Jones Tim Ryan May 1990
The far right crack.

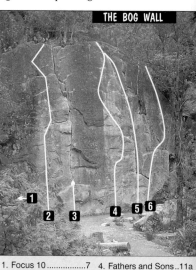

THE BOG WALL

1. Focus 10 7	4. Fathers and Sons ..11a
2. Holy Grail 10a	5. Veils of Illusion...........9
3. Up From The Bog...8	6. Black Butterfly 9

The Highway to Squamish was completed in 1958, the year after the Russians launched Sputnik, the first satellite.

Sugarloaf

An immensely popular and often overcrowded crag due to the easy climbs and user friendly nature of the rough high-angle slab on the south side. It has been used for teaching purposes since the mid-1960s. An unmistakable steel hydro tower sits on top, offering a modest belay anchor. Climbs are described from the toe of the buttress where the trail abuts.

Getting there...   Take the trail that heads up out of the parking lot 20m right of the toilets. 100m to the crag.

■■■■ SUGARLOAF — SOUTH SIDE   ■■■■

The next six climbs represent the most popular lines up the rough slab on the south side of Sugarloaf, although many variations can be worked out. All but one first ascents are unknown, but were likely climbed in the 1960s. A trail winds around below the north side to the top. Climbs are described from right to left on this face.

Lieback Crack   *   .7   20m
Les McDonald and others 1965
At the toe, this prominent corner sports a good crack.

Little Spark   *   .4   20m
The groove just left of *Lieback Crack*. Pass a small bulge at 10m.

Jump Start   .6   20m
Start as for *Little Spark* at the small roof on the left, then up face cracks above.

Magnet   .4   20m
Climb the broken crackline right of the prominent white streak.

Power Smart   *   .8   20m
Directly up the slim wall to the white streak, passing it on the left.

Flat Battery   .4   20m
The obvious crackline left of *Power Smart*.

Diamonds And Spades   .4   x   15m
Unknown
A route up a low-angle cracked slab directly behind the steel hydro tower.

The first climb established on the Apron was Slab Alley in 1961,
by Jim Baldwin and Tony Cousins.

MURRIN

■ SUGARLOAF — NORTH SIDE

The north side of Sugarloaf is made of sterner stuff than the south. 10m right of the toe of the buttress is a distinct corner-groove leading up to a horizontal crack, the start of the first route.

Mandela * 11c 20m
Kevin McLane Joe Turley Mar 16 1986
Climb the groove to a bolt above. Then follow the seam above until possible to move left to the arete.

Thriller Off The Void ** 11b #3 **SPORT**+ 20m
Dave Lane 1978 (Top-roped by Royal Robbins 1971)
Climb the groove, then the vague crackline that trends up right to the top. A fine route. 3 bolts and a wire or two.

> *A top-rope climb at 11d goes up the blunt prow right of Thriller Off The Void (John Howe-Dave Lane 1986)*

Hot Wire * 10c 18m
Tim Holwill 1985   Previously top roped in the 1970s
A popular route. A variation goes right above the bulge.

Heavy Charge 11b 16m
Unknown
Climb into the sentry box, exit up right.

Stairway * .7 14m
John Coope K.Winter 1962
A good climb with a variation start (10b) on the left.

SUGARLOAF SOUTH
oto taken in 1980
vid Harris

SUGARLOAF NORTH

Block And Tackle

An east-facing cliff marked by a prominent bulging roof that splits the crag at mid-height. Popular because of its location beside Sugarloaf, but the climbs are good too.

Getting there...   Take the Sugarloaf trail, 20m right of the toilets, and walk left past the south side of Sugarloaf to the crag.

Holiday In Cambodia   *   .8   18m
Bob Milward   Scott Young   Aug 1983
Start below the the right end of the long roof and climb to the shallow right-facing layback corner above. Finish on the right or the left.

Block And Tackle   **   11b   18m
Unknown   FFA: Perry Beckham   Dean Hart   1982
Long stretches on the lower wall lead to a short strenuous crux through the roof. Deceptively difficult, but good climbing.

Orphan   *   .9   12m
Unknown   FFA: Kevin McLane   Howie Richardson   1978
Climb the right facing corner to the roof and exit left.

Measles And Pestilence   11c   x   25m
Harry van Oort   Rachel McGhee   July 1995
Start up *Holiday*, and traverse left under the roof to finish up *Orphan*. Cool.

Granola Angst   ●   10a   12m
Larry Ostrander   1988
Start just left of *Orphan*, and climb up past a fixed pin.

Tricky Dicky   *   10c   x   18m
Bob Milward   Joe Buszowski   July 1983
A south facing open groove 15m left of *Orphan*. A little gem, actually.

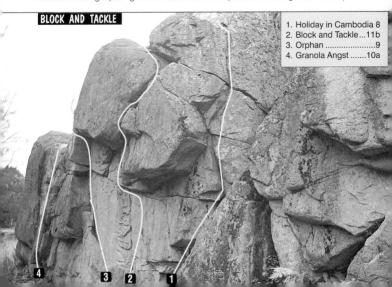

BLOCK AND TACKLE

1. Holiday in Cambodia 8
2. Block and Tackle...11b
3. Orphan 9
4. Granola Angst 10a

The Brunser Area

Fifty metres to the right of Sugarloaf is a 15m cliff with the distinctive stepped roof and corner of *Brunser*. Climbs are described from the left, in the order they are reached. Descend to the north.

Getting there... Walk over from Sugarloaf, or directly up from the parking lot trail that starts 35m right of the Bog Wall.

Sunny Boy   *   10a   *82*   25m
Luc Mailloux Tyler Stayer April 1996
Climbs the prominent dark slab at the left side of the Brunser wall. Start at the foot and climb past 3 bolts. A variation finish goes out left above the salal ledge at 10m *(Luc Mailloux, Robert Korba 1996).*

Washington Bullets   **   10c   *82*   20m
Peder Ourom Daryl Hatten 1982
An enjoyable crackline with good protection and rests.

The Brunser Overhang   **   10d   *82*   20m
Tony Cousins Jim Sinclair 1963   FFA: Dave Loecks Bill Putnam 1975
Brunser Direct: Dave Harris Jim Sinclair '63   FFA Dave Loecks Peter Charak '75
A Squamish classic. Handjam or chimney to the left end of the big flake, and on through the roof above. Quite memorable. The direct start is 11d.

The Washington–Brunser Connection   * 10c   *82*   30m
Gary Korba and Family, Luc Mailloux Oct 15 1994
An excellent route. Climb *Washington Bullets* until just above the crux, then traverse right below the large roof to join the top of *Brunser*.

Psyched For Life   11a   *82*   22m
John Howe Blake Robinson Aug 7th 1985
A long reach (or levitation) is required to gain the upper crack.

Fist   *   10a   *82*   22m
Joe Turley G.Kristiensen 1962
A hard start leads to an easier crack and a roof. Move left to finish. The original finish went out right, and a pin from the first ascent is still there. This climb was the hardest crack at Squamish for almost a decade.

Handful   .9   *82*   14m
Unknown   FFA: Jim Campbell John Coope Sept 1981
Climb the diagonal crack just right of *Fist,* pulling over the roof to finish.

Up For Grabs   .8   *82*   10m
Jim Campbell John Coope Sept 1981
A short diagonal crack at the far right side of the cliff. Zig-zag crack above.

> ▌ *The next climb is actually on the upper section of Xodus Wall, but is best reached from the base of Brunser.*

Flake Off   *   .6   *82*   20m
Jim Baldwin Jim Sinclair KenBaker 1961
Right of *Handful* is a low angle slab. Climb the crack on the left.

BRUNSER AND LOWER XODUS WALL AREA

From Sugarloaf

Photo taken in 1980
by David Harris

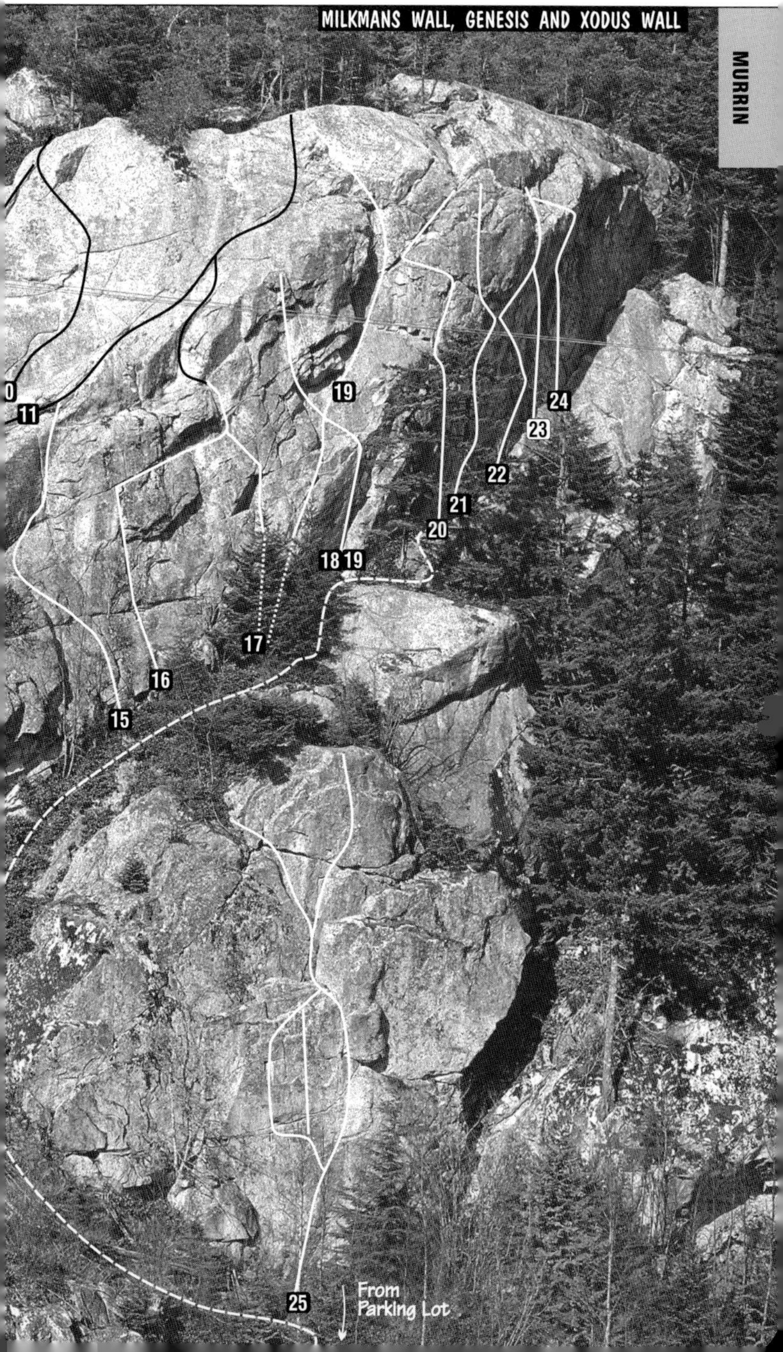

0
11

19

24
23

22

21
20

18 19

17

16

15

25

From
Parking Lot

Xodus Wall

Xodus Wall is the 50m cliff to the right of *Brunser* which is split into upper and lower tiers. Milkman's Wall lies to the right.

Getting there... Approach via a trail from the parking lot that starts 35m right of Bog Wall to the first climb on the lower tier, or walk down from Brunser. Climbs are described from the base upward.

Genesis * 10a-c *83* 25m
Hamish Mutch I.Kennedy 1961 FFA: Unknown
Left-hand Cracks: Rob Rohn 1981 Direct headwall finish: Larry Ostrander D.Dancer 1988
From the base of the wall, gain a crack 10m up to the right and follow it to easier ground. The cracks on the left are 10b and 10c, and the headwall 10a.

Mickey Mantle 10d *82* 12m
Gary Korba and Family, Luc Mailloux Oct 20 1994
The obvious corner high on the left side of the overhanging wall which sports *Betazoid* (12b) and *Beat The Clock* (11d). Chains at the top.

Beat The Clock * 11d #3 *82* **SPORT** 10m
Larry Ostrander D.Dancer 1988
If you're lucky. Goes out to the right. Just a little bit strenuous.

Betazoid * 12b #3 *82* **SPORT** 10m
Dan Jackson Sept 19 1990
Goes out to the left. Just a little bit more strenuous.

Milkmaid * .8 *83* 25m
Blake Robinson John Howe Aug 7 1985
A short climb up a layback corner, joining *Wakey Wakey* above.

Lena ● 10d *83* 25m
John Howe Blake Robinson Aug 14 1985
Short, sharp difficulties.

Fallout ● 10a *83* 25m
Tim Auger Mike Wisnicki 1964 FFA: John Howe Jim Campbell May 1982
A rather vague old line that joins *Lena* at the end of the traverse on that route.

Xodus ** 11a *83* 25m
Jim Baldwin Jim Sinclair Sept 1961 FFA: Eric Weinstein Gordie Smaill 1976
The face crack left of *Tourist Delight*. Climb the crack with some alacrity followed by a long stretch through the roof above.

Tourist Delight * 10b *83* 25m
Jim Baldwin Ken Baker Aug 1961. FFA: Andreas Maurer Kevin McLane Aug 1975
Climbs the deep right facing corner high on the wall. Small RPs help. Start from the terrace on the right or more directly from below on the left.

Flake On * .8 *83* 25m
Unknown
From a ledge right of *Brunser*, climb low-angle cracks up right.

Wakey Wakey .4 *83* 50m
Dick Wilmott and others 1962
A long traverse across the top of Xodus Wall. Sparse protection.

The Milkman's Wall

This gently overhanging wall is home to several outstanding climbs, all of them sustained and exposed. The first ascent of *Horrors Of Ivan* in 1982 (originally graded 5.10c!) was instrumental in opening up the potential of Squamish granite to steep face climbing. The development of the early climbs at Pet Wall in 1984-86, owe much to these gripping climbs at Milkman's Wall.

Getting there... Scramble up rightward from below the upper part of Xodus Wall. Descend back down the slab right of *Milkman*...

Mr Crabbe   **   11c   *83, 86*   35m
Royal Robbins (aid) 1971   FFA: Peter Croft   Mike Beaubien 1982
Follows the long fault splitting the cliff from left to right. Start on the left, as for *Tourist Delight,* at a short corner.

Mr O'Clock   **   11a   *83, 86*   20m
Peter Croft Hamish Fraser 1982
5m right of *Mr Crabbe*. A difficult start leads to a layback flake and a rest at 8m. Pull over a bulge and up a faint groove above. Hand traverse left to finish. A sustained and strenuous route. Excellent. The direct finish straight up the final headwall is 11b *Kevin McLane Ted Marks Mar 1986*.

El Indio   **   11c   *83, 86*   20m
Kevin McLane June 1985
Start just right of *Mr O'Clock* and climb the yellow wall through bulges past a bolt, then up right to join the rising crackline of *Mr Crabbe* and the niche of *Horrors Of Ivan*. Climb directly up the wall above the niche. Poor pro.

Horrors Of Ivan   ***½ 11c   *83, 86*   20m
Peter Croft Tami Knight 1982
A tremendous climb, very sustained. Pull up a line of good holds past 2 bolts. Move left with increasing difficulty to a hostile niche and a poor rest. There was once a block in the niche (now on the ground) that gave a better rest. The crackline above to the right gives a magnificent finish. A Squamish classic. *El Ivan* (11b) is a combination which gives the easiest route up the wall following *Horrors Of Ivan* to the niche, then out left up the headwall of *El Indio*.

The Pass   **   13a   #4   *83, 86*   **SPORT**   15m
Jim Sandford   July 1993
A direct line up the wall midway between *Horrors of Ivan* and *The World's Toughest Milkman*. Powerful bouldery moves topped by a spectacular dyno. Rap hangers at the top.

The World's Toughest Milkman   *** .8   *83, 86*   18m
Peder Ourom Clive Thompson 1981
One of the best climbs of its grade at Squamish, a 5.8 that feels like a 5.10; a sheep in wolf's clothing. From the higher terrace on the right, climb to the overhanging flake, and a committing jug-haul finish on huge holds. Pro to 4".

North Of Milkman's Wall

Three climbs lie on the scattered walls right of Milkman's Wall.

Getting there...   From the parking lot, take a trail 50m right of Bog Wall that leads up right through the trees, passing a prominent boulder with a roof crack. From there, scramble up to the right to a boulderfield and head up it to the base of a white wall *(Wabbit Handcuffs)*. Walk right, then back left. The overhang of *The Baldwin Crack* can be seen above.

Wabbit Handcuffs   12c   #4   x   **SPORT**   7m
Tim Crawshaw August 1994
A short climb up a fractured wall to chains with a very bouldery crux.

The Baldwin Crack   11c   x   25m
Hamish Mutch M.McCuaig 1967   FFA: Tom Gibson George Manson 1979
Hard moves to the lip lead to a much easier corner above.

Cruisin' For Grins   *   10b   x   15m
Perry Beckham solo 1986
20m left of *The Baldwin Crack,* climb the fine juggy wall facing north. A bolt protects the final overhang.

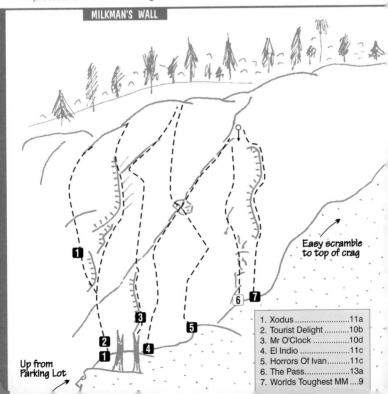

MILKMAN'S WALL

Easy scramble
to top of crag

Up from
Parking Lot

1. Xodus 11a
2. Tourist Delight 10b
3. Mr O'Clock 10d
4. El Indio 11c
5. Horrors Of Ivan..........11c
6. The Pass...................13a
7. Worlds Toughest MM 9

Zoë

This shady little wall offers three fine sport routes–two hard and one not– in the trees just above the main trail along Browning Lake. Climbs are described from the left. The striking feature of the crag is the massive sickle-shaped, hollow arch smack in the centre above the ground. If the line-ups are too much for you on Zoë, the Shaman wall on the right offers more good climbs.

Getting there...   Follow the wide trail out of the parking lot to the lake. Just before the last picnic tables, head up right 40m to the crag. Four minutes from the car. Shaman wall is to the right.

Breathe   **   12b   #6   *89*   **SPORT**   21m
Glenn Payan Jeff Thomson (2pa) July 1998   FFA Jack Fieldhouse July 1998
Undercling the arch to the 4th bolt, then pull the roof and on up the face above.

Jeff And The Giant Reach   **   11c   #8   *89*   **SPORT**   25m
Glenn Payan (1pa) July 1998   FFA Jeff Thomson July 1998
Direct start: Jack Fieldhouse August 1998
Start 2m right of the arch at two obvious juggy flakes. Climb out left to a huge cruxy reach, then face climbing and a short corner lead to the top. A more direct start at 11d (ground fall potential) goes straight up from the second bolt on the arch.

Zoë   **   10a   #7   *89*   **SPORT**   25m
Glenn Payan Jeff Thomson July 1998
A good climb and a soft touch for its grade. Start 5m right of the arch. Climb steeply to a bolt at 5m, then trend leftward into an open corner, finishing through a fine overhang.

ZOE — SHAMAN AREA

Lakeside

Sugarloaf - Brunser
Xodus - Milkmans

Shaman
Wall

Zoe
Wall

Parking
Lot

The Shaman

This fine crag rises above the forest northwest of the lake. It is bigger than it appears from a distance and hosts a number of good climbs and some spectacular firs along the base. Shady and cool.

Getting there...   From the parking lot, walk along the lakeside trail. Shortly before the last picnic table, turn right and hike uphill for 50m to a high, shaded wall rising up the slope. A pair of twin firs at the right side are used as a reference find the starts.

Big Fish In A Little Pond * 11b   22m
Peder Ourom W.Shumka April 1991
A mostly-bolted face climb starting 10m left of the twin firs. Gear to 2".

The first pitches of the next 3 climbs lead to a common belay at 20m.

The Shaman **   10a   2p.
Bill Noble Nick Jones   June 1989
Beautiful climbing, although a bit runout in pitch 1. Start beside the left hand fir, and go up left until it is possible to trend back right to belay in the shallow recess. 3 bolts (10a). Go out left from the belay and up cracks (10a).

Tia *   11c   2p.
Nick Jones June 1989
Goes directly up to the shallow recess past 2 bolts (10d). Climb with difficulty up the wall above on good protection, joining *Medicine Wheel* at a ledge (11c).

Medicine Wheel *   10d   2p.
Nick Jones and others June 1989
Start 8m right of the twin firs on a salal ramp. Step out left, then up past 2 bolt and 2 pins to the recess (10c). Climb up right to a rounded overlap, traversing underneath it past an FP to a steep crack. Pull into the crack and make a few hard moves past an FP gain a ledge. Face climbing leads to the top. An easier finish can be made by continuing the traverse to a join *Fat Lady...*

When The Fat Lady Sings ● 10c   28m
Kevin McLane John Howe May 1992
Start as for *Medicine Wheel,* then right to a bolt. Up past 2 more bolts to gain a crack leading to a ledge belay. Go right to rappel.

Woz On The Edge ● ☺ 10c   40m
Stu Wozney Hamish Fraser Peder Ourom March 1992
Walk up the trail to a block on the ramp 20m up from the twin firs. Go left, then climb discontinuous cracks at the left edge of the wall. Rappel from a tree, or scramble down.

Raven   10d   15m
Nick Jones Bill Noble June 1989
Directly above *The Shaman.* Climb twin cracks then after 10m, pull out right up the first obvious break. Easier face climbing leads to the top.

UPPER SHAMAN

La La Lumpa Lumpa Lae .8   25m
Jia Condon Andrew Howell Aug 2 1992
The right-facing corner above *Woz On The Edge*. Scruffy.

Toenar   10a   27m
Jia Condon Andrew Howell Aug 2 1992
About 6m above and right of *La La Lumpa...* is an obvious overhang (rather like a hole in the rock). Climb up to it and pull over into cracks. Traverse right to more cracks leading to face climbing at the top.

Any Doubt Run It Out   10a   30m
Jia Condon Andrew Howell Aug 2 1992
Traverse up then right below the band of overhangs to reach a short but distinct left-facing corner-ramp. Climb it and then cracks above. Finish with thin moves.

Two hard-to-find climbs have been reported "to the left and uphill from the Shaman"; a thin crack, and a southwest facing corner.

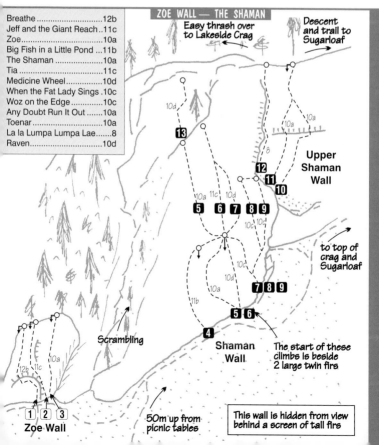

ZOE WALL — THE SHAMAN

Breathe	12b
Jeff and the Giant Reach	11c
Zoe	10a
Big Fish in a Little Pond	11b
The Shaman	10a
Tia	11c
Medicine Wheel	10d
When the Fat Lady Sings	10c
Woz on the Edge	10c
Any Doubt Run It Out	10a
Toenar	10a
La la Lumpa Lumpa Lae	8
Raven	10d

Easy thrash over to Lakeside Crag

Descent and trail to Sugarloaf

Upper Shaman Wall

to top of crag and Sugarloaf

Scrambling

Shaman Wall

The start of these climbs is beside 2 large twin firs

50m up from picnic tables

This wall is hidden from view behind a screen of tall firs

Zoe Wall

Lakeside-In-The-Woods

This long east-facing crag is hidden among tall firs between Browning Lake and Petrifying Wall, stretching up the hill to the right for 150m. There are three sections to the crag: the south end, close to the trail; then a futuristic section of wall (worth a look!); then a lower upper section beyond the *The Reacharound.*

Getting there...   Follow the Petrifying Wall trail which starts 50m past the open beach area at Browning Lake. The crag is on the right, just 100m along the trail. A wide canyon-like gully marks the south end.

Climbs and Gear...   Depending on the climb, you'll need anything from RPs to 4″ CDs. Climbs are described from left to right.

Fearless Fraser   11a   25m
Bruce Langereis May 1991
Start at the toe of the gully. Move up to a bolt, or climb the tree and step left, up left to a flake crack and over a bulge. Easier ground leads to the top.

Free Loader   **   11b   25m
Colin Moorhead John Rosholt July 1997
Start at the tree of *Fearless Fraser*, pass 2 bolts, then go straight up past 2 more to a surprise finish. Short rack, small to medium sizes.

Mister Picklebits   10b   25m
Damien Kelly Colin Moorhead June 1997
Start 25m right of the base of the gully at a limbed tree. Climb the right-leaning crackline just left of the tree.

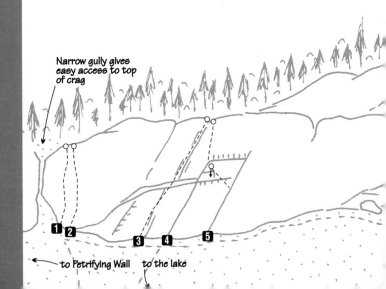

LAKESIDE-IN-THE-WOODS

Narrow gully gives
easy access to top
of crag

1 **2**   **3**   **4**   **5**

to Petrifying Wall   to the lake

Coitus Interruptus   **   12a   25m
John Rosholt Aug 1997
The polished diagonal crack just right of *Picklebits* that leads to a crimpy face above the cave-like recess. Keep a 1" CD for the last move.

The Masses Are Asses   * 12b   18m
Andrew Boyd May 1998
The thin right-leaning seam, 3m right of *Coitus* sporting an FP at 5m. Move left to belay at a tree in the cave.

The Reacharound   **   .9   25m
Colin Moorhead Damien Kelly June 1997
About 100m uphill of the previous climbs is a dramatic cracked corner that provides a fine climb. Don't be concerned about finding it—it will find you.

Hand Over Fist   12b   #4   **SPORT** 10m
Jim Sandford Feb 27 1991
Climb through short bulges to a station, 25m right of *Reacharound.*.

Above Lakeside is a steep east-facing wall with what is believed to be a completed route–a 30m bolted climb that reportedly goes at 11a/b with a bolt for aid. There are a couple of current projects on this wall. Hike up past Hand Over Fist. The climb below is also in that area.

Lost In Obscurity   .9   2p.
Joe Buszowski Craig Thomson 1982
A long-lost climb on one of the highest outcrops, a buttress-type route on a south-east facing wall. Look for a couple of old bolts.

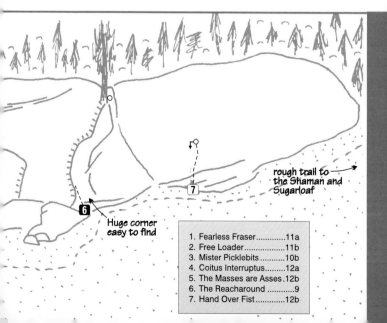

rough trail to the Shaman and Sugarloaf

6 Huge corner easy to find

1. Fearless Fraser.............11a
2. Free Loader...................11b
3. Mister Picklebits...........10b
4. Coitus Interruptus.........12a
5. The Masses are Asses.12b
6. The Reacharound 9
7. Hand Over Fist.............12b

Burning Down The Couch, 5.11d   Climber: Josh Korman

Petrifying Wall

Petrifying Wall is one of the most dramatic single-pitch crags at Squamish with a whole raft of hard climbs. The rock is much more accommodating to hard face climbs than the classic granite of the Chief, but its vertical-to-gently-overhanging nature demands considerable forearm endurance and a high level of technical skill. Of the 47 climbs, 26 offer the best collection of hard sport climbs– from 11a to 13c–in the guide. The cliff is about 200m long, faces east and is a short walk from the car. It is split into two levels, the upper right end with 13 climbs, and the lower lefthand end with 34. The climbs are described right to left along the crag as they are approached. Descents are usually by rappel or lower, but a descent trail goes via the north end.

Getting there... Follow the Petrifying Wall trail which starts 50m past the open beach area at Browning Lake. Eight minutes to the crag.

Climbs and gear... There are so many good to superb climbs it is hard to miss. Just pick one and climb it. There are no thuggish granite cracks here, almost every climb offers a technical challenge for its grade. The most popular moderate sport route is *Pleasant Pheasant* (11a). Four harder sport routes stand out as classics, *No Name Road* (11b), *Black Water* (12a), *Burning Down the Couch* (11d), and *The Flingus Cling* (12b). Of the gear routes *DOA* (11c), *Take No Prisoners* (11d) and *The Flight of The Challenger* (12c) are superb. The 5.13s generally involve long reaches between miniscule edges on vertical terrain. A 50m rope is normal for most routes, but a 60m is helpful for lowering too. Double ropes help on wandering climbs on DOA wall. Take a medium to full rack to the crag, usually small wires to 2½″ CDs. Most of the gear routes will have a bolt or two or fixed pins somewhere. If you're seeking sport climbs only, a sackfull of draws is all you need.

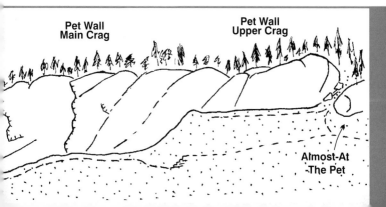

Pet Wall
Main Crag

Pet Wall
Upper Crag

Almost-At
-The Pet

▰▰▰ ALMOST-AT-THE-PET   ▰▰▰▰▰▰

A short vertical wall on the right side of the trail near Petrifying Wall, about 30m before the *Challenger*. Easily spotted by the arching layback corner of *Heart of the Sun* at its left side; a much-neglected little gem.

Heart Of The Sun   ******   .8   10m
Tim Holwill Stu Holwill 1985
A short left facing layback corner capped by a bulge. Great value.

The Karma Police   *****   11d   15m
Unknown (aid?) FFA Andrew Boyd Aug 1998
Six metres right of *Heart of the Sun* is a line of seams and edges. An FP in the first seam and a bolt below the second mark this good route.

If Only I Was Taller   *****   11c   #3   **SPORT+**   15m
Andrew Boyd Aug 1998
Three metres right of *Karma Police*, climb directly past 3 bolts, out left on an easier undercling to finish. Take a CD or two for the undercling at the top.

Monkey See, Monkey Do   *****   12b   #4   **SPORT**   15m
Andrew Boyd Aug 1998
A sustained face-climb with left-facing edges, 5m uphill from *If Only I Was...*

▰▰▰ UPPER PETRIFYING WALL   ▰▰▰▰▰▰

The Wrong Stuff   *****   11c   20m
Perry Beckham John Howe 1986
A wild traverse below *The Challenger*. After 20m, swing left through a roof onto a ledge belay. A 13a TR goes direct to the traverse *(Jim Sandford Aug 1988)*.

Backdoor Santa   *****   12c   20m
Josh Korman 1988
Follow *The Wrong Stuff*, but take the roof more directly past 3 ring bolts.

The Flight Of The Challenger   *******   12c   30m
Dave Lane 1986
An outstanding climb up the right-leaning crack and groove line, guarded by an overhanging start. It is difficult to enter the groove, and little easier above.

Caress Of Steel   *****   13b   #4   **SPORT**   10m
Jim Sandford May 28 1991
Through the bulge left of *The Challenger*. Technical and balancy moves.

Youth Gone Wild   12b   #4   **SPORT+**   12m
Sarkis Vermilyea April 1992
Climbs out of the left side of a cave, above a sharp boulder. Take one 3" CD.

Food Frenzy   11b   20m
Greg Foweraker Jim Sandford 1986
A crackline 15m left of *Caress Of Steel*. Not the best protection.

Panacea   ******   12c   #5   **SPORT**   20m
Jim Sandford Jola Sandford Sept 12 1990
Superb cranking up sharp little edges.

Alistair's Route   *****   12d   #5   **SPORT**   15m
Alistair King 1989
More of the same fine little edges, just a bit harder.

MURRIN

Czech It Out   *   11c   #3   **SPORT**   15m
Tomas Hasal   1989
Left of *Alistair's*, up a dark wall past 3 bolts. Often wet.

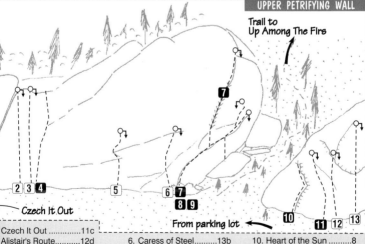

UPPER PETRIFYING WALL

Trail to
Up Among The Firs

Czech It Out

From parking lot

Petrifying Wall - Main Crag

The big rock mushroom is a landmark and lounging spot for the next 4 routes and provides a good view of the lower wall.

Animal Instinct ** 13a #4 99 **SPORT** 16m
Jim Sandford July 1990
The right hand line of bolts. After a hard start through the bulge, move left to join *Animal* at the 3rd bolt.

Animal ** 12c #4 99 **SPORT** 16m
Jim Sandford 1988
A powerful opening to a thin surprise finish, just right of *Flingus Cling.*

The Flingus Cling *** 12b #6 99 **SPORT** 18m
Perry Beckham May 1986
A well-deserved classic. Start off a stump below the mushroom. This is one of the most popular 5.12 sport routes in the guide. Easy to fling yourself at, or to be a belay slave in the sun. Expect lineups.

Mata Hari *** 12d #4 99 **SPORT** 22m
Perry Beckham 1987
Move out left from the start of *Flingus Cling,* and go straight up past a little overlap. Relentless and a tad runout above. Superb.

Burning Down The Couch ***½ 11d #10 99 **SPORT** 30m
Dave Lane May 1986
The classic route of the crag. "*The Couch*" was the first climb on this part of the wall [and still the easiest], although there were many fewer bolts at that time. Follow a line of holds with increasing difficulty to the junction with *The Coffin.* Pull through the bulge above and forge on to a grand finish up a thin crack. 60m rope okay. A shorter version goes only to the chains on *Lost Highway* to the left. Finishing up the *Coffin* to the right needs 2 CDs, 1½-2".

Lost Highway *** 13b/c #6 99 **SPORT** 20m
Marc Bourdon March 1998
The testpiece—currently the hardest climb at Pet Wall.

Rocket *** 12d #4 99 **SPORT** 18m
Jim Sandford August 1988 Right-hand finish (Solid Rocket Booster) Keith Reid 1988
A real blast. Fire up to a bolt station below *The Coffin.* The variation finish out right past the 5th bolt is 13a.

Thinvar * 10d 99 50m
John Howe Perry Beckham 1986
Direct start to *The Coffin.* Good climbing at a moderate grade. Poor protection.

The Coffin * 11a 99 50m
Kevin McLane August 1984
A fine, bold route up the ramp splitting the wall from left to right. Neighbouring routes have much reduced its seriousness.

Second Nature * 12d #5 99 **SPORT+** 30m
Jim Sandford August 1990
Start as for *The Coffin,* then climb through bulges to a good hold at a small square roof. Mantel, step left, then pull out right to finish. Take 3 or 4 CDs.

The imposing dark streaks of black rock down to the left of the Couch wall have yeilded the best group of hard sport climbs in Squamish. A line of bolts at the right side is a project, likely 5.13 (Marc Bourdon).

Baraka   ***   12b   #8   <u>99</u>   **SPORT**+   38m
Kevin McLane August 1986
Climb a left leaning corner and right up a sloping crack to a rest. Straight up the wall above, sustained all the way.

The Fantastic Exploding Rectal Syringe *** 12c #9 **SPORT** 30m
Hugh Lenney Sept 1991
Treads a thin line. Might get more ascents if it had a softer, gentler name.

Black Water   ***½   12a   #11   <u>99</u>   **SPORT**   30m
Dave Lane Sept 1986
Sensationally good. Wonderful technical cruxes one after the other offer sustained climbing, but with adequate rests. 60m rope okay.

Air BC Direct   **   11d   #5   <u>99</u>   **SPORT**+   30m
Perry Beckham 1995
A direct start to *Air BC* starting off the ramp. Some gear ½"-1½" and 5 bolts.

Air B.C.   ***   11c   <u>99</u>   30m
John Howe Dave Lane April 1986
A marvellous climb with a fine airy atmosphere. Climb an obvious left facing corner, traversing through bulges above to the belay. 50m rope okay to lower.

The next two routes are the most popular climbs at the Pet, largely due to the ease of top-roping.

Pleasant Pheasant   *** 11a #7 <u>98</u> **SPORT** 22m
Perry Beckham John Howe March 1986
A very popular classic, with good climbing, good rests, and a crux near the top. As with *No Name Road*, this climb was once a gear route.

Elastic Man   **   11a-c #5   <u>98</u>   **SPORT**+   22m
John Howe April 1986
Good climbing. Graceful style and flawless technique are not as useful as telescopic arms. Grade depends on height. Take a couple CDs ½" to 1½".

Armageddon   ●   11a   <u>98</u>   2p.
Kevin McLane Joe Turley July 1984
Climb to the huge diagonal fault (11a) and follow it to the top of the crag (10a).

Family Ties   *   12d   <u>98</u>   40m
Dave Lane 1987
Climb *Pleasant Pheasant*. Pull through the bulge above and launch off up the wall above, past several bolts and inventive protection. Small gear for the top.

Run For Cover   ** 13b #11 <u>98</u> **SPORT** 40m
Jim Sandford (1pa) 1988   FFA Scott Cosgrove 1989
Takes the left side of the headwall above the long roof. Reachy.

Spargeltarzan   **   12a   <u>98</u>   40m
Jim Sandford T.Emde 1988
Start up *Run For Cover*, finish up *DOA*.

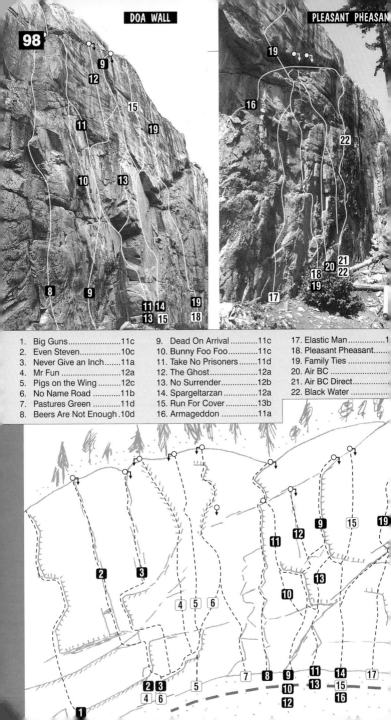

DOA WALL

PLEASANT PHEASAN

#	Route	Grade
1.	Big Guns	11c
2.	Even Steven	10c
3.	Never Give an Inch	11a
4.	Mr Fun	12a
5.	Pigs on the Wing	12c
6.	No Name Road	11b
7.	Pastures Green	11d
8.	Beers Are Not Enough	10d
9.	Dead On Arrival	11c
10.	Bunny Foo Foo	11c
11.	Take No Prisoners	11d
12.	The Ghost	12a
13.	No Surrender	12b
14.	Spargeltarzan	12a
15.	Run For Cover	13b
16.	Armageddon	11a
17.	Elastic Man	1
18.	Pleasant Pheasant	
19.	Family Ties	
20.	Air BC	
21.	Air BC Direct	
22.	Black Water	

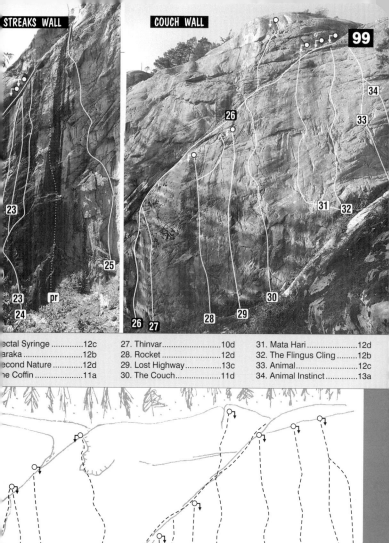

23
25
23
pr
24
26
34
33
31
32
30
26
27
28
29

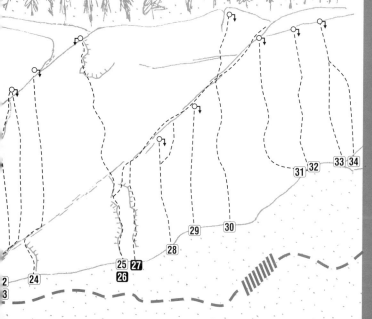

31 32 33 34
29 30
28
25 27
26
24
2
3

No Surrender   *   12b   _98_   35m
Kevin McLane October 1986
A bold and commiting climb up the wall just right of _DOA_. Pull over a roof, up the wall, then out right to hard final moves up a shallow corner to join _DOA_.

Dead On Arrival   ***½   11c   _98_   45m
Kevin McLane Dave Lane Dave Hart (1pa) July 1984   FFA Peter Croft July 1984
A brilliant and intimidating climb that weaves a careful line up through the overhangs. Move right to a slim corner and an exhilarating finish. Double ropes help to reduce rope drag.

Take No Prisoners   ***   11d   _98_   2p.
Kevin McLane Bruce Kay   April 1986
Superb climbing with good rests. Start right of DOA and climb it to the top of the crux corner. Go out left along an undercling line to the base of some vague cracks. Sustained wall climbing above leads to a ledge on the left. Follow pitch 2 of _Beers Are Not Enough_ to the top. Double ropes.

The Ghost   ***   12a   _98_   40m
Kevin McLane Perry Beckham June 1986
The fine direct finish to _DOA_ up the cracks in the headwall. High in its grade.

Bunny Foo Foo   *   11c   _98_   35m
Dave Lane Keith Reid 1988
A cuddly sort of variation left of the corner on _DOA_.

Beers Are Not Enough   * 10d   _98_   2p.
Kon Kraft John Wurflinger (aid—climb was known as Petrifying Wall)
FFA Bruce Kay Howie Richardson Mar 86. p1, Peter Hiltner Mar 86
Left of the _DOA_ wall is an obvious stepped corner system which runs the the full height of the crag. Short cruxes and good rests lead to a large belay ledge (10d). Up the short corner above to finish (10b). As with _Even Steven_, this climb is somewhat overlooked because it is considerably easier than the main attractions at Pet Wall, but nonetheless, it is an excellent climb.

■ _The next six climbs start off an obvious ramp left of the DOA Wall._

No Name Road   ***   11b   #10   _98_   **SPORT**   45m
Perry Beckham Tim Holwill Mar 1986
An outstanding face climb, one of the great climbs of Squamish. Start on the left, move up the ramp to a long sustained central section leading up to an easier groove and a wild pull over a roof. Although is it now a sport route, this climb when first done was a major RP battle and had a fearsome reputation for a long run-out through the crux section.

Through Pastures Green * 11d   #10   _98_   **SPORT**   40m
Jim Sandford 1996
A good alternative start to _No Name_ from the foot of _Beers..._ A rap station at 30m provides a shortened alternative. The grade is height-dependent.

Pigs on the Wing   **   12c   #13   _98_   **SPORT**   45m
Jim Sandford 1996
A good eliminate line that moves directly up to the ramp, crosses it, and takes all the spare rock between _No Name Road_ and _Mr. Fun._

Mr. Fun *   12a #10   <u>98</u>   **SPORT** 40m
Dave Lane John Howe 1986
A hard climb for its grade. Steadily increasing difficulties lead to the final shallow corner. A queer, bouldery high-step at the crux solves the problem. Maybe.

Never Give An Inch *   11a   <u>98</u>   35m
John Howe Dave Lane Mar 1986   Var. J.Buszowski
Or you'll be flying again. Good, varied climbing leads to cracks in the sustained upper section.

Even Steven ***   10c   <u>98</u>   35m
John Howe Dave Lane Feb 9 1986
A Pet Wall classic: a fine steep crackline, with good situations and protection. This is the easiest climb at the crag, and often overlooked in the rush to do the harder routes, but if it were on any other crag, it would be considered a tour de force of 5.10 climbing.

Big Guns *   11c   <u>98</u>   30m
Perry Beckham 1991
The stepped corner and roof system at the far left of the crag. Named in honour of Andy Burnham, who was killed in an accident in Yosemite in 1988.

The first climb established at Petrifying Wall was a route of the same name by John Wurflinger and Kon Kraft in 1970, climbed as an aid route in the general area of Beers Are Not Enough.

The second climb was Dead On Arrival in 1984, which marked the arrival of the modern era.

NO NAME ROAD AREA

Ramp

1. Big Guns 11c
2. Even Steven 10c
3. Never Give an Inch....11a
4. Mr Fun 12a
5. Pigs On The Wing 12c
6. No Name Road 11b
7. Pastures Green 11d

For some folks, a three-hundred foot cliff is a barrier to a destination. For others, a three-hundred foot cliff is a destination.

WHETHER IT'S A MELLOW SUMMER AFTERNOON OF MULTI-PITCHING, AN INTENSIVE MOUNTAINEERING EXPEDITION, OR FRONT-POINTING UP A FROZEN WATERFALL, MOUNTAIN EQUIPMENT CO-OP HAS THE GEAR AND CLOTHING FOR YOU.

FOR OUR LATEST FREE CATALOGUE CALL 1-800-663-2667 VISIT OUR WEBSITE: WWW.MEC.CA

A LIFETIME SHARE IN MEC IS ONLY $5.00

MOUNTAIN EQUIPMENT CO-OP

o by: Matt Jackson

The Sword 5.11a.   Climber: Eve Ruttle

Dead On Arrival 5.11c.   Climber: Jim Sandford

Up Among The Firs

This is the highest crag in Murrin Park, facing southwest with a pleasant and scenic summit area giving views down Howe Sound and over to Mount Habrich. The main feature is an amphitheatre-like bowl with the big corner of *A Little Testis* on the right, and on the left wall, the curious, almost perfectly symmetrical feature of The Pie—six cracks radiating out from the centre of the wall. The crag's name derives from the huge douglas firs at the base—worth a visit to see in their own right. There are three sections to the crag: the main amphitheatre with six climbs; two slabby walls up higher to the right; and around to the left (south) is a small slab of less worthy routes, but suitable for top-roping or escaping the crowds.

Getting there... Take the Petrifying Wall trail, and as soon as that crag is reached, turn right and hike up past *Flight of the Challenger*. The trail winds around, up and down, soon arriving at the crag below the unmistakeable wide corner of *A Little Testis*. 15 mins. from the car. Climbs are listed from left to right on the main crag, then right to left on the left-hand crag

Climbs and gear... The best routes are *A Little Testis* (10b), well worth the hike; *Totally Clips* (10b) an enjoyable face climb; *Wicker Cranium* (.9) a fine moderate crack, well protected; *Poster Boy* (10c); and *The Nose* (10d). Take a dozen draws, and a medium rack to 3″.

Totally Clips	**	10b	#10	*107*	**SPORT**	25m

Glenn Payan Jeff Thomson June 1997
A enjoyable face climb at the left side of the main wall. Good rests.

Youth of Eternal Summers	.8			*107*		10m

Glenn Payan   March 1997
A short crack on a knobby face just around the corner left of the upper arete of *Totally Clips*. Get there from the top of *Zazert*, down a short steep groove.

Wicker Cranium	**	.9		*107*		27m

Glenn Payan John Thompson May 1997
An excellent crack. Start up the left-hand crack of the star feature, and from the centre, take the upper left above the centre. Good rests and pro.

Usual Panic	*	10d	#4	*107*	**SPORT+**	30m

Glenn Payan Jeff Thomson September 1997
Climb the crack of *Wicker Cranium* or the initial bolted face of *Poster Boy* to the centre of the star, and climb the face above past bolts.

Poster Boy	***	10d	#7	*107*	**SPORT+**	27m

Glenn Payan Jeff Thomson July 1997
Start at the foot of the star's right-hand crack and move up the face on the right past 2 bolts. Gain the big arete which provides a psychological challenge, passing a bulge midway by laybacking around to the right. 2½-3″ CU.

A Little Testis *** 10b 24m
Glenn Payan Jeff Thomson July 1997
The corner. Classic granite. Say no more—just do it.

The Nose * 10d # 7 **SPORT** 45m
p2 Glenn Payan Jeff Thomson July 1997 p1 Glenn Payan June 1998
The arete right of the upper part of *A Little Testis.* One long pitch.

> *The next three climbs are reached by scrambling up to the right from the base of A Little Testis, and then up a fixed line to a ledge.*

Seam's Dubious 10d #6 **SPORT** 20m
Glenn Payan Graham Rowbotham December 1997
Start as for *Jaquester,* then step over a mossy groove to the slabby face on the left, which is climbed to the top of the crag.

Jacquester * 11d (11a+3pa) #10 **SPORT** 30m
Jeff Thomson Glenn Payan September 1997
Start from the flat ledge below pitch 2 of *The Nose* and climb the long slab on the right to a superb belay perch.

Wallow Up To The Trough * 10b #5 **SPORT** 18m
Glenn Payan Graham Rowbotham November 1997
From the top of *Jaquester* walk 20m north then 15m east. An obvious "trough" here marks the top of this route. Scramble down to reach the bottom.

> *The next climb starts 25m left of Totally Clips in a square bay.*

Zazert 10c 20m
Glenn Payan Jeff Thomson August 1997
From the back of the bay head out left along a pumpy 6m finger traverse crack (harder than it looks) to the arete, which is then climbed past 4 bolts.

> *The next 4 short climbs are grouped close together on a south-facing slab left of the main crag. Climbs described from right to left.*

Chok'in A Grogan .8 #4 x **SPORT** 20m
Glenn Payan Jeff Thomson September 1996
Step into a slot formed by an adjacent boulder on the right, clip a hidden bolt and move onto the arete. Follow it past 3 bolts to the top.

Nostalgia Ain't What It Used To Be * .8 x 12m
Glenn Payan Jeff Thomson May 1997
Start as for *Zeasi,* go right to a bolt. Follow little edges to a finger crack finale.

Zeasi * .7 x 15m
Glenn Payan Sara Payan April 1997
Start at the centre of the slab up a slim left-facing corner. Climb directly above it past a high bolt to finish.

Collet A Day .8 #3 x **SPORT+** 18m
Glenn Payan August 1997
Surmount an overlap on the left side of the slab past 2 bolts. Move up, then right past the final bolt of *Zeasi.* A direct finish is possible at 10d [TR anchors], *Road Rash* (Payan-Thomson April 1997).

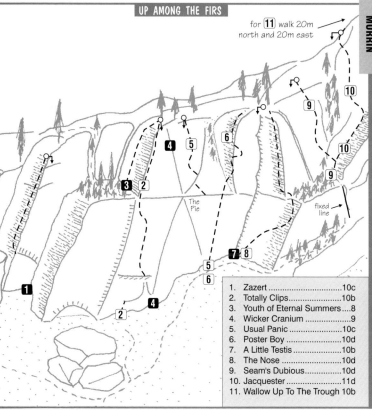

UP AMONG THE FIRS

for [11] walk 20m
north and 20m east

MURRIN

The
Pie

fixed
line

1. Zazert	10c
2. Totally Clips	10b
3. Youth of Eternal Summers	8
4. Wicker Cranium	9
5. Usual Panic	10c
6. Poster Boy	10d
7. A Little Testis	10b
8. The Nose	10d
9. Seam's Dubious	10d
10. Jacquester	11d
11. Wallow Up To The Trough	10b

*In 1980, Hamish Fraser soloed University Wall at the age of 14.
He set off walking the 6km from No Name Road in Squamish in
the middle of the night, haulbag on his back, and got pulled over
by the police who thought he was running away from home. He
convinced them to give him a ride to Psyche Ledge instead, almost
got to Dance before bivouacing, and in the process, did the first
clean ascent of the route.*

Above-The-Lake

This is the rambling series of crags on the hillside opposite Browning Lake. Several hard sport climbs have been established here, but the area's popularity has waned somewhat. Perhaps that will change, as the new trail to the Valley of Shaddai goes right through these crags.

Getting there... Walk along the road from the parking lot, and 30m past the cliff of Browning Bluff, a trail climbs steeply up to the left.

The steep crag on the highway opposite the lake is Browning Bluff. There are two climbs here, long since overgrown.

Route 99 ●   10a   40m
Richard Suddaby Joe Buszowski 1978
Climb up the ramp, then through some blocky overhangs to reach a prominent left-facing corner. Follow it to the top.

Excitable Boy ●   12b   25m
Peter Croft Tami Knight 1979
Climb up the ramp, then the thin vertical finger-crack in the headwall above.

Head up the trail right of Browning Bluff, as for the Valley of Shaddai.

No More Tears **   11d   #10   *SPORT*   28m
Jim Sandford Jola Sandford March 1992
Climb the main corner to a stance at 15m, then step right and straight up the leaning wall. Good rests and protection. A more direct variation leaving the corner at 7m is 12b.

Poltergeist 2 *   11d   #11   *SPORT*   2p.
Mike Tschipper Bruce MacDonald (aid on p2) June 1982   p2 Dean Hart Harry Kettman Sept 92
Start at the lowest point of the cliff as for *No More Tears*, and follow a crackline into a large left-facing corner (10b). Continue up the steepening corner to the top of the cliff (11d). Two rappels off with a 55m rope will work, otherwise scamper down to the top of the *No More Tears* rappel station.

The next climb is a high, wide corner on a dark buttress right of No More Tears. Thrash up from the road through 5.9 bush, or perhaps better yet, rappel in down the north side to reach the foot.

Smell Of Fat Chick ● ☺ 11b   35m
Randy Atkinson Dean Hart July 1984
A powerful layback-stem corner capped by a superb technical roof. Now overgrown, but one of the best 5.11 pitches in Squamish in its former glory.

Just as you enter the heavier timber above the hydro lines, the next climb, up a clean prow can be seen 30m to the left.

Surveillance *   12b   #4   *SPORT*   10m
Jim Sandford March 18 1992
The attractive overhanging prow.

*40m further up the trail a steep cliff lurks behind a screen of trees. Go
up right to its base and five routes. Climbs described from right to left.*

Crack-R-Jack ● ☺ 10c 30m
Rick Leslie Janna Leslie Sept 12th 1992
A prominent crackline right of *A Show of Hands* (11d). Now mossed over.

A Show Of Hands ● ☺ 11d #4 SPORT 26m
Jola Sandford March 18 1992
Climb easily to a bulging wall. Not so easy thereafter.

Fly By Night * 11a #4 SPORT 10m
Jim Sandford Feb 1992
15m left of *A Show Of Hands*. Climb an overhanging wall to a bolt station.

Under Pressure * 11d #6 SPORT 15m
Jola Sandford April 1992
Starts 2m right of *Labyrinth* and heads up the wall on the right.

Labyrinth * 11c+1pa #7 SPORT 15m
Jim Sandford March 18 1992
50m left of *A Show Of Hands* is a prominent blunt prow. Climb the lefthand
line of bolts, using the final bolt for aid.

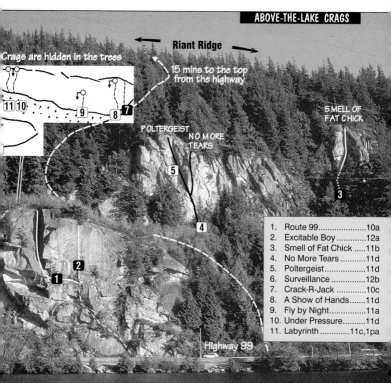

ABOVE-THE-LAKE CRAGS

Riant Ridge

Crags are hidden in the trees

15 mins to the top from the highway

SMELL OF FAT CHICK

POLTERGEIST

NO MORE TEARS

Highway 99

1. Route 99.....................10a
2. Excitable Boy.............12a
3. Smell of Fat Chick......11b
4. No More Tears............11d
5. Poltergeist..................11d
6. Surveillance...............12b
7. Crack-R-Jack.............10c
8. A Show of Hands.......11d
9. Fly by Night................11a
10. Under Pressure..........11d
11. Labyrinth.............11c,1pa

The view from Browning Lake at Murrin Park

Leviticus Area

This is the rambling series of cliffs on the east side of the highway directly opposite the parking lot. There is an eclectic mix of routes. Some hard, some good, some not, some aid and some best forgotten. The main interest is Leviticus, the impressive bulging wall at the right side, as the cliffs become of lesser interest further left. Climbs are described from the far left.

The next two climbs are on a small clean-looking bluff.

Bad Cop No Donut ● 11b   18m
Greg Foweraker Hamish Fraser Peder Ourom March 1992
An obvious cleaned streak up a steep rough wall sporting a fat BC Hydro bolt.

Another Roadside Attraction ● 10b   18m
Kon Kraft and others 1980
Long buried, believed to be just right of *Bad Cop...*

The next climb is directly opposite the entrance to the parking lot.

Show Boat Wall ● 10c   40m
Gene Smith Ted Marks T.McKay Joe Turley Sept 20 1987
A rambly northwest facing steep slab, holding one route up its right side.

SHOWBOAT WALL AREA

1. Bad Cop No Donut 11b	9. Sixty-Nine.....................A3
2. Another Roadside Attraction .10b	10. Shallow Penetration.......A4
3. Showboat Wall 10c	11. Shadows 12b
4. Infinite Decibels...................12d	12. Child's Play A4
5. Vultures Circling...................13b	13. Shock The Monkey......11c
6. Walk The Plank 10d	
7. Another Tourist in Traction....9,A0	
8. Leviticus 12d	

A short gently overhanging featured wall holds two impressive sport climbs, both bolt protected and longer and better than they appear. Described from the left.

Infinite Decibels   *   12d   #6   **SPORT**   15m
Keith Reid May 1991
Climb twin seams up right to the chains. Crux high up.

Vultures Circling   *   13b   #5   **SPORT**   18m
Keith Reid 1989
Follow a distinct left-trending crackline, finishing through a bulge to chains.

The next climb is on a subsidiary bluff left of and below the large bulging wall of Leviticus.

Walk The Plank   10d   20m
Bill Noble Tim Holwill M.Donnelly Stu Holwill Nick Jones June 28 1986
An obvious line of weakness past several bolts, up the high-angle slab just left of and below the main wall.

The next climb is the left-hand route on the main wall of Leviticus.

Another Tourist In Traction * .9 + ropepull _112_   45m
Andrew Boyd Kris Wild June 1998
The prominent left-facing corner at the left edge of the smooth bulging wall.
Excellent climbing, but the present fixed rope is needed to gain the fun stuff.
A prime candidate for an A0 bolt ladder.

LEVITICUS AREA

Leviticus   *   12d   45m
G.McKinnon Dan Tate L.Williams 1964. FFA Andrew Boyd July 1998
An old aid climb, now free. Start 5m right of the bushy ramp below a steep seam, which is bypassed on the right via flakes and edges, then back left at the roof. Pull over it to the start of the difficulties. Sustained crack climbing, good pro and rests, leads to the crux before the crack exits leftward. A slightly easier version (12c) traverses left below the upper crux, into *Another Tourist...*

Sixty-Nine   ●   A3   45m
Neil Bennett Pat Merrill 1969
Aid climb right of *Leviticus*.

Shallow Penetration   ●   A4   45m
Dick Mitten Peder Ourom 1976
Aid climb that branches right out of *Sixty-Nine*. Some 5.7.

Shadows   12b   45m
Neil Bennett Gordie Smaill 1968   FFA Andrew Boyd July 1998
A slim, very steep corner crack that breaks onto the high-angle slab after 12m. Continue up *Shock The Monkey*.

Child's Play   ●   A4   20m
Kim Poehnell Gordon Menzies 1981
The most right-hand seam on the smooth bulging wall, which crosses *Shock The Monkey* after 10m. Belay up to the right.

Shock The Monkey   *   11c   35m
Nick Jones Kirt Sellers Bill Noble (2pa) 1986   FFA: Jim.Sandford 1987
Start at the far right edge of the wall and climb the high-angle slab that diagonals leftward across the upper right side of the cliff.

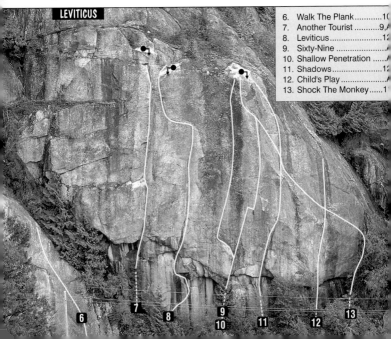

LEVITICUS

Baraka 5.12b, the first ascent.   Climber: Kevin McLane.   Photo: John Howe

Jalap Bluff

Jalap Bluff is a west-facing vertical crag at the side of the highway north of the parking lot. Less favoured than it once was, climbing is most enjoyable in the evening or mid-week when highway traffic is at a minimum. If you are up on the crag, you'll be highly visible to passing traffic. Listen for screeching tires.

Getting there... It's on the east side of the highway, 200m north of the parking lot. Scramble up to the base on the right. Descent for most routes is by rappel from a large ledge below the actual summit of the crag. Climbs are described from the right.

Climbs and gear... The best climbs are *Frail Scales* (11a), *Hellfire Wall* (11c) and *Powerline* (11b). Take a crack rack, small to mid size.

Drive by Drilling ● 11a x 25m
Colin Moorhead Will Dorling May 18 1992
At the upper right corner of the crag, climb a steep slab [bolt] to a block below a prow. Climb it on the right side past 3 bolts to a bolt belay.

Archaeopteryx ● ☺ 10a 40m
Don Serl 1985
Fine climbing [was once, anyway] up a long corner above a roof.

Rush Hour ● ☺ 10a 40m
Scott Flavelle Amy Boyer Sept 1983
Face climbing to the easier arete above. Run out.

Ugly Dwarf ● 10d 40m
Peter Croft Tami Knight Carl Austrom 1982
A thin right-slanting crack that starts as for *Frail Scales*.

Frail Scales ** 10d 40m
Peter Croft John Howe June 1982
Superb climbing up an unlikely series of thin flakes to the crux overhang. Good protection and rests. Double ropes help.

Hellfire Wall ** 11c 40m
Kevin McLane Jim Campbell (1pa) July 1983   FFA: Dave Lane John Howe Oct 1983
Exciting climbing, weaving up a natural line of flakes to a difficult finish. Double ropes help avoid rope-drag. The pancake flake gives a short sharp crux.

The Seventh Dwarf A4 15m
Neil Bennett Kon Kraft 1970
The seam left of *Hellfire Wall*. Tat at the top.

Snow White A4 15m
Dean Lister and others 1980   (Eric Lance Brian Norris, climbed most of it 1970)
The furthest left-hand of several seams on the wall. More tat at the top.

Powerline ** 11b 30m
John Howe Scott Flavelle Aug 17 1985
Climb into a small square niche below a bolt then launch out rightwards across the diagonal cracks that split the wall. A fine, bold climb . Rappel down.

Climbs North Of Jalap

The following two climbs are on opposing sides of the highway just north of Jalap, on really manky little bluffs. Both are short and have long since overgrown.

Rainforest ● .7 x 15m
John Manuel Ross Nichol 1979
On the north side of the highway directly opposite the trailhead for Petgill Lake.

Pig's Trough ● 10d x 10m
Bill Price Mike Boris Daryl Hatten 1978
A short left-slanting thin hand-crack 50m north of the Nightmare Rock trailhead.

The next climb is behind the hydro tower on top of Jalap Bluff, and is reached by following the signed hiking trail to Petgill Lake for 3-4 minutes to a small rock step. Turn right on a rough trail (hard to follow) for 200m to a small crag 100m behind the hydro tower.

Scene Of The Crime * 12b (11a+1pa) x 15m
Jim Sandford Feb 16 1992
Walk along the cliff to its south end and a very steep bolted climb.

JALAP BLUFF

owerline	11b
now White	A4
eventh Dwarf	A4
ellfire Wall	11c
ail Scales	11a
gly Dwarf	10d
ush Hour	10a
rcheopteryx	10a
ive By Drilling	11a

direct start 11a

Presto Area

This imposing 25m wall is hidden behind tall trees 50m from the highway, just south of Nightmare Rock. It holds two spectacular climbs just a few metres apart. They could hardly be more different— a formidable offwidth crack and a fine 13a sport route. All they share in common is stone and difficulty.

Getting there... The trailhead is beside the blue Murrin Provincial Park sign on the southbound side of the road. There is room to park (just) on the shoulder of the northbound lane in front of Nightmare Rock. Otherwise park in the Murrin Park lot and walk.

Presto ***   13a   #5   ***SPORT***   20m
Unknown (aid)   FFA: Jim Sandford   July 20 1990
A striking, shallow corner dominates the centre of the wall. Its left edge is the battleground, with much heavy pinching.

Hypertension **   11a   17m
Dave Nicol Eric Weinstein 1975
A Squamish legend, this mighty offwidth crack saw many attempts, some top rope successes, and many different names before the eventual first ascent. Difficulties increase near the top, just where you need them least.

Cracks left of Hypertension have been aided at about A3.

■ OPPOSITE NIGHTMARE ROCK

Strenotechnic ● ☺   10c   x   15m
John Howe Dave Lane Jean McRae June 1986
This good climb is at the left end of a nondescript crag sporting a few overhangs, which is on the east side of the road. Climb through basalt rock until below the roof. Pull through it with ease to the corner above. Strenuous, technical and surprisingly good.

NIGHTMARE ROCK AREA

HYPER-
TENSION
11a

PRESTO
13a

trail

Nightmare Rock

Nightmare Rock is the most northerly crag in the Murrin Park area, about 300m north of the parking lot on the west side of the highway, facing east and easily identified by its huge roofs. It is made up of four distinct areas: a high wall to the left with three rarely climbed mixed routes; the main cliff with its fine cracks; and a shorter wall with 4 face climbs on the far right. Presto Wall is hidden in the trees down and left of the main wall and described separately. Climbs are described from the left. Rappelling is common off most routes, but a descent trail around the north end provides an alternative.

Getting there... The old trail direct up to *Sentry Box* has all but disappeared from disuse. A good alternative is to approach the crag from *Presto,* starting up the trail from the blue Murrin Provincial Park sign on the southbound side of the road, and scrambling easily up right of that cliff to reach Nightmare at the open area below *Grandaddy.* There is room (just) on the shoulder of the northbound lane in front of the crag. Otherwise park at Murrin Park and walk.

Climbs and gear... This is a crag for heavy hitters. Most of the best climbs are hard cracks offering technical challenge and variety of one kind or another, and one good sport route, *Metal For All* (11d). Highly recommended climbs are *Grandaddy Overhang* (11c), *Sentry Box* (12a), and *Perspective* (11a), all three being entrance exams to their grades at Squamish, and the spectacular *Big Daddy* (12b) and *Sentry Box Direct* (12a). Not a bad haul for one crag. Take along a full-size crack rack from RPs to 3″ cams, and expect to find a bolt or two on most climbs.

▓ *The following three climbs take the high wall, left of the roofs.*

Traumatic Experience ● 11a A4   x   2p.
Fred Beckey Leif Patterson Eric Bjornstad Nov 1965 p1 FFA unknown
Head out left from the base of *Shiver...* and climb the centre of the main wall.

Slam Sandwich ●   A4   x   25m
Perry Beckham 1983
Between *Traumatic...* and *Shiver...*

Shiver Me Timbers ● 11a   x   2p.
Rob Rohn Tom Gibson 1981
Takes the big diagonal fault left of the roofs. Could be a great climb if it was given a retro-scrub?

Have you read How To Use This Guide? Page 12.

Grandaddy Overhang *** 11c   30m
Dick Culbert Eric Lance 1967 FFA Peter Croft Tami Knight 1979 Rebolted Andreas Tayler '98
An undercling traverse right-to-left underneath the biggest roof. Climb easily up a narrow ramp to the roof, then left with increasing difficulty to chains.

Great Grandaddy *   11a   15m
John Howe 1987
Start just right of *Grandaddy*, and make a hard mantel past 2 bolts to gain a curving sickle that leads into the narrow ramp of that route. Rap off.

Big Daddy Overhang *** 12b   40m
Jim Baldwin Jim Sinclair July 1962 FFA: Peter Croft Tami Knight 1981
Sensational climb—awesome position. Follow *Grandaddy* to the roof, then go right. Hard moves gain a small hanging slab in a very exposed position. Pull into the crack above and on to a good rest. Easier to the top.

Sloth   .8 A3   35m
Dick Culbert Alice Purdy 1970
Start up *Sentry Box*. At the top of the corner cracks, go left to *Big Daddy*.

Sentry Box ***   12a (10a)   35m
Jim Baldwin Ed Cooper Oct 1960 FFA: Eric Weinstein 1976
A classic. Easy climbing up a cracked wall leads to small ledge on the face. The thin finger crack above gives technically difficult moves—a crack connoisseur's delight. The initial crack gives an excellent 10a with a rap out.

Sentry Box Direct ***   12a   35m
Peter Croft Tami Knight 1982
Climb the slim pillar from right to left, passing several FPs to join *Sentry Box*. Superb climbing with exciting variety. Low in its grade.

NIGHTMARE ROCK

Perspective   ***   11a   40m

Les McDonald Tony Cousins 1964
FFA: Eric Weinstein 1975, or possible FFA by Dave Loecks and Peter Charak earlier that year.
Splendid handjamming and stemming up a strenuous corner, with a face crack above providing the crux. Well protected with good rests.

Claim Jumper   **   12a   40m

J.Edwards M.Webster 1978   FFA Peter Croft Tami Knight 1982
Climb past 2 bolts just right of *Perspective* to a high FP in a thin crack and a technically problematic crux. Climb it statically or dynamically—take your pick. The crack above is easier. Although the same grade, it is easier than *Big Daddy*.

> *The four climbs on the right hand wall are approached by a scrambly trail along the base the main cliff. Descent is by walking off right.*

And Metal For All   *   11d   #7   **SPORT**   20m

Jim Sandford Jola Sandford April 2 1992
Start 3m left of the arete and climb straight up to join the top of *Mango Bud*.

Mango Bud   ● ☺   10b   18m

Dean Hart Eric Wiess 1985
Start in the deep corner, finish left up the arete. Good.

Captain Hook   *   11b   20m

Kevin McLane solo July 9 1986
A hardish start leads to easier climbing.

Peter Pan   *   11a   15m

Kevin McLane Joe Turley Mar 19 1986
The most obvious line on the right. Committing after the bolt.

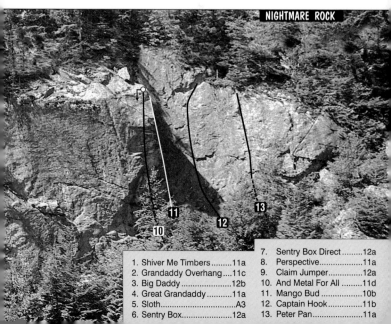

NIGHTMARE ROCK

1. Shiver Me Timbers 11a
2. Grandaddy Overhang 11c
3. Big Daddy 12b
4. Great Grandaddy 11a
5. Sloth...............................A3
6. Sentry Box....................12a
7. Sentry Box Direct 12a
8. Perspective..................11a
9. Claim Jumper...............12a
10. And Metal For All 11d
11. Mango Bud 10b
12. Captain Hook...............11b
13. Peter Pan.....................11a

Petgill Wall

This is the enticing north-facing wall near the top of Gonzales Creek. There is a seven-pitch climb here from 1976 which the difficulty of approach and scarcity of repeat ascents has elevated to mythical status. It is possible to thrash directly up from the highway on the south side of Gonzales Creek to the top of the crag, from which two rappels gain the base. But a better alternative may be to traverse in from the Petgill Lake hiking trail.

Petgill Wall   .9   some aid?   7p.
Keith Nannery Steve Loomer 1976
High adventure. The climb starts deep in the gully and generally follows the right edge of an enormous detached wall. The climbing should all be sub-5.10, but will involve tunnelling, offwidths, aid bolts, chimneys, and tree climbing, as well as the more standard fare of cracks.

Stoney Creek Wall

This cliff is 3km north of Murrin Park, a high dark slab easily seen 250m east of the road at Gonzales Creek with two climbs.

Getting there...   There is no trail to speak of, so bushwhack in from the north, or directly from the hill supporting a Hydro tower just north of the creek. Worthy of more exploration.

Snakes And Ladders ● ☺ 11a   3p.
Carl Austrom Robin Barley 1983
An excellent climb—long overlooked. Scramble up easy 5th class from the right. Continue up the side of a large flake to the base of the slab proper. Trend over left to a sling belay (.9). Move right and up via dikes to a ledge belay (11a). An easier pitch leads to the top (10a). Three raps down, just to the north.

Too Much Effort ●   10b   *x*   30m
Joe Buszowski Peder Ourom Craig Thompson 1982
A climb left of the start of *Snakes...* following grooves and cracks.

The Talisman

A west-facing cliff located behind the Papoose, where a number of top-rope climbs were established around 1991 *(Bill Noble)*, but only one was led. The crag is just above the lowest outcrop on the hillside.

Getting there...   Hike around the south side of the Papoose and bushwhack up.

The Talisman ●   11b   *x*   35m?
Perry Beckham 1991
A climb at the right side of the cliff, right of a fist-offwidth crackline.

PETGILL WALL

oximate
e only

PETGILL
WALL

SNAKES
AND
LADDERS

On Highway 99 just
south of the Papoose

SNAKES AND LADDERS

SNAKES
AND
LADDERS

The first European to arrive in the Squamish area was Captain
George Vancouver, on June 22 1792. He was the commander of
a British naval vessel, and he encamped at Darrell Bay in front
of the Papoose for several days, visiting and trading with the
local native population. The weather was poor. Shannon Falls
Provincial Park—the most heavily-visited park in B.C.—is just a
few hundred metres distant, and to this day, there is no reference
or commemoration of that epoch-making occasion.

Sole Mate, 5.10b. Climber: Unknown. Photo Fieldhouse collection.

Below Left: The Archers Arrows, 5.8 first ascent. Climbers: Tony McLane, Barry McLane
Below Right: A rare photo. March of the Kitchen Utensils, 5.9 Climber: Hugh Lenney

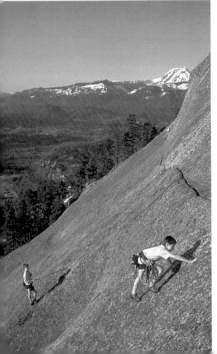

The Papoose

The Papoose is the large west-facing cliff a kilometre south of the Chief, overlooking the highway, Darrell Bay and the Woodfibre pulp mill ferry terminal. There are several worthwhile routes here, and potential for more quality multi-pitch climbs. The Papoose can be thought of as having three sections: the northern end, which is badly overgrown and has never been popular; the large central area where most of the best routes are found; and the lower southern end. The climbing is best characterised by wide open faces, afternoon breezes and lovely views of Howe Sound and the Chief. Descent is possible by rappelling *Centrefold*, or by a bushy trail from the summit down around the south side.

Getting there... From the Shannon Falls parking lot, walk south for 100m to the Woodfibre ferry terminal entrance. 50m south of here, a trail exits the highway and climbs steeply up to the power lines, then south along bedrock below the crag. Climbs are described from the left. A descent trail exists (just) around the south end of the crag.

The first climb is not actually on the Papoose itself, but is on a wall at the edge of the highway, 25m right of the trailhead. Long overgrown.

The Hitchiker ●   .8   x   20m
Ken Marshall summer 1986
An obvious right-slanting crack. Was nice once, but long since reclaimed by the moss. Pity. Take note—this is what your next scrubbing project could look like 5 years later if nobody came to climb it.

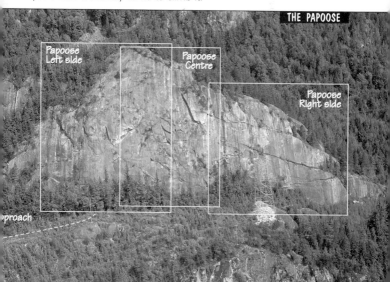

THE PAPOOSE

Papoose Left side

Papoose Centre

Papoose Right side

approach

The following climbs include some of the most exotic esoterica of long-forgotten climbs at Squamish. No line ups...

Hanging Gardens   .6 A3   4p.
John Coope Marion Robertson Oct 1965
Start approximately 50m left of the point where the trail meets the crag. Head left up a diagonal ramp for about 30m (some .7). Scramble up a bush line (4th). Bolts above lead to a crack and corner line directly above (.6 A3).

Overhanging Gardens   .6 A3   5p.
John Coope Tim Auger Jim Sinclair Dietmar Setzar 1967
Follow the first two pitches of *Hanging Gardens*. Bolts above lead out left to a large left-leaning corner (.6, A2). A final pitch of 4th leads to the top.

Hallucination   10b A2   4p.
Fred Beckey Curtis Stout Eric Bjornstad 1965
Start at a distinct 3m flake, leaning against the rock 15m right of the point where the trail meets the wall. Pull up on 2 bolts, then go left, eventually curving back right to join the prominent diagonal crackline (10b, A0). Follow bolts above to a right-trending line of roofs, which is crossed at an obvious 2m crack [12b free, as for *Pamplemousse*], belay above (.6 A2). Easier cracks and some minor aid lead on for 2 pitches to the top, finishing on the left or the right (A1, 7).

Hairpin Turn   A3   20m
Eric Lance Brian Norris 1970
A single pitch of A3 crack to a bolt ladder, joining with *Hairpin*, 15m right of *Hallucination*.

Crossword   .8 A2   4p.
Jim Sinclair Jeannine Caldbeck 1972
Climb *Hairpin* for 2 pitches to join *Hallucination*. Follow a long diagonal crackline up left to join with the top of *Hanging Gardens* (A2, 4th).

Hairpin   10a   4p.
Tim Auger Dan Tate Aug 1965   FFA: Don Serl Vic Coulomb Greg Yavorski '78
40m west of the point where the trail meets the crag, climb a prominent diagonal crackline striking diagonally leftward (.8). Head up right along a bush line (10a). A short section leads into *Papoose One* and a belay (.9). Follow that route 2 pitches to the top (10a).

Pamplemousse   12b   4p.
Peter Croft Greg Foweraker 1987
Start as for *Hairpin*, then after the first pitch, climb the 11a finger-cracks above that lead up to join *Hallucination* at the prominent roof crack (12b).

Howe Sound was named by Captain George Vancouver, after
Lord Howe, a prominent commander in the English Navy.

1. Hanging Gardens 6, A3
2. Overhanging Gardens ..6, A3
3. Hallucination 10b, A2
4. Hairpin Turn......................A3
5. Crossword.........................A2
6. Hairpin 10a
7. Pamplemousse 12b
8. Papoose One 10b

A Duet For Two Hands   ● 11a   40m
Peter Croft Randy Atkinson 1979
Start up *Survival Enhancement*, then go left along a crackline to *Papoose One*.

Survival Enhancement   * 11c   3p.
Nick Jones Tim Holwill June 1992
A good climb in a fine situation. Long pitches. Start 10m left of *Centrefold* and after 15m, move right past 2 bolts up to a station on *Papoose One* (11c). Climb the wide handcrack of *Papoose One*, then where that route goes out left, join *Limbo* above, continue up through the crux of *Limbo* to a good rest. Climb through 2 difficult overlaps on the right (bolts) and join *Centrefold* (11a).

Papoose One   **   10b   6p.
Fred Beckey Eric Bjornstad 1961   FFA: Eric Weinstein Anders Ourom (Alts) 1974
A good climb which sees less traffic than it deserves. Climb *Centrefold* to Moccasin Ledge (10b). Traverse left to gain a wide crack, then left to belay (.8). Easier climbing above and then an awkward chimney slot (10a). Traverse left (.9). Continue traversing, then back right (.6). Up a slab past a bolt ladder to the top (10a).

Centrefold   ***   10b   3p.
John Howe Blake Robinson 1980
An outstanding and deservedly popular climb. Climb a crack and groove past a bolt to gain the left edge of Moccasin Ledge (10b). Climb the corner behind the ledge to a deep groove, move left to gain a smaller groove and a horizontal break. Handtraverse left to a small triangular recess, climb a crack out right then back left to an airy belay ledge: the Playboy Club (10b). Climb the faint groove above to delicate face climbing up the final slab (10a). Walk off to the south or rappel. 2 ropes.

Limbo   ● ☺   11a   4p.
Tim Auger Hamish Mutch 1965   FFA Eric Weinstein Anders Ourom 1976
As for *Centrefold* to Moccasin Ledge (10b) [Original start was over to the right]. Start up the corner above, then out left along a horizontal crack which veers upward, becoming much harder. Up the steep crack above through a small, awkward overhang to a belay (11b). Follow an obvious hand crack to a tricky slab and belay (10c). Continue up *Papoose One*.

Pinup   *   10b   4p.
Ed Cooper D.Hiser 1961   FFA: Don Serl John Wittmayer 1978
Climb to Moccasin Ledge via *Centrefold* (10b). Continue up that route until a traverse is possible to the base of the big left facing corner to the right (10b). Climb it (.9). Easily out right at the top. The original start was on the right up a left-slanting crackline to Moccasin Ledge. It is now hopelessly mossed over but is a good candidate for cleaning up to provide an alternative pitch to Moccasin Ledge.

 Below and right of Moccasin Ledge is a broken area of bush and steep rock. The original starts to Limbo and Pinup began here. It is probably worth cleaning up to provide a second route to Moccasin Ledge.

PAPOOSE — CENTRE

There is a long, prominent line of roofs right of Moccasin Ledge, 20m above the base. The next two climbs cross the left edge of them.

Mixup   .6 A3   2p.
Jim Sinclair Dan Reid 1972
Start 25m right of *Centrefold*. Scramble up to a short section of mid-fifth class that leads to nailing through the roofline. Above, a crack and bolt ladder lead to easier climbing up left to the top of *Pinup*, or an alternative finish is possible out right.

Swinger   A2   30m
Neil Bennett Tony Cousins Jim Sinclair 1972
A variation start to *Mixup*. Start approximately 25m right of the start of *Centrefold*, (just right of the original start to *Pinup*), then cross the band of roofs at its left side and follow A2 cracks before a tension swing into *Mixup*.

Mercury Vapour   10d   25m
John Verbeck and others 1980
30m right of *Centrefold*, climb cracks trending left below the band of roofs, then gain a ramp on the right (crux). Climb on through the roof to a belay and rappel. Bolts, A3, hooks etc. lead to the top.

Wall Street   .7 A3   3p.
Paul Piro Tony Cousins John Burton Jim Sinclair 1972
12m left of the obvious crack of *Mushroom*. Bolts, hooks, flakes.

Mushroom **   .9   20m
Fred Beckey Don Beckstead 1966   FFA: Gordie Smail and others c. 1970
A little diamond among the coal, this is a highly enjoyable thin hand-crack that ends at a horizontal fault and rap chains. The manky bolt ladder leading on to the top is a heritage relic of the first ascent. Gear to 2½".

Horizontally Prone   A3   5p.
Daryl Hatten Eric Weinstein 1974
Climb *Mushroom* to the top of the bolt ladder. At this point, go left along a major horizontal fault for two pitches to join *Mixup* below its last pitch.

Laid Back *   .9   2p.
Steve Loomer Keith Nannery 1976
A crack at the far right end of the cliff.

The next climb is located on the backside of the Papoose. Follow hydro lines around the north end. Difficult to find...

Baby Bum   12a   x   15m
Peter Croft 1987
A short but prominent roof crack.

Construction of the highway from Squamish to

Whistler was completed in 1964.

PAPOOSE — RIGHT SIDE

14. Swinger A2
15. Mixup.........................6, A3
16 Mercury Vapour..............10d
17. Wall Street.....................7, A3
18. Mushroom 9
19 Horizontally Prone.............A3
20. Laid Back...........................9

The first recorded rockclimb at Squamish was Peasant's Route at
the Base of the Grand Wall, by Les McDonald and Jim Baldwin
in May 1958. The final sections on the highway were still under
construction, but they bashed through to beat Fred Beckey.

Local Boys Do Good 5.11a Climbers: unknown.

Shannon Falls

The spectacular falls where Shannon Creek cascades over a 300m cliff provides a fine setting for several excellent multi-pitch climbs–friction routes as good as the best on the Apron. The main cliff is divided into four sections: a slabby wall close to the falls, which is rarely visited and route details vague; the centrepiece slab where the vast majority of climbers can be found, on *Local Boys* and several stellar crack pitches; the long black slab of *Magic Carpet Ride* to its right; and then a more broken, less appealing section of cliff with two old mixed routes. Further uphill to the south, Gobsmacking Wall forms the high southern bastion of this wall of rock. The cliff is easily seen some 500m east of the Highway, a kilometre south of the Chief, and it lies within Shannon Falls Provincial Park. This park, with the falls as its centrepiece, is the most heavily visited park in B.C.

Getting there... The large parking area beside the falls is 5km north of Murrin Park, 1km south of the Chief. Take the wide trail to the falls and after 250m you'll reach a wooden boardwalk. A huge broken log spans the creek here. Cross the creek on or near the log and pick up the steep trail at the other side to the base of a beautiful slab. A new access road to the Park presently being constructed may offer a faster and dryer approach up the south bank of the creek. 10 mins.

Climbs and gear... There are half-a-dozen good to excellent climbs, including the classic *Local Boys Do Good* (11a), *Klahanie Crack* (.8), and *Magic Carpet Ride* (11a). The slab routes require draws and little else, but for the long crack pitches, take a full rack in the 1″–3″ range, including double CDs in the 1½″–2½″ range.

SHANNON FALLS - GOBSMACKING WALL

Gobsmacking Wall

Local Boys
Do Good

Magic
Carpet
Ride

The next three climbs are best approached from the creek. They are rarely climbed, but almost certainly offer climbing as good as Squamish friction gets, especially on thin dykes. Vintage Carl Austrom. Gear will be drilled-on-lead drive-in bolts (or worse), so is probably in bad need of being upgraded.

Vibrating Hands   10d   2p.
Carl Austrom Doug Shinubou summer 1984

This route is so close to the falls, it is under water for much of the year. Details are vague, but expect to find anything from old bolts, rivets, RPs and thin cracks to not much at all. One thing for sure, you'll have quite an adventure and give the tourists something to talk about. Cross the creek high up near the base of the falls. In high summer, the falls can be so reduced in flow that it is possible to have a comfortable shower at the base.

Cafe Flesh   11c   (10d)   45m
Carl Austrom and others summer 1984

Climb up past bolts to reach the lower left end of a prominent dike. From this point, continue up past more bolts to a station (10d). The next pitch is incomplete and much harder, but the first is worth doing in its own right.

I Wanna Be Teased   *   11a   2p.
Carl Austrom and others summer 1984

Start right of *Cafe Flesh* and take a crack that leads to a couple of bolts, then join the prominent dyke. Follow the dyke to a junction with *Jeannine* (11a). Cracks above lead up and out left to a station—a long pitch (.9).

The following climbs are best approached from the base area of Local Boys and Klahanie Crack.

Jeannine   .8 A3   2-3p.
Frank Baumann Doug Herchmer 1975

Start as for *Local Girls*, 15m down and left from *Klahanie Crack*, and climb to the top of a vague pillar (.8). Take a crack above, then bolts and hooks lead rightward to a long crackline that leads directly up to trees at the same elevation as the top of *Local Boys* (A3, hooks, 5th).

Local Girls Are Bad   11a   4p.
Carl Austrom Tim Holwill July 27 1984

Start 15m down and left of *Klahanie Crack*, and traverse up left to the top of a pillar (.8). Up past bolts to belay 10m left of *Local Boys* (10b). Out left to join a thin crack, climb it, then traverse out right to join *Local Boys* (11a). Forge on up the final pitch (10a).

The first occasion on which a 3/8" bolt was placed at Squamish was in June 1985, on Future Shock at the White Cliff by Kevin McLane.

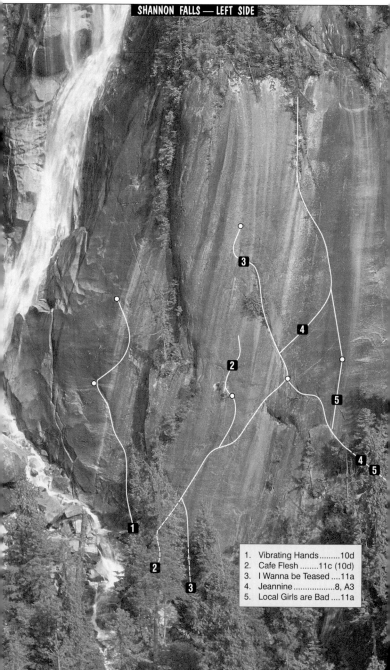

SHANNON FALLS — LEFT SIDE

1. Vibrating Hands.........10d
2. Cafe Flesh 11c (10d)
3. I Wanna be Teased 11a
4. Jeannine 8, A3
5. Local Girls are Bad 11a

Local Heroes **   11c   #5   **SPORT**   28m
Tom Clark David George July 1992
A compelling pitch just left of and parallel to *Local Boys Do Good*. Step onto a thin left-trending dyke. Continue directly to a station 8m left of *Local Boys*.....

Local Boys Do Good *** 11a (10b) #8   **SPORT** (p1, p2)   3p.
p1, G.Smith Joe Turley 1982. p2,3 Dean Hart Carl Austrom Randy Atkinson June 1984
A superb climb in a fine atmosphere. Climb 3m left of *Klahanie Crack,* past bolts up to a welcome dyke. Move left from its top and belay (10b). Pass the troublesome bulge ahead and then plain sailing ahead (11a). The final pitch is a gem, albeit a bit runout. Do it anyway (10a). Rappel.

> *The following three climbs are all excellent, very obvious cracks up a steep slab. The trail meets the crag at Klahanie Crack. Rap off that route—a steep trail descent to the south is possible for the other two.*

Klahanie Crack ***   .7   30m
Unknown
Handjam the beautiful crack just right of *Local Boys*. It takes as many CUs as can be carried. Rappel off the tree.

Urine Too Deep *   .8   50m
Glenn Payan John Thompson July 1996
Climb a thin hand-crack 10m right of *Klahanie Crack* to a bush. Go right up a white dyke to join *Cardhu Crack*. Descend a steep trail to the south or rap.

Cardhu Crack **   .8   40m
Glenn Payan Feb 1997
The fine hand-crack at the right side of the wall above a left-facing corner.

Magic Carpet Ride *** 11c (11a) #10   4p.
p1,2, Scott Flavelle Carl Austrom 1976.
p3,4, Carl Austrom Jim Sandford 1986
A magnificent flight up the long black friction slab 25m right of *Local Boys*. Climb up on the left to a belay. A tad runout at first (10c). Trend up to the right and a long sustained section on small edges (11a). Climb to the left of a bulge then right (11c). A long pitch leads to the top (10c).

Not Your Normal Nightmare ** 11c #9   4p.
John Brodie Mike Campbell August 1996
A fine companion climb to *Magic Carpet Ride*, but more sustained. Start 15m up and right of the base of the black slab, climb up and across *Magic...* to a bolt belay (11b). Three more pitches lead up parallel to *Magic...* (10c, 11b, 11c). Rappel down.

Forked Flume   .8 A2   2-3p.
Dick Culbert Mike Warr 1967
A bush line up and right of *Magic Carpet Ride* that provides 2 pitches of dirty adventure.

Weeping Wall   .8 A1   x   2-3p.
Eric Lance Dick Culbert Einar Hansen 1967
A similar and parallel line to *Forked Flume*, further up to the right, not far from the roof of *Monkey Lust*.

SHANNON FALLS — RIGHT SIDE

Gobsmacking Wall

This is the steep, dome-like wall with a heavily featured west face at the upper right end of the cliffs at Shannon Falls. It is home to several superb climbs, and well worth the effort to visit.

Getting there... Hike to the base of Shannon Falls, and take a rough trail that leads rightward up the cliff base. Continue steeply in the trees, arriving at *Monkey Lust.* For climbs further right, continue to the corner of the west and south faces. A short trail leads off left and scrambles to the base of *Hungry Wolf.* For *Man of Leisure*, continue up the trail a short distance then back left to a ledge by a large root.

Climbs and gear... With few exceptions, this is a crag of long gear pitches. *Hunter's Moon* (11d), *Hungry Wolf* (11b) and *Never Say Never* (11b) are stellar. Two easier routes on the south face are well worth the walk too. Take a full rack–RPs to 3″.

Sneeze   10c A1   2-3p.
Bob Cuthbert Dave Caldbeck John Wurflinger 1973
Climb as for *Monkey Lust* until below the main roof. Turn it on the left and follow cracks above to Dristan Ledge.

Monkey Lust ● ☺   11a   2p.
T.Gibson Mike Alexander 1979
Scramble up the ramp on the left. Climb across the white wall to the roof and traverse with trepidation to its end and belay (11a). Up the corner, out left and up to the belay ledge above (.9).

Sacrificial Lamb ● ☺   10d   2p.
Pete Shackleton Bob Milward (1pa) April 1985 FFA: Kevin McLane Joe Turley May 1985
Climb the dog-leg crack left of the chimney and on up the thin crack above. Belay at the roof (10d). Climb the fine wall above past several bolts to an easier slab finish (10d). Long pitches.

Snot   .8 A1   3p.
John Wurflinger J.Allain 1973
Right of *Sacrificial Lamb.* follow a major crack and chimney line.

> *Follow the trail south and the next 3 climbs quickly come into view. Turn back to the left and scramble onto the belay ledge.*

Hungry Wolf ***   11b   2p.
Dean Hart Randy Atkinson (1pa) Sept 1984   FFA: Kevin McLane Sept 1984
A tremendous climb. Layback up into a treed recess, traverse up left to a dyke then pull right to a good ledge below a large square corner (10b). Up the corner and layback with alacrity through the bulges. Finish up an easier corner (11b).

Hunter's Moon ***   11d   2p.
Kevin McLane Joe Turley Dick Mitten May 1985
An excellent climb in an exposed position. Follow *Hungry Wolf* to reach the arete on the left, climb it and gain easier ground to a ledge (11d). A fine finger crack splits the headwall. Climb it and the slab above to the top (10b).

Never Say Never   ***   11b   50m

Dean Hart Tim Holwill Peter Shackleton Sept 1984

Climb the corner a few metres right of *Hungry...*and exit into a steep crack. Difficult face moves ahead lead to slightly easier ground, trending right to a steep finish up a corner-ramp. A marathon. Rappel or walk down.

The Eyebrow   .8 A2   2p.

Dick Culbert Mike Warr 1967

A diagonal, yellow overhang at the far right edge of the west face.

Man Of Leisure   ***   10a   #7   **SPORT+**   42m

Glenn Payan Jeff Thomson John Thompson May 1997

Awesome. Go out left. After the 2nd bolt, finger traverse the dyke and up. Better take a few pieces to 2".

Poultry In Motion   **   10d   40m

Glenn Payan Jeff Thomson Septmber 1996

A very enticing crackline up the centre of the south face, starting as for *Man...*

SHANNON FALLS — GOBSMACKING WALL

Descent

1. Sneeze 10c, A1
2. Monkey Lust 11a
3. Sacraficial Lamb 10d
4. Snot 8, A1
5. Hunters Moon 11d
6. Hungry Wolf 11b
7. Never Say Never 11b
8. Eyebrow 8, A2
9. Man of Leisure 10a
10. Poultry in Motion 10d

THE MALAMUTE

Upper
Malamute

trails

Parking

Lower
Malamute

Parking

Upper
Malamute

Lower
Malamute

trails

Upper
Malamute

Lower
Malamute

THE MALAMUTE

The Malamute is the dome that rises prominently in front of the Grand Wall of the Chief. This crag is one of the crown jewels of Squamish, with almost 100 climbs up to four pitches in length, some of them rating among the finest in Canada. The significance of the Malamute to Squamish climbing is second only to the Chief. Seen from Highway 99, it appears as a tree-covered hill, but it is the hidden seaward side facing west, where its full grandeur is on display above the Squamish estuary. The easy trail to the summit provides a panoramic viewpoint of the Chief and the surrounding mountains.

The Malamute is divided into 'Upper' and 'Lower', as a result of almost 60 new routes developed here since the last guide was published in 1992, and there are now three different access routes. The only possible approach to the climbs at the Lower Malamute is on railroad tracks owned by BC Rail, a Crown Corporation, and as a result, continued access and a responsible attitude from climbers are very sensitive matters that must be taken seriously. You must take these considerations into account before climbing. **By not observing diligent behaviour in the vicinity of the rail tracks, you will be jeopardising the future of climbing at the Malamute.**

Train crews must be able to conduct their business in safety, and climbers should be aware of this at all times. Trains can arrive with alarming speed, not always with whistles blowing, so act prudently, keep your ears tuned, and stay well back from the tracks. Following these common sense rules will help ensure everyones' safety.

If you are climbing any of the routes near the tracks, keep your gear against the rock, develop the habit of staying off the tracks, and move on elsewhere as soon as possible.

The area which is most sensitive is the north end around *Clean Crack*. Please do your part to minimise usage of those climbs, and keep your gear and yourself away from the tracks at all times. Time spent hanging out top-roping is not a cool way to spend the day here: lead, follow and leave promptly. You read it here.

Always be alert for trains.

Complete your climb and move on quickly.

Do not leave gear or ropes near the tracks.

Avoid unnecessary top-roping.

Do not stand on the tracks watching other climbers.

Getting there... **Upper Malamute.** There are two approaches, from the north and from the south, forming a continuous loop hike of 15 minutes or so over the summit of the hill. Starr Wall is about the same approach time either way, 7-10 minutes. If you are coming from the north, parking in the lot on the west (southbound) side of the highway is safest as it does not require making a hazardous (and illegal) turn into the Chief parking lot. Likewise, if you are coming from the south, using the Chief parking lot avoids an equally hazardous turn across two lanes of traffic into the north parking area. *For the Southern Approach...* From the Chief parking lot take the trail that starts directly opposite the parking lot. Watch out crossing the highway! Once you arrive at the top of the crag at Starr Wall, turn left for 50m to Stooges Slab. For climbs in the summit area, continue north from Starr Wall for 100m. Beyond the summit (Highest Tier), drop down on the right over slabby outcrops to flat bedrock, turn left toward the water, then left again to traverse south below The Cage and Jacob's Wall. The latter can also be reached directly from below Highest Tier by rappel. *For the Northern Approach...* Start from the small parking area on the west side of the highway, 100m north of the Chief parking lot. The trail entrance is 15m left of the trail to the Lower Malamute. Head directly to the summit over open bedrock slabs. It is the fastest way to reach climbs in the summit area, as well as being the most pleasant way to the top. Once on the summit, continue south to the top of Starr Wall.

Getting there... **Lower Malamute.** Park in the large lot in front of the Chief on the east side of the highway, or 100m further north on the west side. Follow a trail down to the tracks to the north end of the Malamute, then head 25m south to the first route.

Climbs and gear... The climbs at the **Lower Malamute** are almost all 5.10 or harder, mostly cracks or face climbs in three general areas: The low north end, with its single-pitch cracks; the larger central section around *Mirkwood Forest*; and the high southern section around the tidal pool that forms on the inside of the tracks. Descents from all climbs are by rappel, but a rough trail exits to the north for climbs at that end. **Climbs on the Upper Malamute** range across half-a-dozen or so west-facing crags, and vary from cracks to face, offering a wide range of difficulty from 5.6 to 5.12, many sport routes and some excellent moderate-grade cracks. Some of the climbs starting from the Lower Malamute that rise the full height of the cliff, such as *Quagmire Crack* can be combined with routes on the upper level.

Lower Malamute - North End

This section covers climbs from the north end to just south of *Caboose*.

Always be alert for trains.
Complete your climb and move on quickly.
Do not leave gear or ropes near the tracks.
Avoid unnecessary top-roping.
Do not stand on the tracks watching other climbers.
Do not leave any garbage - pack it out.

Sacrement C'est Bon   *   11a   *142*   15m
Andrew Boyd August 1998
This is the furthest lefthand line through the band of roofs. Monster holds on the roof lead to a fun lip encounter.

Malamucus   *   11b   *142*   15m
John Ohler Mark Aisbett 1990
Start as for *Sacrement* and pull over the roof to its right.

Horrors Of Zontals   11a   *142*   25m
Greg Foweraker and a cast of thousands 1982
Scruffy. Probably harder than 11a too.

Invertigo   *   11c   #4   *142*   **SPORT**+   20m
Lyle Knight Dave Myers Sept 1989
Easy to the roof, but not so to get onto the wall above.

The Dregs   11a+1pa   *142*   20m
Robin Barley Vicky Earle July 1998
The wall immediately left of *Brown Ale*. From the base of the corner, climb past 3 bolts, using the second for aid. Exit left and finish as for *Invertigo*.

Brown Ale   **   .9   *142*   20m
Kevin McLane Randy Atkinson July 1978
Old-fashioned hand-jamming (euphemism for 5.10) up the corner leads to a small alcove on the right and fine crux moves through the roof.

Awaiting Eternity   **   11c   *142*   20m
Jordan Struthers Rich Wheater Sept 1997
Superb bold climbing up the prominent undercut arete right of *Brown Ale*...
Starting on the left, move across the thin crack, finishing up the wall just left of the arete. Protect with wires in the crack. Easily top-roped from *Brown Ale*.

Exhibition Flake   .8   *142*   20m
Kevin McLane Jim Sinclair Aug 1978
Layback up the flake and traverse easily right to the tree belay.

Exhibition Flake Direct   10a   *142*   15m
Kevin McLane Jim Sinclair Aug 1978
Poorly protected moves up a basalt dyke, then right to tree belay.

> *No details are available on the left-hand bolted face climb on this section of wall. There are three bolts, and difficulty is at least 11+.*

To Glibly Grab *   11a   #4   **SPORT**+   15m
John Fantini Robin Barley May 1998
Go directly to the left end of *Big Eave* traverse. Take a 1" CD and long sling.

Dismal Dreams   10b   15m
Robin Barley Vicky Earle May 1998
Start as for *Glibly Grab...*, then move up right to the start of the *Big Eave* traverse. Rappel out from here or finish left with dismal rope drag.

The Big Eave *   10a   23m
Unknown   FFA: Kevin McLane Robin Barley Aug 1978
Its bark is worse than its bite. The crux is halfway along the traverse.

Penguins In Bondage ** 11a   15m
Hugh Burton Paul Piro 1971 FFA: Bill Price G.Zaccor 1978
A Malamute classic. Layback wildly up into the wide slot. Find the hidden hold. Continue gracefully up the chimney.

Chicken Little *   11d   15m
Andrew Boyd May 1998. (possible FA on aid, Hugh Burton Paul Piro 1971)
Start as for *Penguins...* then pull right around the arete to gain a seam. Serious climbing to the first bolt, crux follows. Finish at the chains on *Penguins...* This is possibly the same line as *Chicken Cacciatori* (A3 1971).

Spook *   11d   2p.
Tim Auger Gordie Smaill 1973 FFA: Peter Croft p1 1979, p2 1987.
Climb the pin scarred seam to a belay in the shallow recess (11d). Continue up easier cracks above (11a).

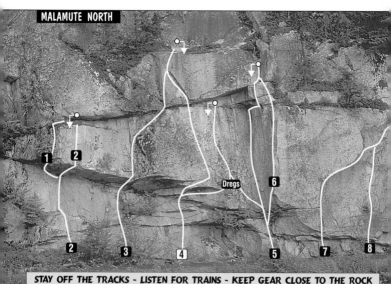

MALAMUTE NORTH

Dregs

STAY OFF THE TRACKS - LISTEN FOR TRAINS - KEEP GEAR CLOSE TO THE ROCK

1. Sacrement c'est Bon.11a
2. Malamucus.............11b
3. Horrors of Zontals 11a
4. Invertigo 11c
5. Brown Ale.....................9
6. Awaiting Eternity 11c
7. Exhibition Flake............
8. Exhibition Flake Direct11
9. To Gliby Grab 11

MALAMUTE

Purple Chicken (aka Get Hooked) 12a   10m
Steve Cosgrove July 1989 FA Dean Lister Jim Campbell July 1979
Steep face climbing past three bolts. Move left to belay on *Spook*. RPs help.

Clean Crack *** 11b   25m
Unknown c. 1967 FFA: John Rosholt Randy Atkinson c. 1977
This famous finger crack is one of the finest pitches at Squamish. Excellent
pro throughout, with technically demanding moves at the mid-height crux.

Clean X ** 11b   25m
Bruce McDonald Tim McAllister August 1988
After the crux of *Clean Crack*, mantel out left and face climb up.

Caboose *** 10b   25m
Tony Cousins Jim Sinclair 1963 FFA: Eric Weinstein J.Haeck W.Hack 1975
A superb complement to *Clean Crack*, this impressive corner gives a sustained
and strenuous climb on good protection. The difficulty increases higher up,
as energy and strength fade away.

The arete right of Caboose is a 12b top-rope (Keith Reid, 1987).

Last Train To Hicksville ** 12b #6   **SPORT** 25m
Perry Beckham c1990
The rather elegant and unlikely wall on the right.

Light Of Day .9   x   10m
Lyle Knight D.Myers June 25 1988
Climb to a crack below the roof, pull out onto the precarious flake above.

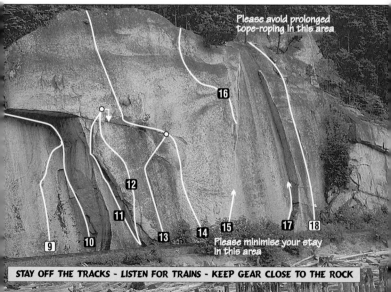

Please avoid prolonged tope-roping in this area

Please minimise your stay in this area

STAY OFF THE TRACKS - LISTEN FOR TRAINS - KEEP GEAR CLOSE TO THE ROCK

The Big Eave 10a	13. Spook 11d	16. Clean X 11b
Penguins in Bond...11a	14. Purple Chicken.......11b	17. Caboose 10b
Chicken Little 11d	15. Clean Crack............11b	18. Last Train Hicksville 12b

Lower Malamute - Central Area

This section covers climbs south of *Caboose* as far as *Hand Jive*. The high wall right of the huge corner of *Sodfanciers*, seamed by slanting overlap-cracks and grooves offers some excellent interwoven multi-pitch routes. Contrived in places, but well worth climbing.

Trainspotting   11d (10d+1pa) #4   x   **SPORT**   20m
Robin Barley (1pa) May 1996   FFA Kevin McCormick July 1996
Start 70m south of *Clean Crack* at a small hanging groove, requiring a long reach or 1pa. Exit left via a hard mantelshelf.

Just A Little Pull   11d (10d+1pa) #5   x   **SPORT+**   20m
Robin Barley Judy Komori (1pa) May 1997   FFA Andrew Boyd August 1998.
The right-hand route. 10d except for a poxy bit at a smooth white bulge.

> *The next climb is a narrow but prominent basalt dyke 100m south of Clean Crack (the seaward extension of the Black Dyke).*

Chasing Rainbows   **   10d   x   2p.
John Howe Randy Atkinson Paul Kindree 1979
A fine route. Climb the dyke on good holds past bolts to a big ledge, and straight up the steepening wall above (10b). Walk into the forest and belay below the continuation of the dyke. The next pitch is an impressive, technically demanding lead, but easier than it appears. Good old-fashioned protection where you can get it (10d).

> *Just south from here is a large open bay. A 15m right-facing corner is prominent on the left, below a long roof—Fungus Razor (a Croft joke about Hamish Fraser), and its direct start Fungicide (12b). Right of here, two pitches climb out of the bay, Canadian Compromise (10a) and Smithereens (10b), offering alternative ways of approaching the climbs on the upper walls.*

Fungus Razor   **   12b (10d)   *148*   2p.
Paul Wood Don Serl 1976   FFA: Peter Croft Tami Knight 1981
RECLEANED: Andrew Boyd 1998
From behind the biggest boulder, pull over a small roof and up the delightful corner, belay on the left (10d). Hand traverse right and pull over the roof by a hard mantel (12b). The first pitch is a fine climb in its own right. Rappel off or continue on one of the routes above.

Fungicide   12b   *148*   15m
Andrew Boyd March 1998
Takes the corner right of the start of *Fungus Razor* to join that route at the roof. Climb directly up the corner (a bit loose), thin crack moves to the roof.

Canadian Compromise   * 10a   *148*   20m
Kris Wild Aaron Black June 1998
The flake chimney-crack below *Quagmire*, at the left edge of the white rockfall scar. Pro to 3". Climb it to reach *Quagmire*. Recent blasting has altered the start of this climb—the best alternative is a scruffy-looking thing on the left.

MALAMUTE

Smithereens   *   10b   *148*   35m
Robin Barely John Fantini Aug 1998
Start 8m left of the scruffy corner on the right side of the giant rockfall scar, and climb a series of left-trending ramps and slabs past several bolts. Finish leftward fo reach the base of *Quagmire Crack,* or rightward for *Sodfanciers* and *Heretical* (10b).

Quagmire Crack   **   10c   *148*   (45m)
Robin Barley Andreas Maurer Kevin McLane 1976 RECLEANED: Andrew Boyd 1998
The prominent steep crack on the headwall above *Fungus Razor*, one of the most exposed and exciting climbs at the Malamute. A major rockfall blew the approach away in 1979, and the best way to start is via *Smithereens* (10a), making a two-pitch route.Take lots of ½"gear.

My Dyke   *   11d   *148*   (2p.)
Andrew Boyd August 1998
This is the right-leaning dyke that joins *Porco's* first pitch at mid-height, above the crux. Good moves (11d). Finish up the 2nd pitch of *Porco* (10d).

Porco   **   12a   *148*   (2p.)
Brian Norris David Bowen (aid) 1974. Yo-yo'd Andrew Boyd Colin Moorhead April 1998
This is the striking thin crack on the headwall left of *Quagmire Crack*. The crux is low on the first pitch (12a). A shorter pitch leads to the top (10d).

Another Man's Dyke   *   11c   *148*   (45m)
Andrew Boyd Kris Wild Marc Bosomworth Steve Leeder July 1998
partial: (aid on 2nd pitch of Unhappy Hooker) Robin Barley Anders Ourom 1976
Start up *Quagmire Crack*, but at the big flake go out left to a thin crack. Good 5.10 crackwork leads to a rest. Then head rightward along a hard dyke, past thought-provoking moves. Take lots of ½"gear.

The Unhappy Hooker   A3   *148*   (2p.)
Robin Barley Anders Ourom 1976
An intermittent crack right of *Quagmire*. Above bolts, pendulum left into Quagmire and belay. The 2nd pitch follows what is now *Another Man's Dyke*.

Heretical   *   11a   *148*   (35m)
John Fantini Robin Barley August 1998
Climb *Smithereens* or *Canadian...* to reach the foot of *Sodfanciers* (10a). Climb a seam on the right wall, then move left into the corner at the base of the Great Salal Sod. Climb the groove above on the left, as for *Sodfanciers*, and continue up the smooth groove in the steepening arete to a station (11a). Somewhat futuristic beyond here, but a superb finale is waiting for someone.

Sod Fanciers Delight   *   10d   *148*   (2p.)
Robin Barley Peter Shackleton (3pa) August 1980   FFA Robin Barley John Fantini August 1998
RECLEANED: Robin Barley John Fantini August 1998.
This is the huge right-facing corner that defines the right side of the *Quagmire* wall. Climb *Smithereens* or *Canadian...* to reach the base of the corner (10b). Climb the corner until it is possible to go left up a thin crack and groove to a belay (10d). Continue up the smooth groove to an FP, traverse right to Giant Salal Sod (some trundle!) and finish up the final arching undercling (10c).

Mirkwood Forest ** 10c+1pa *148* 2p.
Robin Barley Randy Atkinson John Wittmayer 1978   FFA (var.) Peter Croft T.Nakajima 1978
FFA (original) Andrew Boyd 1998   RECLEANED: Robin Barley March 1998
An excellent climb—the original route on this wall and long since overgrown—
has been recleaned. Cracks left of *Id* lead to a belay ledge below the centre
of the clean upper wall (.9). Use a bolt for aid to leave the belay [or 12a, or
climb the 11a corner to the left], then climb the face above, finishing up a
small corner to a tree belay. A fine pitch (10c+1pa).

Renaissance Man * 11b+2pa *148* 4p.
p2,4 Rolf Rybak M.Tygges. p3 Rolf Rybak D.Couperwaithe (2pa) 1997.
Follows a parallel line just left of *The Clearing* to the top of the Malamute.
Start as for *Mirkwood Forest*, then at the point where that route moves left
across a salal groove, belay (.9). Climb straight up the wall above past bolts
to a ledge (11b). Move up, then left to a large overlap-roof trending out left.
Turn it on the left by using 2 bolts then continue with a long, rather nasty
diagonal traverse and up to a ledge system (11a-b, 2pa) *(Top-roped at 12a, Kris Holm).*
Follow a delightful dyke past 6 bolts to the top (10c).

The Clearing ** 11c (10c+1pa) *148* 4p.
Robin Barley Des O'Reagan (1pa) June 1996 FFA Andrew Boyd A.Guinea Pig Aug 1998
A bit contrived here and there, otherwise a fine route. Start up *Mirkwood
Forest*, then at 15m, go up right-trending cracks to a spike [optional belay for
rope-drag] (10b). Or step left to a dyke, then straight up a superb slab and
arete to a ledge (11c or 10c+1pa). Head up right to cracks in an overlap, then
a long narrow slab, moving left to cracks (10c). Finish up *Renaissance* (10c).

Will Power * 11a #6 *148* **SPORT**+ 28m
Will Dorling Nick Watts Robin Barley Oct 1996
Somewhat contrived, but excellent climbing up the left-bounding arete of the
dihedral of *Id*. Start up that route, then go left after 3m onto the arete. Belay
as for *Id*. Also serves as an alternative start to *The Clearing* - watch for rope
drag. Take a couple pieces to 1".

Id ** 10b *148* 35m
Dan Tate Barry Hagen Nov 1965 FFA: Peter Croft Tami Knight 1979
50m right of *Fungus Razor* is a right facing corner, a popular climb. The crux
is low down, small wires help. The original aid route followed what is now
The Clearing and *Renaissance* to the top. A direct finish continues another 10m
along a dyke out right, *Ego* 11c *(Rolf Rybak Sig Isaac Robin Barley August 1996)*

Superego 10c+4pa *148* (2p.)
Sig Isaac Robin Barley Rolf Rybak August 1996
Above *Ego* (the direct finish to *Id*), aid up 4 bolts into a left-trending arch. Follow
it through an overlap as for *The Clearing*, and up a narrow slab. Step right below
a headwall (10c+4pa). Rap, or finish up *Besot and Flushed* (10d).

*Please spend as little time as possible in the Clean Crack -
Caboose area to minimise risk of conflict with train crews.*

A Plague Of Black Bolts   *   11b+5pa   _148_   2p.
Sig Isaac Rolf Rybak Robin Barley August 1996

A good climb despite two aid sections. Takes the wall left of _Hand Jive_ in two
long pitches. From the top of the salal ramp, climb the wall above using three
bolts for aid to reach a curving crack. From its top, make thin moves left to a
dyke (11b+3pa) Follow it precariously up right. Use two bolts for aid to reach
a diagonal crack. Follow it to chains (11b+2pa). The name of this climb is a
fond recollection of _A Plague of Barleys_ at Skaha. Finish up _Besot and Flushed_?

Hand Jive   ***   10b   _148_   20m
Eric Weinstein Carl Austrom 1975

At the right side of this wall is this fine handjam crack and a longtime classic.

Seaside Rendezvous   *   10b   _148_   22m
Anders Ourom Randy Atkinson 1978

Good. Start just left of _Berrycup_, then out left across the curving crack. Hand
traverse across to _Hand Jive_, or walk it if you dare.

MALAMUTE

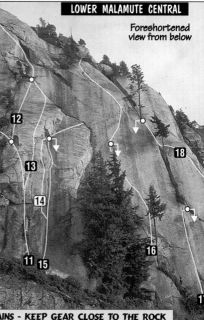

LOWER MALAMUTE CENTRAL

eshortened
from below

Foreshortened
view from below

STAY OFF THE TRACKS - LISTEN FOR TRAINS - KEEP GEAR CLOSE TO THE ROCK

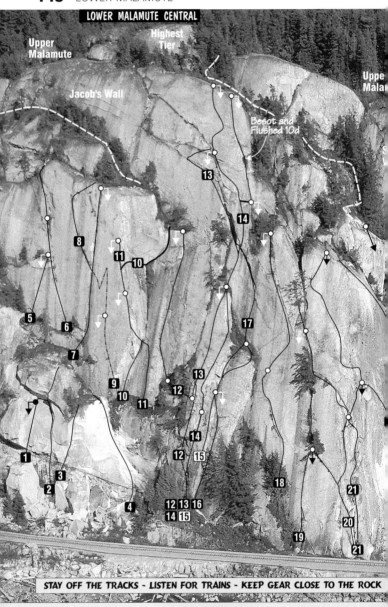

LOWER MALAMUTE CENTRAL

Upper Malamute

Highest Tier

Jacob's Wall

Beeot and Flushed 10d

Uppe Mala

STAY OFF THE TRACKS - LISTEN FOR TRAINS - KEEP GEAR CLOSE TO THE ROCK

1. Fungus Razor 10d-12b
2. Fungicide 12b
3. Canadian Compro 10a
4. Smithereens..............10b
5. My Dyke 11d
6. Porco 12a
7. Quagmire Crack 10c
8. Another Mans Dyke .11c
9. Unhappy Hooker.......A3
10. Sodfanciers Delight .10d
11. Heretical..................11a
12. Mirkwood Forest......10c
13. Renaissance 11b,
14. The Clearing.............
15. Willpower..................
16. Id Dihedral................
17. Superego 10c,
18. Plague of Black 11b,

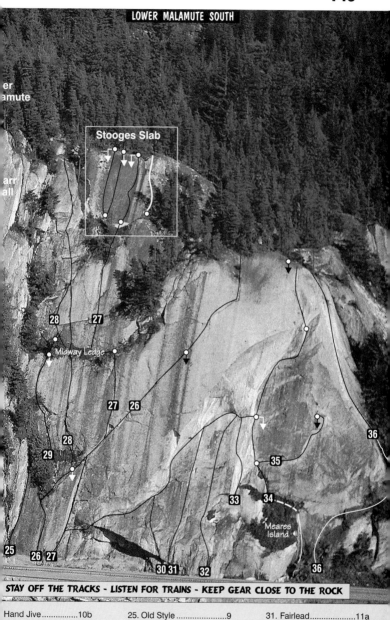

LOWER MALAMUTE SOUTH

Stooges Slab

Midway Ledge

Meares Island

STAY OFF THE TRACKS - LISTEN FOR TRAINS - KEEP GEAR CLOSE TO THE ROCK

Lower Malamute - South End

This section covers climbs south of, and including *Berrycup – Crescent Crack.* Generally longer routes, they include some of the best routes at the Malamute, especially *Crescent Crack* (10d), *Damascus Steel* (11a), *Agonal* (11c) and *Overly Hanging Out* (11b).

Dogberry	11c+3pa	*148*	40m

Robin Barley John Fantini   July 1998

A long, direct eliminate pitch that starts up *Seaside Rendezvous*, then heads up to join *Berrycup* at the station, then on to join *Damascus Steel*.

Berrycup **	10c	*148*	2p.

Gordie Smaill Brian Norris (aid)1970 [Robin Barley Peter Rowat (1pa) 1977] FFA: P.Croft 1979
p1 as described Will Dorling Oct 1996

Excellent for its grade, varied and interesting. 12m right of *Hand Jive,* climb a groove to reach an open corner. Pull out left onto the wall and up to a good belay. An excellent pitch (10c). Continue leftward along the ramp / crack to its end, and climb a short offwidth crack (10a). Rappel. The original FFA at 11d moved left below the roof.

Crescent Crack ***	10d	*148*	28m

Tony Cousins Jim Sinclair Wade Chernekoff 1963   FFA Dave Nicol Paul Piro 1976

This unmistakeable curving corner-crack is one of the most hallowed of all Squamish cracks. The lower ramp is not difficult, but the steep corner above certainly is, with much elegant, pumpy stemming. The thin face crack left of the final corner has been led at about 12a.

Christendom *	10d	*148*	2p.

Robin Barley Luc Mailloux Sept 1998

Climb *Crescent Crack* (10d). Step up right to a thin slab, climb straight up to a generous summit ledge (10d).

Damascus Steel **	12a (11a+4pa)	*148*	3p.

Robin Barley Randy Atkinson (4pa) August 1987
FFA Andrew Boyd Vicky Sullivan Aug 1998

This fine climb has two flavours. All free at 12a; or 11a with 4 bolts for aid. Well worth doing either way. Climb *Crescent Crack* (10d). Go right from the belay, then up and left across the wall to a fine perch at 10b, or better still, climb directly up the slab above the belay (10d). Move up left from the belay to a bolt. Step back down and go left along a very improbable crux traverse (12a) to a blunt arete. Continue up the arete on big holds to another cruxy bit past more bolts to reach a beautiful fingercrack that leads to the top.

To climb this route at an easier 11a+4pa, use the first bolt on pitch 3 for aid to tension to the arete, then use 2 bolts for aid in the 12a section to reach the fingercrack, and one bolt to exit.

The following 11 climbs start in one way or another out of the tidal pool that lies right of Crescent Crack. Ease of getting onto the rock for some will depend on the tide. Only two climbs as described actually go the full height of the wall but numerous variations are possible.

*The following 6 climbs above the tidal pool are vintage late 70s—a network
of interconnected pitches reaching to the top of the crag. Now cleaned up
and accessible by a new footbridge, they offer many superb crack pitches.*

Old Style ★★★   .9   *149*   30m
Peter Croft Tami Knight 1979 RECLEANED: Kris Wild 1998
A superb right-facing corner rising out of the left end of the tidal pool: easier
than it appears. Belay off the bridge at the base of the corner.

Cling Peaches ★★   10d   *149*   3p.
Peter Croft Robin Barley 1978
A fine line. Climb a few metres up *Old Style* and head out right up a dyke to
a ledge (10b). Move up and right again, then climb the peapod groove above
to Midway Ledge (10d). The original route continues up the dirty crack on the
right; better to continue via upper *Grub Street* (10c or 11b), or rappel off. The
original start climbed out of the tidal pool up a prominent right-leaning corner-
fault to reach the peapod groove (10a).

Grub Street ★★★   11b   *149*   3p.
Robin Barley Peter Croft (1pa) 1978 FFA Peter Croft Tami Knight 1978
RESTORED: Robin Barley John Fantini July 1997
Start up *Old Style* and go out right up a dyke to a ledge (10b). Climb the obvious
thin face-crack in the centre of the wall above to Midway Ledge (11b). Move
left and follow cracks, step right to surmount an overlap and follow a slab until
possible to either: move right to Stooges Slab (10c), or stay left up a direct
line to the top (11b). On Stooges Slab, the classic finish is *Rosebud* (.9)

Cider Crack ★   .9   *149*   (30m)
Peter Croft Tami Knight 1978
From the top of *Old Style*, climb a left-trending crackline to the left end of
Midway Ledge.

Knuckleduster ★   11b   *149*   (10m)
Peter Croft Tami Knight 1978
From the centre of Midway Ledge, face moves lead to a thin crack, effectively
a variation start to the last pitch of *Grub Street*.

Rosebud ★★   .9   *149*   18m
Peter Croft Tami Knight Robin Barley 1978
A route that has been superceded by the pitch combinations listed above.
Finish up the dark streaks on Stooges Slab,originally unprotected but now
sporting several bolts (.8). It now makes a good finish to *Grub Street*.

Agonal ★★★   11c   *149*   3p.
Peter Shackleton Robin Barley June 1996
One of the best climbs at Squamish, a superb route up the outrageous diagonal
dyke on the headwall above *Overly Hanging Out*, a test of footwork ingenuity.
Start up *Old Style* and head out right up a dyke to a ledge (10b). Climb on up
right as for *Cling Peaches*, then beyond the peapod groove to gain a very
exposed dyke. Feet or hands on the holds? Belay in the middle of the wall
(11b). Continue, eventually reaching a crack [1″ CD], and then a slab to finish
(10d). Double ropes. Small rack to 2″.

The following three climbs all start from the right side of the tidal pool (not tide-dependent) and end in the huge arch of Overly Hanging Out. Fairlead is the popular choice for starting OHO.

Heel Boom Bay 11b *149* 25m
Kevin McLane John Howe May 1985
Layback the steep left leaning flake. Short and intimidating. Rappel or continue traversing the arch to join *Overly Hanging Out* (11b).

Fairlead * 11a *149* 40m
John Howe Perry Beckham Carl Austrom May 1985
Climb the break 5m right of *Heel Boom Bay* to gain a slim corner. Follow it past a bulge to the big arch above. Traverse right with difficulty to a good stance on *Strawline*. Step right past hard moves to belay on *Overly Hanging...*

Fortified Oatflakes ● 11a *149* 40m
Phillip van Wassenauer C.Conner Sept 1986
From the right end of the tidal pool, climb up to the left end of a big ledge. Step left and up the wall above past a FP. Difficult moves lead left into the arch. Traverse right as for *Fairlead*.

Overly Hanging Out *** 11b *149* 3p.
Eric Lance Brian Norris (aid) 1970   FFA: Peter Croft Tami Knight 1980
The great arch gives a very fine climb through exciting overlaps with a short crux and beautifully exposed climbing. The original 1970 route (on aid) began up the first pitch of *Cling Peaches*, and it is since believed to have been climbed free. Climb the first pitch of *Fairlead* (11a) or *Strawline* (11c) and move right to reach the base of the corner. Climb through the first set of overlaps and traverse right below the second, up to a small ledge (11b). Pull out wildly left into a crack. An easier groove above leads to an unexpected sting in the tail (10a). Rap off chains to *Loggers Are People...* and Meares Island.

 To reach the next three climbs, walk up right of the tidal pool and climb (.7) to the big terrace of Meares Island.

Strawline ** 11c *149* 30m
Perry Beckham May 1985
From the left end of Meares Island, go left to climb a slim wall by technically hard moves past 2FP. Continue up a thin crack to *Fairlead*. Go right to finish.

Loggers Are People Too * 10d *149* 20m
Tim Auger Gordie Smaill (aid) 1969
FFA: Perry Beckham John Howe Carl Austrom March 1985
An unusual climb. From the highest stump on Meares Island, undercling rightward along a pair of cam-eating flakes and up a slanting corner. Rappel.

Three Night Route At The Malamute .8 *149* 20m
Paul Bader Jeannine Caldbeck (aid) 1971 FFA Peter Croft John Manuel 1979
This is the original, direct start to the main corner of *Overly Hanging Out*.

Survival Of The Flatus *** 10b *149* 2p.
Dean Hart Peter Croft June 1984
A superb pitch. Hard to reach, and with a couple of big runouts Climb up into trees at the base of the long arete at the far south end of the cliff (.7).

Upper Malamute

Getting There...   See page 140

Climbs and gear...   See page 140

▬▬▬ UPPER MALAMUTE · APPROACH TRAIL ▬▬▬

Crack Be Nimble   12a   x   8m
Jack Fieldhouse July 1998
This is a thin crack on a small crag right of the approach trail from the Chief parking lot. Walk north along the base of the crag to a clean streak with a hard-looking crack. Gear is adequate but hard to place. Can be top-roped.

▬▬▬ UPPER MALAMUTE · THE CAGE ▬▬▬

This is the first crag encountered when approaching from the north. At the top of the bedrock slabs, the summit trail heads off left around a series of slabby outcrops. Turn right here, and walk out along a narrow ledge. The crack of *Arm Yourself* is encountered after 20m.

Arm Yourself *   12b   #6   *158*   **SPORT**   18m
Jeff Thomson May 1998
A curving, right-leaning crack.

Sparky **   10b   #5   *158*   **SPORT**   18m
Jeff Thomson Glenn Payan Jack Fieldhouse March 1998
A nice climb. After a cruxy start just left of the obvious basalt dyke at the right edge of this wall, traverse up and left across the face.

Pacing The Cage *   10a   #5   *158*   **SPORT**   12m
Glenn Payan Jeff Thomson January 1998
Start as for *Sparky*, but climb directly up.

▌ *The dyke just right of Pacing The Cage is part of the Black Dyke, and is a short third-class romp to the top of the crag.*

THE MALAMUTE

Upper Malamute

Lower Malamute

MALAMUTE

▬▬ *Upper Malamute - Jacob's Wall* ▬▬▬▬

From The Cage, scramble up for 15m, then down to the base of a high-angle slab with two long horizontal cracks at mid-height. The five parallel sport climbs are easy to locate but distinguishable from each other only by difficulty. It is possible, but not essential to place small ¾"-1" CDs in the cracks.

Train Boy *   10c   #5   *158*   **SPORT**   18m
Jeff Thomson Glenn Payan March 1998

Whip Cream Boy *   10d   #5   *158*   **SPORT**   12m
Jeff Thomson Glenn Payan March 1998

Pooshwltyorrfout *   11a   #6   *158*   **SPORT**   20m
Jeff Thomson Glenn Payan Jack Fieldhouse March 1998

Consolation *   10c   #5   *158*   **SPORT**   20m
Jeff Thomson Glenn Payan May 1998

Stone Cold *   10b   #7   *158*   **SPORT**   22m
Glenn Payan Jeff Thomson January 1998

Jacob's Other Ladder * .8   *158*   27m
Glenn Payan John Thompson July 1995

NPCC   10d   *158*   10m
Glenn Payan Jeff Thomson November 1998
From the top of a flake 5m right of *Jacob's*, climb 10m to join in with *Jacob's*.

▬▬ *Upper Malamute - Highest Tier* ▬▬▬▬

This is the small west-facing slab immediately under the summit high point of the Malamute. Walk down to the base on the left (south) side. All four climbs start near the centre of the slab. Yes, the names are longer than the routes.

No Need But A Little Parsley .6   *158*   10m
Glenn Payan July 1995
Trend up to the easier-angled slab on the left side.

Let My People Eat Pasty Lentils 10b   #2 *158*   10m
Glenn Payan Jeff Thomson January 1998
This is the most obvious climb, directly up the middle slab, sporting a bolt.

With Friends Like That Who Needs Enemas .8   *158*   10m
Glenn Payan September 1995
Takes the obvious layback flake right of centre.

I Love The Smell of Nuprin in the Morning ● 10a *158*   10m
Glenn Payan Sept 1995
A nonedescript route up a narrow slab right of *With Friends...*

Name story... *Overly Hanging Out was named after the position of the tongues of the first ascentionists after a previous night in the bar.*

▬ *Upper Malamute - The Terraces* ▬▬

South of Highest Tier, and north of Starr Wall are several climbs on minor walls and aretes.

Below Summit Slab is a large gently sloping granite terrace. The station at the top of Besot and Flushed is at the south end of this terrace, just left of the top of Renaissance, which comes up the major wall from the Lower Malamute. On the left side of the terrace (looking south) are three bolted face climbs.

Besot and Flushed **   10d   #4   *158*   **SPORT**+   35m
Glenn Payan Jeff Thomson Rich Woo May 1996
An excellent climb. Rappel in to the base from a station 20m south of the base of *Featureless Face*, then climb back out up a crack and arete above it. Take a couple CDs to 2".

The narrow slabby wall right of Besot... can be top-roped at 5.10 (Payan-Thomson), rappel in from bolts on top.

Remembrance Day *   11c   #3   *158*   **SPORT**   10m
Jeff Thomson Glenn Payan   November 11 1998.
The left-hand bolted face climb at the back of the terrace.

The Shallow End *   10b   #4   *158*   **SPORT**   10m
Glenn Payan Joe Turley Mark Bombois October 1997
The centre bolted face climb.

Featureless Face *   11a   #4   *159*   **SPORT**   12m
Robin Barley 1996
The right-hand bolted face climb.

Immediately south of Featureless Face is a vertical, knob-and-dyke-infested wall with stations at the top, which as yet is unclimbed.

To reach the start of the next two climbs from the base of Featureless Face, continue hiking down southward to the base of Starr Wall. Below the fixed rope, traverse out toward the west for 20m or so until two bolted, blunt aretes come into view.

Franz's Son   .9   #2   *159*   **SPORT**   10m
Luke Wiedmann 1996
The left-hand arete.

Shockload *   11c   #4   *159*   **SPORT**   10m
Luke Wiedmann 1996
The right-hand arete.

A great place in afternoon sun, the Upper Malamute can be surprisingly brisk and cool in a spring or fall wind.

▬▬ *UPPER MALAMUTE - STARR WALL* ▬▬▬▬

This fine wall is host to several excellent crack climbs. It is a popular place, so don't have high expectations of picking any climb you wish when the weather is good. Starr Wall is exposed to wind and weather and can be surprisingly cool in spring and fall.

Getting there... There are two 'bases' to the crag. To reach either hike down past the Terraces and use a fixed line to reach the foot of *Paul's Crack.* 10m west, away from the base of that climb make a 20m rap (look for chains) to reach the lower base. Please try to avoid rappelling from the top of Starr Wall to the start of the climbs if there are climbers below. Walk instead–it's faster. Climbs are described from the left.

Under The Mercy   *   .9   *159*   20m
Glenn Payan Jeff Thomson John Thompson May 1996
Starts at the base of the fixed handline. Go left at obvious flakes then up.

Gerizim   .8   *159*   18m
Glenn Payan Jeff Thomson June 1996
Start as for *Under...*, then take the open corner on the right to the top of *Pauls..*

Paul's Crack   **   10a   *159*   26m
Glenn Payan Paul Starr June 1995
An excellent crack.

▣ *The following six climbs all start from the lower base level.*

High Mountain Woody   ***   .9   *159*   48m
Glenn Payan May 1996
This is the long finger-to-hand crack that curves up leftward across the face. One of the best cracks of its grade in Squamish, mostly 5.8 except for an adroit 5.9 move low down. A 5.8 variation stays right with *Slap and Tickle* then steps back left. This climb took 100 hours of patient gardening to be in its present impeccable condition, just as it was 9,000 years ago when the glaciers were finished with it.

Slap And Tickle   **   10b   *159*   50m
Glenn Payan Graham Rowbotham September 1995
Superb. One of the best 10b cracks in Squamish with the crux near the top [gotta love that]. Start as for *High Woody*, and exit that route rightwards below its crux. Below View Ledge, step into the crack arching back leftward. Climb it, and then go up right to the flake above, moving right (crux) to the arete a few metres below its top. A good alternative start [55m] is via *Gonch Pull.*

 The following three climbs all have separate first pitches, then join at View Ledge, a fine wide platform at the upper right side of the cliff. There are rap anchors should you wish to head back down.

Gonch Pull ** .9 _159_ 22m
Glenn Payan Jeff Thomson September 1995
A fine crack starting 18m down the slope from _High Mountain..._ Use a hold of generous proportion on a culturally modified cedar to gain a left trending crack. Then move into a right-trending crack after 10m to View Ledge. Continue up _Stefanie's Tears_ (.9), or _Lemming Condition_ (10b).

Neighbourhood Bully ** 11a #5 _159_ **SPORT**+ 25m
Jeff Thomson Glenn Payan July 1996
A direct face climb up to View Ledge. Start as for _Gonch Pull_, and climb past the bolts. Continue up _Stefanie's Tears_, or rap back to the base.

Stefanie's Tears ** .9 _159_ 2p.
p1 Glenn Payan Jeff Thomson Sept 1995   p2 Glenn Payan John Thompson Aug. 1995
Start as for _Gonch Pull_, clip the first bolt of _Neighbourhood..._, then take the right-hand line to finish on View Ledge (.9). Climb the fine corner above (.9).

Lemming Condition 10b _159_ (2p.)
Glenn Payan June 1996
This is the arete right of the second pitch of _Stefanie's Tears_. Climb any of the three previous routes to reach View Ledge.

▬▬ UPPER MALAMUTE - STOOGES SLAB ▬▬

Walk south for 50m from the top of Starr Wall to reach the top of a dark friction slab. Hike around down the left (south) side to reach the base. There are few climbs like these at Squamish–short, easy friction slabs. Climbs are described from the left. _Curly_ and _Larry_ share a belay station at the base.

Easy sport climbs on friction slabs are not common at Squamish and this crag has been setup specifically to encourage novice leaders. Please try to avoid setting up top-ropes on busy days. Bite the bullet and lead the climb first.

Curly .9 #4 _159_ **SPORT** 18m
Glenn Payan Jeff Thomson Joe Turley June 1996

Larry * .9 #5 _159_ **SPORT** 18m
Glenn Payan Jeff Thomson Rich Woo May 1996

Rosebud ** .8 #3 _159_ **SPORT** 18m
Peter Croft Tami Knight Robin Barley 1978
This is the last pitch to a long-lost climb first done in 1978. It was bolted without knowledge of the prior first ascent.

Moe * .8 #2 _159_ 15m
Glenn Payan May 1996
Start in the forest at the foot of the arete on the right side of the slab.

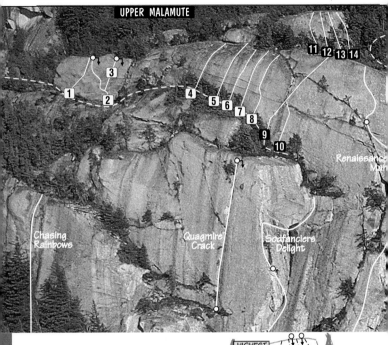

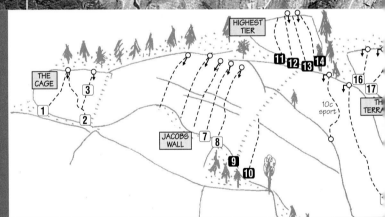

MALAMUTE

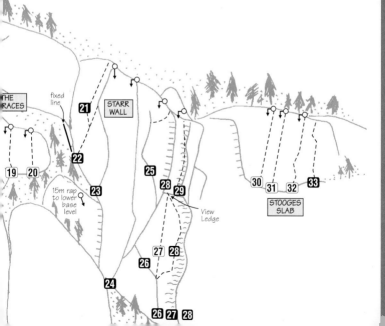

blood, sweat and beers

(we'll supply the beer)

before your climb
check us out at howesound.com
(featuring recreational and weather news)

or even better, come and visit us
afterwards in squamish town centre
at the very end of cleveland avenue

tel: 604-892-2603

beers, beds and burgers
and a whole lot more...

lack Diamond

CK CLIMBING   ICE CLIMBING
CKCOUNTRY SKIING   ALPINISM

4 EAST 3900 SOUTH
T LAKE CITY, UT 84124
NTACT US FOR A FREE
C   A   T   A   L   O   G
ONE: (801) 278-5533
AIL: climb@bdel.com
kDiamondEquipment.com

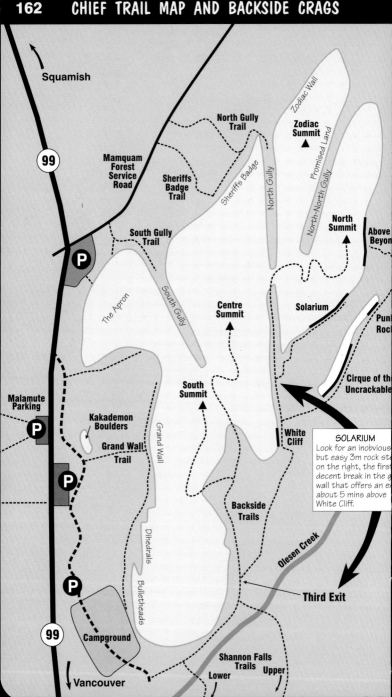

Squamish

99

North Gully Trail

Zodiac Wall

Zodiac Summit ▲

Mamquam Forest Service Road

Sheriffs Badge Trail

Sheriffs Badge

North Gully

Promised Land

North-North Gully

North Summit

Above Beyon

South Gully Trail

The Apron

South Gully

Centre Summit

Solarium

Punk Rock

South Summit

Cirque of the Uncrackable

Malamute Parking

Kakademon Boulders

Grand Wall Trail

Grand Wall

White Cliff

SOLARIUM
Look for an inobvious but easy 3m rock st
on the right, the first decent break in the
wall that offers an e
about 5 mins above
White Cliff.

Backside Trails

Dihedrals

Bulletheads

Olesen Creek

Third Exit

99

Campground

Shannon Falls Trails
Lower   Upper

Vancouver

THE CHIEF

The Chief is the centrepiece of this guidebook, a towering dome of granite rising at the head of Howe Sound to a height of 650 metres. Immense vertical walls, long cool slabs, sinuous dykes and beautiful cracks offer a variety of climbing that is hard to match anywhere. It is a place of spiritual significance to aboriginal people, and indeed to climbers also. The Chief is the cultural icon of Squamish, it dominates the landscape, and has shaped the identity of the town. It has had several names applied to it over time: 'Goose Rock' by the early European settlers; 'Staamish' and 'Sta-a-mus' by the aboriginal people; and now Stawamus Chief Provincial Park. But for climbers there is only one: The Chief.

Around the northern base is a magnificent forest of tall fir, cedar and hemlock—never logged—and the South summit is one of the most popular hikes in British Columbia, with a tradition stretching back over 50 years. It is a special place to all.

The Chief is now a Provincial Park... Since the last guide was published in 1992, the Chief has become a Class A Provincial Park—Stawamus Chief Provincial Park—the result of several years of dedicated work by climbers and local Park staff. It covers an area roughly bounded by Highway 99, the Mamquam Forest Service Road below the North Walls, Olesen Creek on the south end, and the Stawamus-Indian and Shannon Creek FSRs on the east side. BC Parks has given the Climbers' Campground below the Bulletheads a major overhaul and it is now a modern walk-in campground with 60 sites for a fee of $8 per night. The Backside trail to the South Peak has also been given a major and long-overdue upgrade, although trails to the other summits are in as much disrepair as ever at this time. The parking lot at the Apron has been similarly upgraded and expanded. A Rockclimbing Strategy Plan was developed in 1999 by BC Parks and climbers, to serve as an on-going reference as to how the climbs, the trails and new route development are to be cared for.

The Bulletheads... This is a long-overlooked part of the Chief above the campground. Adventurous multi-pitch climbs predominate, and there is potential to absorb many more climbers from the crowded routes of the Apron and Grand Wall base.

Tantalus Wall and the Dihedrals... Huge corner systems and smooth walls mark the right side of the Chief.

The Grand Wall... This wonderful west-facing wall with its striking tones of black and white and gray looms directly over the highway. It is the centrepiece of climbing on the Chief, offering some of the best granite climbs in the world. The slim line of cracks and corners directly up the centre has become the premier rock climb in Canada: the 1961 Baldwin-Cooper Grand Wall route.

The Apron... This is the most popular area of the entire Chief, with its many fine multi-pitch climbs and vast expanses of nerve-chilling crackless rock close to Highway 99. The climbs come in all grades from 5.7 to 5.12, so there is something for everyone.

The North Walls... In the shade for much of the year, the twin walls of the Sheriffs Badge and the Zodiac Wall offer superb long climbs out of the public limelight. Generally hard, they have great potential in future years for many more long climbs.

The Backside... This is the sunny south side of the Chief. The hike is longer, the climbs less crowded, but they are as good as anything in Squamish. Most of the climbs on the Backside have been developed by Robin Barley.

The Squaw... Not strictly part of the Chief, the Squaw is a prominent hill that lies a kilometre to the north of the North Chief. It offers numerous multi-pitch climbs of quality.

The Backside Trail... During the last ten years or so, the popularity among hikers of the Backside trail to the South Summit of the Chief has grown dramatically. As hikes go, it is *steep!* On a busy weekend, all manner of humanity is on display, huge beer guts, high heels and mini-skirts, glassy-eyed tourists who think it is a walk of a few minutes to the top: all gasping, and groaning up the relentless steps. No matter what the weather or season, Squamish people are out there every day for a cardio workout or a quiet hour on the hill. A blast up to the South Peak is the best half-hour workout in Squamish. The fastest known times to the South Peak from the quarry at the trailhead have been reduced to 22:45 minutes by Richard Wheater and 23:15 minutes by Genevieve Leger, both climbers. At that speed, even the steepest sections of trail are run at a full gallop. As for descending, the fastest known time down from the North Chief summit to the base is 16½ minutes, by Kevin McLane in 1986.

*There are just over 400 routes on the Chief, and more
than 1250 pitches of recorded climbing.*

The Four Summits... Most people think of the Chief as having three summits, but in fact there are four: the South Peak, overwhelmingly the most popular as it offers the shortest hike and a neat summit area; the Centre Peak, which is the prettiest; the North Peak which is the highest on the east side of the North-North Gully; and the rocky Zodiac summit, off the beaten track between the North-North Gully and the North Gully.

The Gullies... One of the most striking sights on the Chief are the three awesome chasm-like gullies which give it so much distinctive shape and character, forming immense demarcation lines between the four summits. The South Gully cleaves its way up the Chief just left of the Apron, and the North Gully and the North-North Gully split the North Walls. These chasms provide unusual climbing. There is fifth-class climbing in the South Gully, in addition to loose rock, big trees, big chockstones, and the odd troll and piles of old bones lurking in the shadows. The North and North-North Gullies are heavy-duty scrambles, navigating around and under huge chockstones. The deep and narrow North Gully is the most enjoyable of the three; scrambling interspersed with the occasional rock step; quite easy until the last few hundred feet of 4th class. Beware loose rock! The North North Gully is the largest of all but being the least visible it is rarely visited.

Getting there... The Chief is 60km north of Vancouver–a one-hour drive–most of it along the scenic coastline of Howe Sound. A large parking lot is located right in front of the Grand Wall. Squamish Town Centre is 3km further north.

Camping... A new climbers' campground has been established in front of the Bulletheads, replacing the derelict mess of bacteria that the old site had become after 30 years of free-for-all occupancy. There are now basic facilities such as cooking sheds, gravelled pads, toilets, a telephone and parking adjacent. Drive through the parking area on the highway, past the day-user lots to the parking lots on the west side of the campground. Easy.

A Few Other Things... Peregrine falcons live on the Chief as well as climbers, and as a red-listed threatened species, their needs must be taken into account by all users of the Chief, especially climbers. Please see page 29 for a more detailed appraisal. If you rack up in the main parking lot (the one with the big tacky sign about Squamish), please do so out of the way of cars and non-climbing visitors.

CHIEF

North Summit

Zodiac Summit

Centr Summ

North North Gully

North Gully

Zodiac Wall

Sheriffs Badge

South Gully

THE CHIEF FROM THE ESTUARY

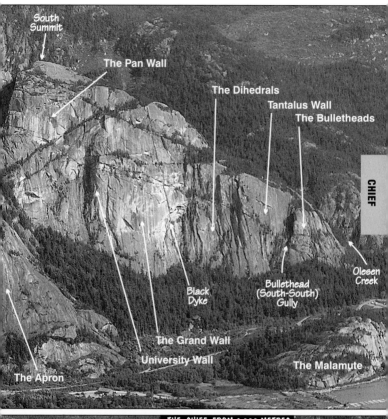

South Summit

The Pan Wall

The Dihedrals

Tantalus Wall
The Bulletheads

CHIEF

Olesen Creek

Black Dyke

Bullethead (South-South) Gully

The Grand Wall

University Wall

The Apron

The Malamute

THE CHIEF FROM 2,000 METRES

North
Summit

Zodiac
Summit

North
North
Gully

North
Gully

Zodiac Wall

Centre Summit

South Summit

The Pan Wall

CHIEF

Caramba Terrace

Sheriffs Badge

South Gully

The Apron

Mount
Murchison

South
Summit

Cent
Summi

The White Cliff
(Mostly hidden)

The Cirque of the
Uncrackables
(Mostly hidden)

The rock of the Solarium is rougher and more textured than that
of the Grand Wall, giving excellent friction and holds.

Mount
Lapworth

Tantalus
Peaks

Mount
Thiestes

Zodiac
Summit
(Hidden)

North
Summit

CHIEF

Solarium
eft Side

The Solarium
Right Side

Above and Beyond

Trail to the
Squaw summit

*The Cirque of the Uncrackables is undoubtedly the most awesome
crag of cracks–nothing but big cracks–at Squamish.*

The Bulletheads

This southernmost bastion of the Chief is easily identified by the large cylindrical buttresses–the 'Bulletheads'–sitting on top of a wide rambling wall of chimneys, bushy cracks and complex ledge systems above the campground. The Bulletheads have always been considered by climbers to be the least of all the jewels the Chief has to offer, but a closer look reveals a number of good to excellent climbs that are well worth the effort of finding and climbing. The rambling nature of the area and lack of popular traffic also has its own charm, at its best on sunny afternoons.

An essential aspect of climbing here lies in becoming familiar with numerous complex ledge systems in order to find the climb you're looking for, especially in the South Bulletheads. The fact that many of these long forgotten routes, particularly in the northern Bulletheads, rely on mixed aid and free climbing in bushy cracks systems is further discouragement, and to climb elsewhere seems to have been a decision often taken. That said, the good climbs in this area are well worth the effort, and this guide attempts to explain as clearly as possible how to find them. Accordingly, the Bulletheads have been divided into five sections.

Getting there... **Campground Wall.**
Page 174. Access to the Bulletheads is through the BC Parks Climbers campground, a short distance from the major parking lot on Highway 99. Follow the BC Parks signs to the campground. Walk into the campground, and 50m past the custodian's house, head left through the sites for 100m to reach the wall at the back: Campground Wall which extends southward toward Olesen Creek and the Backside trail.

Getting there... **Bulletheads North / Bulletheads Gully.**
Page 180 / 184. Head for Campground Wall (above), then take the trail which traverses north to Bulletheads Gully, the chasm that separates the Bulletheads from Tantalus Wall, (also known as South-South Gully). It continues to Tantalus Wall and past the Dihedrals to the Grand Wall, forming a loop with the Grand Wall trail. It is an adequate climbers trail, a bit too burly for the general public, and best kept that way.

Getting there... **Bulletheads Ledge and Bulletheads South.**
Page 176 / 178. Ill-defined trails lead out of the campground for 100m towards the wall at the back. Once at the base, turn right and follow the trail for 50m or so to a pair of short chimney-grooves. Climb the easier right-hand one (5.6) and go right for 40m to a fixed rope hanging down a groove on the left. A trail continues downhill to the south at this point. Ignore it, and pull easily up the fixed rope, scrambling on for 20m to reach a wide, open ledge at the base of the prominent jamcrack of *Slot Machine* .8. You are now in Bulletheads South. To reach the higher routes in this area, such as *Golden Labs*, go left and then after 30m, scramble steeply up a bush ramp immediately right of *Coogee Crack*. North of *Slot Machine* is the major terrace-like ledge system of Bulletheads Ledge, which neatly divides the right-hand side of the Bulletheads into upper and lower sections. Hike out along here for climbs that start from the ledge.

When Olesen Creek was logged in the 1940s, the logs were fired down a flume straight into Howe Sound.

Campground Wall

This is the wall at the back of the campground. There are some worthwhile climbs here, good for hot summer days and times when you want to escape the masses.

Getting there... See page 173 for the approach.

Self Abuse ● ☺   10b   3p.
Dale Caldwell Sept 1987   possibly climbed by Chris Atkinson c.1983.
Layback and undercling the arch (10a). Take the slanting crack above to its left end (.9). Face climb to the top, no pro (10b).

Rainy Day Dream Away   ** 10c   35m
Eric Weinstein Dave Vernon 1975
Climb up 40m right of *Self Abuse* past twin stumps to a fine fingercrack.

Sunshine Chimney North   .8   40m
Unknown
A heinous route starting 10m left of *A Pitch In Time*.

Sloppy Seconds   .9   30m
Gordie Smaill Jim Sinclair 1974
The large, mossy left-facing dihedral just left of *A Pitch In Time*.

A Pitch In Time   ** 10b   15m
Eric Weinstein Dave Vernon 1974
This classic crack is short, but offers excellent hand and fist jamming. It is frequently dry when all else is wet. Rappel.

Hiphugger   .8   45m
Kon Kraft Bert Overt 1973
A zigzagging chimney-crackline just right of *A Pitch In Time*.

> *20m and 35m right of A Pitch In Time are two large chimneys leading up to Bullethead Ledge. Well worth doing. Short pitches.*

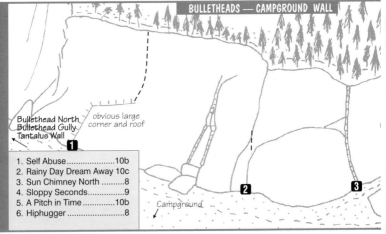

BULLETHEADS — CAMPGROUND WALL

Bullethead North
Bullethead Gully
Tantalus Wall

obvious large corner and roof

1. Self Abuse 10b
2. Rainy Day Dream Away 10c
3. Sun Chimney North 8
4. Sloppy Seconds 9
5. A Pitch in Time 10b
6. Hiphugger 8

Campground

Sunshine Chimney Centre   **   .8   2-3p.
Jim Baldwin Ed Cooper June 1960

This is a neat place, go explore. It appears as a squeeze chimney at first, but soon gives way to a wide chasm. An unusual climb, well worthwhile.

Backsack   *   .8   3p.
FRA Chris Bataille Phillipe Bonin June 16 1993   (Probably climbed long ago)

A major variation of *Sunshine Chimney Centre* where the leader disappears into almost total darkness. Start up *Sunshine Chimney Centre*, belay inside the cave (.8). Go left up an easy ramp into the darkness and through a narrowing to daylight (.6). Climb the chimney-corner above (.7).

The Swedish Touch   **   11a   30m
Simon Thyr and other Swedes encamped at Squamish August 1998

Start at the base of *Sunshine Chimney South* and climb a prominent left-leaning flake. At its top, climb the wall above past 2 bolts to chains.

Sunshine Chimney South   .6   2p.
Jim Baldwin Ed Cooper June 1960

A much less-attractive neighbour to *Sunshine Chimney Centre*, 10m to its right.

Feelin' Groovy   ● ☺   .9   40m
Richard Suddaby Peter Croft 1979

Up 5m to a tree, undercling left along a long horizontal flake for 20m then up to a belay (.9) Follow grooves and cracks to the top (.9). Mossy.

Fungus The Bogey Man   *   .8   2p.
Bob Milward Jim Campbell April 1983

Start as for *Feelin' Groovy* but go right into a deep slanting groove. It cuts sharply back to the left, then right again, then left up to a large fir tree (.8). Continue beyond, until it is possible to go out right across the wall passing a couple of bolts to Bullethead Ledge (.8). Gear to 4". A variation, *Fungus Direct* *Carlos Hatfield Ed Miller July 1998* (.9) starts up an open groove on the right, exiting right from the crack before the large fir at the end of pitch one.

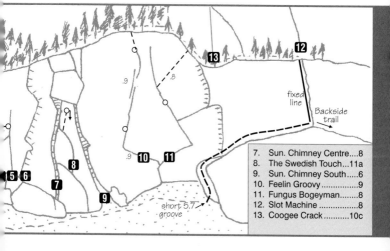

fixed line

Backside trail

short 5.7 groove

The Bulletheads South

These climbs are all located left of, or above the obvious crackline of *Slot Machine*. Many are a bit slow to dry out after heavy rain, but they are an interesting collection, worth an afternoon of exploration. No crowds, and lots to explore.

Getting there... See page 173 for the approach.

Slot Machine ✶✶ .8 2p.
Bob Milward Jim Campbell April 1983
A sturdy and much-underclimbed route. Great handjamming as the name suggests. Follow the crackline for two pitches (.6) (.8). Rappel or walk off.

Arnold Grundlewimp ● 11b 20m
Jim Campbell Bob Milward (some aid) 1983 FFA: Tim Holwill Stu Holwill July 1984
25m left of *Slot Machine* is a rough wall sporting a thin crack.

Coogee Crack 10c 15m
John Howe Kevin McLane June 1983
A face crack splitting the dark wall 25m left of *Slot Machine*.

> *To reach the next three climbs, climb steeply up a ramp just right of the Coogee Crack slab, then scramble up rightward through the bush to a gully with a fine flake crack on the right wall. Climbing Slot Machine and moving left will get you to the same place.*

Golden Labs ✶✶ 10c (.9) 20m
Peter Croft John Howe Blake Robinson Sept 1980
A good climb where the main difficulties can be avoided. The big flake crack is climbed to a small tree (.9). A belay and rappel is possible. Continue traversing with more difficulty to a belay (10c). Rappel.

Mañana ● 10c 40m
John Howe Rolf Rybak Sept 1982
Follows a vague crackline up the buttress to the left. Overgrown.

Nuclear Arms 10c x 25m
Bob Milward Jim Campbell April 1983
An offwidth crack. Hike up to the rightof *Golden Labs*, then left to its base.

In September 1991, Hamish Fraser soloed the Squamish Buttress,
via Diedre, in 38 minutes car to summit.

In 1998, he did it in 34 minutes.

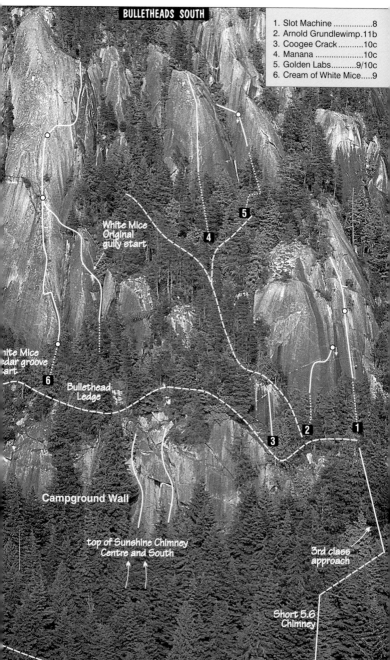

BULLETHEADS SOUTH

1. Slot Machine 8
2. Arnold Grundlewimp.11b
3. Coogee Crack...........10c
4. Manana 10c
5. Golden Labs...........9/10c
6. Cream of White Mice.....9

White Mice
Original
gully start

5

4

hite Mice
dar groove
art

6

Bullethead
Ledge

3

2

1

Campground Wall

top of Sunshine Chimney
Centre and South

3rd class
approach

Short 5.6
Chimney

Climbs Off Bullethead Ledge

The following six climbs start from Bullethead Ledge. *A Cream of White Mice* is well worth doing, but the rest are hopeless. For now.

Getting there... Climb one of the routes on Campground Wall (p.174), or hike up the trail to *Slot Machine* at the far right end of Bullethead ledge, a convenient landmark in this confusing area. Hike north from *Slot Machine* to the following climbs.

A Cream Of White Mice ** .9 3p.
Peter Croft Tami Knight (Alts) 1978

An excellent route, the name is a typical Croft spin on the famous Welsh climb *A Dream Of White Horses*. Scramble up through bush on a rough trail, about 50m left of *Slot Machine* to the base of a rocky gully. This was the original start, deep in the challengingly wet and adventurous chasm (.9). A better alternative is to walk 20m down to the left and around the corner until it is possible to pull up a steep cedar groove. Belay at the trees after 5m.

Scramble on for 10m, then step up and left onto a wide, bolted arete. Climb it past several bolts then make a tricky step back right, and up to join the original route (.9). Climb easily to the next belay below the headwall (.6). Continue on a fine, easy dyke then make a long traverse to the right across the foot of the steep headwall, and finish up a dark corner (.9).

Missing Mice ● .9 x 4p.
Kevin Young Kevin Harrison Aug 1992

Start up the short, dirty gully south of *A Cream of White Mice* (.7). Move left and climb an exposed face with little protection (.9), or scramble through trees to reach the same place. Move leftward until possible to access a corner, which is then climbed for two pitches (.7) (.9).

Triptoe ● .8 3p.
Barry Hagen Mike Wisnicki Dan Tate Alice Purdy 1966

Broken and bushy cracks, just right of *The Black Book* lead in two pitches to the far south end of Stacatto Ledge (.7). Continue directly above up another crackline, possibly the original finish to *Cataract Crags* (.8).

The Black Book ● 11a 25m
Peter Croft Greg Foweraker 1979

An obvious dark left-facing corner crack about 50m north of *Cream of White Mice*. Rappel or continue up *Rainy Day...* or *Triptoe*.

Rainy Day Woman ● 11b 3p.
Gordie Smaill Neil Bennett 1971   FFA: Peter Croft Randy Atkinson Tami Knight (Alts) 1979

A long crackline 10m left of *The Black Book*. Very dirty (11b) (10b) (11a).

Bullethead East ● 10c A1 3p.
Fred Beckey Jim Sinclair 1966

Starting from the very northern end of Bullethead Ledge, climb a finger-hand crackline just left of *Rainy Day Woman* to a ledge belay (10c). Another crack above leads to the Stacatto Ledge (10c). Move left to the final crack (A1).

CLIMBS OFF BULLETHEAD LEDGE

tacatto Ledge

White Mice Original gully start

Bullethead Ledge

Campground Wall

top of Fungus the Bogyman

top of Sunshine Chimney Centre and South

3rd class approach

Despite the persistent local media story, the Chief is not the second largest Granite Monolith in the British Empire, or the Commonwealth, or the world.   The Chief is fine just as it is.

The Bulletheads North

This is the major sweep of rock left of Campground Wall that rises to the top of the tallest bullet, featured with many cracklines and chimneys: very west coast. There are some neat gems here among some of the most esoteric climbs in this guide: even a sport route.

Getting there...   See page 173 for the approach.

Bullethead East Direct   ● .9   *174*   50m
Peter Croft Jim Campbell Allen Tate 1979
This climb takes the high, chossy left-facing corner system that denotes the north end of Campground Wall and the south end of Bulletheads North. It finishes on Bullethead Ledge.

Bullethead Central   ●   11a (10b)   *183*   4p.
Fred Beckey C.Fritch D.Beckstead 1966 FFA: Peter Croft Greg Foweraker 1981
Well, it does have one spectacular finger-crack. Climb a prominent slanting crack, 20m left of the corner of *Bullethead East Direct*, leading in two pitches to a tree groove (10b). Continue to the base of a large headwall. Climb the fingercrack that splits it (11a) or *Vertical Smile*, the chimney to the left (.8).

Third Abortion   ●   A2   *183*   4p.
Neil Bennett Tim Auger 1969
Just up from the start of *Bullethead East Direct*, take a crackline (euphemism for a serious piece of bush climbing) for three pitches to the northern end of Stacatto Ledge (A2). Climb any of the three routes above here to the top.

Vertical Smile   ●   .8   *183*   35m
Neil Bennett Gordie Smaill 1969
A single pitch rising from the northern end of Stacatto Ledge up a prominent chimney line (.8).

Liquid Gold   ●   .9 A2   *183*   5p.
Gordie Smaill Mike Wisnicki 1971
The only liquid you're likely to find here is H_2O. Start approximately 50m south of the *Compression Crack* access ramp, and climb to the rim (.9 A2).

> *The following climbs begin from a prominent narrow terrace just above the base, about 100m north of Campground Wall. Heading north on the trail it is the first decent break, quite obvious and friendly-looking, cutting back sharply to the right.*

The Shortest Straw   *   10d+1pa   *182*   3p.
Colin Moorhead Will Dorling July 1996
p1 Will Dorling Nick Watts Aug 1995 (aka **Sons of Freedom***)*
p1 var. Colin Moorhead Will Dorling Aug 1995 (aka **Pork Soda***)*
The first obvious feature on the approach ramp is a big left-leaning flake chimney—*Constriction Chimney*. Start at its base and head out left across the wall past 5 bolts, then up a widening crack. A long pitch (10d). A strenuous thin crack leads to a blank face move. Pull on the bolt (10c, 1pa). Climb on up easier cracks to a spacious ledge (10a). A major variation on the first pitch exits right after the 3rd bolt and climbs a left-facing corner (10c).

Constriction Chimney * .9 *182* 1-3p.
Joe Turley George Kristiensen 1963
The first obvious feature on the approach ledge is a big flake chimney. Rock on, and move left near its top to the belay by *Shortest Straw*. Rappel back to the base, or continue traversing leftward into Bullethead Gully.

There Goes The Neighbourhood * 11b #6 *182* **SPORT** 25m
Colin Moorhead Will Dorling Tom Gruber June 1995
Sport in the 'heads! A neat-looking face climb 4m right of *Constriction Chimney*.

Bite The Bullet ● 10c *182* 2p.
Jim Campbell Bud Miller... and more. July 1981
Start about 15m right of *Neighbourhood*...up a vague left-facing corner thing, and then scuttle out leftward and climb the face above (.9). Move left, into the upper part of *Neighbourhood*, up a bit, then left along a ledge to a cruxy finish (10c). Rappel from *Shortest Straw*.

Compression Crack 10c *182* 30m
Glenn Woodsworth John Rance 1969   FFA Colin Moorhead Will Dorling Aug 1995
A huge left-leaning chimney-arch.

Mayday ● 11d A2 *182* 4p.
Dick Culbert Barry Hagen 1968
FFA: p1 Peter Croft Rob Rohn 1982   p4 variation Jim Campbell Jim Sedor July 1981.
Climb *Compression Crack* (10c). Follow the hard crack above to bolts that lead right to a belay (11d). Continue to a horizontal ledge (A2?). Above, an aid crack (A1?) with some mid-fifth leads to four choices. A 5.9 traverse leftward to Bullethead Gully; continue up *Into The Void* (11c); climb *Wild Turkey* (10d); or the original A2 crack above. Descend by one rappel and reverse the traverse of *Into The Void* over to Bullethead Gully, or 4 raps down *Mayday* to the base.

Cataract Crags ● .9 *182* many
Hamish Mutch Dick Culbert 1963   FFA: unknown
At the end of the ramp is a huge chasm leading up rightwards, eventually reaching Stacatto Ledge. Find some forty-year old climbing gear to rack up with, and go have an adventure. Hey!—you may never do a sport climb again, or you may sell all your cams and wires the next day.

Half Moon Chimney ● .9 A2 *183* 4p.
Hamish Mutch Mavis McCuaig 1967
Climb to the base of *Cataract Crags*, then after a short distance in the gully (.7), move out right along a traverse line to join *Liquid Gold* (.8). Up the crack and chimney above, to Staccato Ledge (.9, A2). Best finish is up the chimney of *Vertical Smile* (.8).

Chimp Dip * 11b *182* 20m
Peter Croft Tami Knight 1980
An easy-to-find, right-slanting fingercrack on a smooth wall at the side of the trail, just before the trail reaches Bulletheads Gully. Worth checking out.

Start from Bullethead Gully

1. Chimp Dip 11b
2. Sons of Freedom 10d
3. Constriction Chimney ...9
4. There goes the Neig .11b
5. Bite the Bullet 10c
6. Compression Crack ..10c
7. Mayday 11d, A2
8. Cataract Crags 9
9. Eurasian Eyes 13a
10. Into the Void.............11c
11. Wild Turkey 10d
12. Liquid Gold.............9, A2

to Bullethead Gully Trail

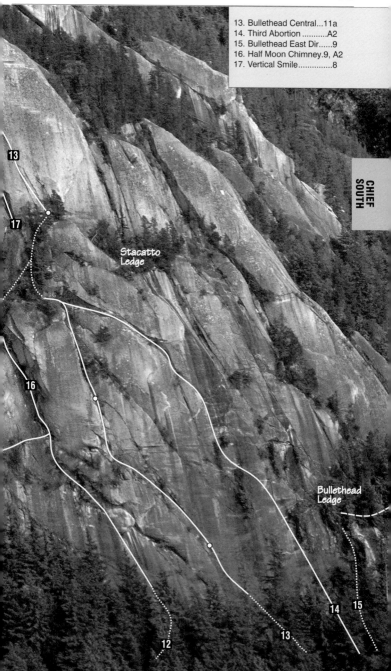

13. Bullethead Central...11a
14. Third Abortion A2
15. Bullethead East Dir......9
16. Half Moon Chimney.9, A2
17. Vertical Smile..............8

CHIEF
SOUTH

Stacatto
Ledge

Bullethead
Ledge

13

17

16

14

15

12

13

Bullethead Gully

Continue northwards along the trail below Bulletheads North, to the base of Bullethead Gully. Hike and scramble up here to a large open bay behind the first Bullet and four fine climbs.

Getting there...   See page 173 for the approach.

Eurasian Eyes   ***   13b   #5   *182*   **SPORT+**   25m
Jim Sandford   1989
This is the stunning arete which forms the left edge of the largest bullet—overhanging, technical, and very exposed. Starting in the bed of the gully, climb up left of the arete to reach a higher ledge, and traverse out to the arete. Climb on the right at first then generally on the left side. Take a couple CDs to 2½"for the crack.

Foreign Affair   **   12c   x   25m
Jim Sandford   1989
Takes the gully wall left of *Eurasian Eyes*. Start on the left to reach a higher ledge, then take the crack system on the wall above, finishing up the face past 3 bolts to reach the top of the arete.

■ *The next two climbs are out on the west face of the Bulletheads.*

Into The Void   **   11c   *182*   2-3p.
Colin Moorhead Nick Watts June 1995
A superb crack climb. From a spacious ledge at the base of *Eurasian Eyes*, hand traverse an exposed horizontal fault to a station (.9). Climb the hand-fist crack above to a small ledge. A finger crack above peters out to a long reach and a difficult mantel (11c). Pro to 4". Descend by a rappel and reverse the traverse, or 4 raps down *Mayday*.

Wild Turkey   **   10d   *182*   3p.
Greg Cameron George Manson Perry Beckham 1979
This is a long chimney-groove high on the wall facing the highway. From Bullethead Gully, at a spacious ledge at the base of *Eurasian Eyes*, hand traverse out right on an exposed horizontal fault to a station (.9). Move up and right to gain a rising ledge system that leads to the base of the long groove (10b). The groove gives classic flaring chimney work and hand-jamming (10d).

Bullethead Gully   .8 A1   x   2p.
Arnold Shives Glenn Woodsworth Tony Ellis Frank de Bruyn 1961
This climb was originally called South-South Gully, but given the use the area now receives, Bullethead Gully is commonly used. Scramble up the gully to the open bay by *Foreign Affair*, and continue, hidden behind the highest bullet, with mixed aid and free to the top.

Entrance Examination   ● ☺   10c   x   25m
Phillip van Wassenaer Dan Sinclair Jim Sinclair 1986
A long-overlooked climb up a whiteish, narrow dike on the Tantalus side of the gully, starting about 30m up from the base trail.

Tantalus Wall

Tantalus Wall is smooth, high-angle sweep of rock at the south end of the Chief. It is divided into a lower and an upper half, with Tantalus Ledge and its trees forming the demarcation line. The lower half is dominated by the mighty crack of Yosemite Pinnacle and the great dihedral of Milk Run.

Getting there...   Follow the Bullethead Gully trail (page 173) to the base of Bullethead Gully. Or approach from the Grand Wall area.

Wrist Twister   Aid   See page 322

Tantalus Wall   12a (11b/c+4pa)   _**187**_   8p.
*Fred Beckey Leif Patterson Mark Fielding 1966   FFA:**Yosemite Crack** Jim Madsen 1968*
Note: Climbed free by Peter Croft and others, although not on one ascent.
A classic wall with fine situations, but long undergraded. The climbing throughout is very sustained at around 11a-c, and using the bolts for aid above the roof is the usual way this route is done.

> Scramble up from the trail just north of Bullethead Gully and belay (low-5th). Awkward cracks [bolt] lead to a small tree (11a). Take the left-hand crack above to reach the base of the impeccable *Yosemite Crack* [the right-hand crack is 11c]. Classic offwidth difficulties are soon encountered in the crack, then it widens and eases—not much though! A long pitch (10a). Easier climbing leads to Tantalus Ledge (.8). Climb the hand and fist corner crack above, then go over a small roof and up face cracks to a belay (11b/c). More fingercracks lead up to the long roof, belay on THE cedar tree. Whoa! (11b). Use the tree to overcome the roof, then use the bolts for aid [free if you can...], tensioning into the base of another crack system. The way in which this pitch was freed is uncertain (12a or 11a+4pa). Up the thin crack on the beautiful headwall to belay (11a). Above the crack, face climbing leads out right then back left to finish (11b). Gear to 4½".

Cerberus   ***   11d   _**187**_   6p.
Daryl Hatten Eric Weinstein 1976   FFA: Dean Hart Randy Atkinson 1989
A magnificent excursion up the headwall, following thin dykes around the long roof. Follow *Tantalus Wall* for 3 pitches to the halfway ledge, or rappel in from the rim for the upper pitches only. Move up right 15m and gain a superb dyke trending right across the wall. All fixed, 8 or 9 bolts (10d). The next pitch, turning the roof is sustained, following more dykes. All fixed, 13-14 bolts. Climb a commiting, enormous hollow flake (scary loose bit!) to a belay (11d). A tricky start to the final pitch leads to easier climbing on the left (11d). Add a few 1"-2½"CDs to the rack, small wires and up to 15 draws. Save a 2½"-3" CD for the last pitch.

Yosemite Pinnacle Left Side .9   _**187**_   3p.
Hamish Mutch Mavis McCuaig Glenn Woodsworth 1965
An unmistakable series of chimneys, the left side of the pinnacle. Rarely climbed, but a classic chimney route nonetheless. Start as for *Tantalus Wall* then go out left to belay at the foot of the chimney. Two pitches lead to the top (.9, .8). Continue up *Tantalus Wall*, or rappel.

Milk Run ***   11d   (10c+2pa)   *187*   4p.

Eric Lance John Wurflinger (aid) 1969 FFA: Peter Croft Tami Knight 1982
RECLEANED: *Matt Maddaloni 1998.*

This is the large north-facing corner system just left of *Tantalus Wall* which
has recently been cleaned up. It is now a superb route. Scramble up as for
Tantalus Wall to a bolt belay (low-5th). Traverse out left for 8m to the start of
a long undercling. An easier start is up *Tantalus Wall* pitch 1 to the first bolt,
then move up left until it is possible to scramble down a groove to reach the
start of the undercling. Follow it out left, using the 2nd and 3rd bolts for aid
[or 11d free], then a few moves down and up to belay at the start of the huge
left-facing corner (11d or 10c+2pa). Two pitches lead up the corner (10b) (10c).
To continue up *Tantalus Wall* at 11b/c, an easier pitch of 5.8 leads up to Tantalus
Ledge. Otherwise, make four rappels back down to the trail.

Crescent Ramp   .9 A1   *326*   (4-5p.)

Fred Beckey Eric Bjornstad 1966

The large diagonal corner-ramp at the left side of upper *Tantalus Wall*. Get there
from Yosemite Pinnacle or *Milk Run*. Rarely climbed in its own right, it is most
commonly used nowadays as an escape off *Cannabis Wall*.

Breakfast Run   Aid   See page 322

Cannabis Wall   Aid   See page 322

Road To Nowhere   11d   *x*   2p.

Andreas Tayler Bruce McDonald Sept 1996

Start just left of the obvious bolt line of *Cannabis Wall* and climb up and left
past 5 bolts to a small bush. Gain the long ramp of *Cannabis Wall* up right and
belay (11c). From the upper end of the ramp climb an easier corner, then go
out left along a dyke past 5 bolts to a belay (11d). Rappel. Gear to 2″.

The upper cracks of Tantalus Wall. Climber: Sig Isaac

TANTALUS WALL

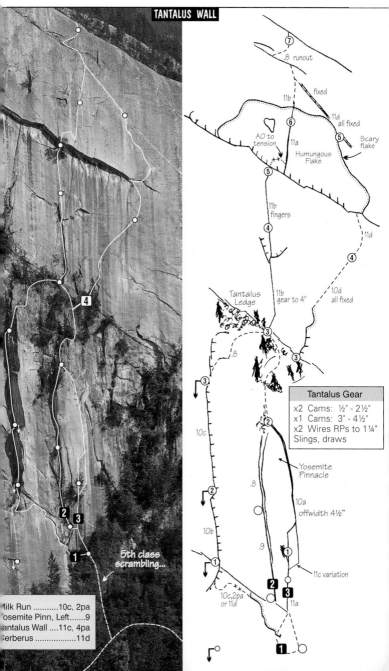

⑦

.8 runout

fixed

11b

11d
all fixed

⑥

A0 to
tension

11a

⑤   Scary
          flake

Humungous
Flake

⑤

11b
fingers

④

11d

④

Tantalus
Ledge

11b
gear to 4"

10d
all fixed

③

③

.8

③

Tantalus Gear

x2 Cams: ½" - 2½"
x1 Cams: 3" - 4½"
x2 Wires RPs to 1¼"
Slings, draws

②

10c

Yosemite
Pinnacle

②

.8

10a
offwidth 4½"

10b

.9

11c variation

①

①

5th class
scrambling...

2 ②

2 **3**

3

①

10c,2pa
or 11d

11a

1

Milk Run 10c, 2pa
Yosemite Pinn, Left.......9
Tantalus Wall 11c, 4pa
Cerberus 11d

Shaved Bum 5.11c. . Climber Colin Moorhead. Photo Richard Wheater

The roof pitch of Freeway, 5.11c. Climber: Jola Sandford.

Freeway

Freeway	***½	✗	11c/d	11p.
Freeway Lite	***	✗	11c	5p.
The Big Slick	***	✗	12a	(3p.)
Express Lane	***½	✗	11a	(2p.)
Diesel Overhang	*	✗	12a	(1p.)

Tom Gibson Rob Rohn 1979 (some aid).
FCFA Dean Hart Randy Atkinson July 1990
Freeway Lite: FFA to "Truck Stop": Dean Hart Randy Atkinson Ian Jones Lindsay Eltis 1989
The Big Slick: p1 Lindsay Eltis 1989   p2 Tom Briggs John Rosholt Aug 1995
Express Lane: John Rosholt Hamish Fraser Aug 1995
Diesel Overhang to the top Peter Croft Dean Hart (by rap-in) 1987

A fantastic climb with two major variations. The climbing is best characterised by long pitches, short cruxes, good rests, good protection, and little respite in difficulty. The shorter "Lite" version to the Truck Stop is quite a bit easier than the full route, despite the grades. Both are excellent.

Scramble rightwards up a long 4th class ramp 150m south of the *Black Dyke* to the base of a long, open corner system. The first pitch, usually avoided, takes a slab left of the corner, moving back into the corner to belay (10d). Tricky moves start and end the next pitch, to a belay in the corner (11a). Swing out right into a fine 10a fist crack. From its top traverse right, along to the base of a slim corner (10c). Climb another long pitch, or split it into two, to a good ledge at the base of a spectacular 50m dihedral (11c). Magnificent climbing leads up the dihedral to a cave under a big roof: the "Truck Stop". 50m - take all the gear you own (11a). This is the end of **Freeway Lite** (11c), 4 raps down.

Move left and pull directly up through two stepped roofs to an airy perch below a larger roof . A very commiting and strenuous pitch, but good protection keeps the wild exposure under control (11c/d). Make a wild, breathtaking traverse rightward along twin cracks that eases into open face climbing on the wall above (11a). Traverse right across the face and up a finger crack to belay (10c). Back left then right to the base of a deep corner (11a). The corner (10a), followed by the sting in the tail up an arete to the rim (10d).

The Big Slick: A major 3 pitch variation left of the main corner below the Truck Stop. Move out left below the crux corner on the 4th pitch. Place a high piece in an arch and cross the wall. A long reach gains a belay ledge (11b). Climb the face past a bolt and up the dihedral above. Traverse left across a dyke to a stunning position on the arete. Climb the arete above to a difficult finish onto a ledge belay (12a). An easy pitch leads to a snag. Go diagonally across the wall to the Truck Stop (.9). Take a rack with plenty of 1" sizes.

Express Lane: A major 2 pitch variation on the upper wall. A bit runout on the easier sections, but well protected where you need it. From the top of the 11a pitch after the roof, step down to a small left-facing corner and climb up left past 2 bolts to a sloping ledge. Up it, then pass 2 bolts to a belay on the arete (11a). Climb on to join *Freeway* at the base of the final pitch (10c). Roll on to the top (10d). The last 2 pitches can make one 55m pitch.

Diesel Overhang: A dramatic roof, an alternative to pitch 8.

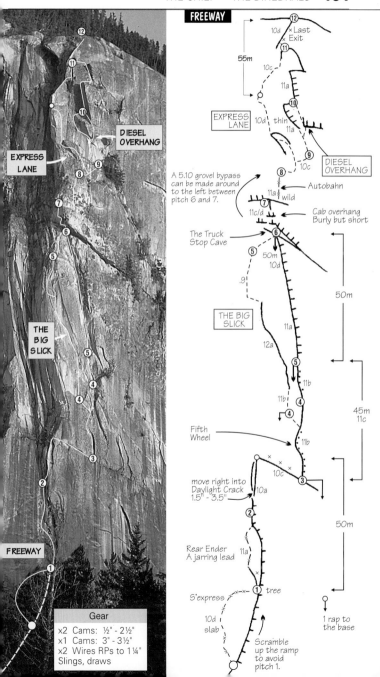

FREEWAY

10d × Last Exit
×

55m

10c

11a

EXPRESS LANE

10d   thin

11a

10

9

10c

DIESEL OVERHANG

A 5.10 grovel bypass can be made around to the left between pitch 6 and 7.

8   Autobahn

11a   wild
7

11c/d   Cab overhang
Burly but short

The Truck Stop Cave   6

5   50m
10d

.9

THE BIG SLICK

11a

12a

5

11b

4

11b

4

Fifth Wheel   11b

× × ×
10c

move right into
Daylight Crack
1.5" - 3.5"   10a

3

2

Rear Ender
A jarring lead   11a
×

S'express   ×-×-×   1   tree

10d slab

Scramble up the ramp to avoid pitch 1.

50m

50m

45m
11c

50m

1 rap to the base

EXPRESS LANE

DIESEL OVERHANG

THE BIG SLICK

FREEWAY

Gear
x2 Cams: ½" - 2½"
x1 Cams: 3" - 3½"
x2 Wires RPs to 1¼"
Slings, draws

The Dihedrals

The Dihedrals are the overlapping series of huge parallel corners, some of which run the full height of the Chief between the Black Dyke and the Tantalus Wall. The centrepiece route is *Freeway*. See page 190.

Getting there... Climbs are described as they are approached from the Grand Wall area. Walk in from either the Bulletheads campground (page 173), or the Grand Wall trail (page 196). The latter offers the quickest approach to climbs at the left (north) end. *Cannabis Wall* and *Road to Nowhere* start off the open forest floor a short distance down from Bullethead Gully. *Freeway* starts up a long right-trending ramp some distance down and left of *Cannabis. Western Dihedral* starts up another huge sweeping ramp further left again.

Peregrine falcons... Some of the routes in this area can intrude on Peregrine falcon nesting sites in the general area of Trichome Ledge. The sites change from year to year, so please check with BC Parks (604) 898-3678 before proceeding. A full explanation is on page 29. Climbs noted with this symbol ⤚ may be affected by closures.

Crap Crags ● ⤚ .7 400m
Dick Culbert Hamish Mutch 1962

A modest climb, still with a lot to be modest about. Start just right of the *Black Dyke* and follow a long, adventurous line of bushy corners, grooves and cracks to Trichome Ledge. Follow chimneys above the left end of the ledge to the top, or *Clean Corner* to the rim. If this climb were to be restored to its original condition, of say 9,000 years ago, it would be the most popular long route on the Chief.

> *The next two climbs are 30m or so down to the right of the Black Dyke off a flat bay: both fine cracks.*

Arrowroot ** 10b 40m
Peter Croft Richard Suddaby Tami Knight 1978

A longstanding classic crack climb. Climb the left hand crack through an overlap. It becomes increasingly difficult and rattly.

Rutabaga *** 11a (10b) 2p.
Petre Hiltner J.Lewis Victor Kramer Aug 1983

A fine crack climb with long pitches. The righthand of the cracks rising from the base ledge is climbed to a tree belay (10b) [rappel]. The enjoyable crack above leads to the base of a long, elegant left-facing corner. Climb it to a memorable crux finish, stemming widely across the walls. Take plenty of small to medium size gear.

Cleaning The Brain ● 10c 20m
Scott Young Craig Thompson Jim Brennan June 1984

A crackline high on the left side of the brushy ramp right of *Rutabaga*.

THE DIHEDRALS

ZONE OF COMMON FALCON NESTING SITES, INCLUDING NEGRO LESBIAN AND FREEWAY. CLIMBING IN THIS AREA IS CLOSED MARCH 15TH UNTIL BC PARKS DEFINES ROUTE-SPECIFIC CLOSURES EACH SPRING.

Trichome Ledge

to the Grand Wall

project

to the Bulletheads

1. Crap Crags 7
2. Arrowroot.............................10b
3. Rutabaga 11a
4. Cleaning The Brain 10c
5. Sticky Fingers.......................9
6. Deadend Dihedral 12a (11a)
7. Slow Duck............................10a
8. Western Dihedral p1,2,3....10c
9. Clean Corner 8
10. Sports Illustrated 11b
11. Cloudburst.........................10d

■ *Walk down another 25m to the base of a high, impressive wall.*

Sticky Fingers   .9   *193*   35m
Ivan Christiansen Rolf Rybak 1987
Climb the obvious crackline at the left edge of the wall, starting with difficult moves off a convenient boulder. Rappel.

Deadend Dihedral   ***½ 12a+1pa (11a)   *193*   3p.
John Rance Frank Baumann Dec 1969 FFA: Pitch 1, Peter Croft Tami Knight 1982
p2, p3 Kevin McLane Perry Beckham (alts) Aug 1984
An elegant climb up a long, left-facing corner system. Take many RPs for pitch 1. Back and foot, and layback the long corner to belay below an arch (11a). A few bouldery undercling moves (crux) lead to the base of a higher corner (12a). Steep laybacking and jamming, followed by an easy pendulum from a bolt gain the arete (11b+1pa). Rappel.

Time Passages   *   A3   x   25m
Chris Atkinson Bill Atkinson 1984
A single aid pitch up a right-facing dihedral. Blades and arrows. Scramble up the bushy ramp right of *Deadend Dihedral* to reach the start.

Slow Duck   ●   10a   *193*   40m
Peter Croft Bruce McDonald 1982
A mossy, right-trending dyke starting just right of *Deadend Dihedral.*

Western Dihedral   10c   *193*   3p.
Fred Beckey Dan Tate May 1966
FFA p1, p2, p3, Matt Maddaloni Ben Demenche Ken Sharpe 1998
The first 2 pitches of this climb, leading into *Sea of Tranquillity*, are now all free (10c, 10c, 10c). Scramble up the long approach ramp to a belay.

Slow Dyke ✗	Aid	See page 322
Illusion ✗	Aid	See page 322
Sea of Tranquillity ✗	Aid	See page 322
Western Dihedral ✗	Aid	See page 322
Getting Down In The Brown ✗ Aid		See page 322

The long run-out to the first bolt on Mercy Me can catch some
climbers by surprise. It was placed on lead—a ¼"—by Eric Lance
on an early attempt at the first ascent. He continued, then took
a big fall onto it. He never went back. Since replaced...

The Dihedrals — Upper Climbs

These short climbs at the top of the Dihedrals can be approached from below, but a much shorter approach is to hike up the Bellygood Ledge trail and rappel in. They offer good climbing.

Getting there... Take the main trail to the Chief summit. At the first fork, continue for 50m, then pull up a short fixed rope on the left. This is actually the descent trail from Bellygood Ledge. Follow the rough, wandering trail above, walk up a big open slab, and turn right at its top into the trees. After 100m or so, a slabby opening in the trees can be seen on the left. From its lower end, make a gently rising traverse for approximately 100m, then down 50m to the large ledge at the top of *Clean Corner*. 40 minutes from the parking lot. Rap in.

CHIEF SOUTH

Clean Corner ** 🪝 .8 *193* (2p.)
Dick Strachan Dick Willmott 1962
This is the big corner rising above the righthand end of Trichome Ledge—a fine outing that offers exposed and exciting climbing. If this climb were more accessible, it would be one of the most popular on the Chief. From Trichome Ledge, climb the chimney until it narrows down to a wide crack. Avoid the crack by delightful stemming across the walls on good holds. An easier chimney above leads to the top. Gear to 4".

Sports Illustrated * 🪝 11b *193* 40m
Perry Beckham Bill Noble Sept 1990
This single pitch climbs the exposed spotted wall wall right of *Clean Corner*. Rather contorted to reach, however. From the large flat ledge at the top of *Clean Corner*, rappel down the arete to a bolt station. Leave a fixed rope here, then rappel down to a ledge at the base of the arete. Climb out rightwards up the wall; unusual but outstanding face climbing over the big black spots of basalt. Back left to the arete and belay. Jumar out! A link pitch back into the top of *Clean Corner* would make this a better climb.

Cloudburst * 🪝 10d *193* 25m
Colin Moorhead Will Dorling Aug 28 1994
This short crack is actually a variation finish to *Western Dihedral*, and can easily be seen from the parking lot. It is best approached by rapping in, about 25m right (south) of the top of *Clean Corner*. Descend to an alder tree alcove, then climb a scrubbed ramp to a finger traverse, followed by a hand crack to the top. Gear to 4".

The first climb to the top of the Chief was the Squamish Buttress,
by Fred Beckey, Don Claunch and Hank Mather in 1959.

The Grand Wall Base — Central Area

This section describes climbs at the Base of the Grand in the area where the Grand Wall access trail meets the rock in the *Apron Strings–Cruel Shoes* area. Climbs are described left to right.

Getting there... From the large parking lot in front of the Chief, walk over to Psyche Ledge (the old highway) and continue 100m to the start of the trail into the trees: 5 minutes up to the base of the Grand.

Climbs and gear... Some great climbs here–this is the home of *Cruel Shoes* (10d)–say no more. In general, gear need be no more than 2½" with an emphasis on smaller stuff, with draws for face pitches. For climbs that end on Flake Ledge, rappel on 2 ropes or walk back down the trail. Take double ropes for climbs right of the Flake.

Cookie Jar   10b A0   *198*   2p.
Jim Sinclair Jeannine Caldbeck 1972
Traverse out left from the start of *Apron Strings*, to a steep wall with a bolt ladder that leads into a left-facing lieback corner. From its top, head up leftward to join the Flake Ledge trail.

Apron Strings ***   10b   *199*   2p.
Tim Auger Mike Wisnicki 1964   FFA: Steve Sutton Hugh Burton 1973
The striking layback flake just left of the previous route. A much fallen-off route and a glorious Squamish classic. Layback up the flake on lovely holds but with increasing difficulty as the crack thins, finishing leftwards and then up an easy groove to a tree belay (10b). Climb the corner above, followed by zig-zag handjam cracks to the top of the Flake (.9).

Sunday Whites ***   11c   #   *199*   (40m)
Hamish Fraser Peder Ourom May 1994
Climb the first pitch of *Apron Strings* (10b), then move out right and climb the fine bolted arete which borders the right-hand edge of the wall. 5 bolts.

The Flake **   10b   *199*   3p.
Jim Baldwin Ed Cooper July 1961   FFA Dave McDonald Kevin McLane Jim Sinclair Sept 1972
A much underrated climb. Climb a short pitch up the chimney behind a tall fir tree to a ledge belay (.6). Excellent laybacking and stemming leads up the corner above to a large ledge (10b). Continue easily up the big flake chimney to the ledges at the top (.4).

The Phew!   10b A0   x   4p.
Jim Sinclair Jeannine Caldbeck Paul Bader 1973.
One of the most difficult mixed free and aid face climbs on the Chief in its heyday, most of it has now been freed as part of *Cruel Shoes* and *War Of The Raptors*. If you want the full experience, climb the bolt ladder, then follow *Revenge...*, then *Cruel Shoes* pitch 2. Traverse right on *Cruel Shoes* for about 15m, then climb the corner above to a large ledge.

Cruel Shoes ***½ 10d _199_ 6p.

p2, Jim Sinclair Jeannine Caldbeck (The Phew!) 1973   p4, p5 ,Eric Weinstein Daryl Hatten 1975 FFA and p3, p6 Perry Beckham Scott Flavelle 1981

A superb face climb that weaves a cunning path to the base of the Split Pillar. Climb *The Flake*, or *Apron Strings*, belaying at the base of the wide chimney above pitch one (10b). After 8m or so in the chimney, traverse rightwards across to a shallow right facing corner and a high bolt. Step down right and climb the face to a belay (10d). A deceptively tricky traverse to the right for 20m leads to the base of a long corner (10b). Climb the corner to a belay on the right of a small pedestal (10c). Pull out left from the corner on good holds and continue more easily, but with little protection, to belay about 10m left of the big sickle above (.9). Follow a line of bolts up to the Split Pillar, an out-standing finish (10d). 3 long rappels down. A popular continuation is to climb *The Split Pillar* (10b) and *The Sword* (11a). 3-5 rappels down.

Revenge Of The Couch Potato *** 11d _199_ 3p.

p1, p2 John Howe Dave Lane Aug 1985
p3 Andrew Boyd unknown belay slave Aug 1998   No redpoint ascent as yet

A hard, bold face route which takes a direct line up through *Cruel Shoes*. Long pitches. Start up *The Flake*, but exit out right to a flake rising across the face to a bolt belay (10b). The next pitch is one of the finest leads on the Chief. Climb up, then traverse out right past a bolt and a pin, then up to make a long diagonal ascent to a small ledge just below the *Cruel Shoes* traverse. Runout (11b). Move up left at first, then directly up in a hard but long and better protected pitch to rejoin *Cruel Shoes* (11d).

War Of The Raptors *** 12a _199_ 4p.

p1, p4 Andrew Boyd Andrew Pedley 1998
p2 Revenge of the Couch Potato (11b)
p3 The Phew! (10b A0) Jim Sinclair Jeanine Caldbeck 1973.
No redpoint ascent as yet

A bold climb which incorporates *Revenge Of The Couch Potato* and parts of *The Phew!* Start just right of *The Flake* and face climb past 6 bolts to join a dyke. Belay at its top as for *Revenge...* (12a) [the right-hand line of ancient bolts is *The Phew!*]. Follow pitch 2 of *Revenge*. Long runouts on a magnificent stretch of climbing (11b). Gain the corner directly above *Cruel Shoes* and follow it to a ledge belay (10a). The final pitch is sustained and devious, weaving its way over to join *The Grand Wall* at the belay below *The Left Side* (12a). Take draws, small-medium wires and a few CDs.

Up From The Skies Direct Start * 11c+3pa _199_ (3p.)

Perry Beckham Peder Ourom (aid) 1978
Free as described: Hamish Fraser Bruce McDonald 1991

This climb is the almost-free version of the direct start to *Up From The Skies*. Climb *Cruel Shoes* to the shallow corner on pitch 2 and lower from bolts to the base of a long sickle arch (.9). The arch is hard and sustained. Move out right from its top [2 bolts aid] to an overlap, and on to a ledge at the base of a higher sickle (11c). The next pitch reaches *Cruel Shoes* (10c). Climb the corner (10c). Go out left, then straight up to the long sickle that denotes the start of the aid (10d).

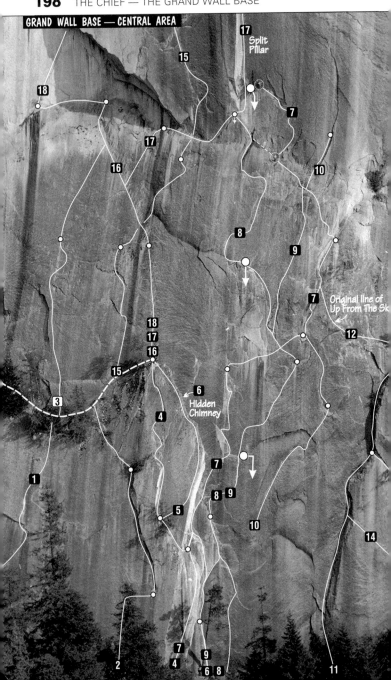

GRAND WALL BASE — CENTRAL AREA

17 Split Pillar

15

18

7

17

16

10

8

9

7

Original line of Up From The Sk

12

18
17
16
15

3

6 Hidden Chimney

4

7

1

5

8 **9**

10

14

2

7
4

9
6 **8**

GRAND WALL BASE — CENTRAL AREA

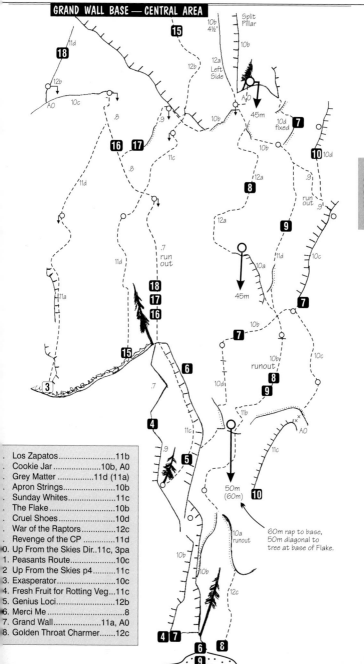

CHIEF
SOUTH

60m rap to base,
50m diagonal to
tree at base of Flake.

The Grand Wall Base — Flake Ledge

This section describes climbs that start off the Flake ledge access trail, a long ledge system that leads from the trail along the Grand Wall Base northern area, cutting sharply back right (south) for about 200m to the top of *Apron Strings*. The Flake is easily identified from the highway by a tall, leaning cedar at its top and the fine dyke of *Merci Me* that rises above the tree.

Getting there... From the large parking lot in front of the Chief, walk over to Psyche Ledge (the old highway) and continue 100m to the start of the trail into the trees: 5 minutes up this to the base of the Grand Wall. Go left for 200m to an easy break that cuts back sharply to the right–Flake Ledge. There are a couple of exposed scrambling sections, down as well as up, and a fixed rope pull.

Climbs and gear... A small but stellar collection. From the dykes of *Merci Me* (.8), to the crack of *Golden Throat Charmer* (12c) and the wide open face of *The First Course* (11a). Take double ropes for rappelling.

Diamonds Or Dust   12a   30m
Jim Sandford 1984.
At the first rock step on Flake ledge, go left to belay near a right-facing dihedral. Climb it, and the thin crack above (crux), to the top of *Seasoned In The Sun.*

The First Course **   11a   #8   SPORT** (p1)   2p.
Kris Holm Sept 1998
An excellent face climb up the huge white streak below *U Wall*. After the fixed rope on the Flake Trail, go right then scramble back left up to the base of the white streak on the long high-angle slab. Face climb past bolts to belay (11a). Pass a bolt to a crack and easier ground leading to the base of *U Wall* (10b). Can be done in one pitch on a 60m rope. Take slings for rope drag.

Grey Matter   **   11d (11a) #7   *199*   SPORT**   2p.
p2 and FCA Perry Beckham Marc Bombois Chris Atkinson Becky Bates Sept 1992
p1 Dean Hart Scott Flavelle July 1984
Start 25m south of the point where the trail starts to descend southward. Climb the arete of a slim, left-facing corner. The difficulties ease higher (11a). Harder climbing joins in with *Merci Me* (11d).

Merci Me ***   .8   #5   *199*   2p.
p1, Jim Sinclair Dave Harris (Eric Lance, Alex Bertulis) 1967. p2, Neil Bennett Jim Sinclair 1969
A real gem. At the top of the Flake, a lovely, elegant dyke rises up to the big roofs. Delightful little finger edges, long pitches, but runout. (#3 .7) (#5 .8).

Golden Throat Charmer ** 12b   *199*   4p.
Hugh Burton Steve Sutton 1970 (aid on Uncle Bens)   FFA: Peter Croft Hamish Fraser 1987
From the belay at the top of *Merci Me*, traverse left to a small tree in a vertical slanting crack (10c). The crack above provides a forceful testpiece of jamming skill. The crux is right off the station, easing above. Rappel out. Gear to 3″.

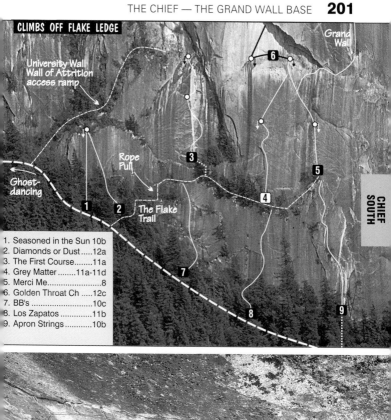

CLIMBS OFF FLAKE LEDGE

Grand Wall

University Wall
Wall of Attrition
access ramp

Ghost-dancing

Rope Pull

The Flake Trail

CHIEF SOUTH

1. Seasoned in the Sun 10b
2. Diamonds or Dust 12a
3. The First Course........11a
4. Grey Matter 11a-11d
5. Merci Me......................8
6. Golden Throat Ch 12c
7. BB's 10c
8. Los Zapatos 11b
9. Apron Strings............10b

The final pitch of University Wall, 5.12a. Climber: Hamish Fraser

The Grand Wall Base — Southern Area

This section describes climbs along the Base of the Grand Wall between *Peasant's Route* and *The Black Dyke,* right (south) of where the Grand Wall access trail meets the rock in the *Cruel Shoes* area,

Getting there... From the large parking lot in front of the Chief, walk over to Psyche Ledge (the old highway) and continue 100m to the start of the trail into the trees: 5ive minutes up this to the base of the Grand. All the climbs listed in this section are south (right) of here.

Climbs and gear... A superb crack, *Exasperator* (10c), a superb face climb, *Java Jive* (10d–11c), and the great *Movin' To Montana* (11a). Take a full rack of crack gear with an emphasis on smaller sizes, and double ropes for rapping off.

Peasant's Route ★★ 10c *198* 3p.
Les McDonald Jim Baldwin May 1958 FFA: Peter Croft John Howe (RH start) Feb 1979
Left-hand start (as described) FFA: Jim Campbell Bob Milward June 1984
This is the open corner-ramp 30m right of *The Flake*. Climb the corner in 3 pitches to a large ledge. The main difficulty is at a small arch 45m up. The original start (1958, aid) is via a thin curving crack (11b) on the right.

Fresh Fruit For Rotting Vegetables ★★ 11c *198* 2p.
Bob Milward Scott Young 1985 FFA: Jim Sandford D.Newman 1985
Climb *Exasperator* to the crux, then go left across thin dikes on the wall, past four bolts to *Peasants* and the top. Rappel.

Exasperator ★★★ 10c *198* 2p.
p1 Jim Sinclair Jim Baldwin 1960 FFA p1 Dan Tate, Rod Crow July 1965
FFA complete Eric Weinstein Dave Nicol 1975
One of the most hallowed of Squamish classics, this outstanding finger crack splits the smooth wall 50m right of *The Flake*. Short cruxes and good protection make it everyone's favourite. It can be split into two pitches (10a-10c). Two rappels down. It is possible to continue up the final pinnacle (.9) and climb a pitch of 11c *(Peter Croft 1983)* that leads across toward *Cruel Shoes*, the original start of *Up From The Skies*.

Iconoclast ★★ .4 A3 *204* 50m
Carl Austrom Anders Ourom (part) c.1975. Dick Mitten Scott Flavelle Keith Flavelle (full) 1977
Mostly aid and some bolts following thin arches and seams up the wall right of *Exasperator*. Tension down into *Exasperator* to finish. Becoming popular as a short aid testpiece, having had the old iron replaced.

Teenage Wasteland ● ☺ (formerly Miners Crack) 11b *204* 25m
Robin Barley 1974 FFA: D.Watson Will Dorling Nick Watts Sept 1989
15m right of *Exasperator*, a slim corner. Rarely dry.

Knacker Cracker ★★ 11b *204* 25m
Peter Croft Randy Atkinson Joe Buszowski 1978
The thin finger crack on the right wall of *Teenage Wasteland*, ending at the same belay station. Rappel.

Movin' To Montana ** 11a—11d <u>205</u> 5p.
Perry Beckham Tim Holwill 1984
A fine route with exceptionally good first and last pitches. A triple set of RPs and hard liebacking are required to succeed on the direct start of the first pitch (11d). [Or scramble in from the right to join in below pitch 2.] A bit troublesome to start pitch 2, then belay at the base of a larger corner (10d). Up this corner easily, then pull out left up to the top of a white pillar and belay (.9). Face climbing and mantelshelves above lead to the base of a long right leaning corner. Belay at its top (10c). Undercling until possible to step up onto the slab. Continue in a magnificent position to the belay (11a). Rappel.

A few metres right, the trail passes below a smooth black wall that leads up to immense overhangs some 90m above.

CHIEF SOUTH

Hangup * .9 <u>204</u> 3p.
Tony Cousins Jim Sinclair 1972 FFA: Jim Campbell Bob Milward June 1984
An interesting, meandering route that heads up highh above *Exasperator*, starting from the layback corner that forms the left edge of the *Java Jive* wall.

Friendly Lizard .8 <u>204</u> (30m)
Jim Campbell Bob Milward June 1984
Continue above *Hangup* for another pitch in the right-facing dihedrals.

Coyote ** 11a #7 <u>205</u> **SPORT** 50m
Rick Clements Peder Ourom July 1995
A long face pitch at the left edge of the *Java Jive* wall. Start at the base of the *Hangup* corner, and follow the bolts leading up to the arch high above.

Java Jive *** 11c (10d) <u>205</u> 2p.
Perry Beckham Dave Lane Scott Flavelle 1979-82 FFA pitch 2, Scott Flavelle June 1984
Superb face climbing up an unlikely line. Climb up the short corner at the left edge of the black wall, runout, to a line up the face above leading to a semi-hanging belay (10d). Continue on the same line of holds until they get scarce near the arch. Move down right into the corner with difficulty. Follow the arch, a few cams to 3", pulling over the top to a belay. Rope drag! (11c). This would be a sport route but for the runout start and CDs needed at the arch.

Miss Led ** 12a (10d+A0) <u>205</u> 2p.
Hugh Burton Jim Sinclair (Jeannine Caldbeck) 1973 FFA: Perry Beckham Hamish Fraser 1982
REBOLTED AND CLEANED: Joe Turley Marc Bombois July 1998
Starts at the line of bolts 15m right of *Java Jive*. Up the bolts on tiny holds (crux), left under a small overlap, and up the open face above to a dyke. Climb the dyke to a belay at the base of a corner above. A long pitch (12a or 10d+bolts). Follow the fine dyke more easily to a large tree (.8). Mostly bolts, take a few small wires. Rappel.

Raindance 10c <u>204</u> 35m
Rolf Rybak Ivan Christiansen 1987
Just above the trail at the base of *The Black Dyke*, pull out left past bolts to gain a shallow groove. Up this, then harder face climbing leads to a belay on the right. Rappel.

GRAND WALL BASE SOUTH

1. Fresh Fruit For 11c
2. Exasperator 10c
3. Iconoclast A3
4. Teenage Wasteland ..11b
5. Knacker Cracker 11b
6. Movin' to Montana .11a-d

7. Hangup ....
8. Coyote ....
9. Friendly Lizard ....
10. Java Jive 10-
11. Misled......10d,A0 or
12. Raindance................
13. Crap Crags ....

The final pitch of Movin To Montana, 5.11a.
Climber: Jill Lawrence

MOVIN TO MONTANA — JAVA JIVE WALL

CHIEF
SOUTH

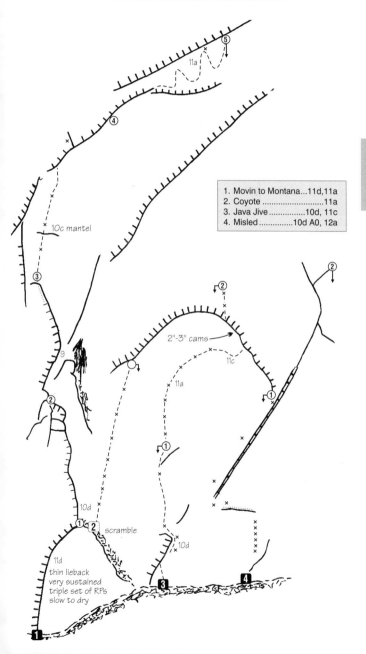

1. Movin to Montana...11d,11a
2. Coyote 11a
3. Java Jive 10d, 11c
4. Misled 10d A0, 12a

11a

10c mantel

2"-3" cams

11c

11a

10d

10d

scramble

11d
thin lieback
very sustained
triple set of RPs
slow to dry

The Grand Wall Base — Northern Area

This section describes climbs along the base of the Grand that lie left (north) of where the Grand Wall access trail meets the rock in the *Cruel Shoes* area. For climbs off the trail to Flake ledge, see page 200. Climbs are described from right to left.

Getting there... From the parking lot in front of the Chief, walk to Psyche Ledge (the old highway) and continue 100m to the start of the trail. Five minutes up this to the base of the Grand Wall. All the climbs listed in this section are north (left) of this point. After 200m of uphill an easy break cuts back sharply to the right–the access trail along Flake Ledge. Another 25m beyond, is a steeper exit up a bushy ramp that leads up rightwards to *University Wall*. The trail continues north for another 100m, about 20 minutes in all from the highway.

Climbs and gear... Multi-pitch climbs predominate here, the finest being *Ghostdancing* (11b). This is also home to *Kneewrecker Chimney* (10a). Take double ropes and a full rack to 3″.

Los Zapatos   **   11b   *201*   50m
Scott Flavelle Dean Hart Keith Flavelle July 1984
An excellent face and friction climb. Bold. 60m up the trail from the central area, climb to a bolt beside a water pocket. Up left past more bolts, then out right up to an obvious overlap (crux). Pull around at its right end, then up to the Flake ledges. 5 bolts and a couple medium CUs for the overlap.

BB's   ●   10c   *201*   30m
R.Barry V.Scott-Polson Sept 1989
30m uphill from *Los Zapatos*, a ramp cuts sharply back to the right. Climb the thin dykes above, trending right, then back left.

Seasoned In The Sun   ***   10a   *209*   35m
Anders Ourom Dave Lane 1977
A classic rattly finger crack which splits the wall, getting harder all the way.

Aged In Oak   **   11a   *209*   2p.
Neil Kirk Ernie Nomeland Sept 16th 1992
Scramble up the *University Wall* access ramp for 30m until below the righthand edge of the big wall above. Climb up the right edge of the face for 10m to a bolt, traverse left on small ledges for 6m or so, then directly up past more bolts to belay chains (11a). Trend left and up past 5 bolts and on to a small stance and station. Two rappels down. You can traverse left lower down into *Kneewrecker* (some gear and fixed aid) to reach *Ghostdancing* (10c). Take a few small to medium size CDs and wires as well as many draws.

Kneewrecker Chimney   10c A2   *209*   5p.
Robin Barley Peter Koedt 1973
Start 10m up the *University Wall* ramp at a bolt on a black wall. Follow corners with some aid pins, crossing *Ghostdancing* to reach the prominent chimney.

Never Were Warriors   ** 11b+5pa   _209_   5p.

p1-p2 Robin Barley Judy Komori Aug 1996   p3-p5 John Fantini Robin Barley (alts) July 1997

Lots of worthwhile climbing. Start 5m left of the U Wall access ramp, and climb under an arch (often greasy) onto the face above. Climb it, using the 3rd bolt for aid to belay at a cedar tree (10c+1pa). Continue up a short groove to a thin crack above a roof (11b). Difficult climbing leads rightward over an arch system to the long sustained groove above *Aged In Oak*. Belay on the left above (11b+1pa). Climb the big groove on the left, then a strange ramp (10c). A final 3-bolt ladder leads to easier climbing up rightwards (10a+3pa). Rappel.

Ghostdancing   *** 11b   _209_   3p.

Peter Shackleton Robin Barley (alts) July 1985

A wonderful, well protected climb which has earned the reputation of being a sandbag, so the grades are adjusted. Start at an obvious pancake flake 35m left of *Seasoned....* Climb over a trick overlap and a flake above to a ledge belay (11b). Go up on fine, delicate face climbing that leads to an easier corner (11b). From a large ledge, finish up the tremendous dihedral above (10b) or go left to the final superb back and foot pitch of *Kneewrecker Chimney* (10a). Better still, do both. 3 rappels down. Great stuff!

CHIEF SOUTH

Arthroscopy   * 10c+2pa   _209_   3p.

Robin Barley Judy Komori Aug 1996.

A good wandering line left of *Ghostdancing*. Climb steep black rock past 2 bolts to reach a slim, left-trending ramp until a dyke leads out right to a ledge belay (10b). Lovely rough rock above leads up almost to a junction with *Ghostdancing* at a blank bulge. Move up and leftward, pulling on 2 bolts to a long shallow dihedral, which is followed to the base of *Kneewrecker Chimney* (10c+2pa). Finish up this classic Squamish chimney, and learn what real old-style 10a is all about. Rappel.

The Spectre   ** 11c   _209_   5p.

Colin Moorhead Will Dorling Nick Watts Aug 14 1994

A fine route up the main corner at the left side of the wall. Climb the first pitch of *Ghostdancing* (11b). Traverse easily left to belay below the main corner system (.7). A short sharp pitch of face climbing leads to an excellent ledge (11c). Climb the fine, exposed ramp system to the base of the chimney (10b). Finish up the last pitch of *Ghostdancing* or *Kneewrecker* (10a). Take a small rack of CDs to 2", a few wires and draws.

Green Thumb   ● .8 A2   _209_   many

Dick Culbert Bob Cuthbert 1967

A meandering climb that starts left of *Ghostdancing*, and takes the line of least resistance (and most bush) to Vulcan's Artery.

Trouble In Paradise   * 11c   #4   x   30m

Peder Ourom John Rosholt (Luc Mailloux) summer 1995

A face climb 60m uphill beyond *Ghostdancing*. Moderate at first up small ledges, then difficult face climbing leads to a belay station.

Jingus The Cat   * 10b   x   20m

Scott Young Jacquie Beaubien 1986

An obvious, open right facing corner 80m beyond *Ghostdancing*.

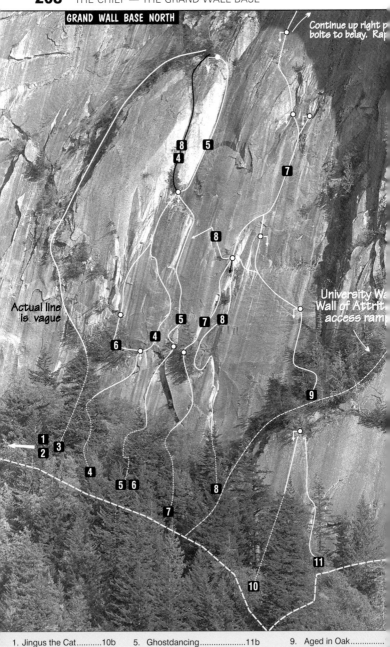

GRAND WALL BASE NORTH

Continue up right p
bolts to belay. Rap

University Wa
Wall of Attrit
access ramp

Actual line
is vague

1. Jingus the Cat...........10b
2. Trouble in Paradise ..11c
3. Green Thumb...........8,A2
4. Arthroscopy........10c,2pa
5. Ghostdancing...................11b
6. The Spectre 11c
7. Never were Warriors ..11b+A0
8. Kneewrecker 10c,A2
9. Aged in Oak.................
10. Seasoned in the Sun..
11. Diamonds or Dust ....

CHIEF
SOUTH

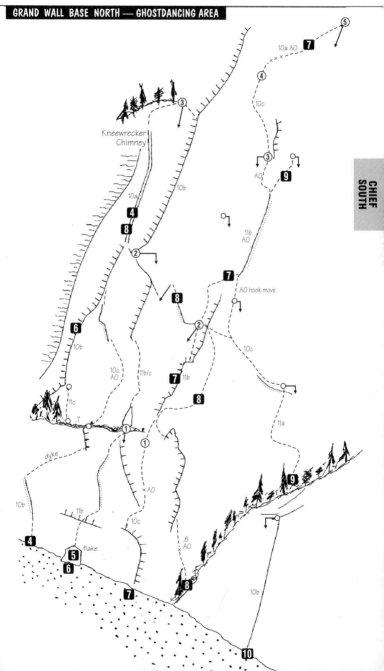

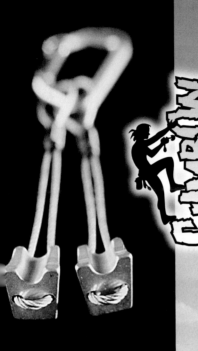

The Split Pillar, 5.10b.
Climber Keith Reid

The Grand Wall

The Grand Wall is the vast sweep of smooth vertical rock facing west over the highway, stretching from the Dihedrals to the shadowy recesses of Northwest Passage. It has been the centrepiece of climbing on the Chief for over 40 years. To climbers '*The Grand*' represents the spiritual soul of Squamish. Three spectacular free or almost-free climbs rise the full height of the wall; *The Grand Wall* (11a) up the centre; bounding the left edge is *University Wall* (12a) and *Wall of Attrition* (11b). *The Grand Wall* has numerous variations and collectively they form the most esteemed collection of routes in the guide, the stuff that climbers aspire to. Its reputation is well-deserved, superb cracks, wonderful exposure and the cheeky audacity of a stunning line up an awesome wall at a very moderate grade.

CHIEF
SOUTH

The Grand has been climbed in every month of the year, done 5 times to Bellygood in one day by Hamish Fraser and Peder Ourom in August 1993, and in 1996 raced the full 16 pitches to the top of the *Roman Chimneys* in an incredible 1 hour 44 minutes by Sig Isaac and Guy Edwards. The latter eclipsed Perry Beckham and Peter Croft's 1986 time of 2 hours 45 minutes. If combined with *Cruel Shoes*, it makes for a continuous climb of 17 pitches, 11 of which are 5.10 and 4 are 5.11a. Aid is still required on an exposed, vertical bolt ladder above the Sword. One day, someone will succeed in linking the top of the *Underfling* to the top of the bolt ladder, (hey, it's there...) and history will be made. Beware the wind, a characteristic that catches many climbers off-guard, whipping across the barren wall. Even on a sunny day in spring, it can be deceptively cold and windy.

Getting there... From the large parking lot beside the highway in front of the Chief, walk over to Psyche Ledge, and continue 100m to the start of the trail, then a few minutes up this to the base of the Grand Wall. A beautiful granite sculpture of a climber created in 1970 by Jack Richardson can be seen along the way on a small boulder.

Descents... There are two descents. Scrambling off along Bellygood Ledge after 10 pitches is the most common. At the southern end of Dance Platform, traverse out right (keep the rope on!) for 150m, until a regular trail leads down over bedrock slabs to a final scrambly drop to join the Backside trail about 15 minutes from the base.

If you finish at the top of the *Roman Chimneys*, head up right along a wide ledge below the Penthouse crag, soon joining the Backside trail near the top of the Chief.

The Grand Wall ***½	11a+A0	<u>217</u>	12p or 17p.
The Roman Chimneys **	11a - d	<u>217</u>	(4p.)
The Left Side ***	12a	<u>217</u>	(2p.)
The Underfling ***	12c	<u>217</u>	(18m)
To The Hilt ***	12d	<u>217</u>	(40m)
The Grinning Weasel ***	11a	<u>333</u>	(35m)

ORIGINAL:
JimBaldwin Ed Cooper July 1961. A 40 day sieged aid epic to the top of the Chief.

The Flake	Dave McDonald Kevin McLane September 1972
Mercy Me-Pillar	Dave Loeks W.Putnam 1975
Split Pillar	Eric Weinstein Daryl Hatten 1975.
Sword	Peter Croft Greg Foweraker March 81
Perry's Lieback	Kon Kraft (aid) mid 1970s. FFA Perry Beckham Jan Daly 1982.
Flats to Bellygood:	Peter Croft Greg Foweraker March1981
Flats variations: (LH)	Perry Beckham, Will Dorling 1989
Flats variations: (RH)	Alistair Veitch Lee Purvis July 1998
Bellygood Ledge Traverse:	Tim Auger Mike Wisnicki 1964 (second ascent of the Grand Wall)
Roman Chimneys:	FFA: Peter Croft Greg Foweraker Tami Knight 1981
	FFA p2 as described: Don McPherson 1985
	FFA Direct p3: Peter Croft Hamish Fraser 1985
The Left Side:	Dick Culbert Tim Auger 1972 FFA: Nick Taylor Peter Peart 1975
The Underfling:	(from upper Sword belay) Dave Lane Bob Alison 1987
To The Hilt:	(from Split Pillar belay) Peter Croft 1988
The Grinning Weasel:	Peter Croft Greg Foweraker 1982

The climb is most commonly started up *Apron Strings* [page 196] to reach Flake Ledge (10b, .9), although a longer day out can be made via *Cruel Shoes*, and a shorter one by walking to the top of Flake Ledge.

From the top of the Flake, climb *Merci Me* (.7), then shortly after beginning the 2nd pitch, trend up rightwards to belay below large roofs (.9). A traverse follows, down a little at first, then up to an airy perch on a small ledge (10b). Belay here, or continue up right with 3 bolts for aid to the base of the *Split Pillar* (10b). Handjam this brilliant, exposed corner crack, described as "a 10b with an 11a feel" finishing up a small chimney to a perfect ledge (10b). Continue laybacking up *The Sword* to a small ledge, move out left into a good face crack and dramatic exposure. Climb the crack then pull back into the corner and out left at its top to a hanging belay (11a). Climb the 10-bolt ladder above to a stance down and right of an ominous offwidth crack. Layback or aid the protection bolts, up this strenuous crack to the Flats (11a). From the right side of the Flats, traverse up right and along a fault to belay (.9).

Up into a short right-leaning corner above and belay on top (10b). Undercling the final strenuous flake to Bellygood Ledge and Dance Platform (10c). Two good variations are possible from the Flats that climb directly to the start of the last pitch. One is to climb directly up the right-leaning corner above (10c). The other goes up from the left end of the roof band traverse on the standard pitch off the Flats, and requires a long reach (#6, 10a).

For the **Roman Chimneys**, go left across Dance Platform to its north end. The great chimneys rise overhead. Climb through overlaps and short walls to belay at the left end of the big 'Boot Flake' (11a). Climb it [4"CD], enter the main chimney and belay on top of a huge chockstone (11a). Move up, then go left into a vague corner [small wires] to reach a large horizontal fault. Roll into it and crawl back to the main corner and belay on a good ledge. A demanding, rather bold pitch (10d). A very direct line can be taken to reach this same ledge, up the dramatically overhanging groove to the right—rarely dry, but can be partly aided on fixed gear (11d). Climb the last classic corner to a big ledge on top, a fine place to reflect on a great day (10b).

The Left Side: This is the awesome face crack that forms the left side of *The Split Pillar*. Belay below the small roof. Pull out left from the roof into the crack. Fingerjamming or laybacking through the thin hand-crack crux are equally difficult, then the crack widens and gets progressively easier above. The 5.10 offwidth section is alarmingly runout unless several big CUs are taken. A tremendous pitch. Continue up *The Grinning Weasel*, *Genius Loci,* or make a wild traverse around to the top of the right side of *The Split Pillar* (.9).

The Grinning Weasel: This is the left-facing corner that rises above the top of *The Left Side*. Presently, there is no belay-rappel anchor at the top of this climb. No word on what happened to the last climber down. The climb continues as an aid route [page 323].

The Underfling: This is a spectacular continuation of the Sword from the station on the Grand Wall below the bolt ladder. Continue rightwards along the curving flake to its end. Desperately strenuous, technical underclinging, above which is the possibility of linking back into the Grand Wall all free.

To The Hilt: Starting from the top of the Pillar this ups the difficulty of *The Underfling* a grade to 12d. A tremendous 45m pitch.

Genius Loci   ***   12b   <u>*217*</u>   5p.**
Hamish Fraser Peder Ourom Mark Gandy 1991.
Believed to have not been freed on a single ascent.
A magnificent excursion up the open walls left of the Pillar, bolted on lead. Start 15m left of *Merci Me*. Difficult face climbing leads to a station above a small overlap (11d). Up rightwards across *Merci Me* to belay on the slab below the end of the big roof (11c). These first two pitches are unrepeated and rather bold. Climb up to the bottom of the thin face crack and go out right to a slim dyke. Follow it back to the crack and up it to join a wide dyke, good holds and a belay (12b). Follow the dyke in a sensational position to the top of *The Left Side* (10d). Continue up *Grinning Weasel* until a pull out right into a hand crack is possible. Face climb to a hard mantel onto the small ledge halfway up *The Sword*. Continue up that pitch (11b).

Negro Lesbian ✈	Aid	See page 323
The Black Dyke	Aid	See page 323
Zorros last Ride	Aid	See page 323
Under The Gun	Aid	See page 323
Up From The Skies	Aid	See page 323
The Grinning Weasel	Aid	See page 323
Ten Years After	Aid	See page 323
Humpty Dumpty	Aid	See page 323
Uncle Ben's	Aid	See page 323

THE GRAND WALL

Dance Platform

The Roman Chimneys

Bellygood Ledge

The Flates

Perry's Lieback

Bolt Ladder

The Underfling

The Grinning Weasel

Sword

Split Pillar Ledge

Left Side

Split Pillar

Genius Loci

Merci Me

Baldwin Cooper Bolt ladder

Merci Me

Top of Apron Strings

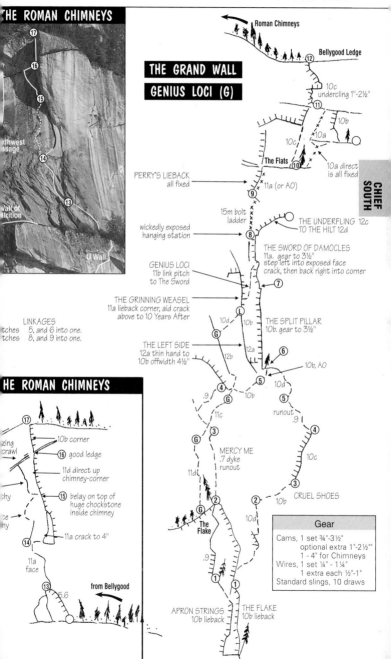

THE ROMAN CHIMNEYS

Roman Chimneys

Bellygood Ledge

⑰

⑯

⑮

Northwest Passage

⑭

Wall of Attrition

⑬

U Wall

THE GRAND WALL
GENIUS LOCI (G)

⑫

10c
undercling 1"-2½"

⑪

10b

10c   10a

The Flats   10a direct
⑩   is all fixed

PERRY'S LIEBACK
all fixed   11a (or AO)   ⑨

CHIEF
SOUTH

15m bolt
ladder   THE UNDERFLING 12c
wickedly exposed   ⑧   TO THE HILT 12d
hanging station
                              THE SWORD OF DAMOCLES
                              11a. gear to 3½"
                              step left into exposed face
GENIUS LOCI   crack, then back right into corner
11b link pitch
to The Sword   ⑦

THE GRINNING WEASEL
11a lieback corner, aid crack
above to 10 Years After   Ⓛ
                              10d   10b   THE SPLIT PILLAR
                    Ⓖ   10b. gear to 3½"
THE LEFT SIDE   12b   12a   ⑥
12a thin hand to
10b offwidth 4½"   ④   ⑤   10b, AO
                   .9 Ⓖ   10b   10d
MERCY ME   ③   ⑤
.7 dyke   Ⓖ   11c   runout
runout   .9   ④

                   ③   10c
              11d
                   Ⓖ ②   ②   CRUEL SHOES
            The   10d   ③   10b
            Flake
             Ⓖ ②
                  .9   10d

                   ①   ①
APRON STRINGS   THE FLAKE
10b lieback   10b lieback

THE ROMAN CHIMNEYS

⑰   10b corner
              ⑯ good ledge
sizing
crawl   11d direct up
              chimney-corner
          ⑮ belay on top of
chy   huge chockstone
              inside chimney
ce
hy   ⑭   11a crack to 4"

      11a
      face
   ⑬   5.6

from Bellygood

LINKAGES
tches   5, and 6 into one.
tches   8, and 9 into one.

Gear
Cams, 1 set ¾"-3½" optional extra 1"-2½"" 1 - 4" for Chimneys Wires, 1 set ¼" - 1¼" 1 extra each ½"-1" Standard slings, 10 draws

University Wall Area

This is the far left side of the Grand Wall, noted by the long line of corners of *University Wall* and the dark recess of *Northwest Passage*.

| **University Wall** | ***½ | 12a | 11p. |
| The Shadow | *** | 12d | (2p.) |

Tim Auger Dan Tate Hamish Mutch Glenn Woodsworth May 1966
FFA to Dance Platform: Peter Croft Hamish Fraser Greg Foweraker 1982
FFA to the summit via Roman Chimneys: Peter Croft Hamish Fraser 1982
***The Shadow:** Peter Croft Geoff Weigand Aug 1988*

This towering line of overhanging dihedrals at the left edge of the Grand Wall gives a magnificent climb. The main difficulties are in the first three pitches. Hike up the access ramp from the base of the Grand Wall to a belay just left of the major corner system of *UWall*. Move right onto the rock and the start of a powerful crackline leading into the dihedral above—often wet at the start, but that seems be no deterrent (12a). Up the corner, undercling out left into a flake chimney. Belay here to minimise rope drag (12a). Climb a burly flake chimney to its top (11c). Move up into the main corner, go left past a roof to a small ledge and tree belay (10c). Climb a short offwidth crack above followed by more laybacking and stemming to a hanging belay (10d). Wide stemming across the corner leads to a flake on the left. Traverse out, then onto a ramp leading back into the corner. Continue to a ledge (11b). Trend right up across the wall and break through the roof above, belaying around the corner on a ledge (10d). A sting in the tail. Face climb up left of 2 bolts—scary long reach!—to gain a flake crack leading up right to Dance Platform (11c). Continue up *The Roman Chimneys* (11a) or scuttle off over Dance Platform and Bellygood.

   The Shadow comprises 2 very direct variations: the stunning dihedral on pitch 2 (12d), which is climbed by full-on stemming with both arms and legs; and on pitch 5, avoiding the flake traverse out left and remain in the main corner to the belay (12a).

| **Wall Of Attrition** | ** | 11b (10d+1pa) | 6p. |

Bob Milward Jim Campbell (1pa) Oct 1984 FFA p3 Scott Young 1985
FCA and FFA p5, p6, John Rosholt Peder Ourom 1996

Left of the central section of *University Wall* is a huge white dihedral. This route climbs to its top, offering excellent climbing in a fine situation. Take the same approach as for *University Wall*, but nearing the high point, veer off to the left, scrambling up to the base of a small chimney. Climb it to a ledge (4th). Continue up mixed face climbinges, passing the left edge of an overlap to belay (10a). A thin crack and face moves above form the technical crux of the route, beyond which climb over into the main corner and belay a little higher (11b or 10d+1pa). A short pitch leads up to the base of the big dihedral (10b). Climb it in a fine position (10b). A dramatic pitch leads on upward through bands of stepped roofs; bold, with suspect rock and old fixed gear (10c). A short final pitch leads to the far north end of Dance Platform (10c).

Northwest Passage	Aid	See page 324
Drifter's Escape	Aid	See page 324
The Non Wall	Aid	See page 324

WALL OF ATTRITION — UNIVERSITY WALL

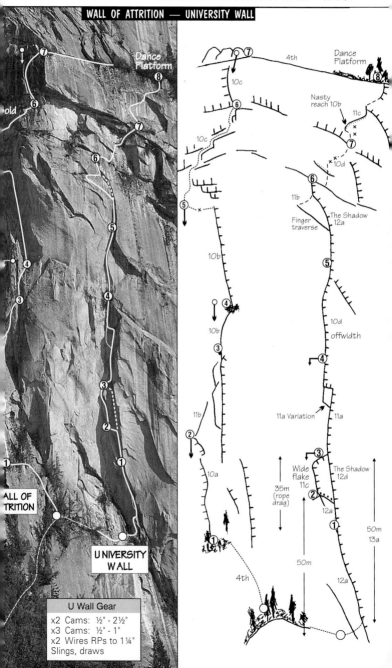

Dance Platform

4th

Nasty reach 10b

11c

10c

10d

11b

The Shadow 12a

Finger traverse

10c

10b

10d offwidth

10b

11a Variation

11a

11b

Wide flake 11c

The Shadow 12d

35m (rope drag)

50m 13a

10a

12a

50m

4th

12a

ALL OF TRITION

UNIVERSITY WALL

U Wall Gear
x2 Cams: ½" - 2½"
x3 Cams: ½" - 1"
x2 Wires RPs to 1¼"
Slings, draws

Climbs Off Bellygood Ledge

Bellygood Ledge is the demarcation line on the Grand Wall between the main Grand Wall climbs and the upper, less travelled areas. Despite being in full view of the highway below, there is a distinct feeling up here of being way high, removed from the teeming masses below.

Getting there... The shortest approach to these climbs is up the Backside trail. Follow the trail as for the South Summit of the Chief, then exit left to take the Bellygood descent trail (page 297)–travelling the opposite way to climbers walking down from *The Grand Wall*. Needless to say, all of these climbs can be conveniently added on to an ascent of *The Grand Wall*.

The Roman Chimneys ** 11a - d   <u>217, 222</u>   (4p.)

The Upper Black Dyke ● ☺ 10a   <u>223</u>   4p.
Greg Shannan (solo aid) 1974 FFA: Robin Barley Gordie Smaill 1974
Variation finish: Alan Agopsowicz Mathew Maddaloni July 1996
Above Bellygood Ledge, the *Upper Black Dyke* offers fine exposed situations and excellent climbing, but is generally scruffy and loose. If you're prepared to overlook this, you'll enjoy it. If it were to be cleaned up and bolts replaced, this climb would become a popular and moderate extension to *The Grand Wall*. A variation finish goes out left down an undercling just before the final steep section on the final pitch, then up a 5.8 crack to finish.

On Tilt ● ☺   11c   <u>223</u>   2p.
Dean Hart John Rosholt Scott Young 1985
A short distance right of *The Black Dyke* is a major left leaning corner system which is an excellent, if rarely climbed route. Climbed in two pitches (11c, .9). From its top, traverse off right.

Shaved Bum ***   11c+1pa   <u>223</u>   3p.
Colin Moorhead Kai Hirvonen June 1998
An incredible crackline splitting the prominent ass-like feature at the right side of the cliff. It is possible to rap in from the top of Skyline Slab, or to approach from Bellygood Ledge by scrambling up 4th-class ledges then climb a scruffy corner and traverse to the base of a golden-orange dihedral (.8). A sustained thin crack [wire for aid] leads to a chimney and a rest, overhanging jamming and an easier corner. A stellar pitch, heavy on thin gear (11c). Climb on up the easier corner above (10b).

Colon   .9   <u>223</u>   3p.
Dick Culbert Alice Purdey Nov 1965 FFA: John Coope Jim Campbell Sept 1981
From Bellygood a 3rd class scramble, left then back right is necessary to reach the start, or a more direct line to the base of *Shaved Bum* (.8). Head out right (.8). Climb the left-hand feature above (.9). The right-hand feature is also 5.9. Scramble up left for 150m or so to rejoin the Chief Summit trail. Take a double set of CDs from 2″ to 4″.

Skyline Slab

This is a high-angle wall below the rim of the Chief, just south of the top of *The Black Dyke*. The climbs require rappelling in, so they hold a sense of adventure. At this time, it is not possible to reach these routes from Bellygood Ledge, but tantalising opportunities exist.

Getting there... Head up the Backside trail for the South Summit of the Chief (page 297) and exit as for the trail as for the Penthouse (page 222). At the point where it crosses *The Black Dyke* walk southward to a notch, and descend the slab to the rim. A 30m rap-in is necessary for each route.

Gold Medal Ribbon **   11a   #9   <u>223</u>   **SPORT**   30m
Colin Moorhead Will Dorling April 1998
Sustained dyke walking and pinching. An excellent climb.

Up From Nowhere *   10c   <u>223</u>   30m
Kai Hirvonen Craig Rankin July 1998
Undercling and lieback. Good.

CHIEF SOUTH

UPPER SOUTH PEAK

Raven's Castle

Penthouse

Skyline Slab

Bellygood Ledge

Grand Wall

The Penthouse

This is a west-facing cliff near the summit of the South Chief, in a fine airy position with a collection of excellent face climbs–well worth a hike. Sport climbs with a view. The climbs all start off the long ledge system that runs from the top of the *Roman Chimneys* south to the hiking trail up the South Peak of the Chief. When climbing here, please consider that anything you drop or dislodge will fall with hardly a bounce to land on the trail at the base of the Grand Wall...

Getting there...   About 35 minutes. Take the Backside Trail (page 297), and fork off as for the hiking trail to the South Chief. After the second major fork, the trail climbs steeply again, passing beneath a prominent line of roofs just above the trail, then emerges into the open with views to the south. The trail then veers right (north), and after 50m arrives at a short section of basalt bedrock. Go left here, and walk easily for 50m along a narrow trail to reach a sudden dramatic viewpoint down to the valley. Continue northward along a narrow ledge below an undercut cliff for 40m to the first climb.

CHIEF — ABOVE BELLYGOOD

Raven's Castle

Backside Tra
to South Pea

12

11   8

10   9

10b

10d

11a

11a

1   Dance Platform

University Wall

Grand Wall

Bellygood Ledg

The Trimark Years ** 11b (10c+1pa) #10 SPORT 40m
Peder Ourom Anders Ourom March 1998

An obvious line of bolts trending up right. Step up to the roof, clip a bolt and go. The crux is a long reach at the third bolt. Don't be afraid to use it.

Bad Religion ** 10d #10 SPORT+ 40m
Colin Moorhead Will Dorling March 1998

Pull over the roof left of *Trimark*, and climb up to a line of bolts. Gear to 2".

Chickenhead Soup * 11a 40m
Colin Moorhead Kai Hirvonen Oct 1997

Pull over the roof as for *Bad Religion*, then go left out along an obvious handrail of holds for 10m, then straight up. A tad runout. 5 bolts, gear to 2½".

> *The next two climbs, noted by a pair of bolts at their common start, begin off a small terrace 10m up and left of the start of Chickenhead...*

High Society ** 11c #9 SPORT+ 30m
Colin Moorhead Rich Wheater March 1998

Climb the crack to the tree, and climb the right-hand line of bolts above. Take a couple CDs to 2".

Now With Wings ** 11b #8 SPORT+ 30m
Colin Moorhead Nov 1997

Climb the crack to the tree, and climb the left-hand line of bolts above. Take a couple CDs to 2".

CHIEF SOUTH

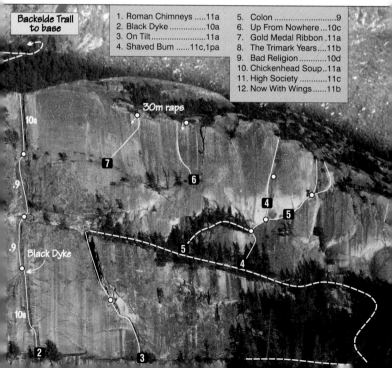

Backside Trail to base

30m rape

Black Dyke

1. Roman Chimneys 11a	5. Colon 9
2. Black Dyke 10a	6. Up From Nowhere ...10c
3. On Tilt.........................11a	7. Gold Medal Ribbon .11a
4. Shaved Bum 11c,1pa	8. The Trimark Years....11b
	9. Bad Religion 10d
	10. Chickenhead Soup..11a
	11. High Society 11c
	12. Now With Wings......11b

Raven's Castle

This is the beautiful low-angle apron of friction slabs at the summit of the South Chief, with spectacular views looking west over the Squamish Estuary and the mountains. It is bigger than it appears–the full 60m length is best appreciated from below. When looking up from downtown Squamish, Raven's Castle is the Chief's 'nose'.

The rock on the lower apron is unusually polished, and can be a bit eerie at first for some climbers. However, most of the climbs are modest in difficulty, offering good leading experience for novices, as well as an excellent finish to the *Squamish Buttress*.

Getting there... Take the Backside Trail and exit as for the Penthouse (page 297). After 50m, head right up an easy gully to the top of that crag and continue northward over open bedrock until the sweeping slabs of Ravens Castle come into view on the right, 45 minutes approach. The first 4 climbs start from the same bolt station at the base of the centre of the slab. Traverse below the slab to reach the 2 climbs at the far left side. Climbs are described from the right.

Descent... The angle at the right side of the polished slab is uncomfortably steep for most climbers–low 5th class–so walk around way on the south side, or rappel on two 55m ropes.

The Flight Of The Fledgelings ** .7 #5 **SPORT** 2p.
Tony McLane Barry McLane (alts) April 1999
Climb up right over polished rock to a bolt station in a scoop #2 (.6). Pad up the wide arete above on good holds #5 (.7)

The Archer's Arrows *** .8 #3 **SPORT** 2p.
Barry McLane Tony McLane (alts) April 1999
Climb directly up to belay in a scoop #3 (.7). Move right to a bolt, then directly up a wide scoop to finish—a bit harder than the first pitch # 3 (.8)

The Bow * .9 #3 **SPORT** 2p.
Kevin McLane Tony McLane Barry McLane April 1999
A direct finish to *The Archer's..* Try it in one pitch of 55m.

Slesse's 500 **. .9 #5 **SPORT** 2p.
Kevin McLane Tony McLane Barry McLane April 1999
Trend up leftward and belay in a scoop #3 (.7) Continue to cross *Joe's Dyke*, then finish out left #5 (.9). The climb is named after the author's dog (pronounced as in the mountain), who hiked over the summits of the Chief at least 500 times, and possessed uncommon adroitness on 4th class rock.

Welfare Daze ** 10a #3 50m
Peder Ourom Jim Brennan 1982
This climb wanders up easy flakes left of *Slesse's 500* before crossing *Joe's Dyke*. Head directly up on good holds to reach a short, steep headwall. Cool moves lead to the rim.

Joe's Dyke ***½ .7 #6 *SPORT* 2p.

Joe Turley Jim Sinclair (solo) c.1978

This is the long dyke that cuts left to right across the crag: the best easy sport face climb in the guide. Belay as for *Talking Crack*, then head up right on a dyke to the base of the steepening wall (.6). Move right and up onto the head wall. Continue in a fine position along the dyke to the rim (.7).

Talking Crack ** .7 2p.

Joe Turley 1962

A short S-shaped hand-crack in a beautiful position at the far left of the crag. From the trail, step up a short groove to reach a low-angle flake and a bolt belay. Climb the flake (4th) to a belay at a tree below the crack. Gear to 3½".

CHIEF
SOUTH

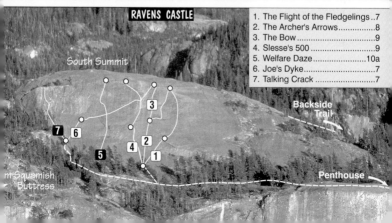

The Grand Wall Boulders

The forest of old-growth fir stretches below the Grand Wall for a kilometre, from the Apron on the left to the Backside Trail on the right. Hidden within the trees are hundreds of boulders, some as big as houses, that have fallen off the Chief over the last 10,000 years.

Since the first days of climbing, the caves and walls of the boulders closest to Psyche Ledge (the old highway), have been the scene for an eclectic mix of ancient overgrown aid routes, ancient overgrown half-freeclimbs, bolt ladders, and in more recent times, some hard sport routes from Jim Sandford and Marc Bourdon. In 1996 a major new development evolved, its genesis being a small group of highly talented Victoria climbers lead by Nick Gibbs, Stu Worrall, Tim Doyle and Peter Michaux, whose home base is the modest little crag of Fleming Beach on Vancouver Island. Fleming is 'too short' to use a rope, and too high to be ignored, so for bored Victoria climbers, cut off from the real thing at Squamish, it became the training ground for a hard-core bouldering ethic. No ropes, no gear, just get good at jumping if you fall...

The boulders at the base of the Grand Wall, and the even larger ones below the north walls, are a treasure house of untapped fun waiting for a time such as this. Several hundred problems now exist, and new ones are being worked whenever the forest is dry. The difficulty of the recognised problems generally starts around hard 5.10, although easier ones are there to do. A detailed listing of all the boulder problems is being published in a guide by the climbers involved. It should be available in 1999.

Getting there... **For the roped climbs**, walk over to Psyche Ledge from the parking lot in front of the Chief, and take a short path 70m left of the start of the Grand Wall trail leading to Kacademon Rock and Eleven Bolt Rock. **For the bouldering...** a good start is to head in on the Grand Wall trail and within the first 50 metres turn right at the carving of the climber and follow a winding trail that travels southward from boulder to boulder. The Black Dyke boulder (no relation) along the way is a popular warm-up area. Alternatively, just after entering the forest from Psyche Ledge, another trail heads north up behind Kacademon Boulder in a rising traverse toward the Apron, with numerous interesting problems enroute. Take a chalk bag, and a crash mat if you have one. Meet other climbers in the quiet forest and have fun working the problems. Please stick to the defined trails– no shortcuts–to help retain as much natural forest floor as possible.

▬ *KACADEMON ROCK* ▬

This is the largest boulder, much bigger than most houses and some crags in the Smoke Bluffs. It is easy to find. Walk in on the approach trail and there it is, among the trees at the edge of the hydro lines. Climbs are described from the north face around leftward. The first two are on either side of the huge prow that juts out toward Squamish.

Bravado   *   13d   #8   229   **SPORT**   15m
Jim Sandford   Oct 1991
From the big ledge below the prow, pull up onto a good juggy flake and handrail along out to the right past many bolts but shrinking holds to the lip crux. Long reaches give no respite above.

Young Blood   *   13a   #5   229   **SPORT**   10m
Jim Sandford   May 1991
On the left side of the prow. Start as for *Bravado* then pull up onto a good juggy flake, and straight up to a powerful lip sequence. A delicate finish.

Rurp Riot   A3   229   18m
Bob and Glenn Woodsworth 1967
In the large cave on the north side of Kacademon, nail out rightward along an almost horizontal crack on the north face of the boulder to a dyke. Hook back left to a higher crack, then on to finish at the the top of the northwest corner of the boulder.

Kloset Klimb   A2   229   18m
Graham Barber and others c. 1969
Start just left of *Rurp Riot*, then go out left up a bolt ladder. *Gavin's Purple Sweater* A4 *(Daryl Hatten and others, 1980)*, joins in after nailing up the thin corner below.

Tarzan   ●   A3   229   15m
Carl Austrom Keith Flavelle 1981
An old stud and hook problem in the centre of the east face, just left of a defunct best-forgotten chipped line of a bygone era.

Permanent Waves   ***   13c   #10   229   **SPORT**   18m
Jim Sandford   July 1993   (formerly Carl's Problem A4 Daryl Hatten Carl Austrom c. 1977)
An impressive line up a wave-like feature at the left end of the east wall of Kacademon. Start up a tree [honest] and finish with a crux.

Creepshow   **   13b-c   #10   229   **SPORT**   15m
Marc Bourdon 1998
A hard climb up the central section of the west face of Kacademon.

Natural Reflex   **   13a   #9   229   **SPORT**   18m
Jim Sandford April 1995   (formerly Seaside Misery A3 Carl Austrom Randy Atkinson 1978)
On the left side of the west face of Kacademon. After a burly start in the centre of the wall, left of *Creepshow*. Go out left to a tricky finish to *Bravado*.

Rainmaker   ●   A4   229   12m
Carl Austrom John Stoddard 1977
A left-right diagonal thin crack with 2 hidden bolts at the start, above a low roof on the north-east face of the boulder just north of Kacademon.

CHIEF SOUTH

▬▬ *ELEVEN BOLT ROCK*   ▬▬▬▬

This boulder is north of Kacademon and has a distinct pointed summit. A trail leads along its west side to the north arete and *Panic*.

Archives ***½   12d   #8   <u>229</u>   **SPORT**   15m
Jim Sandford Aug 1991 (Formerly West Face A3 Graham Barber and others c. 1969)
The leftwards leaning dyke, over the roof to a good ledge. Harder than it appears.

Technical Ecstacy **   13b   #8   <u>229</u>   **SPORT**   15m
Jim Sandford Aug 1991
A direct line up the rib, joining *Archives* at the lip.

Panic *   10a   #6   <u>229</u>   **SPORT**   18m
Jim Baldwin Jim Sinclair Ann McKenzie Don Mostowy (aid) Nov 1961
FFA Gordie Smaill Tim Auger c. 1970 REBOLTED: Jim Sinclair Kevin McLane Jan 1999
The north prow of Eleven Bolt, finishing up the east side hosts an ancient climb which was recently cleaned up into a decent sport route by Jim Sinclair, 38 years after he was on the first ascent [made under two feet of snow and with a six-month pregnant woman]. It is one of the few climbs in the guide that ends on a true summit. After a bouldery start, the difficulty eases.

Button ● ☺   10d   <u>229</u>   12m
Jim Sinclair Jeannine Caldbeck 1972 FFA Peter Croft Blake Robinson 1980
Somewhere in the moss, just right of the southeast corner of the boulder.

Munginella ●   10c   <u>229</u>   15m
Carl Austrom 1978
A crack and face climb up what is now a wall of moss on the highway face of the boulder just north of Eleven Bolt. Long since reclaimed by the forest.

▬▬ *ANIMAL MAGNETISM*   ▬▬▬▬

Animal Magnetism   13a   #3   <u>229</u>   **SPORT**   7m
Jim Sandford Mar 1992
A short overhanging wall left of the trail, just before Kacodemon Rock.

▬▬ *GILLIGAN'S ISLAND*   ▬▬▬▬

These 2 climbs are located close together on the north side of this single boulder about 100m directly uphill from Kacodemon.

Neurotica   13b   #4   <u>229</u>   **SPORT**   8m
Jim Sandford Sept 1992
This is the dyno route from hell. Lots of fun.

Force Of Habit   12d   #5   <u>229</u>   **SPORT**   8m
Jim Sandford   August 1992
After a heinous start, follow a handrail into *Neurotica*, or finish out right (easier).

Name story. *The Daily Planet, on the Sheriffs Badge was the*
newspaper where Superman worked.

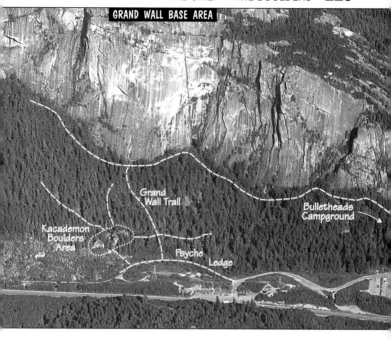

GRAND WALL BASE AREA

Grand Wall Trail

Bulletheads Campground

Kacademon Boulders Area

Psyche Ledge

GRAND WALL BOULDERS

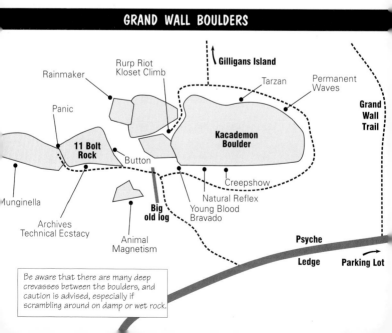

Rainmaker

Rurp Riot
Kloset Climb

Gilligans Island

Tarzan

Permanent Waves

Grand Wall Trail

Panic

Kacademon Boulder

11 Bolt Rock

Button

Creepshow

Munginella

Natural Reflex
Young Blood
Bravado

Archives
Technical Ecstacy

Big old log

Animal Magnetism

Psyche

Ledge

Parking Lot

Be aware that there are many deep crevasses between the boulders, and caution is advised, especially if scrambling around on damp or wet rock.

The Grand Wall Boulders. Photos: Fieldhouse collection.
Climbers: top left, Tyler Jordan: top right, Shannon Price:
bottom left, Scott Milton: bottom right, Jack Fieldhouse

The late, great Catherine Freer on the Split Pillar, 5.10b

Name story. Silent Ladies, on the Backside was named in honour of two deaf and dumb Japanses women who the first ascentionists encountered on the trail.

Name story. Pipeline, on the Squaw is so named because the first ascent team employed several dozen home-made aluminum pipes as pins for the wide off-width crack.

The Grand Wall via the Roman Chimneys was climbed in 1 hour 44 minutes by Sig Isaac and Guy Edwards in 1996. Must have been a lot of simul-climbing going on.

The Apron

The Apron is the long, compelling sweep of slabs that reach down to the highway north of the Grand Wall. It was here that some of the earliest Squamish free climbs were established. Today, the Apron is enormously popular with over 40, mostly friction climbs, ranging from pleasant romps to desperate grippers. The friendly angle of the rock combines with the feel of the wide open spaces and afternoon breezes to create a unique experience that lies close to the heart of Squamish climbing. The easy angle of the rock is non-threatening, but the runouts on some climbs can put the grip into everyone. Euros either love or fear the Apron, as there is very little climbing like it over there. It is very Squamish.

Getting there... **The Main Parking Lot.** Hey, this is easy. The climbers parking lot is beside the highway north of the main public lot in front of the Grand Wall. Exit onto the logging road and you're there. There are three basic approaches to the climbs and a descent common to all routes.

Getting there... **Slab Alley area.** A trail begins 200m south of the main parking lot at the north end of Psyche Ledge about 30m off the highway, giving access to the original start to *Slab Alley* and the climbs on the upper Apron (which is also the descent trail from Broadway). For *Slab Alley*, head up the trail for 40m then go left across to a treed ramp. Walk up the slab on its left into the trees and up to a large open bay where the climbs begins.

Getting there... **Upper Apron Climbs.** For the upper Apron, reverse the descent trail. Start as for the Slab Alley trail but continue across the boulderfield (some markers) into the trees. The trail soon cuts back to the left, out onto the open slabs and a pleasant hike up to the base of *A Question Of Balance.*

Getting there... **The Central Apron Climbs.** This is the access to most of the climbs. Take the obvious trail past the large pointed boulder and up an ancient cedar log into the trees (this would have been a substantial tree before Christopher Columbus' time). At its top, the trail forks to the left and right. The left trail goes to the many climbs that begin near *Snake,* and north along the base. The righthand fork gives access to climbs around *Diedre* and all other climbs to the right, including *Slab Alley.* It scrambles up steeply to the right, then back left, and finally right again to the base of a beautiful welcoming slab. The weight of traffic is causing this trail to erode badly.

Getting there...   **The Northern Apron and South Gully Climbs.**
For access to the climbs on the northern buttress of the Apron above
Baseline ledge, and in the South Gully, walk 50m along the logging
road and turn right into the trees. After a short distance, the trail forks.
Keep left for the South Gully, about ten minutes up to the climbs.
For the climbs off Baseline ledge, go right at an obvious fork a minute
up the trail and climb a pitch of 5.7 tree-and-rock climbing to a clean
corner. Climb this corner (5.8) to the left side of the Baseline, a
prominent tree ledge below several long crack systems.

Descent...   Almost all Apron climbs end at Broadway, the long
tree ledge that cuts across the top of the slabs. From any point on
Broadway, traverse right to the south end until below the inviting slab
of the Upper Apron. There are two ways down from here. The most
common (and fastest) is to turn right and walk straight down open
slabs for 150m until they steepen (perhaps a bit much for novices),
then turn left into the forest and down the trail. The other is to
scramble down directly into the forest, to join the trail down through
the woods.

Combination routes...   About half the climbs listed here on the Apron
are actually direct starts and finishes, or variations major and minor,
to the dozen or so climbs that run the full height of the slabs. These
combinations give some of the best and most popular routes on the
Apron. Where the number of pitches is shown like this: (3p.) it
indicates the climb as described does not run the full height of the
Apron and is dependent on other routes to reach Broadway.

Climbs and gear...   There are so many good climbs here, it is hard
to know where to start. Climbs on the open slabs are almost entirely
bolt-protected, but some gear, mostly smaller sizes of wires and CDs
will be needed on almost all climbs to deal with corners and cracks.
Despite the proliferation of bolts, there are only two sport climbs as
the runouts are generally a bit too much for that comfort zone. A
couple of short climbs are noted as such, both accessed by the same
easy pitch of 5.7 (Sport on the Apron? ...whatever next).

*Uncle Bens, the classic aid route on the Grand Wall, was named
after a popular B.C. beer of the time. To drink and toss a 6-
pack from the bivi was a rite of passage.*

The Lower Apron

This is the 100m sweep of slabs just south of the parking lot, the lowest rock on the Apron. There are three climbs at the left side of this slab— two long-forgotten and one recent. All are worth a look.

Getting there... Walk up the trail to *Diedre*, but turn right at the start of the big cedar log to follow a trail that winds south for 100m to the slab, then stays close to the rock along base of the climbs. *The Bottom Line* offers a good direct start to any of the easier climbs on the Apron above, making a 9-10 pitch climb to Broadway.

Crystal Burst ● 10b 2p.
Ed Seedhouse Hamish Fraser 1979
Largely overgrown, this route lies 8m left of *Mickey Mouse*. Gear to 3".

Mickey Mouse 10d 2p.
Peter Charak Joe Turley 1979
This the central climb, easily identified by its wide scrubbed line and an old station at the top of the first pitch (10d, 10a).

The Bottom Line * .9 3p.
Anthony Chahal Brian Finestone June-Sept 1998
Sorry Joe: *Anthony Chahal Brian Finestone August 1998*
A worthwhile venture that links with the upper routes, providing up to nine pitches of continuous climbing. Head out right along the base of the wall to the obvious start. Climb the scrubbed-off slab past various cracks to a bolt belay. CDs to 2" (.9). Climb up, move right through small trees and negotiate a tricky slab. Continue more easily to a belay below a steepening bulge (.9). Traverse right from here until it is possible to go directly up to trees. A fine pitch (.8). Scramble up 10m, then walk left from here for 40m to the base of *Diedre*. An alternative, but harder last pitch (*Sorry Joe,* 10c) goes out left then up to trees. All pitches but the first are bolt-protected.

LOWER APRON

Slab Alley Trail

Thrash

The South Apron

These are the climbs best accessed from a trail approach at the south end of the Apron (page 233, photo on page 235).

The Chacha Crack　　13a+2pa　　*235*　　12m
Andrew Boyd Sept 1998
A left-leaning hand traverse in an easy-to-see diagonal crack on the wall below the wooden hydro towers. Chains at the top. Bushwack in from the highway.

The Groove　　.7　　*235*　　3-4p.
Mike Wisnicki Arnold Shives 1963
This is the large low-angle groove that cuts left to right at the lower right side of the Apron—easy to see from the Highway. It joins in with *Slab Alley*.

Happy Trails　●　☺　　11b　　*235*　　2p.
Gordie Smaill and others c. 1974   FFA Peter Croft Joe Buszowski Tami Knight 1979
Part way up the lower part of *The Groove*, head out right aiming for a distinct roof out of a large alcove. That's it.

Slab Alley　**　　.9　　*235, 239*　　6p.
Jim Baldwin Tony Cousins 1961   FFA: unknown
A pleasant but much neglected climb, which for the most part is considerably easier than 5.9. There are two approaches. The most popular is via the long, easy traverse across from *Banana Peel*. For the better original start from the right, climb easily up the back of the open bay, and belay at a tree (.4). Traverse right, pull steeply over the overlap and then go back left to belay at the south end of the *Banana Peel* approach: a steep, un-Apron like pitch (.8) Climb up to where the slab bulges, move left up past bolts, then diagonally right to belay (.9) [the steep section above can be climbed direct at 5.10d]. Go left on easier climbing to gain the unusually deep water runnels which are a nice feature of this climb. Continue easily along delightful water worn solution grooves.

Mobius Variation　　10a　　*239*　　(35m)
Dick Mitten Carl Austrom 1976
A bold direct start to *Slab Alley*. From the overlap above the open bay, climb straight up to rejoin on the right of the bulge (10a). Continue up and right, eventually joining *Slab Alley* (.9). Runout.

Pineapple Peel　*　　.8　　*239*　　(4p.)
Terry Rollerson Frank Baumann 1969
A good start to *Banana Peel*. Take the original start to *Slab Alley*, but pull steeply up the layback flake above the tree and out left to belay (.8). Gain a higher fault, then climb open slabs, joining a groove line that leads up to a tree ledge, 2 pitches (.8). Continue easily to join *Banana Peel* at its final tree ledge (.4).

Between Heaven And Earth　●　　11c　　*x*　　40m
Tom Clark Tiemo Brand Sept 1993
An unusual climb on the descent trail. In the woods, 40m above the descent trail's entry onto the talus, a distinctive, dark wall on the left is split horizontally by a long groove underneath a 2-3m roof. This groove provides a deceptively hard and varied climb. Start a little uphill from the foot and climb past 3 FP to the end of the groove and easier face climbing. Take small CDs and nuts.

The Central Apron — South of Diedre

Hike up the main trail that leads up out of the parking lot (page 233).

Banana Peel ****** .8 _239_ 7p.

Dan Tate Barry Hagen July 1965

An excellent moderate climb with few difficulties and much variety, this route sees less traffic than it deserves. When the lineups are too much on _Diedre_, head this way. Take the Apron centre trail to the foot of _Diedre_. Pad up the short first pitch and trend out right to a tree belay (.6). Traverse easily right along a horizontal fault for almost 100m to a birch tree, just 10m below the upper horizontal fault. Stem off the tree and pad up to the upper fault (.6). Climb up leftwards across rounded waves, using delightful small pockets [crux] to the base of a short corner and FP below a tree ledge (.8). Move up left into a groove, belay at the last tree (4th). Up a few metres, then go right across the open slab to good flakes—runout. Trend back left across the slab to a tree island (.6). Easier climbing up pleasant flakes leads in 2 pitches to Broadway (.4). Note that halfway along the traverse to the start, it is possible to climb an excellent 5.8 pitch [but no pro], trending right up vague scoops to the upper fault, and on to the base of the waves pitch.

Sparrow ****** .9 _239_ 7p.

Terry Rollerson G.Loset 1970

A long-time Apron classic that offers a considerable amount of varied and interesting climbing. Start as for _Diedre_ up the short slab. Climb up rightwards through depressions to belay at a higher horizontal fault (.8). Climb past a tricky bulge, then easier terrain leads left then back right to a big tree island (.9). This pitch can be climbed more directly above the bulge, but with little protection _(Slim Pickins 5.10b Tim Auger Gordie Smaill 1970)_. Scramble down to a thin crack splitting the slab on the right. Climb it and a short slab to another tree ledge (.9). From the left end of the ledge, follow a line of weakness trending up right to belay at a small corner (.8). Move left past a curving flake and straight up to the base of a corner leading to Broadway (.8). Climb it a short distance, then step out right and follow the slab to the top (.8). Take wires and CDs to 2".

Black Bug's Blood 10c _239_ (4p.)

Peter Croft Richard Suddaby 1977

Start from _Banana Peel_ and climb to the large overlap right of _Sparrow_, joining that route at the thin crack pitch (10c). Follow _Sparrow_ for 2 pitches, then finish directly up two more pitches of unprotected 5.9 left of _Banana Peel_.

Sickle ***** .9 _239_ (5p.)

Bob Woodsworth Ashlyn Armour-Brown 1962

From the top of the second pitch of _Diedre_ go right, up a right-leaning corner system to its top (.7). A tricky bulge above gains a large tree ledge (.9). From the left end of this ledge, climb two or three more pitches to Broadway (.6). Better climbing is obtained by padding up _The Stirling Moss Variation (Gordie Smaill Tim Auger 1970)_ from the right end of the tree ledge [runout] to join _Sparrow_ for the final pitches (.8).

**CHIEF
APRON**

White Lightning ** 10c (5p.)

Gordie Smaill Steve Sutton Paul Piro 1973   Direct finish Ed Spat Dean Hart Sept 1990

A revered classic and a hard route in its day. Start up *Diedre* and climb 3 pitches to the base of the long dihedral. Climb the slab on the right and belay by a flake (.9). Surmount the overlap above. Thin edging leads up to a ledge with a lone pine tree. This well protected pitch has seen a great many falls and much cussing over the years (10b). Head back out left, weaving through the bulges, moving back right into the prominent dihedral (10c). These two pitches are best combined into one. The wide arete above gives a fine direct finish (.9). Alternatively, traverse into *Diedre* at 5.9: no protection, or go right and finish up Sickle for an easier exit.

Wildebeeste 10d (45m)

Peter Croft Tami Knight 1978

From *Sickle*, climb straight up to *White Lightning*, then hook right to cross the overlap and end at the trees above.

Diedre *** .8 7p.

Jim Baldwin Jim Sinclair (much aid) July 1962   FFA Bob Woodsworth Monty Lasserre 1963

The most popular climb on the Apron, this lovely dihedral line gives a highly enjoyable climb, but is subject to heavy overcrowding and lineups, unless you're willing to climb at night or in the rain. Pad easily up the first short slab and belay beside a large birch tree (.6). Move left, then up a short open groove, to a large slabby alcove and belay (.7). Step up to the left, and across to the base of the main dihedral (.6). Two very fine sustained pitches of well protected laybacking lead to a belay on the right of a small roof (.8, .8). Step into the upper, more open dihedral (sometimes wet) and continue (.6). Easier climbing follows, but a sting in the tail gives a brief struggle just below Broadway (.8).

Diedre Direct * .9 (30m)

Dick Mitten, Carl Austrom 1976

Climbs very directly to the base of the long dihedral on *Diedre*. From the top of the first pitch of *Diedre*, traverse left 20m to a single tree. Climb directly up from there to the base of the main corner system. One bolt for protection.

Straight Up * .9 (40m)

Carl Austrom Dick Mitten 1975

An equally bold twin to *Diedre Direct*, climbed long before the days of sticky rubber. Climb the open friction slab right of the second pitch of *Diedre*, to rejoin that climb at the slabby alcove (.9).

When Mount Garibaldi was first climbed in 1907, the party of six men walked in from Howe Sound, a two-week round trip.

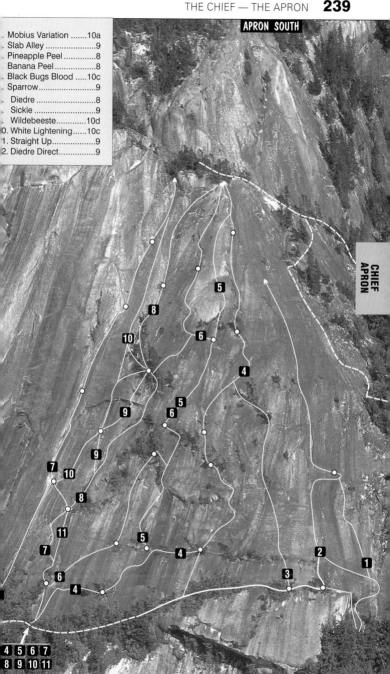

APRON SOUTH

CHIEF
APRON

The Central Apron — North of Diedre

These climbs are accessed from the main trail that leads up out of the parking lot (page 233).

Bloodlust Direct ******   11a   _**243**_   6p.
p1,2 Dick Mitten Carl Austrom 1975   FA p3, Scott Flavelle Dave Lane 1976
Find some old EBs to enjoy the full no-sticky-rubber adventure of this bold and visionary climb, which as described also combines two older routes. Climb the first pitch of _Dream On_ (10c) or traverse across from _Diedre_, to a single tree at the base of the long smooth slab left just of _Diedre_. Three very direct pitches lead to a point where it is possible to move right into _Diedre_ mid way up the dihedral (11a, 10d, 11a). The 3rd pitch is the original _Bloodlust_ (_Gordie Smaill Eric Weinstein 1975_), which started out from _Diedre_ at that point. Continue on _Bandwagon_ (_Jack Bradshaw Garret Gardner 1971_) up vague cracks for a pitch (.9). Continue padding to join _Diedre_ near the top (.8).

Dancing In The Light *******½ 11b   _**243**_   6p.
Dave Jones Don Serl (Alts) 1988
An outstanding climb offering pitch after pitch of superb friction, up a very direct line on the prominent white streak left of _Diedre_. Runouts between bolts, although not excessive, are stretched enough to ensure a healthy dose of respect for life. Start from the rocky terrace at the top of the first pitch of _Dream On_. Pull out right over a bulge and climb directly up to belay bolts (10a). Three more pitches of the same thin padding lead to the alcove below the crux pitch of _Dream On_ (10b - 11a - 10d). Straight up out of the alcove (a small wire is useful), and forge on to a bolt belay (11b+). An easier pitch follows (.9), and a final stroll off to Broadway. One to remember.

Firewalk ******   11c   _**243**_   (5p.)
p1, p2 Peter Croft Randy Atkinson 1978   FA p3, p4 Dave Jones Don Serl 1990
Left of the first pitch of _Dancing In The Light_ is a mossy, grass filled groove. _Firewalk_ takes the cleaned streak to its left. Climb the first pitch of _Dream On_. From the rocky terrace climb up in 2 pitches to the righthand side of the overlap below the looming headwall (10a - 10d). Cross the overlap and enter a wide scoop. Follow it, trending left to a belay at the junction with _Dream On_ (11b). Continue up the same line to join _Dirty Little White Boys_, move right and belay (11c).

Dream On *******½   12a   _**243**_   7p.
Scott Flavelle Carl Austrom et al. (1pa) 1976 to 1981 FFA: Scott Flavelle Dean Hart 1984
An inspiring climb up the line of least resistance that cleverly breaches the daunting headwall between _Diedre_ and _Unfinished_. The final 2 pitches can be avoided by finishing up _Dancing In The Light,_ reducing the grade to 11b. Start as for _Snake_, then go easily up to a good ledge on the right. A long pitch leads to the rocky terrace (10c). From its left edge, a flake leads to a bulge and belay (10a). Step left, and up to an overlap (10d). Cross it to a depression. Follow the natural line rightward then straight up to a large alcove (11b-11a). Climb out of the alcove trending left to the centre of the wall, up past a very thin section (12a). One more lead (.9). Dream on.

Dream Weaver   **   10c   _243_   (3p.)

p1 Bob McGowan M.Smelser 1977   p2 p3 Dave Jones Bill Betts Paul Cournoyer July 1991

Good and sustained. Start as for *Snake*, but climb up to the left of *Dream On* to the rocky terrace (10c). Climb up just left of *Firewalk* to belay at the bulge on *Dream On* (10c). Turn the bulge on the right and go straight up to the overlap belay. (10c).

Dirty Little White Boys   ** 12a   _243_   (6p.)

Rolf Rybak Ivan Christiansen Dave Jones (various) 1986 - 91

A nebulous line between the *Dream On* wall and *Unfinished Symphony* becoming progressively harder with each pitch. Start as for *Snake*, then climb the obvious white streak in 2 pitches to reach a large tree island (10a - 10b). Move up to the left and climb 2 pitches up the narrow slab right of the corners, to a tree ledge below the open upper corners of *Unfinished* (10b-10c). Climb the slab towards a flake pinnacle and belay (11c). Trend rightwards about 15m, then back up left to belay (11b). Continue straight up for another 15m, sustained and steep (11c). Easier ground leads right into *Dream On* (10c).

Unfinished Symphony   *** 11b   _243_   8p.

p1-3 Jim Baldwin Hamish Mutch 1962   FA complete Fred Beckey Jim Sinclair 1966
FFA: p2-5 Kevin McLane Einar Hanson Aug 1973   FFA complete Peter Croft Tami Knight 1979

The striking line up the long dihedrals in the centre of the Apron. The lower pitches are somewhat scruffy, so the best approach is via the lower pitches of *Dream On* or *Anxiety State*. Follow the first 2 pitches of *Snake* to the top of the initial corner (.7 - .8). Pull right around the overhang, to a tree belay beyond a second roof (.9). Continue to the final tree ledge (10a). Up into the upper corners and stiffer climbing to a sling belay (10d). More of the same good stuff to belay below the final small roofs (10d). Pull out past the roofs and pad with more difficulty up to a belay in a corner (11b). Easy to the top.

Anxiety State   *   10d   _243_   (5p.)

Robin Barley Carl Austrom 1977

A good and varied climb, taking in some of the best pitches on the Apron. Start up *Snake*, and climb *Dirty Little White Boys* [or move right near the top of the first pitch of *Snake*] to the large tree island (10a - 10b). Follow a moderate corner crack to belay at its top (.7). Enter the bigger corner above, and exit left into a small groove. Up this, and across to the tree ledge (.9). Climb the next pitch of *Unfinished*. (10d). Move boldly left across the wall at a break to belay on the arete (10d). A long rising traverse is made, then straight up, moving left to finish. A fine pitch (.9).

Dream State   ***   10d   _243_   7p.

Dean Hart Bruce McDonald 1986

A fine combination, very sustained at mid-5.10, offering the easiest line up the central part of The Apron. Long pitches. Follow *Dream On* until a traverse above the overlap on pitch 4 leads to the narrow tree ledge on *Unfinished*... Continue upwards, finishing as for *Anxiety State*.

Dream Symphony   ***½ 11b   _243_   7p.

Another superb combination climb. Above the overlap on pitch 4 of *Dream On*, traverse left to *Unfinished Symphony* and continue up that route.

CHIEF APRON

APRON NORTH

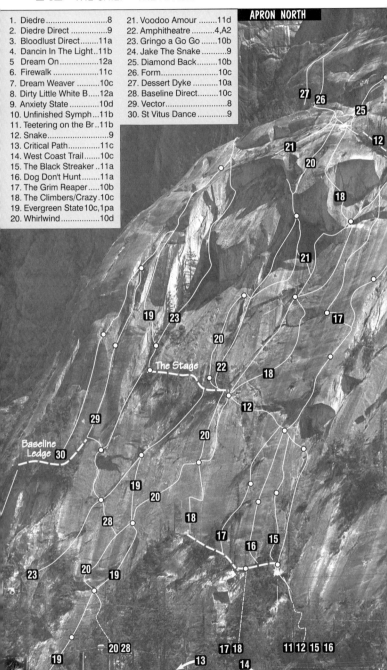

The Stage

Baseline
Ledge

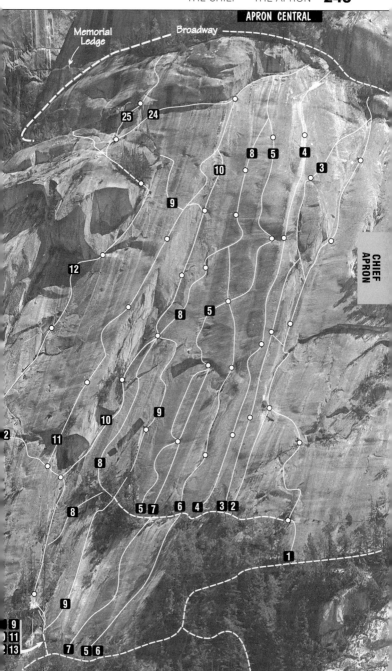

APRON CENTRAL

Memorial Ledge

Broadway

CHIEF APRON

25 24

8 5 4

10 3

9

12

8 5

10 9

2

11

8

8 5 7 6 4 3 2

1

9

9
11
13

7 5 6

APRON NORTH

Not all climbs are shown on this topo.

Baseline Ledge

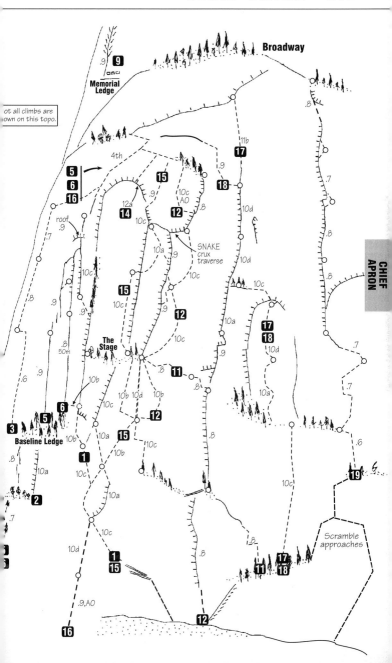

Broadway

.9 **9**

Memorial
Ledge

ot all climbs are
own on this topo.

4th

5
6
16

15

roof
.9

11b

17

18

10c
A0

.8

10d

12a
14
10c

.7

15

10a

SNAKE
crux
traverse

10d

.8

.9

10d

15

10c

.8

.9

.9

10c

.8

.9

.8

10c

12

.9

The
Stage

.8

10a

17
18

10a

11

10d

.8

50m

10b

.9

.6

10b 10d 10b

10c

12

10a

.8

.9

.7

6

10b

5

10c

15

3

10a

10c

Baseline Ledge

10b

1

.8

.8

.7

10a

2

10c

10a

.8

19

10d

1
15

10c

.8

10c

Scramble
approaches

11 **17**
18

.9,A0

16

12

CHIEF
APRON

The North Apron

These climbs are accessed from the main trail that leads up out of the parking lot (page 234).

Teetering On The Brink Of Madness   **   11b   _242_   (4p.)
Carl Austrom Bruce MacDonald Jean McRae 1984

This brilliant and bold line takes the striking left edge of the *Unfinished...* corner system. Best approached via a short flakey corner above the trail (.8), followed by *The Black Streaker* (11a). Otherwise climb the first 2 pitches of *Snake*. At the start of the traverse move up to the tree above and belay in the long crack (.9). Move on up more difficult padding, first to the left, then back right again to the edge (10d). Stay close to the arete for another pitch (11a). Move up, then right along a ramp and up to a belay (10d). Move up right to join *Unfinished...* for the final pitch (11b). Lurch off along Broadway.

Snake   ***   .9   _242_   7p
R.Willmott P.Botta (much aid) July 1962

A Squamish golden oldie, this is one of the most popular climbs on the Apron when it's dry, winding a cunning route through steep slabs and big overhangs. Unfortunately, it is rather slow to dry after prolonged rain, especially the crux pitch. Take the left fork trail at the top of the stepped log, and walk a short distance to two large dead cedar trees. Scramble up a well worn groove on the right for 30m to a break in the slab above. (Or climb the slabby .8 corner left of the ramp). From the flat ledge at the top of the groove climb a short wall across to ledges on the left. Belay at the base of the long, wide corner above (.7). Climb the corner to belay at large flakes below a roof (.8). Go left across a short steep wall onto the arete and a stance. Short but sweet (.8). Traverse leftwards to the base of a second corner system. A bit tense near the end (.9). Climb the open corner to a short delicate section below a belay ledge (.9). The crux pitch follows. Up the wide groove above to the overhangs, and then traverse right with difficulty past a small tree and gain a large flat ledge. A very fine pitch (.9). Continue laybacking up the corner-flake above to trees on the left (.8). From the highest point of the trees, scramble up leftwards to join Broadway. Gear to 3".

The Black Streaker   **   11a   #±6   _242_   **SPORT**   (2p.)
Robin Barley Sept 1987

This is the arete left of the second pitch of *Snake*. Climb the first pitch of *Snake*, and just below the belay ledge, go out left a few metres and belay. Climb a slim, easy groove, then past 3 bolts to belay (10c). Continue on to anchors on the *Snake* traverse (#±6, 11a). Can be done in one long pitch.

That Dog Don't Hunt   **   11a   #9   _242_   **SPORT**   (2p.)
Richard Davis Karl Ritter 1997

A parallel climb just left of *Black Streaker*. Exit left out of the first easy pitch of *Snake* and belay by the skinned log bridging the top of the first pitch of *Climbers Must Be Crazy*. Step up onto the slab and climb to anchors (#6, 10c) Continue to *Snake* Traverse (#9, 11a). Can be done in one long pitch.

Whirlwind   **   10d   242   7p

Colin Moorhead Will Dorling Nick Watts April 29 1995

This excellent climb starts north of *Snake* and winds its way up to Broadway via *Voodoo Amour*. On the trail 25m north of *Snake,* step up onto 2 downed cedars at the base of the cliff, walk along them and scramble up the scrubby ramp beyond to the foot of the route. Make a 3rd-class traverse across to the top of the 2nd pitch of *Evergreen State*. Climb left over a bulge and continue, rejoining *EState* and belay (10c). Make a rising traverse rightward over the exposed slab to join *The Climbers Must Be Crazy* (10b). Climb a fine direct pitch up to the tree ledge of the Stage (10d), or more sketchy climbing on the wall to the left *[Benetier Bypass]* at 10b. Above the Stage, climb the arete (10c). Move right over a corner and across the slab, a bit sketchy, to join *Voodoo Amour*. Belay below the steep corner crack (.9). Climb the corner to reach the slab above (10c). Climb the slab above to easier ground (.9). Take 10 draws, a light rack with some hand to fist-size CUs for the *Voodoo Amour* crack.

Baseline Direct   **   10c   #8   242   **SPORT**+   3p.

Will Dorling Nick Watts July 1995

A good, sustained link between *Whirlwind* and the Baseline ledge. At the 7th [?] bolt on pitch 1 of *Whirlwind*, move left and up to a large belay ledge (10c). Continue directly up the face, turning a roof on the left to another ledge. Watch for rope drag (10b). Move up, then make an airy traverse left to the base of *Vector* [gear] at the right-hand end of Baseline (10b). 10 draws, one 2½" CU.

The Grim Reaper   *   10b   242   6p.

Gordie Smaill Neil Bennet 1970

This famous route, first climbed in stiff soled boots, is one of the great legends of Squamish. Its fearsome reputation for the huge runout on the crux pitch, done on-sight, remains undiminished. Gain the start via the first pitch of *The Climbers Must Be Crazy*, and step up the tree ramp on the left for 5m. Climb a thin crack and flake to a tree, continue up the face above past a bolt to belay at a tree (10b). An easier pitch follows up a flake crack to join the *Snake* traverse (.9). Continue to the top of the crack on *Teetering...* then traverse left to a small tree under an overlap (10b). Go over the overlap to gain a series of shallow scoops leading up right to eventually move left to the belay ledge on *Snake*. A tad runout... (10b). Continue up the last pitch of *Snake* (.8). This route offers excellent climbing and clever route finding. Modern sticky shoes will likely dull the Reaper's blade even more.

The Climbers Must Be Crazy   ** 10c+2pa 242   6p.

Nick Barley Robin Barley (Alts) Aug 1987

A good climb that takes a direct line to the main dihedral on *Snake*, then climbs the slab on the right, near *Grim Reaper*. Climb the large 5.8 corner left of the start of *Snake* [the one with the long fallen log spanning its top], moving left from the log up a tree ramp to the base of a long open slab. Climb in 2 pitches to the main corner on *Snake* (10c, 10b). Move out right across the slab, then straight up and back left to belay on *Snake* (10c). Go out right and then climb direct to the belay at the end of the traverse pitch on *Snake* (10c). Start up the last pitch of *Snake*, then pull out left up a wall to an overhanging scoop, climb its left wall, then easy slabs above (10c+2pa).

CHIEF
APRON

Evergreen State   *   11c   (10c+1pa)   *242*   9p.
Robin Barley Peter Croft Randy Atkinson (1pa) 1978 FFA unknown
A long, worthwhile route from the lowest point of the Apron. Climb a greasy crack (.9+1pa or 11c). Three more sustained pitches lead directly to a corner which gives access to the Stage (10d) (10a) (10a) (10c). Climb a bushy pitch leftward, then break out left on fragile flakes to a prominent white corner (9). Two more pitches lead to easy ground (10c) (.9).

Amphitheatre   ●   .4 A2   *242*   (3p.)
Glenn Woodsworth Tim Ellis Oct 1965
At the point where *Evergreen State* moves out left on the pitch above the Stage ledge, stay in the main corner and belay below the roof above. Another pitch (aid) leads through the roof to easy terrain above.

Voodoo Amour   **   12a   *242*   (3p.)
p1 p3 Dean Hart Randy Atkinson Ed Spat Sept 1990   FA: p2 Gordie Smaill Vic Coloumb 1977
A short climb with oddly enough, two roof cracks. Climb *Snake* to the start of the crux pitch. Halfway up, go out left across a slab and belay below a very steep corner crack (10a). Handjam up this crack into a deep alcove above (*Gringo-a-go-go*), making aquaintance with an even steeper crack (10c). Climb this fine roof crack out of the alcove to easy ground above (12a).

The West Coast Trail   ●   10c   *242*   15m
Peter Croft and others 1979
A single long-overgrown crack at the trailside on the way to *Snake*.

Critical Path   ●   11c   *242*   45m
Dave Jones Don Serl Sept 1987
A single pitch 30m left of the start of *Snake*. Step off two windblown trees 5m left of a prominent black streak, and climb the steep slab above to the tree ledge.

Gringo-A-Go-Go   10c   *242*   5p.
Hamish Mutch G.Dunham B.McKnight 1963 FFA: Gordie Smaill Vic Coloumb 1977
An old and bushy route largely superceded by more modern climbs. From the tree ledge below the Baseline, at the same level as the clean .8 corner, go diagonally up right to join *Evergreen State*, and to the Stage in 2 pitches (.8 - 10a). Follow the bushy corner system above, to join *Voodour Amour*. Climb the overhanging crack (10c) and finish as for *Whirlwind* to easy ground (.9).

■■■■ **CLIMBS OFF BASELINE LEDGE**   ■■■■■■■

The following climbs begin off Baseline Ledge, a small tree ledge below several prominent cracklines running up the north buttress of The Apron. See the approach for the northern Apron, page 234.

Vector   **   .9   *242*   2p.
Glenn Woodsworth R.Woodsworth 1964 FFA: unknown
RETROSCRUBBED: *Will Dorling 1996*
An excellent climb above Baseline—the main pitch is one of the best in Squamish of its grade, a stellar 50m of handjamming, some fist, some offwidth, 4 or 5 pieces 3"- 4" to a ledge (.9). Continue to join *St. Vitus' Dance* (.9).

St. Vitus' Dance   ***   .9   <u>242</u>   4p.

Robin Barley Gordie Smaill 1974

A fine climb which offers 3 sustained pitches of hand jamming. Take some larger CDs and nuts. Scramble up steeply to the Baseline ledge, 4th class at first, then some 5.8. Climb the obvious crack splitting the fine wall above, belay in a small scoop at its top (.9). Trend up right, crossing from crack to crack, belay on a ledge above a corner (.9). Climb the short sharp roof crack on the right to easy ground (.9). Scramble on to Broadway.

St. Vitus' Dance Direct Start   *   10a   <u>242</u>   22m

Robin Barley Peter Shackleton 1986

A good pitch that gives a direct start up the corner below the Baseline (10a).

South Arete   .8   x   2p.

Fred Beckey Hank Mather Don Claunch 1959   FFA: unknown

Climb the green crackline left of *St.Vitus' Dance* in 2 dirty pitches to easy ground below Broadway.

Calculus Crack   **   .8   <u>245</u>   3p.

Fred Beckey D.Beckstead Oct 1966

At the far left side of the Apron is a fine crackline starting from the left side of Baseline. Three nice pitches (5.6, 5.8, 5.7), then easier climbing to Broadway.

▉ *CLIMBS BELOW BROADWAY* ▉

The following 4 climbs are short routes which are high on the Apron below Broadway and require climbing other routes to get there.

Dessert Dyke   *   10a   <u>242</u>   30m

Nicholas Watts Will Dorling May 3 1994

An excellent finish to *Snake* or *St. Vitus' Dance* up a basalt dyke immediately underneath the Baldwin Memorial Ledge. Steep at first to a small bush on the left, then friction and edges to a bolt station. A 1" CD will be useful.

Form   10c   <u>242</u>   30m

Will Dorling Nicholas Watts   Sept 14 1994

A harder alternative to *Dessert Dyke*. Start 6m to the right and join *Dessert Dyke* at the final bolt.

Diamond Back   **   10b   <u>242</u>   2p.

Dave Jones Don Serl Sept 1987

This climb is a possible direct finish to *Snake* for those so inclined. From the left end of the trees at the top of *Snake*, go up to a pine tree beside large blocks. Follow the thin slanting cracks above up rightwards to Broadway. Take many small wires.

Jake-The-Snake   .9   <u>243</u>   25m

Tom Clark Linda Nordick Aug 1993

From the last belay on *Snake*, go up left from the tree ledge and onto the open slab. Head easily up right to the base of a large right-facing layback corner which leads to the impressive undercling traverse to the top of *Unfinished Symphony*. Take a 3" CD for near the end.

The Apron — Climbs Above Broadway

A welcome bonus for many climbers on reaching Broadway is the opportunity to climb one of the fine routes on this 100m slab.

Getting there... Walk up, or climb a route on the Apron.

Pig Dogs On Parade   ***   .8   #3   2p.
D.Whelan P.Simmons July 1980
The righthand scrubbed line curving around in 2 pitches of 5.8, joining into *A Question Of Balanc*e on pitch 2.

Dances With Pigs   **   10a   #4   (50m)
Mitch Thornton Nola Stewart April 26 1995
A fine top pitch to *Pig Dogs On Parade* up the wide arete. This climb makes a good start to the *Squamish Buttress* with easy fifth into the trees above.

A Question Of Balance   ***   .9   #3   2p.
Anders Ourom Paul Peart 1977
A very popular climb. Fine padding for two sustained pitches. A head spinning run-out on the first pitch tests your self-worth as a climber (.9). A new, longer finish to pitch 2 heads up right to the top of *Dances With Pigs* (.8).

Bran Flakes   *   10a   #1   2p.
Peter Croft Tami Knight Anders Ourom 1978
A slightly harder and bolder climb. Two pitches (10a - .9).

Eric's Route   *   10a   #2   40m
Eric Weinstein Gordie Smaill 1975
A poorly protected route stretching up to *Granville Street* in one lead.

Granville Street   .6   4p.
Jim Baldwin Ken Baker 1961
This long groove that defines the left side of the main slab is the standard descent, rappelling off trees (chains needed!) or downclimbing. Move up into the groove from the left, 5.6 friction, and an exit is possible past a bolt, some 5.8 to reach the forest on the *Squamish Buttress*.

Boobie   *   10c   #2   2p.
N.Humphries S.Lynn 1977
A nebulous line left of *Granville Street*. Start by the first tree.

John 3:16   **   10c   #±5   50m
S St. Louis M.Davis 1987
Excellent climbing. Start up *Boomstick..,* go right into a scoop, pray for some help, and continue up left past bolts.

Boomstick Crack   *   .4   2p.
Jim Baldwin Jim Sinclair P.Neilson 1961
A hard start to a nice flake, otherwise the easiest climb off Broadway.

Boomerang   11a   *x*   30m
Mark Aisbett John Ohler June 1989
About 50m north of the top of *Diedre*, at a level section on the trail, is a curious, almost circular flake recess in the wall just above the trail. Climb the left side of this feature and up the face above, trending leftwards.

Afterthought   *   10d   <u>254</u>   27m
Peter Charak H.Bauer Jack Bryant 1980
RECLEANED: Jason Camp Maurice Brennikmeijer Angie Pollon August 1998
The obvious thin handcrack 4m left of *Boomerang*.

> *The crackline north of Afterthought just right of Memorial Ledge is believed to have been climbed free, but little information is known. It was top-roped in 1992 (Andy Cairns), at 10c with 2pa, but appeared to have been climbed previously. At the northernmost end of Broadway, just above the trail is a beautiful balcony . There are memorial plaques here to Jim Baldwin, Andy Burnham and Grace Wong, who all died in climbing accidents.*

Memorial Crack   *   .9   <u>254</u>   35m
Fred Beckey Hank Mather Don Claunch 1959 (FFA unknown)
Well worthy of attention for anyone climbing the *Squamish Buttress* or completing *Snake* or *St. Vitus' Dance* with energy to spare. Start from the left side of Memorial Ledge at the north end of Broadway and climb a corner up the headwall to the forest above.

> *Descent: Just south of the top of Memorial Crack, on open bedrock is a rap station–35m down to Broadway. Further south, and a short scramble down, is a 27m rappel down Afterthought. See page 254.*

CHIEF APRON

UPPER APRON

Squamish Buttress

Broadway

The Apron — Squamish Buttress

The Squamish Buttress	***½	10c	<u>255</u>	(7p.)
Cornered Rat ● ☺		11b	<u>255</u>	(18m)
Heatwave ***		12a	<u>255</u>	(45m)

Buttress: *Fred Beckey Hank Mather Don Claunch 1959   FFA: Peter Charak Joe Turley 1979*
Cornered Rat: *Peter Croft Richard Suddaby 1979*
Heatwave: *Hamish Fraser Greg Foweraker John Rosholt Val Fraser (Kris Wild) Aug 1998*

This is one of the classic climbs of Squamish. Generally of moderate difficulty and quality, but the fine crux pitch and the highly enjoyable position of the climb make it very popular. Although it is considered a "full-day" route, it can be shortened into a 2-4 hour climb car-to-summit by hiking up to Broadway, and climbing one of the routes on the Upper Apron.

Arguably, the best way to reach the upper buttress is via *Rock On* [page 256], otherwise climb any of the routes on the Apron that lead to Broadway. From there take any route to reach the large forested area. Wind upward on a trail, trending right near the end onto the start of Vulcan's Artery, and the start of the upper wall just as the trail narrows. Start up through blocky roofs, a short section of 5.9 face past a bolt, then trend up left over easier ground towards the crest. Head back right up 3rd class terrain to grooves and ramps and a terraced area overlooking the gully. A steepish crack leads up to easier ground on the left and a huge terrace at the base of an elegant headwall. It is split by two corners on the left and three long cracks to the right. Take the right-hand of the two corners, a fine 25m crux pitch that sucks up nuts well and is easier than it appears. It can easily be aided on wires. The next pitch zig-zags across the gully wall, left, then back right, then left again to easy ground. Walk up easy slabs to the summit.

Cornered Rat. The shorter corner left of the crux pitch of the *Buttress*...

Heatwave. Right of the crux pitch on the *Buttress* are three long cracks. This is the central one, and a fine pitch. Take many small CDs, up to 2.5"

Pan Tease ***	10c	<u>255</u>	5p.
Pan Tease Upper **	11c+ A0	<u>255</u>	(2p.)

Marc Gandy and many friends 1998

An intriguing route that is a good alternative to the *Squamish Buttress*. The climb trends up rightward from the forested shoulder and after five sustained pitches at 5.10 joins the big terrace on the *Buttress*. An exposed and exciting traverse from here (Upper Pan Tease) leads out right to the rim of the Pan Granitic Wall. Several points of fixed aid and 11c.

Kashmir *	11c	#10	<u>254</u>	**SPORT** (28m)

Jola Sandford Jim Sandford   Feb 8th 1995

Kashmir Wall is the triangular white wall easily visible two-thirds of the way up the South Gully below the top part of the Squamish Buttress. Near the top of the forest, pick up a trail which leads left to the base. This is an interesting and varied pitch: liebacking, face and arete climbing, and even a crack or two. One 55m rope will get you up and down. Gear is needed to finish *The Buttress*, otherwise hike back down to Broadway and rappel off.

CHIEF
APRON

SQUAMISH BUTTRESS — PAN TEASE

The last moves to the summit 5.8

See Inset

Kashmir Wall

Easy scramble into South Gully

35m rap

27m rap

Broadway

From the Upper Apron

Looking down on the last pitch

Terrace

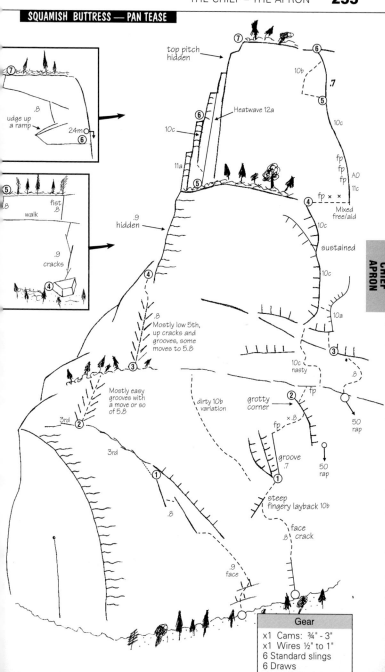

SQUAMISH BUTTRESS — PAN TEASE

top pitch hidden

Heatwave 12a

10b

.7

10c

10c

fp
fp
fp   A0

11a

fp × ×   11c

Mixed free/aid

.8
udge up a ramp

24m

10c

sustained

.9 hidden

10c

10a

.8
Mostly low 5th, up cracks and grooves, some moves to 5.8

fist .8
walk

.9 cracks

10c nasty

.8

.8

Mostly easy grooves with a move or so of 5.8

dirty 10b variation

grotty corner

fp

50 rap

3rd

fp ×.8

3rd

groove .7

50 rap

.8

steep fingery layback 10b

.9 face

face crack .8

Gear
x1 Cams: ¾" - 3"
x1 Wires ½" to 1"
6 Standard slings
6 Draws

CHIEF APRON

South Gully — Rock On

At its northern end, The Apron drops off dramatically into the great chasm of the South Gully. The climbs are divided into three areas, the left (north) side, known as the Opal Wall, the right (south) side with the superb 5-pitch *Rock On*, and the higher walls on the southwest side of the Centre Chief.

Getting there... Take the trail to the South Gully (page 234). 10mins.

The Terror   .8 A2   x   2p.
Hamish Mutch Tim Auger November 1965
A short roof pitch climb about 100m below *Rock On.* Knifeblades.

Where The River Bends   *10d   (10a)   x   2p.
Will Dorling Nick Watts June 1997
An interesting dyke climb, useful as a warm-up for *Rock On*. Start down right of *Rock On*, and climb a dyke to a fault. Go left then up another dyke to belay bolts (10a). Move right, then go straight up the dyke above (10d).

Rock On   ***½   10a   5-6p.
p1-2-3 Steve.Loomer Dave Harris (aid) 1977 (may have been Bastille)
FFA p1 Peter Croft A.Johnson 1981
FFA continuous Bob Milward Jim Campbell July 1983
This classic climb threads a line up a series of impressive left-facing corner systems on the right wall of the South Gully, just at the point where it narrows. Difficulty rises as height is gained, with continuous hand and finger cracks, excellent rests and belays, several laybacks and a lot of fun corner-work. All the belays except the last are on gear. It is slow to dry, but many a climber has dealt with the crux in damp conditions (like pulling on gear).

    Start by climbing a stepped left facing corner for 40m to a belay (.8). Layback up a fine crack above and belay on a spacious ledge below a large arching chimney (.9). Grovel up the cracks in the back of it and on the left wall, exit left—possible belay—then traverse 8m left to a belay ledge at the foot of the final corner system (.9). One long pitch (or two 20-25m) leads up with increasing difficulty. The crux near the top can be damp, but such is life (10a). A short final pitch exits up left into the forest above the north end of Broadway (.8). To descend, hike south to either of two rappel stations above Broadway on the Apron. Rapping the route is possible [2 ropes], but messy if there are other climbers below. Better to descend via Broadway on the Apron.

Rock On Direct   ● ☺   10d   2p.
Bob Milward Bruce Kay 1983   FFA Jack Lewis Peter Hiltner Valerie Rosner July 83.
A variation that leaves and then rejoins *Rock On*, traversing out left at the start of pitch 2 into a long, parallel left-facing corner (10d). A short pitch then leads to the belay below the long final pitch (.9).

Bastille   .9   (30m)
Hamish Mutch Bob Woodsworth (much aid) May 1966
An old climb which followed what is now *Rock On* to the traverse on the third pitch. At that point, continue up under a huge chockstone to the top of a pinnacle—The Bastille. Rappel.

The Great Arch ** 13a 24m
Keith Reid 1994

A remarkable and very strenuous climb which goes part way up the huge arch system left of *Rock On* in the South Gully. Pull up a fixed line 10m left of *Rock On* to a belay ledge. The crack in the back of the corner slowly widens. Take a full range of gear from small wires to large CDs to a bolt station.

The South Gully .8 x many
Hank Mather Jim Archer (right fork) 1957   Ashley Armour-Brown Peter Crone (left fork) 1961

The South Gully is the most prominent of the 4 gullies on the Chief—easily seen from the highway—with several major chockstones blocking access to the upper gully. The first is climbed on the left at 5.8 and perhaps some aid moves; the second is 4th-class and the 3rd is bypassed by 4th-class ledges on the right, often muddy. The gully forks above. The left is 5.6 and loose, the right is 5.8 and loose [the joy of choices!], and leads to a 5.8 exit chimney. If you find an old leather belt up there it's mine, a back-off sling from a solo attempt in 1973. My pants stayed up.

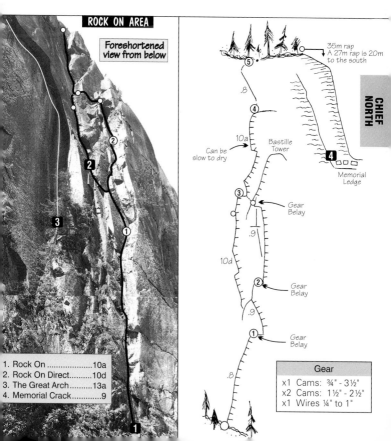

ROCK ON AREA

Foreshortened view from below

35m rap
A 27m rap is 20m to the south

CHIEF NORTH

.8

10a Bastille Tower
Can be slow to dry

Memorial Ledge

Gear Belay

.9

10d

Gear Belay

.9

Gear Belay

.8

1. Rock On 10a
2. Rock On Direct.........10d
3. The Great Arch.........13a
4. Memorial Crack.........9

Gear
x1 Cams: ¾" - 3½"
x2 Cams: 1½" - 2½"
x1 Wires ¼" to 1"

South Gully — The Opal

This is the dramatic wall in the South Gully, directly opposite *Rock On*. Entering the main gully, the lefthand wall looms in a smooth, mighty sweep of dark granite. This is it. An obvious series of overlapping ramps and corners signal the climbs. The most prominent is *Mercy Street*, comparable in character to the *Split Pillar*. However, it is the *Opal* which is the prima donna. Were it not for the dismal atmosphere in the gully when wet (which it often is), this crag would see a considerable amount of traffic.

Getting there... Take the trail to the South Gully (page 234). About ten stiff minutes from the car.

Bong King   *   11a   30m
Kirt Sellers Nick Jones Sept 12 1986
Start up the easy right side of a 5m flake, and go into the left hand corner groove. Follow it to a pedestal at its top. Rappel off.

The Opal   ***½   12d   (12a)   6p.
Nick Jones Phillip Wassenaer 1986.
FFA p1 p2 p3 Perry Beckham 1988
FFA p4 p5 p6 Andrew Boyd May 1998
No continous free ascent to date.
One of the most dramatic climbs on the Chief, up a series of right-facing corners leading to a smooth upper wall. The first 2 or 3 pitches make a fine climb in their own right. Take the same start as *Bong King*, but climb the central ramp, to a belay below the roof (11a). The ramp now becomes very narrow and exposed, the climbing technical and much harder. Flop onto a ledge at the top (12a). Step left and climb down, traversing across a ledge to a bolt station and rappel (11b). [The previous 2 pitches can be combined, and a rap-off is possible.] Hard face climbing above leads to a narrow ledge (12c\d). Climb directly above to a station (12a). Trend left, then back right to finish (11d). Take small to medium nuts and CDs and 10 draws. Rappel the route.

Mercy Street   ***   10b   2p.
Kirt Sellers Bill Noble 1986
This climb boasts a superb second pitch, comparable to the right side of the *Split Pillar*, but unfortunately it is the last climb to dry out here. Start as for *Bong King* or *Dude Lips* up to the main ramp. Belay at a small ledge (.8). Power up the remorseless layback corner above. A real blockbuster for its grade (10b).

Dude Lips   10c   12m
Phillip van Wassenaer Nick Jones Peter Cooper Sept 12 1986
Start 8m to the right up a steeper flake crack, which soon curves back into the main corner of *Mercy Street*. Belay and rappel out (10c).

THE OPAL

Gear
p1,2 med. CUs, nuts
p3 #5
p4 #10
p5 #3
p6 #8
Small CUs useful
on upper pitches.

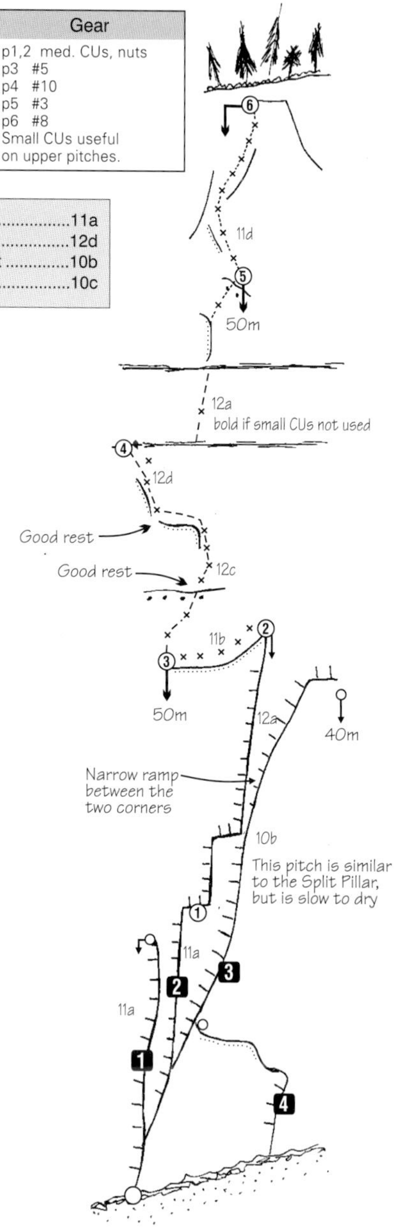

1. Bong King 11a
2. The Opal 12d
3. Mercy Street 10b
4. Dude Lips..................10c

⑥

11d

⑤
50m

12a
bold if small CUs not used

④
12d

Good rest →
Good rest → 12c

③   11b   ②
50m

12a

40m

Narrow ramp
between the
two corners

10b
This pitch is similar
to the Split Pillar,
but is slow to dry

① 11a

11a

■1 ■2 ■3

■4

posite Image
Rock On

Koyaanisqatsi ** 10c+4pa 5p.

Phillip van Wassenaer Nick Jones Sept 1991

An interesting but little-known climb which has seen several repeat ascents. Adventurous to say the least, but worth doing. Approach by traversing across from the point where the South Gully trail enters the bed of the gully: very bushy. Pull up on trees and a fixed line to reach the base of the rock. Walk left to a hump of rock. Start in the centre of the face, up a long easy pitch (.7+2pa). Pendulum off a tree past the first roof, into a left facing corner. Up it, and the face above to the top of a big flake system (.9). Low angle rock leads to a bulging slab and a major left leaning fault. Belay in a big alcove (10c). Stay on the face to the left of the big fault, following the line of least resistance. Traverse right into the main corner system below two roofs (10a). Undercling right to a high CD placement, and pendulum 10m into a prominent crack on the right. It widens slowly to the top (10c). Take a large CD, and get ready for long pitches.

To get off *Koyaanisqatsi*, hike 100m or so up to the right. The rappel station (at the top of *The Opal*) is just before a big cave fault. Three long rappels lead down into the South Gully.

OPAL WALL — KOYAANISQATSI

Rough trail

10c
1pa

10a

10c

.9

.7
2pa

THE
OPAL   ROCK
ON

KOYAANISQATSI   Rough
Trail

OPAL WALL FROM HIGHWAY 99

ROCK
ON

THE
OPAL

KOYAANISQATSI

South Gully — Upper Left Side

The three climbs below represent the cutting edge of Squamish esoterica–long, adventurous and deserted. Although they cover much bushy terrain, there is no doubt that there is plenty of good rockclimbing to be had too.

Getting there... Take the trail to the South Gully (page 234) for *Echelon* and *Amazon Slabs*. For *The Prow*, climb the *Squamish Buttress* and traverse into the gully at the top of the forested area.

Echelon .7 A2 <u>**270**</u> many
Dick Culbert Alice Purdy 1965
This long route up the full height of the Chief takes the big rambling wall of bushy ledges and steep slabs, high on the left side of the South Gully. Generally speaking, the route exits the South Gully near the 3rd chockstone, in the location of the south end of Caramba Terrace. When in doubt above this point, remember the words from Glenn Woodsworth's 1967 guide: "... the route traverses left on ledges until able to climb to the next ledge system above. Climbing is mostly class 4, with a few class 5 and aid moves. Many variations are possible". No need to hurry to beat the line-ups on a sunny weekend.

The Prow .9 A2 <u>**270**</u> many
Dick Culbert Bob Cuthbert May 1968
This huge left-facing corner system high up on the smooth walls at the top of the South Gully, easily noted by its jutting prow. Approach from the *Squamish Buttress* by walking into the gully at the top of the forested area below the upper buttress. Climb cracks and traverse ledges to gain height to reach a prominent corner which arches left to the top.

Amazon Slabs .7 A1 <u>**270**</u> many
Dave Harris Jeannine Caldbeck 1970
One of the least-known climbs on the Chief. Hike up to the top of Caramba Terrace close to the South Gully, or just climb the gully to reach the same point. Pick a line, any line you think you can get up, left of and roughly parallel to *Echelon* (if that's any help!), eventually reaching the middle summit of the Chief. This is a surprisingly big wall, with a lot of good rock pitches to offer between bush ledges and ramps.

CHIEF NORTH

> ***Name Story****: Joe's Dyke (5.7) at Raven's Castle has two meanings–take your pick. It was first climbed by Joe Turley, but not named until the early 1980s in honour of another Squamish Joe (there have been a few) who made a second "first ascent", and whose male psyche had just been tweaked as his girlfriend had left him for a woman.*

THE CHIEF IN 1920

The Skaomish C.
Squamish B.

The above photo of the Chief was taken in 1920 from Squamish town centre. Compared with the photo of today on the right, note how few trees there are on the Squamish Buttress above the Apron, Caramba Terrace, Amazon Slabs, and on the Angel's Crest. Other archival photos from that era at the Squamish Public Library indicate a similar tree cover in other areas on the Chief and the Squaw. This thin tree cover is also evident in some of Fred Beckey's photos of the 1960s, particularly *Northwest Passage*. The reason for today's heavier tree coverage on the Chief are speculative, but are most likely caused by climate change: things are getting warmer. Just imagine– all that vast expanse of open granite, while every winter the Chief would have been a frozen ice-palace.

The photo on the right is of Cleveland Avenue as it was in 1914, looking north toward Mount Garibaldi, and the Smoke Bluffs as they were before being logged. The restaurant is on the approximate site of the present-day post office, and the foreground bridge was over what was then an estuary slough. The building on the left is on the site of the present-day Chieftain Hotel.

Historial photos courtesy Squamish Public Library Archives.

THE CHIEF IN 1999

CLEVELAND AVENUE IN 1914

Cleveland Ave.
SQUAMISH, B.C. 1914

We repair:

Rockshoes
Hiking Boots
Expedition Boots

and more…

Suite 105, 38012 2nd Avenue
Squamish, BC V0N 3G0
(604) 892-7463

Alaska Highway pitch 1, 5.11c. Climber Perry Beckham

Daily Planet, 5.12b.
Climbers Jordan Struthers, Colin Moorhead.
Photo Richard Wheater

The North Walls

The quiet, brooding north walls of the Chief are divided into two great cliffs—the Sheriffs Badge and the Zodiac Wall—divided by the awesome chasm of the North Gully. Both gaze serenely over the glaciers and mountains that stretch beyond Squamish into Garibaldi Park. The unmistakeable Sheriffs Badge is clearly marked by the giant white rock scar (a bird? a witch?) and a huge band of roofs. The first European settlers in the Squamish valley in the 1880s called the Chief "Goose Rock" as a result. The Badge is home to several superb hard climbs (including the legendary *Daily Planet*) above the Terrace, a big ledge system 60m above the base. The Zodiac Wall, with its mighty dihedrals, boasts the brilliant *Northern Lights* up its full height and several outstanding climbs above Astro Ledge. These two climbs, along with most of the others on these walls, are for heavy hitters only, but at the left edge of the Sheriff's Badge is one of the best moderate long climbs on the Chief—*The Angel's Crest*.

Climbing on the North Walls is a very different experience from that on the Grand Wall or Apron. It is quiet, no noise from traffic and bustle below, shady most of the year, but with afternoon sun from late spring till early fall.

The great slash of the North Gully can be clearly seen from the northeast–likewise the similar chasm of the North-North Gully. Understanding the nature of this gully brings an appreciation of the little-known fact that the Zodiac Wall is actually a gigantic fin of rock, with a backside to it rising from the gully. This is seen to good advantage when climbing on the Squaw.

Getting there...   **North Walls Trails.** There are two trails, both of which start from the Mamquam Forest Service Road, about 600m from the Apron parking lot. The trailheads are 80m apart, the left-hand heading up to the *Angel's Crest*, North Gully, and Zodiac Wall Base, the right-hand to the Sheriffs Badge and Caramba Terrace.

Getting there...   **The Sheriffs Badge.** Take the right-hand trail and follow it up through the forest. As it approaches the main wall of the Badge, it turns right, then sharply back left for a steepish scramble up to the base of *Philistine Groove*. 15 minutes. The mess of trees in this latter section are due to a colossal windstorm that hit Squamish in December 1991. It was considered a one-in-a-hundred year event. Nearly lifted the roof off my house too.

Getting there...   **The Angel's Crest, Zodiac Wall Base, North Gully.** Take the left-hand trail, and climb steadily for 15 minutes until the lower left side of the Badge is reached and the short routes along the base. The gully is reached a couple minutes later. Cross the wide, bushy gully to reach the base of the Zodiac.

Getting there...   **The Upper Zodiac Wall and North-North Gully.** Take the Angel's Crest trail until the North Gully is reached. Go leftward below the Zodiac (rough) to the entrance of the North-North Gully. Scramble up it a short way until it is possible to exit out right, up the last possible, obvious ledge system out of the gully. Above this point, the gully narrows and the least-known wall on the Chief– the Promised Land–rises from the gully floor. The trail traverses around to Astro Ledge, the major fault that divides the Zodiac Wall into Upper and Lower regions.

CHIEF NORTH

Until Glenn Payan and Jeff Thomson arrived at the top of the Malamute in 1995, it was a deserted, little-known scenic summit visited by fewer than a half-dozen people each year.

Climbs off Caramba Terrace

Caramba Terrace is the major forested ledge that reaches from the base of the Sheriffs Badge into the South Gully, an adventurous and rarely-visited place. Approach from the base of the Sheriffs Badge. The climbs listed are little-known and an ascent today would be high on both the adventure and thrashing scale. Difficulty is low by today's standards, and the likelihood of meeting other climbers remote.

Getting there... Take the trail for the Sheriffs Badge (page 269), and once at the base of *Philistine Groove*, head up right on an ill-defined trail until it disappears. Thrash on.

Caramba Crags   .8 A1   many
Bob Woodsworth Arnold Shives 1963
An adventurous and rarely climbed route up the broken ramp-like wall that denotes the right edge of the Sheriffs Badge. Hike up Caramba Terrace until the steepness of the Badge on the left relents and becomes bushy. After a couple pitches of steepish rock, involving some 5.8, trend up right, then back left for 3 pitches. At roughly mid-height on the wall, take a lower line (tension traverse?) on the left, thereafter a rising diagonal line eventually meets with the Acrophobes on *Angel's Crest*.

Caramba Crags Two   .8 A1   many
Alice Purdey Dan Tate Dick Culbert Sheila Pilkington 1965
As for *Caramba Crags*, but avoid the tension traverse and stay to the right all the way to a big white corner system that leads up to *Angel's Crest* above the Acrophobes.

EAST SIDE OF SOUTH GULLY

Approximate Lines only

Thrash

Top of The Opal

Sheriffs Badge

1. Caramba Crags 8
2. Caramba Crags 2 8
3. Amazon Slabs.........
4. Echelon ....
5. The Prow...............9

The Sheriff's Badge

The climbs on the Badge can be thought of as being of three groups: those that start from the large terrace some 60m above the base, (reached via *Philistine Groove* or *Borderline*); the aid routes up the huge white rock scar; and two developing long climbs up the wall at the left side, reaching up toward the lower section of *Angel's Crest*. Some of the routes climbed in the mid-1980s are getting a bit green due to lack of traffic. This is due in part to a shorter climbing season here than most other Squamish areas–generally May to September. There is considerable scope here for more long climbs.

Getting there...   Take the trail for the Sheriffs Badge (page 269).

A & W Wall   11c+A0 ladders   275   6p.

Tom Clark Don Phillips Dave Merrick Mike Henry May 1997

A lengthy climb up the great expanse of smooth rock at the left side of the Sheriff's Badge, hanging out above the great cleft corner. Climb the first pitch of *Borderline* (10a). From the bolt station, lower down 5m to a bolt, then traverse the wide ledge [bolts] to an airy stance and station. Rappel possible, 55m (10d). A hard start to the next pitch leads to difficult, exciting climbing up large featured holds—the best pitch on the wall (11c). The next pitch uses many bolts for aid (.9 A0). An easy traverse to the left leads to a hanging station (.9). A combination bolt ladder and bat hook pitch leads to the high point. (.9, A0, hooks).   To descend, make a short rappel of 15m to a station above the huge overhung corner, followed by a free-hanging rap of 55m to the trees below, and a third rap to the base.

THE SHERIFFS BADGE

CHIEF NORTH

Borderline ** 11c (10d) <u>275</u> 4p.

Susan Bolton David Harris Eric Hirst (alts) May-August 1997.

Blazing Saddles connection: *Susan Bolton David Harris May 1997.*
Hired Gun: *original aid ascent unknown. FFA Robert Cobb (Eric Hirst 1997) Jun 1997.*

A good climb which gives four pitches up to 11c, depending on variations chosen. It is also offers an alternative access to the climbs starting off the Terrace. When combined with *Blazing Saddles*, this route makes a recommended adventure at 5.10b. Scattered old bolts and tatty slings indicate other explorations on this wall, but no details are known. As with *Philistine Groove*, the lower pitches can suffer from becoming plugged up with falling debris from trees, especially evident early and late in the season.

Start 15m left of the base of *Philistine Groove* where the base ledge peters out. Move up left up past two bolts to reach a crack then a long obvious corner which is climbed to a small ledge with belay bolts out on the left wall (10b). Continue up the corner to the prominent flake overhang, finishing up an easy left-slanting ramp to a belay (11c). A much easier alternative is to climb the corner for 10m or so, until possible to move out right to a small ledge, from which a crack is followed to the left edge of the Terrace, and access to *Blazing Saddles*. Go out left above to rejoin the route (.8). The arete left of the corner has been top-roped at 11c-d *(Eric Hirst 1997)*. The 3rd pitch is long and sustained. Follow bolts left and up to a finger-hand crack. Finish on an arête then step right to belay bolts on a good ledge (10d). Climb the blocky corner above the belay to an obvious alcove. Go straight out the top, cool moves, then easier up to the station (10a). Rappel out.

Borderline-Blazing Saddles Connection. Follow *Borderline* to the junction with the Terrace (.8). Follow *Blazing Saddles* from here (10a, 10b).

Hired Gun. A major variation up to the right off the third pitch is possible at 11b, starting about 15m up the 3rd pitch. Move into a thin crack. Follow the crack past a bulge then continue up the thin seam, sustained to a belay.

Blazing Saddles *** 10b <u>275</u> (2p.)

Mike Beaubien John Simpson Perry Beckham 1982

The white corner above the left side of the Terrace sports a tremendous hand-crack flake on its left wall. Climb the corner off the Terrace and step left under a blocky roof to belay on a cracked slab below a fine crack (10a). Continue to a giant poised flake, then climb the jam crack, mostly laybacking with some assistance from an off-width to the left to the roof. Undercling left to a station around the corner. (10b). Rappel. Gear to 3". Double 2-2½" CDs.

Philistine Groove ● ☺ 11a <u>275</u> 2p.

Dave McDonald Les McDonald Kevin McLane (1pa) Sept 1972
FFA: Mike Beaubien John Simpson Perry Beckham 1981

This climb has been the main access to the climbs that begin off the Terrace, and is still the fastest, despite its rather scruffy demise as a repository for fallen leaves off the Terrace. At this time, it is still equipped with my fixed rope of 1986. From the trail, climb a short corner to belay below the main groove (.7). Follow it past a roof up to the Terrace. One difficult move passing the roof, otherwise easy to a belay tree (11a).

Hot Rod   ● ☺   11c   <u>275</u>   (3p.)

K.McLane P.Beckham March 1985

A spectacular excursion through the roofs above the Terrace. Above *Philistine Groove* is a prominent deep corner capped by a roof. Climb it, followed by a stiff undercling past the roof to a belay (11c). The crack above is easier and leads to a belay below the upper roofs (10b). Make a wild hand traverse leftward across a long, very detached block to a tricky exit onto the wall above and a few more moves up to a belay (11b). Rappel.

The next two climbs lie in the bay immediately left of the main corner of The Daily Planet, and offer two very steep cracklines that gain access to the large right-facing corner that leads to Gunsmoke Ledge.

The Big Scoop   **   11b   <u>275</u>   (35m)

P.Croft D.Hart (Alts) July 1984

Strenuous jamming. Truly. Just left of the start of *The Daily Planet*, climb a overhanging hand-crack to an alcove below a square roof. Traverse right below the roof to a difficult mantel onto a ledge and continue more easily up the right side of the flake above, into the upper corner of *Astronomy*.

Astronomy   **   12a   <u>274, 336</u>   (2p.)

p1 Dave McDonald Les McDonald Kevin McLane Sept 1972.
p2-5 Karl Karlstrom M.Baxter Kevin McLane Aug '73
FFA: p1 Peter Croft Aug 1984 (aka Mad Englishman And Dog)
FFA: p2 Daryl Hatten Kevin McLane Aug 1984

Start in the same place as *The Big Scoop* and go into the left side of the alcove up a fine finger-crack, below the square roof. Turn the roof on the left to belay at the base of the long upper corner (12a). Climb this corner in a fine position to Gunsmoke Ledge (10c). Rappel out. The original ascent continued for 3 more mixed pitches before traversing off to *Angel's Crest*.

The Daily Planet   ***½   12b (12a)   <u>275</u>   (4p.)

p1 Perry Beckham Blake Robinson (aid) 1981
(p1 free) *Perry Beckham Mike Beaubien John Simpson July 1982*
p1 After a hairline broke at the crux, freed by Peter Croft July 1982
p2 (aid) John Simpson July 1982: **(p2 free)** *Perry Beckham Mike Beaubien July 1982*
p3 Mike Beaubien (yo-yo) Perry Beckham July 1982: **(p3 free)** *Peter Croft to top of 10d flake.*
First Continuous Free Ascent p1, p2, p3: *Peter Croft Hamish Fraser July 1982*
First Continuous Free Ascent p1, p2, p3, p4: *Perry Beckham Brook Sandhal 1986*

A magnificent climb up the soaring corner system at the left edge of the rock scar. Your 5.12 portfolio is not complete without *"The Planet"*. Heavy on the laybacking, stemming and jamming. From the top of *Philistine Groove*, hike up right. A few easy moves up a short wall lead to a belay below the first pitch up the main corner. Stem widely past several FP to a rest at the bottom of an intimidating layback. Forge on up, into a technical crux passing the flake above. A stunning pitch, low in its grade (12a). Up the chimney to the roofs (10b), and belay here or continue muscling along the fine undercling to the end of the roof (11a). Rappel from here, or continue up the short flake above (10d). A final pitch continues almost to the roofs: long reaches (12b).

The Sheriff's Badge   Aid   See page 325

Skullfuck   Aid   See page 325.

Cowboys and Indians   Aid   See page 325.

CHIEF NORTH

THE SHERIFFS BADGE

Approx. Line 10a A2

4 Gunsmoke Ledge

4

5 →

3

2

9

8

6

7 The Terrace

10 ←

8 **7**

1

THE SHERIFFS BADGE

1. Philistine Groove 11a
2. The Daily Planet 12a
3. The Big Scoop 11c
4. Astronomy 12a/10c,A2
5. Englishman's Dog............12a
6. Hot Rod 11c
7. Blazing Saddles 10b
8. Borderline...................11c/11a
9. Hired Gun........................11b
10. A & W Wall................11c,A0

23m   12b Reachy

11a

10b

Gunsmoke Ledge

50m

10b

10c

1

12a

Twin face cracks on left wall. 10b.

50m

11b

Huge hanging flakes

10b

11b/c

4

5   12a fingers   11c hand

10a

finger

Bolts and batholes

8

11b

9

10d

11c

4   **3**   **2**

5.7

.9 AO (many bolts)

.7

7

11c

.8

6

The Terrace

45m

.9

tension

10

10d AO (bolts)

11c

.8

11a
Usually dirty, sometimes a fixed rope is in situ

55m base

45m

10b

1

8 **7**

45m

The Angel's Crest — North Gully

The *Angel's Crest* is one of the great Squamish classics. Generally, the northern aspect means it is a late-spring until early fall route, but in that time it will see many ascents.

Getting there... Take the Angel's Crest trail from the Mamquam Forest Service Road (page 269).

The Angel's Crest ★★★ 10b   12p.

FA above Acrophobes (via North Gully) Les McDonald Hank Mather Fred Becky (some aid) 1962
FA below Acrophobes Fred Beckey Eric Bjornstad (some aid) May 1964
FA (1pa) R.Barley R.Edwards 1974 FFA: D.Loecks P.Charak L.DuBois 1975
FA p8 offwidth variation R.Rohn D.Lister 1979
FA p 11 crack variation Kevin McLane Chris Murrell 1978
FA p12 final chimney Robin Barley Peter Koedt 1974

This climb takes the long arete at the left edge of the Sheriff's Badge. Despite a fair bit of greenery on the route, it is very popular, offering grand views and fine situations and is especially pleasant in the heat of summer. It is longer and more tiring for most climbers than it may appear. A small forest at two-thirds height divides the route into upper and lower sections.

At the entrance to the North gully, turn right and head up it for only 10m before stepping up right for 5m to reach a ledge. From here, climb an easy groove with small trees to reach a long ledge (.7). Walk right to the start of the first pitch. Six pitches lead to a tower and a big ledge where an escape is possible. Two pitches then lead to a small forest below the Acrophobe Towers. Climb the lower tower, make a short rap [bolts] down the gully side, cross back to the west side, up a bit, then climb down again [fixed line] on the gully side. Scramble up to the notch behind the highest tower. The next pitch regains the crest, then three more excellent pitches lead to the top.

The North Gully   4th   many

Jim Baldwin Dick Culbert Adolf Bitterlich Bren Moss John Owen Elfriga Pigou Feb 1958

This is the huge chasm that splits the Sheriff,s Badge and the Zodiac Wall. Partly visible from Squamish and the highway, it is best seen in its full glory from the Mamquam Forest Service Road [or outside my house]. The climb is mostly a stiff hike, with occasional sections of 4th class. There are several chockstones, easily bypassed. The final one is enormous, and quite intimidating when seen from below. All is well though, as a cute tunnel exists below it. Above it, a narrow but easy ramp on the right wall cuts up right onto the *Angel's Crest*. The final section in the gully has much loose and rotten rock. This is one Squamish route where helmets are preferred.

High Plains Drifter ★★★ 11a   30m

Perry Beckham 1990

At the top of the Sheriff's Badge, facing across to the *Angel's Crest* is a long, impeccable handcrack. Unfortunately it is an epic to reach, with rappel stations very questionable at present. From the top of the *Angel's Crest*, walk up 50m along the rim until it begins to drop off into steep slabs. Two rappels from trees (very exposed!) lead to the base of the crack. Leave your ropes fixed! Climb the sustained handcrack, then jumar back up the fixed rope.

ANGEL'S CREST

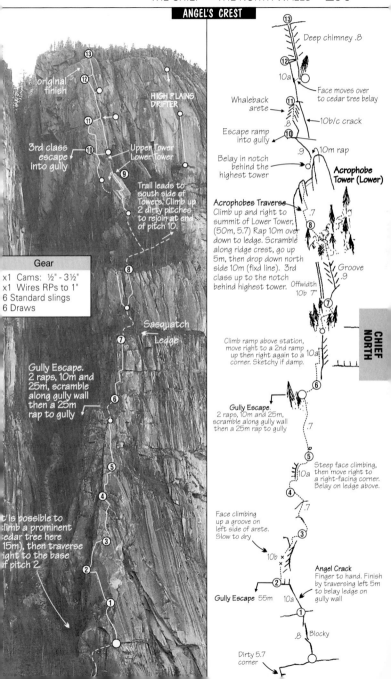

original finish

⑬

⑫

HIGH PLAINS DRIFTER

⑪

3rd class escape into gully

⑩

Upper Tower
Lower Tower

⑨

Trail leads to south side of Towers. Climb up 2 dirty pitches to rejoin at end of pitch 10.

⑧

Gear
x1 Cams: ½" - 3½"
x1 Wires RPs to 1"
6 Standard slings
6 Draws

Sasquatch Ledge

⑦

Gully Escape. 2 raps, 10m and 25m, scramble along gully wall then a 25m rap to gully

⑥

⑤

④

③

② ① It is possible to climb a prominent cedar tree here (15m), then traverse right to the base of pitch 2.

---

⑬ Deep chimney .8

⑫ 10a

Face moves over to cedar tree belay

Whaleback arete ⑪
.8 — 10b/c crack

Escape ramp into gully ⑩
.9 — 10m rap

Belay in notch behind the highest tower

Acrophobe Tower (Lower)

Acrophobes Traverse
Climb up and right to summit of Lower Tower, (50m, 5.7) Rap 10m over down to ledge. Scramble along ridge crest, go up 5m, then drop down north side 10m (fixd line). 3rd class up to the notch behind highest tower.

.7

⑧

Groove 9

Offwidth 10b 7"

⑦

Climb ramp above station, move right to a 2nd ramp up then right again to a corner. Sketchy if damp.

⑥ 10a

CHIEF NORTH

Gully Escape.
2 raps, 10m and 25m, scramble along gully wall then a 25m rap to gully

.7

⑤ 10a

Steep face climbing, then move right to a right-facing corner. Belay on ledge above.

④ .7

Face climbing up a groove on left side of arete. Slow to dry

③

10b ✕
✕

② ✕

Gully Escape 55m   10a

Angel Crack
Finger to hand. Finish by traversing left 5m to belay ledge on gully wall

①

.8   Blocky

Dirty 5.7 corner

Angels Crest Trailside Climbs

One the way up to Angel's Crest, a number of short climbs at the base are passed along the final approach to the North Gully.

Getting there... Take the Angel's Crest trail from the Mamquam Forest Service Road (page 269). The first climb is encountered right where the trail meets the wall.

Calculated Risk .4 A2 *x* 10m
Gord Menzies Kim Poehnell 1980
The right-hand line, starting up a stepped left-facing corner. Go left to finish as for *Well Hung Roof*.

Well Hung Roof .7 A2 *x* 10m
Jim Campbell Jim Brennan John Manuel Nov 1980
A few metres left of *Calculated Risk*, climb a seam that splits the roof.

Copperhead Road A3+ *x* 10m
Tom Clark Don Phillips May 1996
A similar, parallel seam located 4m left of *Well Hung Roof*. Usually dry.

Nostromo .6 A2 *x* 20m
John Manuel Bruce Fairley 1982
Part way up the North Gully is a right-facing corner on the north side which offers a short pitch of free and aid. No further details. Not much help, I guess.

> *The next two climbs are about 80m right of the entrance to the North Gully, and can be seen down off to the right at the point where the approach trail meets to main wall.*

The Reward ● ☺ 10b *x* 2p.
Kevin McLane David Harris (Nancy Henderson)   Sept 1992
This climb is probably the same as Dave's Route A2 c.1970 (different David Harris).
A major 70m left-leaning crack and corner system. Overgrown, but nonetheless an excellent climb with some fine-looking unclimbed cracks above. Face climbing leads into the corner, which is cruxy at first then easier. Laybacking and jamming, very nice stuff, leads to a good belay ledge and rappel (10a). Layback with increasing difficulty to the base of the offwidth above (10b).

The Redeemer ● 10a A1 *x* 40m
David Harris solo 1984
The left-leaning arch right of the start *The Reward* has been climbed on aid, joining the latter in the main corner above. Could go free at 5.11.

Please join the Climbers Access Society, and lend your support to helping protect and improve access to the crags.

Angels Crest, 5.10a   Climber Jim Sinclair

Zodiac Wall — Lower

Along the base of the Zodiac are four routes: two short, one 4-pitch chimney and *Alaska Highway*, the lower half of the outstanding *Northern Lights* (page 284).

Getting there... Take the North Gully trail from the Mamquam Forest Service Road (page 269). At the entrance to the North Gully, head up for 30m until the trees thin out, then turn left and traverse about 30m until below *Astrologger*.

The Forgotten Flake * 10a   25m
Colin Moorhead Tom Gruber Sept 1995
This is an obvious wide flake 3m right of the start of *Alaska Highway*. Take gear to 4".

Astrologger *** 11b   25m
P.Beckham J.Turley July 1983
This is a little gem tucked away at the base of the wall, across and a little downhill from the start of the North Gully. Look for a short, striking prow which sports on its left side a deep back and foot groove containing a beautiful thin hand crack. From below the groove, walk left 30m, scramble up [fixed line] and traverse across to belay just left of the groove. Even steeper than it looks. Take 3-2" CUs.

Tall Skinny People * 10c   4p.
Kris Holm Andrew Boyd May 1997
This is a prominent chimney immediately right of the start of *North-North Arete*, leading up to just below the left side of Astro Ledge. Possibly easier than 10c if the rock is dry. Climb at mid-5th into base of chimney. Stem widely into a squeeze chimney at the top of the pitch and belay in an alcove below a large chockstone roof (10b). More wild stemming and handjamming past the roof – easier than it looks. Continue to next steep section and belay (.9). Stem and squeeze wildly onward—runout (10c). Easier (.9). Two #4 Camalots were used on the first ascent. Descend by continuing up *NN Arete*, or exit left and down *NN Gully*.

Alaska Highway / The Calling / Northern Lights *** 11c (page 284)

On August 8th 1996, Sig Isaac climbed Freeway, The Grand Wall and Northern Lights in 14 hours 40 minutes car to car. He led every pitch and ran down the Backside each time.

Different partners each climb...

1. The Forgotten Flake..10a
2. Astrologger 11b
3. Northern Lights 12a
4. Tall Skinny People.....10c

North Summit
ZODIAC WALL
Zodiac Summit

Rockfall

Upper Zodiac

CHIEF NORTH

NORTH NORTH ARETE

ANGELS CREST

3
2
1

4

Rough Trail

This area is now a talus slope resulting from a rockfall in January 1999.

Zodiac Wall — Upper

The upper left side of the Zodiac Wall is home to 7 hard climbs off Astro Ledge, the great 4th-class faultline that divides the Zodiac into upper and lower sections. Astro Ledge is narrow and very exposed, definitely no place for the faint-hearted. Just as well, as the climbs are too. They are full-on crack climbs—strenuous, technically demanding, steep and with long exposed pitches.

Getting there...   The climbs all start from Astro Ledge, reached in one of two ways: by climbing *Alaska Highway;* or the rough trail up the North North gully. See page 269.

Visionquest ***   12a   3p.
R.Atkinson D.Hart 1987
A beautiful dihedral just left of the chimney line of *Public Image*. Climb to the top of a pie shaped pedestal from the left (.7). Face climb to a sling belay (10b). A more direct start can be made from the right up a fingercrack to reach this point (11a). Layback up the corner with difficulty, easing above. A wonderful pitch (12a).

Public Image   ● ☺   11c   4p.
R.Atkinson D.Hart (Alts) May 1985
The obvious big crack and chimney line at the left edge of the wall. Climb the initial crack (11a). Chimney and offwidth in a fine position (11b). More of the same, but easier (10c). Pleasant stemming up to Indica Point (10b).

Tattered Tights ● ☺   10c   40m
R.Atkinson D.Hart June 1985
Rappel in from the North-North Arete at Indica Point and climb back out to the top up a crackline.

Gone Surfing   ***½   11a   2p.
D.Hart R.Atkinson (Alts) July 1985
Classic cracks through an overhanging white and orange wall right of *Public Image*. Start up a fingercrack widening from fingers to fists with good rests (11a). A fist crack in the corner above widens to a chimney. Belay on the arete by a big roof (10b). It is essential to leave a fixed rope for rappelling back out to the top of the first pitch. Gear to two 4".

Endangered Species   ● 11d   2p.
R.Atkinson D.Hart (Alts) Aug 1986
Poor faceclimbing and handcracks right of *Gone Surfing*.

The Ron Zalko Workout   ** 12a   2p.
Randy Atkinson Dean Hart July 1986
Strenuous power laybacking up the dihedral line just left of *The Calling* (12a, 11b). Unfortunately it cansuffer from dampnesss low on the route, and the 2nd pitch is ovegrown. Belay above a small roof. Rappel out. The line of bolts above is an abandoned project. Gear is mostly small wires to 1½", some larger to 3½"".

ZODIAC WALL UPPER

1. Tattered Tights 10c
2. Visionquest 12a
3. Public Image..................11c
4. Gone Surfing 11a
5. Endangered Species ...11d
6. Ron Zalko Workout ...12a/b
7. The Calling 12a

approximate line
North-North Arete

Indica Point

10c

10d

10b

12a

10d

11b   11d

10c

12a

10b

12a   11c

10b   11d

11a

rth
rth
lly

2

3

4   5   6   7

Astro Ledge   4th class
(very exposed)

Alaska
Highway

CHIEF NORTH

Zodiac Wall — The Northern Lights

This climb is arguably the most demanding long route at Squamish. *University Wall* is technically harder, but *Northern Lights* is longer, more sustained in difficulty, and the crux pitch comes high on the wall after a considerable amount of heavy crackwork.

Northern Lights is the combination of two climbs: *Alaska Highway* (11c), which takes a long line of cracks and chimneys from the base up to Astro Ledge; followed by *The Calling* (12a), up a brilliant series of dihedrals to the top of the wall. Both climbs are superb individually, but the combination makes one of the finer long freeclimbs in the universe. And one of the better climbs at Squamish.

Getting there...   Take the Angel's Crest trail from the Mamquam Forest Service Road (page 269).

The Northern Lights	***½	12a	*281*	12p.
Alaska Highway	***	11c		5p.
The Calling	***	12a		7p.

First Continuous Ascent P.Beckham E.Winkleman 1987
The Calling*: D.Hart R.Atkinson (1pa on p4) 1986   p4 was freed by D.Hart by rappelling in.*
Alaska Highway*: P.Beckham R.Atkinson (some aid) 1987   FFA P.Beckham D.Dunaway '87*

Start 30m left of *Astrologger* [page 280] by scrambling and pulling up fixed ropes to a belay by a tall gnarly snag. Climb a rather poor pitch, including a Squamish tree shimmy, up right to belay below a big line of roofs (10c). Fire on through the large overhanging groove that splits it. This pitch is something to really sweat over for both the leader and second—it is much more over-hanging than it appears from below (11c). A burly pitch of cornerwork leads to a gear belay (11a). Fire up a strenuous layback corner and an awkward chimney, then face moves to a ledge (10c). A short, thin flake leads to a sloping hand traverse, then runout 5.8 to a belay on Astro Ledge (11a). Once on Astro Ledge, a 4th-class escape to the North-North Gully is possible, but the rappel route is faster. Stations can require care to find, as they blend with the wall.

Above Astro Ledge is ***The Calling***. A pitch of crack and face climbing leads to a belay at the base of a long towering corner capped by roofs (11d). Take a deep breath and start up the most elegant and breathtaking dihedral at Squamish—the heavy hitter's version of the *Split Pillar*. Lieback and jam the crack in the dihedral; triple up on 1½"-2" CDs (11d). Turn the roof above on the left, then back right and belay (10d). Then follow a long pitch of face climbing up to 11b [bolts] followed by a difficult crux [more bolts] before the difficulty eases (12a). The rock begins to deteriorate in the bushy corner above (10b). Traverse left along a ledge filled with loose blocks to the final pitch (4th). Go fairly directly up the wall above to the last belay (10d). Traverse off to the right (south) through the trees until you are forced up left. Keep your eyes peeled for the trail back out leftward to the summit area. Wander off down the Chief trail, your lights well and truly punched out.

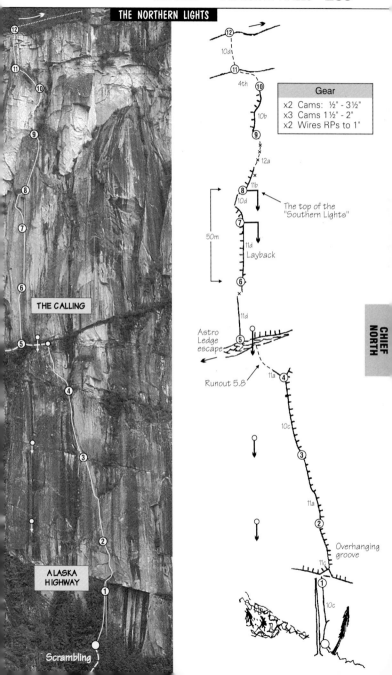

THE NORTHERN LIGHTS

Gear
x2 Cams: ½" - 3½"
x3 Cams 1½" - 2"
x2 Wires RPs to 1"

10d

4th

10b

12a

11b

10d

The top of the
"Southern Lights"

11d

Layback

50m

11d

Astro
Ledge
escape

Runout 5.8

11a

10c

11a

Overhanging
groove

11c

10c

THE CALLING

ALASKA
HIGHWAY

Scrambling

**CHIEF
NORTH**

North North Arete — North North Gully

The North-North Arete is the great prow at the left side of the Zodiac Wall, and one of the least-known climbs on the Chief. It is a better route than generally thought, offering good, interesting climbing, mostly steep cracks and chimneys, and secluded situations on the left side of the crest of the arete. The climb is mostly east-facing, in the sun for most of the morning.

Getting there... See page 269.

North North Arete ** .9 ±6p.

R.Woodsworth W.Chernekoff 1964   FFA: Eric Weinstein Dave Vernon 1973

This long arete bounding the Zodiac Wall at its left edge is divided into two sections; a lower half that offers bush scrambling then increasing amounts of bush 4th-class, ending abruptly on the trail to Astro Ledge (Zodiac Wall). The upper arete has been climbed by a number of variations, and holds many more impressive cracks yet to be climbed. The route as described here is the easiest line, no more than 5.9, and as such is the easiest climb to the top of the Chief. Gear to 3½". Many pitches are rather scruffy and could use a good cleanup, rather like *Angels Crest* was many years ago.

From the high point of the Astro Ledge trail, climb three short, mostly easy pitches over broken terrain, ledges and short walls until the arete proper rears up into a steep tower of large blocks. Belay on a ledge at the left side (5.7/8). Climb cracks over flakes and blocks, trending slightly leftward away from the crest onto an open wall. Belay at a niche below some impressive hand cracks: a long pitch (5.8). To the left is a parallel, harder-looking crack above a square roof. Step out right off the belay, up fine handcracks and grooves to a great Yew tree, then traverse left 10m and up a chimney-recess to a large treed ledge (5.9). There is a great view of Squamish from the pedestal over to the right. Scramble up 10m and belay in a deep, impressive bay, full of jammed blocks. Stem up out right to a ledge just left of the crest, 15m (5.7/8). Walk and scramble leftward for about 70m, below a steep wall of cracks, and belay at the top of this slope. Climb into a deep chimney and back-and-foot up it to a ledge (5.7). Belay, or continue up a rather nasty pitch of loose rock and dirt to a good ledge on the left below a steep groove and cracks (5.8). Layback and stem up here (the"Guillotine" has now gone) to the base of a slabby corner (5.8/9). Belay here, or continue up the corner (FP) awkward if wet, and enter a cave below a chockstone. Squeeze through for a few metres, aiming for an opening to the sky above. This is the "birthing pitch", and will give you some idea of what lies in store for you at the start of your next life. It may even help you remember the last one.

North North Gully .7 many

F. deBruyn Glenn Woodsworth 1961

An adventurous scramble through some remarkable terrain in a huge chasm.

NORTH–NORTH ARETE

The Promised Land

hike off in a rising
traverse, keeping left
through bluffs to the top
of the Zodiac summit

*Wherever you go,
there you are.*

Yew Tree

Blocky
Tower

Astro
Ledge
trail

orth
ummit

Zodiac
Summit

to
Above and
Beyond

Centre
Summit

North
North
Gully

Zodiac
Wall

Astro
Ledge

Trail to Astro Ledge exits
the gully at the last possible
exit. Easy to find.

4th
thrashing

The Promised Land

It is not commonly known that the Zodiac Wall has a backside. It appears to be a very solid part of the Chief, but in fact it is more in the nature of a colossal and none-too-solid fin that separates the North Gully from the North-North Gully. The backside is hard to see clearly, although the Squaw offers a decent vantage point, and this big southeast facing wall is packed with interesting potential. But it is a long way from anywhere in Squamish terms, so the journey to the Promised Land is long and adventurous. Such is the nature of nirvana. But you will never get there unless you try...

Getting there...   Take the Backside Trail to the North summit of the Chief, up past the White Cliff and Solarium trailhead. Once you get to the area around the top of the North Gully, head out onto the open bedrock slabs of what is the top of the Zodiac Wall, an intriguing sidetrail where you won't meet many hikers. In fact, this is a summit of the Chief no less so than the commonly known South, Centre and North summits. Walk on down past the high point, trending leftward. At the point where a sketchy trail from *The Northern Lights / The Calling* comes up from the left, stay right for another 200m or so, contouring around to the northern side. Look for a flake sticking out and set up a rappel. A second rappel down will get you to the base of the climb. Jumar back out.

The Promised Land   ***   11b   x   (50m)
Perry Beckham Elise Kelly August 1998
A stunning crack. Lots of mid-size gear.

The Legend of Mike Boothroyd: In September 1991, Squamish ace Mike Boothroyd was riding his trials motorbike (not to be confused with the heinous moto-cross) at the top of Burgers and Fries, practising that gentle art riding loops, down to and back up from the ledge at the top of the 5.7 classic. He did it one time too many. Landing on the ledge, a fork broke, the throttle jammed and his bike lurched over the top of the climb, with Mike still on it. A nasty demise was imminent, but he was able to remain on the bike, just, as it clattered and scraped down the crag, and made a fine landing, two wheels flat. There were a few broken bits on the bike (on Mike too), but surviving such an unexpected test of bike control levitated him to near-diety status in the trials world.

The Squaw

Northeast of the Zodiac Wall is a detached summit of the Chief massif, the Squaw. The climbing action is concentrated around the southern, lower end of the vast expanse of rambling walls, a huge buttress beautifully carved into dihedrals, aretes and walls. Like the North Walls, the Squaw looks out over the mountains of Garibaldi Park, and the residential area of Valleycliffe below. Some of the best multi-pitch routes in this guide are found here, and for that reason, they tend to be popular. Acres of very steep rock grace its northern flanks, which have some remarkable lines yet to be climbed, but protected by steep forested slopes below.

Getting there...   From the Apron parking lot, drive 1.5km up the Mamquam Forest Service Road below the north walls to a turn-out on the right. Park here and take a trail that leads into a small clearing. Exit on the left side. Continue for 15 minutes, arriving at the base of a steep, blunt arete–*Godforsaken Land.*

Indian Queen   10b   *293*   2p.
Will Dorling Nick Watts April 1996. FFA p1 Bill and Marci (Americans) April 1996
Scramble left for 10m from the start of *Eagle's Domain* to a slab. Climb a fist crack and walk up a diagonal crack. The short corner above leads to a belay (.8). Climb left along a sickle past bolts to a stance. Traverse left under a small overlap, mantle and on to belay at a tree (10b). A traverse over to *Birds of Prey* is possible.

Eagle's Domain   **   .8   *293*   2p.
Jim Campbell Bob Milward July 1983
This is the first two pitches of *Birds of Prey*, a fine finger and handcrack in the steep dark slab; each is .8 with a gear belay in the crack. Rappel via trees on the left or *Bump Pumice* on the right.

THE SQUAW

Mamquam
Forest Service Road

Birds Of Prey   **   10b   _293_   6p.
R.Milward J.Campbell (Alts) July 1983
A very popular climb which winds its way up the cliff at a mostly moderate grade. 40m left of the trailhead is an obvious dark slab. Climb the fine crack that splits the slab [*Eagle's Domain*] for two pitches [gear belay], to a tree belay below a vertical wall (.8) (.8). Go up rightwards and jam a steep corner crack, exiting onto the long ramp below *Pipeline*. A difficult step up leftward gains a slab and a tree belay (10b). Move easily up to a higher belay beneath the final corner system. Two nice pitches lead to the top (10a) (.8).

Bump Pumice   10c   _293_   3p
Will Dorling Nick Watts May 1993
Start a few metres right of *Eagles Domain*, and climb a long narrow slab in 3 pitches (10c) (.9) (.7) to tree ledges right of *Birds of Prey*. Gear to 2".

Frayed Ends of Sanity * 12c (11a)   _293_   **SPORT** p6   6p.
p1-2 Colin Moorhead Will Dorling (2pa aid on pitch 2) August 1991
*p3 (**Heart of Darkness** pitch) Marc Bourdon 1997.*
FFA p2 Peder Ourom Greg Foweraker Hamish Fraser May 1994
This climb takes the huge arete left of *Pipeline*. Climb *Birds of Prey* to the top of the third pitch (.8) (.8) (10b). From the belay, step out right and climb a crack and slab past 2 bolts to reach an overlap. Tenacious underclinging past a bolt lead out right to a ramp and belay (10c). Follow strenuous cracks and lieback flakes in a wonderfully exposed position to a cruxy bulge. Move up right to a corner, on top of which is a lovely little ledge (11a). Look into the gaping jaws of *Pipeline's* crux. A rappel off is possible from here, keeping the difficulty to 11a. The pitch above is one of the finest sport pitches at Squamish, up the smooth, exposed prow (12c). A short step leads beyond to the top. The top pitch can be done alone by climbing up the descent trail (which is no sport route!) and rapping in. Take CDs to 2", some medium wires and 8 draws. To descend from the 11a high point, rap 25m down to the top of the 10c pitch. Then make a long, free-hanging rap to bolts on *Bump Pumice*–one of the most hairy-chested rappels on the Chief.

**Pipeline ***½   10c   _293_   5p.
L.Patterson B.Hagen G.Woodsworth 1966 FFA: G.Cameron (solo) 1979
A magnificent squeeze chimney in a majestic curving dihedral. The first free ascent was an amazing free solo, which has contributed much to the climb's fearsome reputation. In fact, this reputation far outweighs its actual difficulty, given the availability of wide crack protection today. Follow *Birds Of Prey* onto the slim ramp, and belay. Continue up the steepening ramp, and its offwidth crack. Belay inside the crack as it widens (.9). Climb the overhanging squeeze chimney in a position of great exposure. The difficulty eases off gradually. A very long pitch (10c). Awesome.

**Right Wing ● ☺   10c   _293_   7p.
F.Beckey D.Beckstead A.Givler 1970   FFA: D.McPherson R.Suddaby July 1983
Climb *Birds Of Prey* and go right with difficulty up into the base of the great arch. Sometimes wet (.8) (.8) (10c). Three pitches of mid-10 lead to the final 10b steep corner with the obvious beak-shaped flake. This climb just needs a good scrub and a tree pruning and it will be excellent.

Godforsaken Land   ***   10c+9pa   *293*   5p.
R.Barley P.Shackleton 1985 FFA: p2 (5.11c) D.Lane S.Flavelle 1986.
p1 variation start Nick Watts Will Dorling Aug 1996
This climb offers tremendous value for the effort expended, despite a few
aid bolts. The position is splendid, the difficulty sustained, and the final pitch
is one of the best. Long slings help for the aid. Start on the right of the blunt
arete above the trailhead and continue to a belay on the right below a short
steep wall (10a). One bolt for aid, or free at 5.11c, leads to easier terrain to a
tree belay on the ramp of *The Great Game* (10b +1pa). Climb a bolt ladder on
the left, then across into the white corner, belay at its top (10a+6pa). Go left
to a thin crack, then back right to a small roof. Two bolts for aid lead to a hard
overlap then easier climbing to the base of the final pitch (10c+2pa). Follow
the wildly exposed, exhilarating flake up right, the original finish to *Right Wing*
(10c), or the beak-shaped, flexing flake in the corner the left (10b).

Checkmate Arete   10d+1pa   *293*   (3p.)
Will Dorling Nick Watts Aug 1996
A route with some fine situations that joins *Birds of Prey* with *God Forsaken
Land*. Climb the first pitch of *Birds of Prey* (.8), then traverse right out of the
second pitch to climb the first 12m of *Right Wing* [can go free, but often wet]
(10b+1pa). Traverse right across the great wall to a belay near the arete (10b).
Climb left of the arete join *God Forsaken Land* (10d).

The Great Game   ***   10d   *293*   4p.
R.Barley B.McDonald P.Shackleton 1985
Quality climbing and sustained. Start 25m left of *God Forsaken Land*, up a
lieback which zigs and zags to a long hand crack (10d). An easier pitch leads
up a ramp to the main dihedral (.8). The difficulties grow as the crack thins
out, an excellent pitch. Belay below a headwall (10d). A few muscle moves
gain a grand exit ramp (10d).

Supernatural   ● ☺   11a   *293*   2p.
R.Barley P.Shackleton D.Jones (1pa) April '83 FFA: P.Shackleton '84
Uphill from the trailhead 50m is an inviting corner sporting a crux roof at 5m
(10a). A fine pitch, a rappel is possible. To continue, traverse right across the
wall to a thin crack leading to a leaning arch, joining into *Jungle Warfare*.
Continue up left to belay (11a).

Adrift   11a   *293*   3p.
Colin Moorhead E.Werker May 8th 1994
Climb *Jungle Warfare* until possible to traverse left into the first belay of
Supernatural (10a). Climb steep flakes left of *Supernatural*, then a corner crack
until possible to move back right into the crux of *Supernatural* (11a). Gear to
3". Finish up *Jungle Warfare*.

Jungle Warfare   **   10a   *293*   5p.
R.Barley K.McLane April 1983
The easiest climb in this area. 10m right of *Supernatural*, a steep crack leads
to an easier groove (10a). Continue up the groove (.7). Left up a ramp to tree
belay (.8). Two pitches up yet more cracks and the final slab (.9) (.7). Good
value for its grade. The original start is up a large flake just right of *Supernatural*.

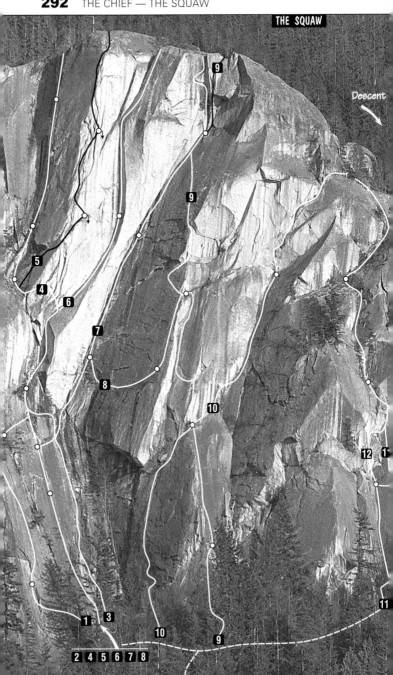

THE SQUAW

Descent

THE SQUAW

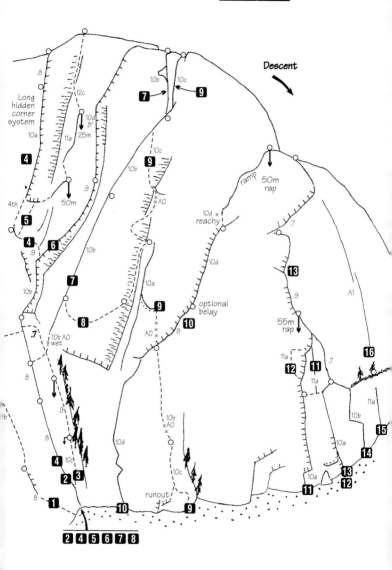

Descent

Zig Zag ● ☺   10b   _293_   40m
R.Milward D.Jones J.Campbell June 1983
Just right of _Jungle Warfare_, a single pitch zigs and zags. (10b).

Freedom Fighter ● ☺   11a   25m
R.Barley D.Jones (1pa) 4/83   FFA: J.Lewis P.Hilltner P.Post 8/83
Offset cracks just right of _Zig Zag_. Dirty. (11a).

Insurrection   10 A2   _293_   3 or 4p.
Robin Barley David Davies 1983
From the top of _Freedom Fighter_, move right and nail cracks for a pitch, trending left to finish near the top of _Jungle Warfare_.

■ _The next climb is on the west side of the descent trail in the big chimney._

Anxiety **   12a   #9   _293_   **SPORT**   25m
Tyler Jordan Oct 15th 1994
Hike uphill on the descent trail from the base of the main cliff. As you enter a deep and impressive chimney formed by huge jammed boulders, an excellent climb can be seen on the right where the angle of the wall changes with a curiously featured "wave" in the rock. The bolts are easy to see. Climb past 2 bolts to gain the ramp created by the wave, which is followed with increasing difficulty to the crux at the top.

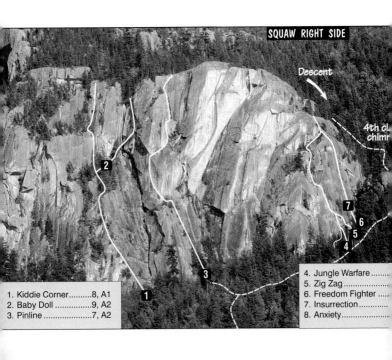

SQUAW RIGHT SIDE

Descent

4th cl. chimr

1. Kiddie Corner..........8, A1
2. Baby Doll 9, A2
3. Pinline 7, A2

4. Jungle Warfare........
5. Zig Zag ....
6. Freedom Fighter ....
7. Insurrection.............
8. Anxiety....................

Left of The Squaw

Left of the main climbing area on the Squaw is a vast amount of untouched rock which will yield many good climbs over time. Only the following routes are known to have been climbed.

Klootch Buttress .8 A3 many
Dick Culbert Paul Starr 1970
Climb face cracks on the major buttress just right of a huge cleft which runs the full height of the Squaw, well to the left of *Birds of Prey*.

Kiddie Corner .8 A1 many
Glenn Woodsworth Arnold Shives 1964
Climbs the left side of the huge brushy slab which forms the left side of the major corner cleft left of *Birds of Prey*.

Baby Doll .9 A2 many
Hamish Mutch Jim Sinclair 1968
A major variation to *Kiddie Corner*, heading out right and crossing below the great chimney cleft before taking a more direct line to the top.

Pinline .7 A2 many
Dick Culbert Alice Purdy 1970
Climb the cracks left of *Eagles Domain* for two pitches. Head left around onto the north-facing side and climb a striking, curving crackline that reaches back up into the recess below the final pitches of *Birds Of Prey*. Finish up the left wall.

Haley's Comet 10c 2p.
J.Turley T.Marks 1987
A long crack at the left edge of a wide black streak, on a prominent big black slab, 150m to the left of *Birds Of Prey*. Adventurous.

CHIEF NORTH

The Backside

In the mornings, when the great west and north faces of the Chief are deep in the shade, and climbers are abuzz with where-to-go talk, the Backside is basking in warm sunshine and likely not a climber is in sight. The climbs are varied and of quality. They are centred on four cliffs on the Centre, and the North Chief. The White Cliff and the Cirque of the Uncrackables offer short crag climbs and great cracks, whereas the Solarium and Above and Beyond offer multipitch climbs in a position of grandeur, high up below the summit. All of the crags on the Backside are worthy of a visit, there is quality rock that sees very little traffic, and plenty of scope for more new route development.

Getting there, the Backside Trail...   This is arguably the most popular summit trail in British Columbia. On a busy summer weekend, upwards of a thousand people make the steep trek each day. Or try to, anyway. The grindingly steep buffed trail heads for the South Summit, with major forks branching off to the Centre and North

THE BACKSIDE — THE SOLARIUM, AND ABOVE AND BEYOND

Solarium Left Side

Solarium Right Side

Summits. Drive through the main Chief parking lot to the day hiker's parking area near the climbers' campground. Walk along the gravel road a short distance to the small quarry by Olesen Creek and the start of the Backside trail to the summits of the Chief. This trail can also be reached by walking over from Shannon Falls Park. See also page 164.

Bellygood Ledge Trail...   This is used to reach those climbs which start off Bellygood Ledge (page 222), and is the descent trail off the Grand Wall routes. About 50m above the first major fork on the Backside trail (for the North Chief), look for an 8m fixed line on the left side, where the steep slabs relent a little. Pull up here and follow a faint, rough trail to a huge slab (easily visible from the highway). Walk up here, and at its top, take the trail off rightward into the trees. Walk north to Bellygood. You'll know when you're there.

North Chief trailside climbs...   See page 299.

Solarium trail...   See page 307.

White Cliff, The Cirque, Above and Beyond trails...   See page 302.

North Summit

CHIEF BACKSIDE

Above and Beyond

South Peak Trailside Climbs

The following two climbs are right on the main Backside trail, a short distance up from the base.

Getting there...   Take the Backside Trail (page 296). *Enchimeggs* is about 10 minutes from the car; *Sherry's Crack* 15 minutes.

| **Enchimeggs** | ● ☺ | 10c | x | 20m |

Peter Croft (solo) March 1983

This long-forgotten climb is at the trailside about 20m beyond the second, shorter flight of stairs on the Backside Trail. Look for a steep groove behind a couple of skinny trees, with a sentry-box at 10m, still sporting an ancient sling.

| **Sherry's Crack** | | 10d | x | 10m |

Joe Buszowski Bruce McDonald June 1983

A short distance beyond *Enchimeggs*, the trail leaves Olesen Creek and climbs steeply up leftward for 30m to a short hand-railed section. Immediately above is a clean little wall, projecting from the mass of rambling bush crag above, and split by this short finger and hand-crack. Often wet.

> *Continuing up the trail from Sherry's Crack, the fork for the North Chief is reached within a 100m or so. Beyond this point, the South Peak trail passes below a wide expanse of high dark slabs, easily visible through the trees. Sharp eyes will spot an occasional ancient bolt and station, but no record of any climb is known.*

> ***So it goes in Squamish.*** *On October 17th 1995, the Chief was declared a Class A Provincial Park at a public ceremony and celebration in Squamish. Government dignitaries, First Nations, local businesses, media, politicians and climbers were all represented. But the loggers of Squamish also turned up in large and very noisy numbers to protest, (something about not enough jobs), and largely succeeded in wrecking the Chief's big day, even to the extent of fisticuffs on the side.*

North Peak Trailside Climbs

The following three climbs are scattered along the trail between White Cliff and the Solarium. Worth checking out.

Getting there... Take the main trail up the Backside (page 296). to White Cliff. The first route is a short distance above, 50m above the trail fork to the Cirque of the Uncrackables. It faces south.

A Walk In The Park   10d   30m
Marc Bombois   Joe Turley   May 1998
A crack and groove system with a burly start past a bolt.

> *The next two climbs overlook the North Chief trail in the wide gully a few minutes past White Cliff. They lie up on the right (east) side of the gully, but are approached off the trail to the Solarium. See page 307, and the map on page 162. At the top of the rock step out of the gully head immediately left, up a narrow groove for 20m to a flat terrace below a steep south-facing wall.*

Silent Ladies   *   10b   20m
Joe Turley   George Hanzel   March 1998
The offwidth corner-crack at the left side of the terrace.

British Bricklayer   *   .9   20m
George Hanzel   Joe Turley   March 1998
Left of *Silent Ladies* is a facecrack overlooking the North Chief gully. Climb it, past hidden flakes. The thin face crack between the two routes is unclimbed.

Trailside Distraction   10c   x   8m
Robin Barley   Aug 1995
This climb is right on the trail to the Solarium, 50m past *Bricklayer*, a deceptive, right-leaning thin crack on the left side of the trail.

NORTH PEAK TRAILSIDE CLIMBS

A WALK IN THE PARK

BRITISH BRICKLAYER

SILENT LADIES

The White Cliff

This crag is a worthwhile destination with an interesting array of short quality climbs to offer. Well worth a vist. Climbs are described from the left as they are approached. Rappel descents.

Getting there...   Take the main hiking trail up the Backside (**page 296, map page 162**). At the third fork go right for the North Chief, a major junction just past the minor trail exit off right to the top of Shannon Falls. The cliff is reached in about 30 minutes up from the campground, very obvious at the trailside.

Future Shock ******   12a   25m
Perry Beckham 1982   FFA: Kevin McLane June 1985
Fine climbing where the trail first meets the cliff. A short steep wall leads past 2 bolts to an impending ramp. Technically difficult moves up the ramp lead to a final strenuous crack.

Alien Discharge *****   12b   27m
Josh Korman 1988
Layback up the flake line to the right, joining into *Future Shock*.

Conventional Arms ●   10b   2p.
Robin Barley Bernie Protsch 1985
Start 5m right of a cedar snag, and climb into a sentry box. Traverse left along a crack to a small ledge. Pass a detached block then more easily up the ledge above (10b). Above the belay, move up an open corner, then left to climb a good crack (10c).

Vital Transformation ******   12c   *304*   20m
Jim Campbell R.Gordon (Wee Stoppers) Dec 1978   FFA: Perry Beckham July 23 1986
Start as for *Conventional Arms*, but climb the fierce thin crack right of the sentry box. It is sustained and quite desperate. RPs etc.

Backwoods Beebop ******   10d   22m
Perry Beckham Jan Daly Mar 1983
An excellent climb, easier than it appears. Climb the shallow corner just right of *Vital Transformation*, to a basalt dyke and up the steep face above on beautiful jugs. Ledge belay above.

Bush Doctor ● ☺   11b   *304*   20m
Perry Beckham R.Kusera Mar 1983
10m right of *Backwoods Beebop*, a steep groove leads up to a ramp and an even steeper crack above.

Transmigration ● ☺   10b   *304*   2p.
Robin Barley Dave Jones April 1983
A varied and exciting climb. Take the flake that crosses *Bush Doctor* leftwards up to the basalt dyke, then follow fine holds straight up to the belay ledge (10a). Traverse left along a steep, exposed crack to a FP. Pull up on better holds to reach a dyke leading to a ledge (10b). Rappel down.

Fungus Flare ● .8 12m
Perry Beckham 1983
The left-leaning chimney-groove the leads to the top of *Bush Doctor*.

The Grip Of The Kaffir Dog ● ☺ 11b 40m
K.Smith Robin Barley (1pa) 1984 FFA: Jim Brennan Greg Foweraker 1988
A compelling line up the flaring crack 5m past *Fungus Flare*. Cross a small roof and up the crack to a higher corner, pull through the roof and up the flake crack above. Rappel.

Everyone's A Guide * 12b 35m
Hamish Fraser Peder Ourom Jan 1994
Face climb right of *The Grip of the Kaffir Dog* past 4 bolts to a 10b crack.

> *A little higher, the trail forks. The right fork goes to The Cirque of the Uncrackables, the left to the Solarium. At the fork, there are three climbs on the upper White Cliff wall.*

Fragility Test * 10c 20m
Robin Barley Nick Barley April 1987
Start up the prominent crackline, but soon go left up flakes on the left wall. Belay at a small tree.

Urinary Incontinence * 10a 30m
Robin Barley Nick Barley April 1987
Follow the main crackline.

Diagonal Gang .8 20m
Robin Barley Nick Barley April 1987
Start on the right, join *Urinary...* then exit left along large blocks.

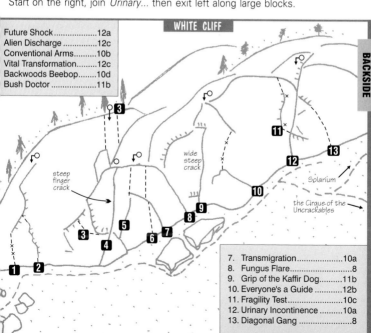

WHITE CLIFF

CHIEF BACKSIDE

Future Shock	12a
Alien Discharge	12c
Conventional Arms	10b
Vital Transformation	12c
Backwoods Beebop	10d
Bush Doctor	11b

steep finger crack

wide steep crack

Solarium

the Cirque of the Uncrackables

7. Transmigration 10a
8. Fungus Flare 8
9. Grip of the Kaffir Dog 11b
10. Everyone's a Guide 12b
11. Fragility Test 10c
12. Urinary Incontinence 10a
13. Diagonal Gang 8

The Cirque Of The Uncrackables

This is an impressive south-facing cliff which houses a number of superb long cracks across a range of grades. The atmosphere is one of being deep in an open forest, as the tall trees reach almost to the top of the crag–good for hot summer days. If this entire crag could be seen as one, it would be one of the most impressive sights at Squamish. The crag lies below and slightly left of the Solarium, but travel between the two crags is fraught with steep 5.10 bush.

Getting there... Take the main hiking trail up the Backside, turning right at the first fork for the North Chief (page 269). Just beyond the White Cliff, turn right again at a trail fork onto the hiking trail to the Squaw. In 3 minutes the first route is reached.

March Of The Kitchen Utensils ** .9   35m
John Howe Joe Buszowski Blake Robinson 1981
Grand stuff. Climb the obvious and friendly offwidth crack. Layback or jam.

Ivan Meets GI Joe *   10a   20m
Hamish Fraser Craig Thomson 1981
Start as for *March...*, but climb the overhanging flake on the left.

> *30m further along the trail is a impressive square bay on the left. Hike up into it, and discover two awesome climbs.*

The Scimitar ***   11b   *305*   40m
K.Swedin Todd Bibler July 1984
The corner at the left side of the back of the bay, hidden from the trail, houses this awesome wide crack. Naturally, it overhangs near the top, just where you don't need it. It is the hardest offwidth yet climbed at Squamish.

The Scimitar Right Side ● ☺ 10b   30m
Peter Croft Tami Knight 1981
Climb the large flakes on the right side of the bay facing across to *The Scimitar*. It is uncertain exactly where the route goes, but it sure looks good.

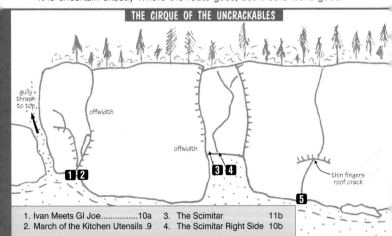

THE CIRQUE OF THE UNCRACKABLES

gully thrash to top

offwidth

offwidth

1 2   **3 4**   thin fingers roof crack   **5**

1. Ivan Meets GI Joe..............10a	3. The Scimitar	11b
2. March of the Kitchen Utensils .9	4. The Scimitar Right Side	10b

Just beyond The Scimitar, the cliff rears out into a great curving roof above the trail – Cobra Crack.

Cobra Crack A2 40m
Peter Croft Tami Knight 1981
This rates as one of the most awesome Last Great Problem finger cracks at Squamish. Worth a hike just to look at the way the finger crack up the wall arches out to overhang the trail.

The next, unmistakeable feature is a big dihedral east of Cobra Crack.

Bop 'til You Drop ★★★ 10b _304_ 40m
Dave Lane Scott Flavelle 1981
The huge right-facing dihedral. Hand and fist jamming above a chimney lead to an easier finish. A good climb for its grade: real 5.10 jamming.

Boogie 'til You Puke ★★★ 10c _304_ 40m
S.Flavelle D.Lane 1981
Immediately right of *Bop 'til You Drop* is an impressive right-in-your-face offwidth face-crack, a worthy companion to *The Scimitar*.

The next feature is an impressive face-crack that curves across from left to right.

Magical Dog A3 .8 2p.
John Howe Blake Robinson Jan 1981
The striking left-curving crack that almost reaches into *Boogie...* Aid, followed by some face climbing.

Big Mouth ● 11b 15m
Peter Croft Mike Beaubien 1981
A thin crack leading into an ugly flake chimney.

Hidden Umph ● 10a 15m
Robert Gordon Jim Campbell Dec 1978
Move up a ramp right of *Big Mouth* to reach this off-width crack.

CHIEF
BACKSIDE

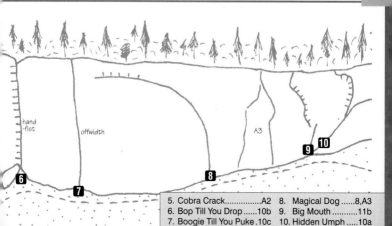

WHITE CLIFF — CIRQUE CLIMBS

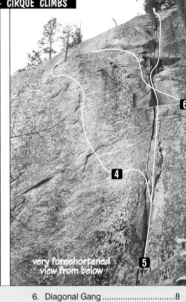

very foreshortened
view from below

1. Vital Transformation 12c
2. Bush Doctor 11b
3. Transmigration 10b
4. Fragility Test......................10c
5. Urinary Incontinence 10a

6. Diagonal Gang 8
7. Ivan Meets GI Joe 10a
8. March of the Kitchen Utensils 9
9. Bop Till You Drop 10b
10. Boogie Till You Puke 10c

foreshortened
view from below

very foreshortened
view from below

Slesse

THE CIRQUE — PUNK ROCK — ABOVE AND BEYOND CLIMBS

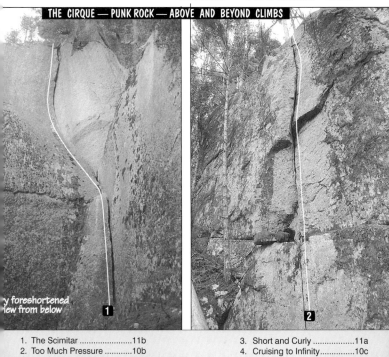

very foreshortened
view from below

1

2

1. The Scimitar 11b
2. Too Much Pressure 10b

3. Short and Curly 11a
4. Cruising to Infinity..............10c

3

CHIEF
BACKSIDE

4

very foreshortened
view from below

Short and Curly

This is a small crag directly above the right end of the Cirque of the Uncrackables. Hard to reach, but no crowds.

Getting there... Take the main hiking trail up the Backside (page 296). and head for the Cirque of the Uncrackables. The best approach is to thrash up a steep gully at the left side of The Cirque, just left of *Ivan Meets GI Joe.* Or climb *Boogie* or *Bop* to reach the same place.

Too Drunk To Fuck   11b   *x*   15m
Bruce McDonald Dean Hart May 1983
What a let-down for the unfortunate lass. A short distance left of *Short and Curly*, this climb is in an area of blocky flakes and cracks.

Short And Curly *   11a   *305*   12m
Peter Croft Greg Foweraker 1981
A curving finger-crack above an open terrace.

Punk Rock

This little outcrop is east of the Cirque of the Uncrackables, and is actually a continuation of that same line of crag. Some new route potential–worth a visit if you're climbing on the Solarium or White Cliff with time to spare.

Getting there... Take the main hiking trail up the Backside (page 296). to White Cliff. It's an easy walk of less than 10 minutes from White Cliff–just 3 minutes past the last route on The Cirque. The trail to Above and Beyond passes below this crag.

Too Much Pressure *   10b   *305*   18m
Peder Ourom John Howe Blake Robinson 1981
The obvious handjam crack. Excellent value.

Safety Valve ● ☺   10b   *x*   15m
Unknown, c 1983
A short corner immediately right of *Too Much Pressure.*

Stone Flower ● ☺   10b   *x*   15m
Unknown, c 1983
A thin face-crack 20m right of *Too Much Pressure*, leading to a blocky, right-facing ramp.

> ***Name story...*** *March of the Kitchen Utensils was named in honour of the first nude ascent of Diedre in 1979 by Dave Lane, Dave Fulton, Paul Kindree, John Kindree and John Howe. Dressed with paper bags covering their heads, pots as helmets and kitchen utensils as protection.*

The Solarium

This cliff forms the major climbing area on the Backside, facing south and offering fine routes up to 3 pitches long below the summit of the North Chief. The open, sunny aspect and sense of quiet space and elevation are unmatched by any other crag at Squamish. The rock is rougher than that of the west and north faces of the Chief, allowing steeper face climbs and padding. Approaching from the west, the initial slabs steepen into walls split by several corners, including *Scatterbrain.* A major bush ramp splits the Solarium into two crags. Continuing on, the base is steep with long slabs hidden above, then the cliff rears up into a large prow and the stunning finger-handcrack of *Sunblessed* comes into view.

Getting there... Take the main hiking trail up the Backside (**page 296, map page 162**). Continue beyond White Cliff (**see page 300**) on the trail up into the canyon-like gully that leads to the summit of the North Chief. The gully is steep, and the wall on the right side is craggy. Five minutes (200m or so) above White Cliff, an easy exit to the right is possible up a short, 3m rock step. This is the first practical place to get out of the gully. At the top of the step, either continue east on a rough trail that scrambles up 100m or so to the open slabs west of the Solarium, or turn immediately left and scramble up a narrow groove for 20m to a flat sunny terrace below a steep south-facing wall (*British Bricklayer* and *Silent Ladies*). Go right here to rejoin the main trail. Traverse 150m along the base of the slabs to the west end of the Solarium. Allow 45–60 minutes car to crag.

Another Imperfection   *   10c   #6   <u>309</u>   **SPORT**   30m
Robin Barley   Anthony Silva   May 1994
This bolted face climb is encountered left of the trail, immediately upon entering the trees again after crossing the slabs. A good warm-up.

> ▮ *The next group of climbs is about 40m right, just as the wall steepens. If the climbs don't make you feel silly, the names will.*

Dafter By The Day   *   11a   #8   <u>309</u>   **SPORT**   30m
Robin Barley   1995
At the left side of the high wall, climb a short hand-crack past a block then a slabby ramp trending up right to the base of a dyke. Continue up left on the vague, intermittent dyke to a tree belay.

Dimmer Still   **   11a+1pa   #7   <u>309</u>   **SPORT+**   35m
Robin Barley   1995
Just right of *Dafter* is an open, right-facing dihedral with a bottoming crack and bolts on its left wall. Gain the dihedral by using the first bolt for aid. Tenuous climbing then leads up the dihedral and a thin crack to a palatial balcony.

Dancing With The Village Idiot ** 10c   2p
Robin Barley Judy Komori 1995
The easiest climb around here, taking in some of the best climbing on three other routes. Start up *Dafter...* moving right at 15m to the dihedral of *Dimmer Still*. Belay at the palatial balcony (10c). After wandering a bit on the right, join *Dimwitted*. Pass the belay and finish up an arete (10c).

About 25m further right along the base from Dafter and Dimmer is a short obvious corner. Four climbs begin here. Dimwitted starts up the corner, the other three up the slab to its right.

Dimwitted *   11c   2p.
Guy Edwards Robin Barley August 1994
Climb the easy left-facing corner to the left edge of the ramp above, then go left up an abrasive crack to gain a black overhanging bay (10c). The lieback seam above is mainly bolt-protected, but save a 1½" CD for pro. Belay on the left on a narrow ledge (11c), or continue to the top of *Village Idiot*.

Scatterbrain ***   11a   2p.
Robin Barley Nick Barley (1pa) June 1988 FFA Lindsay Eltis May 1993.
Start up a mossy slab right of the short corner to reach the right end of the ramp above and belay (10a). Excellent sustained climbing follows up a crack and corner line. Climb the bottoming corner-crack then difficult moves into a wider crack and a good ledge above. Climb the steepening headwall (11a). Rappel or scramble down the big ramp on the right.

Anencephalic   *   10d   2p.
Robin Barley Anthony Silva June 1994
Climb the initial slab of *Scatterbrain* to gain the ramp and belay (10a). Move right up a long pitch to the headwall, up shallow dihedrals and seams (10d).

Nick's Trick *   10a   3p.
Nick Barley Robin Barley June 1988
Climb the initial slab of *Scatterbrain* to gain the ramp and belay (10a). Climb diagonally up the unsteep ramp on the right and gain a crack leading to easier ground and a ledge belay (10a). An easier crack leads to slabs.

Fissure Fiend   10d   *x*   25m
Robin Barley Luc Mailloux 1995
About 50m right of the *Scatterbrain* area is a rough, discontinuous crack above a culturally modified cedar. Climb it, past an awkward overlap to a distinctly raspy finish.

Last Will And Testicle ** 10d   *x*   3p.
Robin Barley Nick Barley 1988
About 100m right of the *Scatterbrain* area, at the end of the long roof, step up off another culturally modified cedar to gain a left facing corner. Strenuous climbing up the finger crack to a tree belay above. A good pitch (10d). Go across left and up an easy crack, veering left over slabs to belay beside flakes (.7). Friction climbing past bolts leads to the top of the descent ramp (10a).

THE SOLARIUM — LEFT SIDE

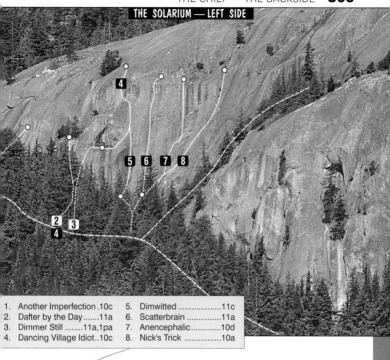

1. Another Imperfection .10c
2. Dafter by the Day 11a
3. Dimmer Still 11a,1pa
4. Dancing Village Idiot..10c
5. Dimwitted 11c
6. Scatterbrain 11a
7. Anencephalic.............10d
8. Nick's Trick 10a

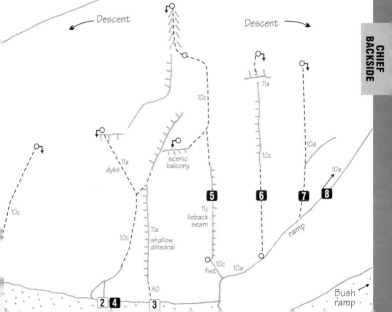

CHIEF
BACKSIDE

The trail along the terrace at the base of the cliff narrows down toward the east end and the final group of climbs, including Sunblessed and Message from the Stars. Several routes here share the same two starts— a thin bolted seam and a dike to the right.

The Velocity Of Darkness   * 11a   2p.
Robin Barley Peter Shackleton 1996
Start up the seam. From its top, step left to a shallow groove then a hard mantel up leftward, then up to belay (11a). Follow a short groove then a lovely rough wall to a shallow dihedral (10c).

Mere Mortals   **   11c   (11a+2pa)   2p.
Robin Barley Luke Mailloux (alts, 2pa) July 1994   FFA: John Rosholt Peder Ourom 1997
Start up the seam, and continue past bolts to a tree. Traverse right to a bush in the main corner (11a). Go up a rib and steep face above to a ledge, past a hard crux at two bolts (11c). A final groove on the left leads to the top (10a).

Message From The Stars ***½ 11c   #10?   **SPORT**+   3p.
Guy Edwards Robin Barley (Alts) August 1994
A tremendous climb which takes the great prow right of *Sunblessed*, sharing the same belays. The 2nd pitch, hidden from view, is one of the finest face pitches in this guide. Start up the seam, and follow the diagonal dyke out right to join *Sunblessed* at the belay (11a). Move up the crack above then traverse right on the dyke to the exposed prow. Climb the narrow face to its right. Sustained (11b). Rappel, or climb the arete above (harder than it looks), left of the deep corner. Take some wires and CDs to 1″ for this pitch (11c).

Enlightened   ***   10c   3p.
Robin Barley Judy Komori 1996
Climb the initial dyke of *Sunblessed* and continue leftward up the slab to belay below a tree (10a). Step left and climb a gritty groove then up to the base of a superb corner crack (10c). Climb it—long and beautiful (.9).

Sunblessed   ***½   10b   4p.
Robin Barley Dave Jones (Alts) May 1988.
Right-hand finish David Vocadlo Tamara Rusnak 1995
This beautiful climb is a must-do. Climb a steep but delicate dyke to belay below a superb crack (10a). This long sustained finger and hand crack splits the wall above in a very fine position (10a). An easier pitch leads up right, then back left to the base of a steep open corner (.6). Hand and fist jamming lead up to better holds and an excellent finish through a slight bulge at the top (10b). An alternative finish is possible up the arete to the right (10c), and an excellent finish is possible out left up the last pitch of *Mere Mortals* (10a), keeping the grade of the climb to 5.10a on every pitch.

Helioproctosis   10d+1pa   2p.
p1 Robin Barley Nick Barley 1986   p2 Robin Barley Judy Komori 1996
This climb, where the sun shines from a dark place, follows the huge left-facing corner that defines the left edge of the *Sunblessed* wall. Start right of *Sunblessed* and climb to a pedestal. Cross a smooth wall (1pa) to a hand-crack the leads to a belay on *Sunblessed* (10b). Follow the large corner above, passing through the belay of *Mere Mortals* (10d).

THE SOLARIUM — RIGHT SIDE

CHIEF
BACKSIDE

he Velocity of Darkness.........11a
ere Mortals ....11c (11a+2pa)
essage From the Stars 11c
lightened...............................10c
unblessed................................10b
alioproctosis............10d 1pa

Above And Beyond

The 1992 guide said this was "A big mysterious crag lurking in seclusion behind the North Chief". Well, it still is. But its day will come, as there is a lot of unclimbed stone there.

Getting there... Take the trail up the Backside (page 296). Just beyond the White Cliff, turn right along the trail to the Squaw. Hike on below The Cirque, and about 10 minutes further, the trail crosses a huge rockfall. A short distance beyond, a rough trail heads up for a few minutes to the base of Above And Beyond. About 60 minutes approach.

Cruising To Infinity   ★★   10c   *305*   2p.
Robin Barley Peter Shackleton May 1985
A tall east facing wall, is split by a long impeccable finger and hand crack, albeit dirty. Climb up to belay in an alcove (.8). Good protection in the crack, balance left to finish (10c). Rappel. Full rack.

> *To reach the start of the next climb, crawl out leftward from the start of Cruising to Infinity along a bedding plane.*

Ad Infinitum   10c   30m
Robin Barley June 1998
From the top of a huge pillar an obvious hand crack beacons upward.

The Fissure Flavelle   ★★   10c+1pa   2p.
p1 Perry Beckham 1982   p2 Scott Flavelle Robin Barley Aug 1988
Right of *Cruising To Infinity* is a monster square roof. A difficult start with an aid point leads up to the roof and a bolt. Traverse left to the end of the roof and up an excellent hand crack to a constricted belay (10c+1pa). The next pitch is a magnificent 5" offwidth crack (10c). Bolts beside the crack were scorned by Flavelle, hence the name given by his peers. Rappel down.

Mustafa Rides To The Stars   ★   10b   25m
Bob Milward Peter Shackleton 1987
Just right of *The Fissure Flavelle*, climb a fine crack to a tree belay (10b). Rappel, or climb two poor pitches to the top (10a).

Exploring Uranus   ★   10c+1pa   40m
Robin Barley Bernie Protsch July 1986
How interesting. Walk up along the base until below an obvious triangular roof. Start here, climbing up to a ledge at 15m. Tension left into a larger corner system, and up to a small ledge and spike belays. Rappel.

The fastest known time up the Backside trail to the top of the South Summit is 22 minutes 45 seconds, by Richard Wheater in 1998.

ABOVE AND BEYOND

from Squaw Trail

1. Ad Infinitum........................10c
2. Cruising to Infinity..............10c
3. Fissure Flavelle............10c,1pa
4. Mustafa Rides to the Stars .10b
5. Exploring Uranus.........10c,1pa

Canadian Compromise, 5.10a
Climber: Gordon Addison
Photo: Aaron Black

Negro Lesbian, A4
Climber: Sean Easton
Photo: Jia Condon

THE LONG AID CLIMBS

Since the last guide was published in 1992, there has been a renaissance in big-wall aid climbing at Squamish, coming after more than 15 years of inactivity. It began about 1993-94, and by the summer of 1998, climbers up on the walls had become a routine sight again, often several parties on three or four climbs at once. This is a welcome and exciting trend.

The early years of exploration at Squamish left a legacy of outstanding aid routes scattered along the great walls of the Chief, a testament to some of the qualities that have shaped Squamish climbing–typically bold and adventurous, to which another 6 climbs have been added since 1996. The new climbs of recent years are all quality enterprises from Luc Mailloux, Sean Easton, Perry Beckham, Damien Kelly and Matt Maddaloni, and include *Under The Gun; Skullfuck, Cowboys and Indians* and *The Raven.* Other climbers who have contributed to the high-energy psyche include Jia Condon, Rich Prohaska, Chris Geisler and Rob Munro. Not just the dudes either: Laura Hellyar, Elise Kelly and Page Bell have shown it is a woman's game too, swinging leads on difficult climbs.

This trend back to aid climbing at Squamish poses some interesting questions as to why. Some things seem obvious: a new generation looking for adventure and horizons; uncrowded places to climb where challenge and ingenuity can be tested; and as rock-climbers have embraced the low-risk fun of sport climbing, so the game has naturally expanded at the other end of the scale to embrace high-risk adventure. Improvements in gear have helped too, especially micro-cams and beaks.

Aid climbing has some less-obvious attractions too: climbing can continue in poor weather and living on the walls costs a lot less than rent; it will certainly ensure a high level of competence at rope-management and gear organisation; and on short easy practice climbs, it is a fast way for novice climbers to gain confidence at gear placing and becoming comfortable with real exposure.

The three great easier classics are unchanged: *University Wall, Uncle Ben's,* and *Cannabis Wall.* They are by far the most popular long routes, by virtue of their moderate difficulty and fine settings. Long-established quality climbs at a higher level of difficulty and commitment are: *Breakfast Run, Negro Lesbian, Up From The Skies, Ten Years After, Humpty Dumpty, Edge of Pan* and *The Sheriff's Badge.*

CHIEF AID

Squamish granite is very compact for the most part, but the climbs generally have common features, particularly the proliferation of expanding flakes, from thin flakes to entire corner systems, tiny micro seams, thin cracks, basalt dykes and tiny edges for hooking. The hardest climbs demand the full arsenal of modern technique and ingenuity, typically sketchy hooking on tiny edges, long top-step stretches, tiny cam placements, and very sustained sections. The nature of the available unclimbed rock means that classic aid cracks are becoming harder to find, so the trend is toward the open walls, linking micro seams, hooking, drilling the occasional rivet, using tiny peckers and beaks (kinda like rurps shaped into tiny ice-tools) and major amounts of hairy off-balance top-stepping, hands reaching up to feel around for something... a bathole, anything. A bolt kit is advisable for replacing rivets and upgrading belay stations on the less-travelled routes.

A trend has developed toward long pitches, often linking what was previously two by means of 60m ropes. Until the mid-1980s, 45m ropes were standard fare. Larger and heavier racks are required of course, but it does allow faster climbing.

Grading aid routes is an esoteric and uncertain process. Today, aid climbs come with three grading flavours: standard A1 to A5 grades, **C** grades (Clean) for hammerless climbing, and new wave grades which are being exported from Yosemite Valley, generally half to a full grade lower than their standard counterpart. All of the climbs listed prior to 1996 are standard grades, one of the new climbs is new wave.

A1 traditionally means "will hold a truck", interpreted as meaning that several placements will make a bombproof belay.

A2 requires a good knowledge of a wide variety of gear, especially micro cams for less secure placements, but with A1 placements never far away.

A3 ramps up the difficulty to demand experience at marginal placements, expanding cracks and flakes, and potential for falls up to 10 or 15 metres.

A4 will require considerable experience at using all the modern modified gear, route-finding, perhaps bad rock, and definitely potential for long falls.

A5 is similar to A4 except that the difficulty is even more sustained, to the point where full rope-length falls must be anticipated: very serious stuff.

Below is a checklist for starting your aid career, and suggested racks for the long aid walls. Most climbers will adapt these lists to suit their own preferences. To this can be added more specific gear for each climb as you choose, bivi gear if you need it, and your own favourite tools, devices and gadgets, as well as exotic stuff like beaks and aliens. Consider 55m ropes, kneepads, fingerless mitts and helmets, rivet hangers and swaged loops to be standard equipment, as well as a bolt kit for less-travelled routes and 60m ropes for the modern ones.

Rurps , 2
Angles ½", 2
Angles ⅝", 2
Angles ¾", 1
Angles 1", 1

Knifeblades (mix), 10
Lost Arrows (mix), 8
Leepers, 2
Hooks (each size), 1
Bathooks (each size), 2

Cams, 2 of each size, micros to 3"
Sawed-off angles, 1 each ½" to ¾"
Rivet hangers, 3
Copperheads, 10 assorted sizes
Hand-drill bolt kit

Wrist Twister
Cams, 2 each to 2"
Cams, 1 each 3½"-4½"
Rurps, 2.   Heads, 10
Knifeblades, 8
SO angles, 1 at ¾"
Nuts, RPs, hooks

Breakfast Run
Cams, 2 each to 2"
Knifeblades, 10
Lost Arrows, 10
Heads, 10
Angles, 2 each ½" - ¾"
Nuts, RPs, hooks

Cannabis Wall
Cams, 2 each to 2½"
Heads, 3
Lost Arrows, 3
SO angles, 1 each ½" & ¾"
Nuts, RPs, hooks

Negro Lesbian
Cams, 2 each to 4"
Heads, 10
Rurps, 2. Beaks, 2
Knifeblades, 8
Lost Arrows, 10
Angles, 2 each ½" & ¾"
SO angles, 1 each ½" & ¾"
Nuts, RPs, hooks

The Black Dyke
Cams, 2 each to 1½",
Cams, 1 each 2"-3½"
Knifeblades, 5
Lost Arrows, 5
Angles, 1 each ½" & ¾"
Hooks

Zorros Last Ride
Cams, 2 each ½" to 1½"
Rurps, 2
Knifeblades, 20
Lost Arrows, 15
Nuts, RPs, hooks
Rivet hangers, 5

Under The Gun
Cams, 1 each to 3"
Knifeblades, 10
Lost Arrows, 10
Heads, 10
Nuts, RPs, hooks

Up From The Skies
Cams, 2 each to 3"
Knifeblades, 8
Heads, 6
Lost Arrows, 8
Angles, 2 each ½" to ¾"
Nuts, RPs, hooks

Ten Years After
Cams, 2 each to 2½"
Knifeblades, 4
Lost Arrows, 5
Angles, 2 each ½" to 5/8"
SO angles, 1 at ½"
Nuts RPs, hooks

Humpty Dumpty
Cams, 2 each to 1",
Cams, 1 each 1½" to 3"
Knifeblades, 8
Lost Arrows, 10
Heads, 10
Angles, 2 each ½", 2 each 5/8"
SO angles, 1 each ½" to ¾"
Nuts, RPs, hooks

Uncle Bens
Cams, 2 each to 4"
Knifeblades, 2
Lost Arrows, 3
Angles, 1 each ½ to ¾"
SO angles, 1 each ½" to ¾"
Nuts, RPs hooks

University Wall (clean)
Cams, 2 or 3 each to 1½"
Cams, 2 each 2" to 3"
Cams, 1 each 3½" & 4"
Knifeblades, 2
Nuts, RPs, hooks

Edge of Pan
Cams, 2 each to 2"
Knifeblades, 8
Lost Arrows, 8
Nuts, RPs, hooks

Pan Granitic Frogman
Cams, 2 each to 3"
Rurps, 20
Knifeblades, 20
Lost Arrows, 15
Angles, 3 each ½" to ¾"
Nuts, RPs, hooks

Son of Pan
Cams, 2 each to 3"
Rurps, 20
Knifeblades, 8
Lost Arrows, 8
Angles, 2 each ½" to ¾"
Nuts, RPs, hooks

Sheriffs Badge
Cams, 2 each to 3½"
Heads, 20
Rurps, 3
Beaks, 3
Knifeblades, 8
Lost Arrows, 8
Angles, 2 each ½" to ¾"
SO angles, 1 each ½" & ¾"
Nuts, RPs, hooks

Skullfuck
Cams, 3 each to 1½"
Cams, 2 each 2" to 3"
Cams, 1 each 3½" & 4"
Heads, 40
Rurps, 5.   Beaks, 10
Knifeblades, 10
Lost Arrows, 15
Angles 2 each ½" to ¾"
Angles, 1 at 1"
Nuts, RPs, hooks

Cowboys and Indians
Cams, 3 each to 2½"
Heads, 20
Knifeblades, 16
Lost Arrows, 10
Angles, 4 each ½ to ¾"
Angles, 2 each 1" to 1½"
Nuts, RPs, hooks
¼" bolt hangers / loops, 15

The Raven
Cams, 3 each to 2"
Cams, 1 each to 4"
Lost Arrows, 15
Knifeblades, 15
Rurps, 4
Beaks, 4
Heads, 30
Angles, 3 each ½" to ¾"
Angles, 1 each 1" to 1½"
Nuts, RPs, hooks
Rivet hangers, 10

LONG AID CLIMBS ON THE CHIEF

Bivouacs... Assume that all of the climbs that go to Bellygood or the top of the Dihedrals will require a bivouac, unless you are very fast and confident of a one-day ascent. *Sea of Tranquillity*, *Cannabis*, *Breakfast Run* (via rap-in), and *Wrist Twister* are considered one-day routes. *Breakfast Run* via *Cannabis* will require a bivi. One-day ascents of climbs on the Pan Wall are pushing it, given the haul up from the base. The climbs on the Sheriffs Badge and Zodiac Wall will also require a bivouac. Or two. It is essential to practise no-impact bivis, and always tell someone responsible (that could be hard) which climb you are on and when you hope to be back.

Notes on the topos... The topos have been picked over and checked by many climbers, and can be considered accurate for the most part, although opinion will always vary on the grade of some pitches and on the rack required. Grades change too, as pitches gain more (or less) fixed gear, and the rock changes. Not all bolts are marked, as it is not practical in the available space. However, the intention is that a bolt or bolts are marked where they matter, and as an aid to routefinding. Successful aid ascents demand resourceful climbers, for whom the topo is a guide only–there is no substitute for your eyes, good judgement and a vivid imagination as to what to do next.

CHIEF AID

Tantalus Wall

Wrist Twister   A3   C4   **327**   3p.
Paul Piro Brian Norris 1974
A popular aid route. Short and sweet up a line of thin bottoming cracks at the right side of Tantalus Wall. Take lots of small stuff, hooks, bathooks and copperheads. Look for batholes on the last pitch!

Breakfast Run   A4   .7   **327**   4p.
Tim Auger Neil Bennet (to the roof) 1972; Hugh Burton Steve Sutton (complete) 1975
A high quality route up cracklines at the left side of Tantalus Wall. Best approach is via *Cannabis Wall*, for a total of 9 pitches. There is a thin, awkward crux described as "talus food potential".

Cannabis Wall   A3 or C3   .7   **327**   5p.
Eric Lance Brian Norris T.deGuistini 1969
Along with *Ben's* and *Wrist Twister*, this climb is a great first wall. Just south of *Freeway*, a bolt ladder indicates the start. Finish by rapping down [most common] or up *Crescent Ramp* or *Breakfast Run* [harder].

The Dihedrals

This group of rarely-climbed long routes suffer from being either terminally damp (except in summer), or too much bush. But it is an intriguing area, with lots yet to be done.

Getting Down On The Brown   � A2   .9   **328**   ±9p.
Daryl Hatten Cam Cairns 1978
Never repeated, this is a much-looked at line of long, parallel corners left of *Freeway*. Climb *Freeway* to the top of the *Daylight Crack* and launch.

Western Dihedral   ✽   A2   .8   **328**   ±9p.
Fred Beckey Dan Tate May 1966
The enormous corner system at the right side of the Dihedrals Wall, left of *Freeway*. Often wet and danky. Rarely climbed, but it could have a major new lease on life as a freeclimb if given a thorough clean and good stations.

Sea Of Tranquillity   ✽   A3   **328**   (3p.)
Matt Maddaloni Ben Demenech Ken Sharpe January 1999
Three pitches up *Western Dihedral* (10c), then out left to take an often-looked at corner system to the base of *Clean Corner*. Some excellent nailing.

Illusion   ✽   A2   .8   **328**   10p.
Bob Woodsworth Dan Tate June 1966
Another rarely climbed route, it branches left out of *Western Dihedral* to climb big corners up to Trichome Ledge. Finish up *Clean Corner*.

Slow Dyke   ✽   A3   .8   **328**   10p.
Tim Auger Mike Wisnicki 1970
A climb that lost its best pitches when *Deadend Dihedral* was freed, but there is a pitch and a half of interesting climbing before it merges with *Crap Crags*.

The Grand Wall

The Negro Lesbian 🐾   A3+ .8   *331*   8p.
Daryl Hatten Clive Thomson Rick Baudains 1982
One of the great climbs of Squamish, this long, classic wall has almost everything, including major exposure through the roofs.

The Black Dyke   A3+ 10a   *331*   8p.
Al Givler Mead Hargis 1970 (to Bellygood)
The great basalt dyke that streaks the right side of the Grand Wall. Difficult aid through the first roof band. Watch for loose rock and sharp edges. Many bolts from a free attempt through the upper roof have drawn *The Dyke's* teeth.

Zorro's Last Ride   A3+ 10c   *331*   (8p.)
Perry Beckham Dave Lane 1979
Rarely climbed, it offers 6 pitches of aid between the top of *Movin' To Montana* and *The Grand Wall.* Start up *Movin' To Montana* or *Exasperator.*

Under The Gun   A3 (New Wave) 10c *333*   (5p.)
Luc Mailloux Rob Munro 1997
A major variation to *Up From The Skies*, it sneaks off right to some good terrain in that great expanse of rock left of *Zorro's.*

Up From The Skies   A4 10c   *333*   (4p.)
Daryl Hatten Eric Weinstein July 1975
Expanding flake horrors have given this route a formidable reputation. Climb *Cruel Shoes* to reach the start, and check the picture of Luc before you go. The last pitch to the Flats has been reported as the hardest on the Chief.

Grinning Weasel   A3 12a   *333*   (50m)
Peter Croft Greg Foweraker 1982
This single pitch of thin crack aid links *The Left Side* with *Ten Years After*, a climb of 9-10 pitches in all to Dance Platform.

Ten Years After   A3 10a C4   *333*   7p.
Hugh Burton Dick Culbert Paul Piro 1970
A prominent line of face cracks and expanding corners left of *The Grand.* A popular climb because of its generally moderate difficulty and fine exposure, but the first aid pitch is shared with a freeclimb—*Genius Loci*—and the hammering and hooking is breaking holds. ***Please tread very lightly here.***

Humpty Dumpty   A4 10a   *333*   (4p.)
Scott Flavelle Carl Austrom 1977
One of the great climbs of Squamish, *Humpty* takes an elegant line joining *Uncle Ben's* to *10 Years After.* The *Yellow Sickle* pitch is wickedly expanding and the highlight of the climb.

Uncle Ben's   A2+ or C3 10c *333*   10p.
Hugh Burton Steve Sutton 1970
The most popular classic aid wall, this is the route where most local wall climbers cut their baby teeth—a rite of passage to higher realms, although that passage is easier than it used to be due to so much fixed gear—all in the full blast of tourist awe. It has been climbed without hammers.

CHIEF AID

University Wall Area

University Wall   C2   *333, 335*   7p.
Tim Auger Dan Tate Hamish Mutch Glenn Woodsworth May 1966
One of the great freeclimbs of Squamish, this route still sees many more aid ascents than free. Considerably easier than *Uncle Ben's* technically, it nonetheless offers a strong sense of commitment through the overhanging rock in the lower section, a bivi, fine exposure, and the length ensures that a lot will be learned. Hand-placed gear only - **no hammers**! Follow the line of the original aid ascent, which varies here and there from the modern free route. Long pitches. The next time your parents give you a hard time about staying out late, or doing strange teenage things, gently point out that Hamish Fraser soloed *U Wall* when he was 14. And he grew up to be quite nice too.

The Non Wall   A4   *335*   3-4p.
Bruce MacDonald John Simpson September 1984
An abbreviated attempt to climb the great expanse of wall left of *U Wall*. Another few pitches to link with *Drifters Escape* may produce a stellar route.

Drifter's Escape   A3   .9   *335*   ±6p.
Eric Weinstein Bill Thompson Dave Nichol 1975
Another mysterious route from a bygone era which heads out right from the base of the huge dihedral on *Wall of Attrition* into some intriguing stone. It is worthy of more exploration.

Northwest Passage   A2   .8   *335*   ±15p.
Fred Beckey Alex Bertulis Hank Mather Leif Patterson May 1965
A long-lost climb that takes the huge shadowed depression left of *University Wall*. It is the longest inescapable route on the Chief and judging from Fred's photos, there was a lot less bush on the route too. Head up to the top of pitch 2 of *Wall of Attrition*, then launch out left into the unknown. If this climb was cleaned up and saw a few ascents, perhaps all-free, it would likely become much better regarded.

Pan Granitic Wall

The three climbs on the Pan Wall are some of the most intriguing and exposed on the Chief, but only *Edge of Pan* has seen repeat ascents. There is a long approach up from the highway. The finishes offer a grand sense of arrival at the rim of the South Chief.

Edge Of Pan   A2+   .8   *334*   (4p.)
Jim Brennan Clive Thomson Mar 1983

Pan Granitic Frogman   A3+   .8   *334*   (4p.)
Daryl Hatten John Simpson 1978

Son Of Pan   A4   .8   *334*   (4p.)
Daryl Hatten Greg Foweraker 1982
The master at his best, this is a daunting-looking line.

The Sheriff's Badge

The Grand Wall gets all the attention, but that's where climbers learn the skills to get onto the real thing–The Badge.

Descent... From Sasquatch Ledge, go left to *Angel's Crest*, see *Angels Crest* topo for the descent into the gully.

The Sheriff's Badge   A3+ .6   *337*   10p.
Paul Piro Greg Shannan 1976
This great line offers a lot of nailing and copperheads with relatively few bolts ladders, a hallmark of its quality. No aid climber's tick list is complete without this route, developed over several years in the 1970s, and for almost two decades was **the** hard aid climb of Squamish.   Enjoy the huge roof pitch. Immaculate rock.

Skullfuck   A4 (New Wave) .6   *337*   8p.
Sean Easton S.Isaac July 1996
The hardest route on the Badge. Very modern, with all the tricks of the trade required. Beware the fourth and the last pitch... It was the first new aid wall of the modern era at Squamish—14 years after *Negro Lesbian.*

Born Slippy   A3 .4   *337*   (70m)
Matt Maddaloni solo October 1998
This route takes the often-looked-at seam on the wall above Sasquatch Ledge immediately above *Skullfuck*. One long pitch, although a midway belay is possible. A good finale to any of the other routes.

Cowboys And Indians   A4 .8   *337*   6p.
Perry Beckham solo 1989—1999
Completed in two attempts in 10 years, this excellent climb takes the right side of the Badge before taking a direct line to Sasquatch.

No Name   A3   *336*   3p.?
Perry Beckham, mid 1980s
A route that weaves up on the far right side of the Badge to the roofs.

Astronomy   A2   *336*   (3p.)
Kevin McLane Karl Karlstrom Mike Baxter Aug 1973
An early attempt at the Badge which failed amid major loose rock. The 3 lower pitches to Gunsmoke Terrace are now part of *Mad Dogs...* and *The Big Scoop.*

Zodiac Wall

Zodiac Wall   A3   *338*   ±10p.
Fred Beckey Alex Bertulis Eric Bjornstad Leif Patterson June 1967
A climb that held a big reputation for many years, it has had only two known repeats. It is there to find again, and probably deserves a closer look.

The Raven   A4 .9   *338*   8p.
Perry Beckham Damien Kelly Summer 1998
Hard to believe that after all these years, this is only the second aid route developed on the big Z. Clean and direct with long pitches, take a 60m.

CHIEF AID

TANTALUS WALL — AID CLIMBS

Crescent Ramp

Breakfast Run

Wrist Twister

Cannabis Wall

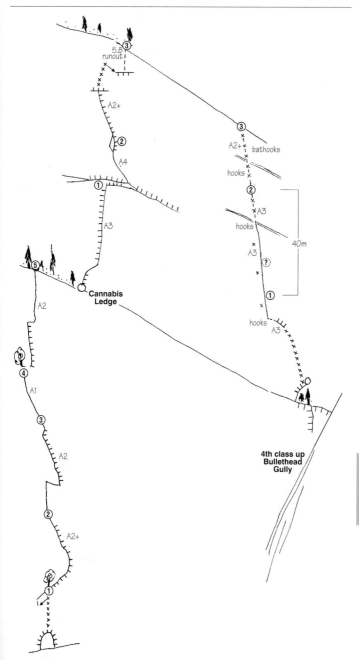

5.8
runout

A2+

②

A4

①

A3

⑤

A2

Cannabis Ledge

④

A1

③

A2

②

A2+

①

③

A2+   bathooks

hooks

②

A3

hooks

A3   ?

40m

①

hooks

A3

**4th class up
Bullethead
Gully**

THE DIHEDRALS— AID CLIMBS

Clean Corner

A3

Illusion

A3

Western Dihedral

Sea of Tranquillity

Getting Down On The Brown

10c

10c

10c

10a

11a

Freeway

all free to 11a

Slow Dyke

WESTERN DIHEDRAL
All pitches are A2, some free up to 5.8, and 10d for the last pitch.

DOWN ON THE BROWN
All pitches are A2 except the last, A3.

ILLUSION
All pitches are A2, with 2 pendulums on pitch 2.

SLOW DYKE
Pitches 1 and 2 are A3, mixed A2, easy free above.

Zorros last Ride, A3+
Climbers: Sean Easton, Dave Edgar
Photo: Jia Condon

Negro Lesbian

Zorros Last Ride

The Black Dyke

wet weather
alternative
via
Exasperator
(original start)

normal
start

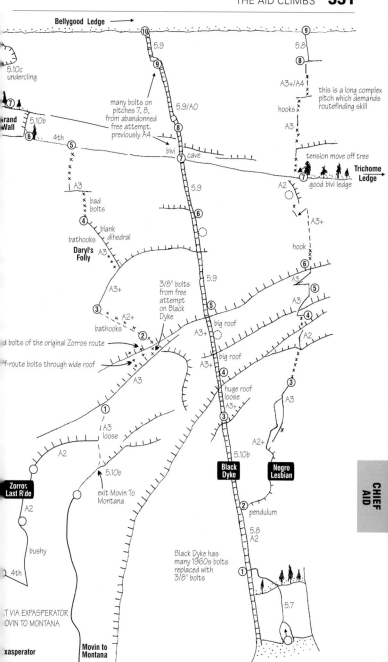

Bellygood Ledge →

5.9

5.8

5.10c
undercling

A3+/A4

this is a long complex
pitch which demands
routefinding skill

5.9/AO

hooks

A3

many bolts on
pitches 7, 8,
from abandonned
free attempt.
previously A4

Grand
Wall

5.10b

4th

tension move off tree

bivi
cave

good bivi ledge

Trichome
Ledge →

A3
bad
bolts

5.9

A2

A3+

blank
dihedral

bathooks

hook

Daryl's
Folly

A3

A3

A3+

A3

3/8" bolts
from free
attempt
on Black
Dyke

5.9

A2+

bathooks

big roof

old bolts of the original Zorros route →

A3+

off-route bolts through wide roof →

A2

big roof

A3+

A3

huge roof
loose

A3

A3+

A3
loose

A2+

A2

Zorros
Last Ride

5.10b

A2

exit Movin To
Montana

Black
Dyke

Negro
Lesbian

bushy

5.10b

4th

2

pendulum

T VIA EXPASPERATOR
OVIN TO MONTANA

5.8
A2

Black Dyke has
many 1960s bolts
replaced with
3/8" bolts

5.7

xasperator

Movin to
Montana

**CHIEF
AID**

GRAND WALL — LEFT SIDE AID CLIMBS

Rapp Route
requires a
60m + 55m
to Flake Ledge

50m↓

Dance
Platform

Bellygood Ledge

Gra
Wa

University Wall

45m↓

55m↓

Under
The Gun

Uncle Ben's

Humpty
Dumpty

Ten Years
After

Up From
The Skies

58m↓

Mercy Me

Cruel
Shoes

Up From
The Skies
Original
Start

35m↓

60m↓

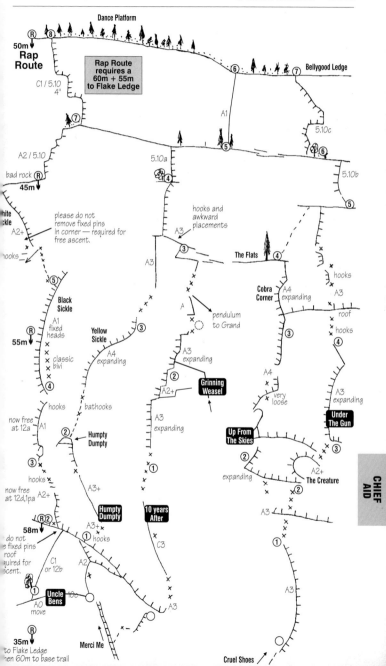

Dance Platform

50m
Rap Route

Rap Route requires a 60m + 55m to Flake Ledge

C1 / 5.10
4"

Bellygood Ledge

A1

5.10c

A2 / 5.10

5.10a

bad rock
45m

5.10b

hite ickle

please do not remove fixed pins in corner — required for free ascent.

A2+

hooks and awkward placements

A3

The Flats

hooks

hooks

A3

Cobra Corner

A4 expanding

roof

Black Sickle

A1 fixed heads

Yellow Sickle

A4 expanding

55m

classic bivi

A4 expanding

A3 expanding

pendulum to Grand

A3 expanding

A

hooks

A4

A3 expanding

now free at 12a

A1

hooks

bathooks

Humpty Dumpty

A3+

A3 expanding

A2+

Grinning Weasel

very loose

Under The Gun

now free at 12d,1pa

A2+

hooks

Humpty Dumpty

A3+

10 years After

C3

Up From The Skies

expanding

A2+

The Creature

A3

58m

do not e fixed pins roof uired for scent.

A3+

hooks

C1 or 12b

A2

A0 move

Uncle Bens

10c

35m

to Flake Ledge hen 60m to base trail

Merci Me

A3

A3

Cruel Shoes

CHIEF AID

PAN GRANITIC WALL — AID CLIMBS

A3

A2

Edge of Pan

5.8, A1

5.7, A3

5.6

A3+

A4

A3+

Pan Granitic Frogman

A4
rurps

A4
rurps

A4

Son of Pan

A3

from Squamish
Buttress

UNIVERSITY WALL AREA - AID CLIMBS

Dance
Platform

⑦

⑥

① ⑤

Drifters
Escape

④

Northwest
Passage

③

University Wall

②
① ②
Non Wall

①

①
Wall of
Attrition

CHIEF
AID

NORTHWEST PASSAGE
The exact route is un-
certain, and has not been
repeated. Expect 1960s
bolts, lots of dirty A2 and
mixed free\aid.

DRIFTERS ESCAPE
Unrepeated. Expect A3.

UNIVERSITY WALL
Clean, no hammers. All
pitches are C1 or C2.

THE NON WALL
Little-known. A3 on pitch
1, harder on pitch 2.

SHERIFFS BADGE — AID ROUTES

Born Slippy

Angels Crest

Sasquatch Ledge

8 8

7

7

7

6

5

3

A2

2

A2

1

A2

Astronomy

6

5

5

4

4

4

3

3

3

2

2

Skullfuck

1

Sherrifs Badge

2

1

7

5

4

3

2

approximate st and finish of an incomplete rout

1

Cowboys & Indians

1

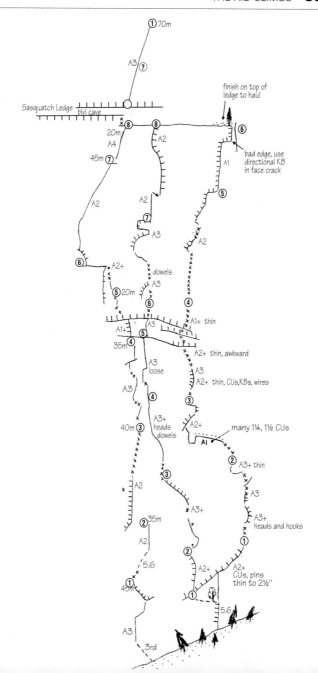

① 70m

A3 ⓘ

finish on top of
ledge to haul

Sasquatch Ledge
bivi cave

⑥

20m ⑧   ⑧
A4   A2

45m ⑦

bad edge, use
directional KB
in face crack

A1

A2   A2   ⑤
              ⑦
              A3   A2

⑥
     A2+   dowels
                 A3   ④

⑤ 20m   A1+ thin
         ⑥
   A1+ ⑤ A3   A2+ thin, awkward

35m ④
         A3   A3
         loose   A2+ thin, CUs,KBs, wires
A3
              ④   ③
                     A2+
40m ③   A3+   many 1¼, 1½ CUs
         heads   A1
         dowels
                    ②   A3+ thin

              ③
     A2   A3

              ③
                    A3+   A3+
                          heads and hooks

     ② 35m   ①

     A2   ②
              ⑤ 5.6   A2+
                    ②   A2+
① 45m   ①   CUs, pins
                          thin to 2½"

                          5.6

A3
         3rd

ZODIAC WALL — AID ROUTES

See Northern
for descent b

8 35m
A2   A1
10   7 40m
          × A2
A3
9   A3   A1
A3   ×
          6 40m
variation   A2 lo
          ×
5 35m
8
A3
5.7
7
A2   4 35m
6   × A2+
5.8
5   A1
A1   3 4
4   ×
A3
3   big
×   ledg
×   2 55m
A2   × A4
2   ×
A2   A3+/A4
          1 55m
          loose × A3+
1   × A3+
5.9

Zodiac Wall

The Raven

Angels
Crest

ZODIAC WALL
Expect to find numerous
1960s vintage bolts,
loose and dirty rock,
freeclimbing up to 5.9.

Cowboys and Indians, A4
Climber: Rich Prohaska
Photo: Jia Condon

Some of the crags in the Smoke Bluffs are close to residential areas. For this reason a code of conduct was developed in 1996 by the Climbers Access Society of BC, local residents and the Municipality. Please read it, inform others, and at all times, try to adhere to it. Please make a special effort at Burgers & Fries, Alexis, and Neat & Cool, as these crags are close to residences. The limitations are common courtesy, applicable to all users of the Smoke Bluffs.

- ◆ **Do not disturb residents. Be courteous to all users.**
- ◆ **Please minimize your noise impact.**
- ◆ **Please use toilets provided.**
- ◆ **No Fires - No Camping - No Garbage.**
- ◆ **Do not park at any time in residential areas, use the Smoke Bluff Parking Lot on Loggers Lane.**

AT BURGERS AND FRIES, AND ALEXIS.

These longstanding beginner crags are close to several residences. Please be especially diligent in these areas.

- ◆ **Avoid gathering in large groups on the clifftop.**
- ◆ **Minimize your presence.**
- ◆ **Try to avoid climbing in these areas during early mornings and evenings. Please consider climbing on other crags at these times.**

The Victoria boulderers in the Smoke Bluff Parking Lot: Photo: Peter Michaux

THE SMOKE BLUFFS

This delightful collection of crags on a large hill close to downtown Squamish offers a year-round climbing area, thanks to the low elevation, sunny exposure and quick drying rock. The volume and variety of routes in the weekend warrior grades ensures there is something of interest for everyone. There are over 400 routes in all, about 35% of the total climbs in the guide. Although they do not receive the accolades of the Chief or the Malamute, the Smoke Bluffs fill an essential role in the repertoir of what's to do at Squamish.

The atmosphere in the Bluffs is that of an urban park, albeit unkempt, situated within walking distance of downtown and adjacent to Hospital Hill, a pleasant residential area. The rock is a little different from the classical granite of the Chief, rougher and more rounded. But the same sinuous little dykes are evident, and so is that Smoke Bluff hallmark, the thin crack. Most of the crags are pitched at a friendly angle, many with good ledges at the base and top, so it is not at all surprising the Smoke Bluffs is the favoured place for teaching novices. The popularity of the area continues to grow. It now requires steady rain to deter climbers, whatever the month or season. In fact, so many residents of Squamish own climbing gear now (estimates are upward of 500), that all it takes is a lull of a few hours in wintertime rain and a few locals step out for a rock fix. Even when a big freeze descends, out come the ice tools, the parking lot fills, and *Alice*, Bughouse Heights and Krack Rock come into their full glory, laden with non-too difficult ice.

It is worth noting that the Smoke Bluffs are by far the most popular visitor destination in Squamish–count the cars–and that the once-generous space in the lot is now barely enough. Despite this popularity, the areas potential as a unique civic asset has never caught on with the local government and business leaders, so it remains a mess of eroding trails and scraggy bush. Only the climbers love it.

Land Ownership... All of the crags above the Smoke Bluffs Trail are on land which is owned by the Municipality of Squamish, extending to the top of the hill. The benchlands in front of Burgers and Fries and the Smoke Bluff Wall, down to Crag X are owned by climbers through the Federation of Mountain Clubs of BC. Some of the crags along Blind Channel may be on undeveloped private land. The parking lot and its tortured history is a long-running saga almost worthy of a not-very-good TV soap, but presently is leased by the District of Squamish from a local landowner.

BLUFFS

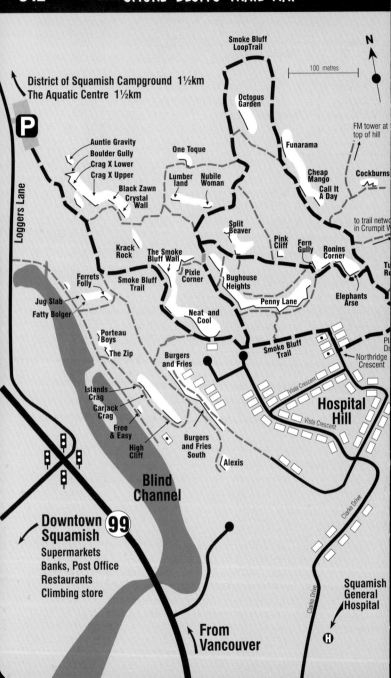

N

100 metres

Smoke Bluff
LoopTrail

Octopus
Garden

Funarama

District of Squamish Campground 1½km
The Aquatic Centre 1½km

P

FM tower at
top of hill

Cheap
Mango
Call It
A Day

Cockburns

Auntie Gravity
Boulder Gully
Crag X Lower
Crag X Upper

One Toque

Lumber
land

Nubile
Woman

Black Zawn
Crystal Wall

Split
Beaver

Pink
Cliff

Fern
Gully

Ronins
Corner

to trail network
in Crumpit W

Loggers Lane

Krack
Rock

The Smoke
Bluff Wall

Pixie
Corner

Bughouse
Heights

Tu
Re

Ferrets
Folly

Smoke Bluff
Trail

Penny Lane

Elephants
Arse

Jug Slab

Fatty Bolger

Neat and
Cool

Porteau
Boys

The Zip

Burgers
and Fries

Smoke Bluff
Trail

Pl
Dr
Northridge
Crescent

Vista Crescent

**Hospital
Hill**

Islands
Crag

Garjack
Crag

Free
& Easy

High
Cliff

Burgers
and Fries
South

Alexis

Vista Crescent

**Blind
Channel**

**Downtown
Squamish** **99**
Supermarkets
Banks, Post Office
Restaurants
Climbing store

Clarke Drive

Clarke Drive

**Squamish
General
Hospital**

H

**From
Vancouver**

The Main Trails Around The Smoke Bluffs

So Where Would You Like To Go?   The crags in the Bluffs are linked by a complex network of trails. Most are heavily travelled. New ones appear every year. Very few disappear. It is never far from one to another. Only the principal routes are described below, all starting from the parking lot. The Smoke Bluffs Trail is the main highway through the crags, connecting the parking lot to Plateau Drive and Crumpit Woods to the east. It is a heavily used recreational corridor for not only climbers but hikers, mountain bikers, dog walkers, the annual Test of Mettle mountainbike race, and the occasional lost horse.

Parking...   **The Smoke Bluff Parking Lot**   Easy. Head for the main intersection at the entrance to the Town Centre on Highway 99. Turn right (if heading north) onto Loggers Lane and continue for less than half a minute to the Smoke Bluff Parking Lot on the right side, at the north end of the Bluffs.

The Smoke Bluffs Trail.   Head south out of the parking lot and up the hill. Along the way on the left side, the main crags you'll pass are Crag X, The Black Zawn, the Smoke Bluffs Wall and Neat and Cool. Beyond Neat and Cool there is a major fork to the left (north) which marks the start of the Smoke Bluffs Loop Trail (see map). Keeping right will take you to Northridge and Plateau Drive.

The Loop Trail.   This is a major thoroughfare that passes by many crags, starting and finishing on the Smoke Bluffs Trail. Between Neat and Cool and Penny Lane, take the well-hammered trail branching northward. It climbs up to Octopus Garden and Funarama before dropping back down past Ronins Corner to Plateau Drive and a link trail past Northridge back to Neat and Cool.

Pixie Corner - Ronins Trail.   This is a similar, parallel trail to the main Loop Trail, but at a lower elevation on the hillside, linking the top of the Pixie Corner stairs with Ronin's Corner.

Blind Channel to Burgers And Fries.   This is a new trail that could become a major avenue from Hospital Hill to Blind Channel. Walk back south along Loggers Lane from the parking lot, and turn left through the yellow gate onto a quiet trail along the side of Blind Channel. At the Zip, turn left onto a trail that rises up the hillside below Islands In The Sky and High Cliff to Burgers and Fries.

Boulder Gully
Crag X Lower
Crag X Upper
The Black Zawn
Crystal Wall
Krack Rock
One Toque Wall
Lumberland
Smoke Bluff Wall
Octopus Garden
Pixie Corner
Nubile Woman
Funarama

Parking Lot

Fatty Bolger
Ferrets Folly
Boys of Porteau
The Zip
Island Crag
Car Jack Crag

Bughouse Heights
Split Beaver
Neat and Cool
Penny Lane
Ronins Left
Ronins Centre
Ronins Elephants Arse
Mount Crumpit

High Cliff
Burger and Fries
Burger and Fries South
Alexis

The Blind Channel Crags

Blind Channel is the tidal salt water inlet that lies between the Bluffs and Highway 99, and this section describes the crags that lie between Blind Channel and the main Smoke Bluffs trail.

Until 1921, Blind Channel was actually the lower part of the Mamquam River. In October of that year, a major flood re-aligned its course directly into the Squamish River (the same storm caused a dam at Britannia to burst, killing 37 people). Prior to that flood, the Mamquam River flowed through the Squamish Leisure Centre and the ballfields, down Highway 99 and passed just south of the Smoke Bluffs Parking Lot to enter what is now Blind Channel. Must have been a cool thing to see.

There is a small buttress at the side of the trail north of Fatty Bolger. The two lines here are presently overgrown, but can make decent little top-rope climbs. Both have been soloed.

▓▓▓ BLIND CHANNEL — FATTY BOLGER ▰▰▰

The Leading Edge ** 11a #6 **SPORT** 24m
Will Dorling Elise Hunt 1996
Start up *Fatty Bolger*, then go right after the second bolt to climb the arete.

Fatty Bolger * 11a #6 **SPORT** 35m
Tami Knight Peter Croft 1981
Start on the right side of the wall and follow a natural line on the rock to gain a shallow flake line on the upper wall.

Bumper * 11c #5 **SPORT**+ 23m
Jeff Thomson Glenn Payan (1pa) March 1996 FFA Jeff Thomson Toby Froschauer Sept '96
A face climb 4m left of *Fatty Bolger*. Take a CD.

Rumours * 10a 25m
Glenn Payan Jeff Thomson March 1996
The left-hand buttress of the crag. Start up cracks, then face climb past a small roof. Easier slab to finish.

The next four climbs are on the less intimidating, featured slab to the left. Described from right to left. Good novice sportleads.

Hamish's .6 #3 **SPORT** 14m
Jeff Thomson Glenn Payan May 1996

Moominland .9 #4 **SPORT** 14m
Jeff Thomson Glenn Payan May 1996 (Drew Brayshaw David Vocadlo)

Stepladder .7 #4 **SPORT** 12m
Jeff Thomson Glenn Payan May 1996 (Drew Brayshaw David Vocadlo)

David's .6 #2 **SPORT**+ 12m
Jeff Thomson Glenn Payan May 1996

▬ BLIND CHANNEL — FERRET'S FOLLY ▬

A steel hydro tower sitting at the top marks this clean little cliff above Fatty Bolger. The trail that joins Blind Channel Trail to the Smoke Bluff Trail passes just to the south of the cliff.

Ferrets Folly .7 x 10m
E.Spat P.Paquette 1980
Climb the right wall up obvious face holds, finishing on the left.

It's Green And Bright .9 x 10m
L.Ostrander C.Oliver 1988
A right hand finish to *Ferrets Folly.*

Earth Trip * .6 x 10m
E.Spat P.Paquette 1980
The obvious and inviting corner in the middle of the cliff.

Cold Metal 11a #3 x **SPORT** 10m
L.Ostrander 1988
Follows bolts up the steeper left hand wall.

▬ BLIND CHANNEL — FREE AND EASY ▬

This is a small outcropping at the trailside 150m south of the Municipal water pipeline. Look for the obvious twin roof-cracks 5m above the ground, both short.

Protein Eater 11b x 10m
Randy Atkinson John Howe Sept 1979
The harder, right-hand roof.

Free And Easy 10a x 10m
John Howe Randy Atkinson Sept 1979
The left-hand roof.

Range Ball Record Wreckers 11c x 20m
Rolf Rybak Ian Wigington May 1998
A face-climb around to the left on the north-facing side of the outcrop.

1. The Leading Edge.....11a
2. Fatty Bolger.............11a
3. Bumper....................11c
4. Rumours..................10a
5. Hamish's..................6
6. Moominland 9
7. Stepladder...............7
8. David 6

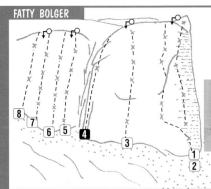
FATTY BOLGER

BLUFFS

Have you joined the Climbers Access Society yet?

▬▬ BLIND CHANNEL — THE BOYS OF PORTEAU ▬▬▬

This is a clean, sweeping crag by the Blind Channel road just south of the water pipeline. Climbs were established as top-ropes by students of the Porteau Boy's Camp in May 1992 under the direction of Rich Woo and John Harvey, who later returned and led them. The top of the cliff can be reached by walking up the pipeline and traversing across. The best climb is the main corner, *Boys in the Wood*, easily noted by the tall birch tree in front of it.

Pushup City ●   10a   10m
Dave Richards (solo)
A short climb up the prow at the left edge. Step up, mantel and go.

Do It Right The First Time ●   .8   18m
A nice face climb up the centre of the wall left of the main corner.

Boys In The Wood   10b   20m
The wide corner which is the main feature of the cliff.

Naughty By Nature ●   10d   25m
Follow the slanting crack to a bulge, a bolt and a stiff move. Continue up the headwall above past two bolts at 5.9.

Hydrotherapy ●   .6   28m
The wide slab on the right, ascended from right to left. No pro.

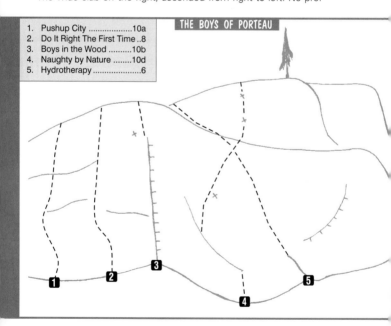

1. Pushup City 10a
2. Do It Right The First Time ..8
3. Boys in the Wood 10b
4. Naughty by Nature 10d
5. Hydrotherapy 6

THE BOYS OF PORTEAU

■■ *BLIND CHANNEL — THE ZIP* ■■

This fine little crag lies 60m south of the Municipal water pipeline, hidden in the trees where a small spit reaches into Blind Channel.

Outside Edge   .9   x   10m
Robin Beech Oct 9 1994
A short, steep corner 30m left of *The Zip*. Handjams and liebacking.

Gaia **   12b   #7   **SPORT**   25m
D.Hart Oct 1989
Superb face climbing up the steep bolted wall at the left of the cliff.

The Zip ***   10a   25m
Ward Robinson Blake Robinson 1979
The beautiful finger and hand crack splitting the face.

Sole Proprietorship *   11a   20m
Rolf Rybak M.Tygges Aug 31st 1994
A 3-bolt face climb between *The Zip* and *Crystal Ball*. Take a couple of medium size CDs. Finish up the crack to chains.

Crystal Ball *   10b   22m
D.Nicol A.Ourom 1979
A groove right of *The Zip*, leading to a roof. The lefthand finish is .9.

No Name Route   .9   15m
Anders Ourom 1979
The most right-hand route on the wall.

Impulse   .7   x   13m
Robin Beech Ian Blakeman March 1996
This climb is at the top of *The Zip*, a corner crack behind the big boulder.

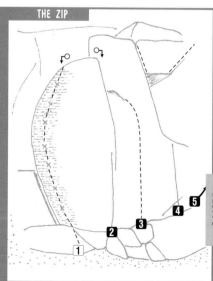

THE ZIP

Fatty Bolger was a cartoon character in an English public school, made famous in a schoolboy's magazine. Yes, he was fat and nasty, but he lives on.

BLUFFS

▪▪▪ BLIND CHANNEL — ISLAND IN THE SKY ▪▪▪▪▪

This is the first crag encountered on the Blind Channel trail south of the Zip. Although well hidden in the trees, the crag is easy to find and navigate. At the top, look for the steel hydro tower at the north end of Burgers and Fries, and 30m to its west are a pair of wooden power poles. These poles are at the top of *Edgar Allan Pro*. The prominent left-leaning roof at the top of *The Kip* can be easily seen too, directly ahead when exiting Squamish on Cleveland Avenue, just before the traffic lights on Highway 99. Climbs are described from left to right.

Fissureman's Friend   *   .8   25m
Chris Trautman Bill Kipper   2 July 98
A fine, west-facing open dihedral rises above a pair of short hand to fist cracks. Intimidating, but surprisingly easy.

Gang Of Foreplay   10b   25m
Bill Kipper Chris Trautman July 98
The short crack left of *Fisherman's Friend*, leading to 2 ring bolts.

▪ *To reach the next three climbs, scramble up a treed groove on the right and step left onto a ledge below a fine little slab.*

Mossy Tongue   *   .8   20m
Bill Kipper Kelly Santaga   29 July 97
Tread delicately up the left side of the slab past 2 bolts and then pull through the easy roof feature.

The Kip   *   .7   20m
Bill Kipper Dean McGregor Harry Young   1 August 97
The delightful crack which splits the slab. Finish up *Mossy Tongue*.

Belays Of Glory   10a   20m
Bill Kipper Brad Robison 13 July 97
Climb the right side slab past 2 bolts to gain a steep groove. Layback up it, or climb the left hand wall.

Edgar Allan Pro   10b   15m
Bill Kipper Ian MacNeill Harry Young 17 May 97
Start a little higher up the right side of the crag. Climb the right-hand of several flakes, or go uneasily up the weirdly leaning corner to the left. Pull the overlap, marvel at the bizarre knobby granite and follow the easy crack to the top.

University Wallet   .8   12m
Bill Kipper Chris Trautman July 1998
Scramble up higher to the right, to a short slab starting off the ledge right of *Edgar Allan Pro*.

Have you read Conservation and Courtesy? Page 22.

■ *BLIND CHANNEL — CARJACK CRAG*

This crag is immediately right of Island In The Sky. Take the Blind
Channel trail up from The Zip, or down from Burgers and Fries. *Dirty
Route and Scoundrels* is an obvious feature.

The Anty Crest   .9   25m
Bill Kipper Kelly Santaga   May 1997
Left of *Dirty Route*... is a steepish slabby wall just right of an arete with cracks
and a small tree. Climb it to the lone bolt, which protects some thin face
moves. Scamper up to a bolt anchor.

Dirty Route And Scoundrels   .7   25m
Bill Kipper Valerie Denike May 98
Climb a somewhat grainy slab to gain a right trending, stepped undercling-
dihedral. Go under a small roof and make a tricky move left (crux) to gain an
easy dihedral to the top.

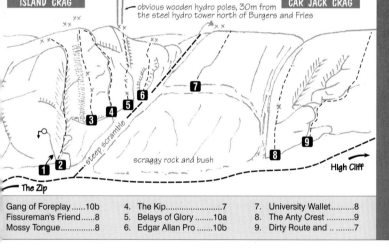

Gang of Foreplay 10b	4. The Kip.........................7	7. University Wallet...........8
Fissureman's Friend......8	5. Belays of Glory 10a	8. The Anty Crest 9
Mossy Tongue..............8	6. Edgar Allan Pro 10b	9. Dirty Route and 7

Name story... Los Zapatos, a climb at the base of the Grand
Wall means "The Shoes" in Spanish, and refers to the first
sticky-rubber shoes—the legendary Fires—that took the climbing
world by storm in the early 1980s. Made in Spain.

▰▰ *BLIND CHANNEL — HIGH CLIFF* ▰▰▰

This well-hidden crag lies immediately in front of Burgers and Fries below three wooden power poles. It is the last (third) crag met when walking up from the Zip. Or, from Burgers and Fries, walk down a trail 40m south of the hydro poles. This will place you at the south end of the crag. Climbs are described from left to right. An obvious feature is the overhanging finger-crack of *Red Nails,* rising out of an overhung bay in the centre of the crag base.

This cliff now offers a number of good climbs, making it a useful alternative to more established but crowded Smoke Bluffs crags, although it has taken almost two decades to get there.

Please note... Below High Cliff is a private residence, so **Do Not** head down directly to Blind Channel. Stay on the trail to the Zip!

Beware the Fiends of Starch!   .9   22m
Bill Kipper Dean McGregor Mia Monsoir Harry Young Mike Damgaard Aug 1996
A diagonal crack and face climb at the north end.

▰ *The face right of Fiends... has been top-roped at 10d (Bill Kipper).*
The next three climbs start left of Red Nails, offering some good climbing,
but are a bit confusing to figure out - give them a try anyway.

Miner Details   *   10c   15m
J.Black   June 1992
Step up off a small boss at the base 8m left of *Red Nails* . Follow a line of weakness rightward to a lieback crack left of an overhang. Face climb past two bolts to the top (crux). Protection to 3".

Miner Matters   *   10a   15m
J.Black   June 1992
In the centre of the cliff, 6m left of *Red Nails*, climb a 5m vertical crack to a small tree. Climb the bulge above into a scoop then up the wall.

Are You A Frond Or Anenome?   10d   15m
Bill Kipper John Smith Guylaine Gauthier 1995
2m right of *Miner Details*, climb a shallow right-facing corner. A few strenuous moves gain a right-trending series of cracks. Face climbing above.

Red Nails   *   11c   15m
P.Croft T.Knight 1980
An overhanging finger crack past a fixed pin. A fine testpiece.

▰ *The next two climbs start just right of Red Nails.*

Splat   10d   15m
DaveSarkany Mike Spagnut June 1985
The overhanging cracks immediately right of *Red Nails*.

Run Like A Thief   10a   15m
John Howe Joe Buszowski S.Meakin Richard Suddaby 1979
A short wall 5m right of *Red Nails*.

Step n' Stump .7 x 10m
Paul Paquette Ed Spat 1980
A lost right-leaning crackline somewhere between *Red Nails* and *20 Minute..*

The next climbs are the the south end of the crag.

Severe And Unique Disciplines 10b 18m
Bill Kipper Stephanie Daigneaulp 1998 Direct Start: Gary Henning George Hanzel Sept1998
This is the corner immediately left of *Looney Fringe*. Climb it, then go left to a slim left-facing flake-line. Climb the slab on its right. A very direct start on the left, through a small roof, [bolt] is 12b.

Looney Fringe * 10c 18m
John Smith Bill Kipper 1995
The flake crack immediately on the right side of the arete at the south end.

Twenty Minute Workout * 10b 8m
T.Holwill April 1984
A short, clean left facing corner.

Convolutions Of Felicia 10c 15m
Bill Kipper Derek McGuire John Smith 1995
The low-angle arete 8m right of *20 Minute..* with a high bolt. This is the first climb encountered when walking down from Burgers and Fries.

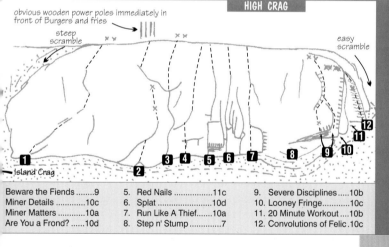

Beware the Fiends 9	5. Red Nails 11c	9. Severe Disciplines 10b
Miner Details 10c	6. Splat 10d	10. Looney Fringe............10c
Miner Matters 10a	7. Run Like A Thief.......10a	11. 20 Minute Workout 10b
Are You a Frond? 10d	8. Step n' Stump 7	12. Convolutions of Felic.10c

BLUFFS

Name story. *The first ascentionists of Run Like A Thief*
arrived at the top of the crag and discovered two big marijuana
plants set out by their owner to dry in the sun.

Burgers And Fries

This cliff bears the distinction of being the most heavily used crag in Canada, given its friendly ambience, ease of top-roping, year-round climbing and the speed with which it dries after rain. Low angle face climbs predominate, and the fine views from the top of the cliff across to the Chief and Howe Sound contribute to everyone's enjoyment. From the top of the cliff, scramble down an easy ramp at the north end. Hardly a square inch of the cliff has not seen the hand of a top-roping climber, so lower your expectations of more first ascents here.

A Foot In The Gravy	10d	10m
S.Tooley S.Bracken 1979		

Left of Foot in the Gravy is a top-rope climb: Foot In The Soup (10b).

Lone Rhino	11a	10m
Unknown		
Pink Panther ★	11c	20m
Jim Bahnuk Oct 1989		
Burgers And Fries ★★	.7	20m
J.Manuel E.Spat B.DenHertog 1980		
Peaches And Cream ★★	10a	20m
D.Jones J.St Amand 1982		

BURGERS AND FRIES

Genetically Superior Neighbour   * 11a   20m
George Hanzel   Joe Turley   March 1998

Frying Brownies   10a   20m
P.McKernin   J.Black   Sept 1993

Dusty Eyes   .4   30m
K.Rajala   D.Harris   1981

Wisecrack   *   .7   22m
B.Wiseman   B.Wilson   T.Spurrell   1980

Catch Me   10b   22m
J.Turley   G.Smith   1980

Catch Me Quick   *   10b   22m
J.Turley   G.Smith   1980

Over Forty   *   11a   22m
D.Hutchinson   D.Jones   Aug   1989

Catch Me Quicker   *   10c   22m
J.Turley   G.Smith   1980

Movin' On Over   *   .9   22m
S.Tooley   J.Beekman   1981

Short And Sweet   10a   12m
Unknown

▦ *BURGERS AND FRIES — SOUTH*　▦▦▦

South of Burgers and Fries is a broken but inviting wall about 100m long, with a variety of pleasant climbs for leading or top-ropes.

▦ *The white wall at the left of the crag has two pleasant face climbs.*

Casey *Unknown*	.7		10m
Mr Dressup *Uknown*	.8		12m

▦ *The next 3 similar climbs are grouped on a smooth high-angle wall just right of Burgers and Fries. A face leads to a crack in each case. They are described left to right.*

Who Needs Bolts? * *R.Milward J.Campbell April 1984*	10a		18m
Who Needs Pro? * *R.Milward J.Campbell May 1984*	10b		18m
Predator * *Glenn Payan Dec 1995*	10c		17m

▦ *The next 2 climbs are on the next wall to the south.*

High Boltage Line * *Glenn Payan Jeff Thomson Nov 1996*	10a	#5	**SPORT**	15m
French Leave * *Glenn Payan Jeff Thomson March 1996*	10b	#3	**SPORT+**	15m

Take a couple of CDs to 1½".

BURGERS AND FRIES

Burgers & Fries　　Wisecrack　　Movin On Over

The Smoke Bluffs trail map is on page 342, and the crag
overview photo on pages 344-345

There are two pleasant handjam cracks on a distinctive white wall about 50m south of Burgers & Fries.

Bilbo Baggins   .9   15m
Unknown

Gollum   .7   15m
Unknown (possibly Toe Jam, Keith Rajala Ken Willis 1982)

Rugosite ●   10d   x   8m
Gene Smith 1980

A short climb on an overgrown boulder somewhere in front of the main wall.

The next 5 climbs are grouped together near a residence. Please be quiet in this area.

Libya Sucks *   .9   20m
J.Campbell R.Milward April 1984

Nookie Monster *   10a   20m
R.Barley P.Shackleton 1981

One Mistake, Big Pancake 11c   20m
S.Young 1985

Hot Cherry Bendover *   11b   15m
W.Price 1978

Gigolo ● ☺   10a   15m
D.Jones R.Nichol July 1984

There are two short thin handcracks just right of Gigolo. The lefthand crack is Bert 5.10d, and the righthand is Ernie 5.10b

BURGERS AND FRIES SOUTH

8 9

10 11 14 15
12 13

BLUFFS

Photo was taken before current tree growth occured

▰▰ BURGERS AND FRIES — ALEXIS ▰▰▰▰

This small cliff is underneath a steel hydro tower, and sports some short cracks and face climbs. Climbs on this crag are every close to a friendly nearby residence, so best behaviour please. To descend, walk down to the left along a ramp below the hydro tower, or rappel.

All You Need Are Jugs .8   10m
S.Young J.Campbell April 1982 (possibly earlier)

The Alexis Cracks * .7   12m
Unknown
Three fine hand cracks to choose from. You can't go wrong.

White Streak * 10c   12m
Unknown

Groundward Bound 10d   12m
P.Post B.Kay Feb 1982

Halcyon Days 10d   12m
R.Barley G.Shannan 1973

Brick's Crack .8   10m
G.Shannan R.Barley 1973

ALEXIS

1. All You Need Are Jugs ..
2. The Alexis Cracks..........
3. The White Streak 1
4. Groundward Bound 1
5. Halcyon Days..............1
6. Brick's Crack................

*The Smoke Bluffs trail map is on page 342, and the crag
overview photo on pages 344-345*

Racking up. Climber: John Rosholt
Photo: Richard Wheater

The Daylight Crack on Freeway
Climber: Chris Bonington

White Lightning, 5.10c
Climber: Kai Hirvonen
Photo Richard Wheater

The Flight of the Fledgelings, 5.7, first ascent
Climbers: Barry McLane, Tony McLane

The Shadow, 5.12d
Climber: Peter Croft

Family Ties, 5.12d
Climber: Dave Lane

Unfinished Symphony, 5.11b
Climber: John Howe

Boulder Gully

This area is the closest to the Climbers Parking Lot, and is well endowed with good climbs, a mix of crack and face. There is less emphasis on thin cracks and seams and a greater abundance of steeper, technically interesting climbs.

Loose Lady *   .9   35m
J.Howe R.Atkinson Sept 1979
Climb cracks just left of the arete to the top of *Cold Comfort.*

Lust   10c   #4   **SPORT**+   22m
Nick Jones Tim Holwill Bill Noble Aug 22 1992
The narrow wall between *Cold Comfort* and *Loose Lady.* Start between the two and head up past bolts to join the final crack of *Loose Lady.*

Cold Comfort **   .9   20m
J.Campbell A.Hughes Feb 1980
An excellent finger crack. Good protection and rests.

Triage Arete **   10a   #4   **SPORT**   22m
Kevin McLane John Howe Chris Murrell June 1983
RECLEANED AND BOLTED: Kevin McLane Barry McLane July 29 1998.
An unusual arete climb. Originally led with almost non-existent natural protection, the climb also became almost non-existent due to regrowth of moss and lichen. Hence, it was rescrubbed and 4 bolts placed.

Picket Line *   .9   35m
K.McLane T.Marks Mar 1984
A popular crack climb up the groove left of *Triage.*

True Love **   11c - 12b   40m
D.Hart April 1984
A good face climb with some enormous reaches.

Supervalue **   10c   40m
R.Barley J.Turley 1982   FA direct finish J.Howe C.Murrell April 1984
Excellent varied climbing. After the delicate crux moves into the upper cracks, an unprotected variation finish is possible on the left.

Public Menace   11d   40m
K.McLane C.Murrell (1pa) July 1983   FFA: K.McLane June 15 1985
Straight over the roof on *Supervalue* and up cracks above.

Sensitol ● ☺   10b   30m
R.Barley J.Howe Sept 1982
Takes the cracks up the left side of the prow.

The original Climbers Parking Lot was in the open area at the foot of Vista Crescent, between Neat and Cool and Penny Lane until 1992.

BOULDER GULLY

top of
Golden Mongrel

Auntie Gravity 10b	5. Public Menace...........11d	9. Triage Arete...............10a
Turbocharger 11b	6. Supervalue................10c	10. Cold Comfort 9
Talking Holds 10a	7. True Love 11c-12a	11. Lust 10c
Sensitol 9	8. Picket Line 9	12. Loose Lady 9

BLUFFS

In August 1985 a dramatic bush fire just below Alexis, started by errant
local youths, swept up the busy crags as far as Pink Cliff (the Forest
Service bombed the area, hence the pink colour).

Boulder Gully — Turbocharger Wall

This is the steep, north facing wall above the parking lot. Rappel descents are possible from *Turbocharger* and *Stroll On*. Climbs are described from right to left as they are approached. Most of the climbs are well worth doing, and *Turbocharger* is one of the most convenient 11b finger workouts in the Bluffs. Climb *Talking Holds* to the belay.

Sideshow   10c   x   15m
K.McLane C.Murrell Jan 1984
An uninviting crack at the right side of the wall.

Talking Holds **   10a   15m
R.Rohn J.Howe April 1982
The fine handjam crack that curves across from right to left.

Turbocharger **   11b   12m
K.McLane D.Lane Oct 1983
A short testpiece offering fingery, technical climbing past 3 fixed pins. Start as for *Stroll On* and finish at the top of *Talking Holds*.

Stroll On **   10c   40m
K.McLane S.Flavelle D.Hart Sept 1983
The striking diagonal crackline. Climb to the roof, then straight up.

Golden Mongrel ● ☺   .9   x   25m
K.McLane L.McLane April 1984
A deep groove and wide crack in the steep prow left of *Stroll On* .

Wallflower ● ☺   .8   x   10m
J.Howe solo May 1984
A hand crack at the top of the gully, 10m left of and facing across to the large block at the top of *Golden Mongrel*.

Phlegmish Dance, 5.8
Climber: John Howe

Boulder Gully — Auntie Gravity

The small, obvious buttress 40m above and north of *Supervalue* holds four routes.

Silly Putty ** 11a 25m
J.Howe D.Lane April 1984
A stunning climb along a strenuous diagonal crack on the left wall, bold and strenuous. Finish up *Auntie Gravity*.

Auntie Gravity * 10b 18m
J.Campbell C.Doig Oct 1979
The obvious crackline right of the prow. Good climbing.

Don't Believe The Hype * 11a #4 **SPORT** 18m
Dean Hart Ed Spat Aug 3 1992
The blunt arete immediately left of *Auntie Gravity*. Finish on the right up *Auntie Gravity*. There is a rap. station at the top.

Crag Rat * 10a #3 **SPORT** 18m
K.McLane J.Howe June 1983
A face climb at the right side of the face.

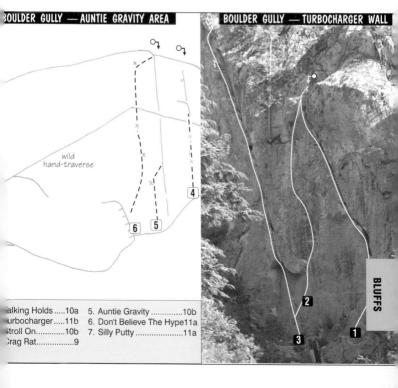

BOULDER GULLY — AUNTIE GRAVITY AREA

BOULDER GULLY — TURBOCHARGER WALL

wild hand-traverse

BLUFFS

Crag X

Immediately south of Boulder Gully are two high, west facing triangular walls easily visible from the Climbers Parking Lot. The lower wall is seamed with thin cracklines. The upper wall to the right sits above a terrace. Short paths to each lead from the Smoke Bluff Trail.

▬ CRAG X — LOWER WALL ▬▬

Side Street *   10c   2p.
Joe Turley Ted Marks March 1996
Climb a prominent handcrack [*Piece of Pie* R.Atkinson J.Howe Sept 1979] then the crack of *Baby Lizard* (10b). Climb arete above (10c).

Baby Lizard   .9   20m
J.Campbell J.Rollins Oct 1981

Centre Street **   10c   45m
J.Campbell A.Hughes Mar 1980
A good climb, cruxy above the tree.

Oregon Express   10c   40m
J.Kokotailo L.Kokotailo Aug 24 1986

Gord's Block   10d   8m
J.Campbell G.Menzies Oct 1980

Grunt ● ☺   .9   15m
J.Rollins J.Campbell Oct 1981
This climb is worthy of cleaning up as a good start to *Sniffler* and *Snorter*.

Chargex   .9   15m
J.Campbell J.Coope Oct 1981

Bellevue Drive   .7   15m
J.Coope M.Coope Oct 1981

▬ CRAG X — EASTER ISLAND AREA ▬▬

Easter Island *   .8   15m
J.Coope M.Coope C.Doig H.Doig J.Campbell P.Croft Oct 1979
A good crack climb with an obvious bulge at 10m. It is possible to hand-traverse in from low down on *Out to Lunge* (.8) *(M.Bosomworth D.Horne April '98).*

Payanoia   .9   12m
Drew Brayshaw (solo) Oct 1998
A crack to a ledge, just right of *Out to Lunge*, and a contrived arete finish. The name reflects the stress of trying to find a good new climb before Glenn Payan gets there.

Out To Lunge   10a   18m
J.Campbell J.Rollins Nov 1981
A curving crack which joins into *Easter Island*. Easier to walk the crack than hand-traverse it.

▬ CRAG X — SNIFFLER AND SNORTER ▬

Two short parallel roof cracks can be seen in a small bay at the left side of the terrace below the upper crag. Both offer good climbs. *Grunt* (.9) is immediately below, and would make a good first pitch if it were cleaned up.

Snorter *	.8	12m
R.Atkinson J.Howe A.Tate Sept 1979		

Sniffler *	.7	12m
J.Howe R.Atkinson A.Tate Sept 1979		

CRAG X — LOWER

BLUFFS

■ CRAG X — UPPER WALL

This crag has a half-dozen pleasant climbs, and deserves more traffic. A place to check out on a busy day in the Smoke Bluffs. Several good link-ups can be made, even a three-pitch route. Climbs are described from right to left as they are encountered. The first three all start off the trail to the Black Zawn.

Sunny November * .8 x 15m
J.Campbell J.Coope Nov 1979
The wide, square corner to the right of the arete. Pleasant climbing.

Castle Creep * 11b #3 x **SPORT+** 15m
Tom Clark Tiemo Brand May 1995
Climb on the right side of the arete of to join *Up From Despair*.

Up From Despair ** 10c 15m
R.Barley P.Shackleton 1982
A shallow curving dihedral on the left side of the arete. Tenuous.

Fingerlicking Good * 11a (18m)
R.Barley P.Shackleton (2pa) FFA: K.McLane J.Campbell June 1983
Another good fingercrack, best gained via *Up From Despair*.

■ *The next 2 climbs make an excellent linkage above Up From Despair.*

Friction Addiction * 10b #2 (12m)
Andrew Boyd July 1997
The short arete immediately above *Up From Despair*.

Bucky ki-yea * 10c (18m)
Jeff Thomson Glenn Payan Aug 1997
This climb is on the left edge of the uppermost arete at the right side of the crag. It offers an interesting 3-pitch 5.10 linkage up the lower aretes, *Up From Despair* (10c), and *Friction Addiction* (10b).

■ *The next 5 climbs are on the main wall to the left. Described right to left.*

Easy Does It ** 10c 2p.
J.Campbell J.Coope (2pa) Nov1979 FFA: P.Croft T.Knight Nov 1979
A good fingercrack, past 2 pins (10c) And an easier second pitch (10a).

Cosmik Debris 12b 18m
Andrew Boyd July 1997
Climbs a roof and a thin seam left of the first pitch of *Easy Does It*.

Outer Mongolia * 11c 35m
K.Duck R.Barley (2pa) Oct 1981 FFA: P.Croft R.Suddaby Oct 1981
Starts with an undercling and mantel. Some good climbing.

Virgin Soil 10c 22m
R.Barley F.Baumann 1982
A hand crack, a puzzling offwidth and a perplexing wall.

X-Ray ● 10c 12m
G.Smith J.Turley June 1981
A dirty crack, a bulging overlap then a right-facing corner.

CRAG X — LOWER AND UPPER

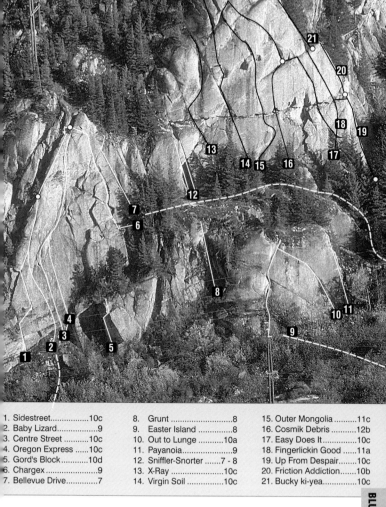

BLUFFS

Crag X was so named by John Howe and Randy Atkinson in 1979, as they thought they had discovered a secret crag.

The Black Zawn

Above and right of Crag X is a steep triangular recess about 30m high, seamed with grooves and bulges. Several good climbs are found here. Hike up past Crag X to the base of the cliff. The first two climbs are on the high, steep slab on the left. Scramble up to a small ledge.

Slipping Clutch ★★ 10b **SPORT**+ 30m
K.McLane D.Hart S.Young Mar 1984
A good face climb on small holds. Sustained. Take some wires, small CUs.

Joe Hill ● ☺ 10d 30m
K.McLane C.Murrell Mar 1984   FA direct start J.Howe 1984
Climbs the right side of the wall to join into the final crack of *Token Brits*. A harder direct start is possible from the right.

The next two climbs are among three short parallel corner-ramps located at the left side of the ledge below Slipping Clutch.

Chronicle Small Beer ● .7 10m
Glenn Payan Nov 1994
Start 8m left of *Slipping Clutch*. Climb the righthand of the three corner-ramps, traversing below a large roof at 6m.

Isaac Air Freight ★ 10a 15m
Glenn Payan April 2 1995
The narrow, central ramp of the three corner-ramps left of *Slipping Clutch*. A bouldery start.

The next four climbs are in the main trianglar bay.

Token Brits ★★ 10d 28m
R.Barley P.Rowat (1pa) Sept 1982 FFA: J.Howe K.McLane Aug1982
Direct finish: K.McLane D.Lane B.Kay Sept 1983
The fine groove up the left side of the main recess. Start at the base.

Perfidious Albion ★★ 10d 18m
R.Barley P.Shackleton (1pa) Sept1982 FFA: K.McLane J.Howe 6/83
FA direct variation J.Howe M.Fish 1985
A harder climb than it appears. Technical, steep and good. A direct variation at 11a avoids the traverse to the left. Scramble up to the ledge at the base.

Black Flag ● ☺ 10d 18m
K.McLane J.Howe July 1983
Layback onto the ramp right of the corner. Up through the bulges.

The Crucifix ● ☺ 10d 28m
K.McLane C.Murrell J.Howe Sept 1983
Impressively steep and intimidating.

General Strike ● 10c 28m
K.McLane P.Shackleton Sept 1983

Ladybug ● .8 x 8m
Jim Campbell John Coope 1979
A short crack on boulder a few metres below and right of the Black Zawn.

THE BLACK ZAWN

1. Isaac Air Freight 10a
2. Chronicle Small Beer 7
3. Slipping Clutch 10b
4. Joe Hill 10d
5. Token Brits 10d
6. Perfidious Albion 10d
7. Black Flag 10d
8. The Crucifix 10d
9. General Strike 10c

Have you read Conservation and Courtesy? Page 22.

Crystal Wall

This is the high wall south of the Black Zawn and above Krack Rock, now boasting some excellent climbs. Approach from the Black Zawn or to the left of Krack Rock.

Evaporation   ***   11a   #7   **SPORT**(p2)   2p.

p1. W.Dorling N.Watts C.Moorhead R.Dorling B.Moorhead March 24 '95
p2. Colin Moorhead Will Dorling Nick Watts March 17 1995

The top pitch is one of the best face leads of its grade the Bluffs. Start 5m left of a pair of pine trees and climb a crack to a slab to the big ledge above and chains (10c). Move right, go up to a small ledge then directly up the open wall moving right to finish (11a). 2 or 3 1½"-2½" CDs.

Natural Carpet Ride   *   10c   2p.

R.Barley J.Turley (Alts) April 1983 RECLEANED: Drew Brayshaw 1998

Corners and grooves at the left side of the cliff. Worth doing.

Supernatural Carpet Riders   *   .9   30m

Drew Brayshaw Shane Cook May 1997

A direct finish to *Natural Carpet Ride*.

Sublimation   10c   22m

Myles Holt Javier Pereda April 1996

A left-hand variation start to the first pitch of *Evaporation*.

Roca Diablo   *   11a   #6   **SPORT**+   (30m)

Will Dorling Nick Watts Feb 1996

An alternative 2nd pitch to *Evaporation*. Clip the first bolt on that route, then go out right past bolts to belay on the arete. Take a couple pieces to 1½".

1. Evaporation.................11a
2. Sublimation.................10c
3. Natural Carpet Ride ...10c
4. Supernatural Carpet 9
5. Roca Diablo 11a

Will Dorling drilling on lead, FA of Evaporation, pitch 1.

CRYSTAL WALL

trail up to Lumber and Octopuc Gar

Krack Rock

South of The Black Zawn, and close to the main trail, this small crag is seamed with many cracks. It merits much more attention that it has received. With a little re-scrubbing and some stations, it would make an excellent teaching area. Descend by walking and scrambling around on the south side.

Fairy Ring .6 20m
D.Jones June 1989

Turkey Dinner .7 20m
J.Kokotailo L.Kokotailo Oct 12 1987

Lonely Thunder .9 20m
E.Clemson June 1989

Koko Krack 10a 18m
J.Kokotailo L.Kokotailo Oct 12 1987

Popsickle .7 18m
D.Jones June 1989

Pieces Of Eight .7 - 10c 12m
D.Jones S.Sheffield June 1989

Hornet's Delight 10b 10m
D.Jones S.Sheffield June1989

Gumby's Inversion .8 12m
M.Sample J.Palaty C.Palaty   1993

Start up the deep corner groove on the upper south side of the crag (the descent route). Halfway up, step right to the base of another, higher wall then climb obvious twin cracks for 12m to the top.

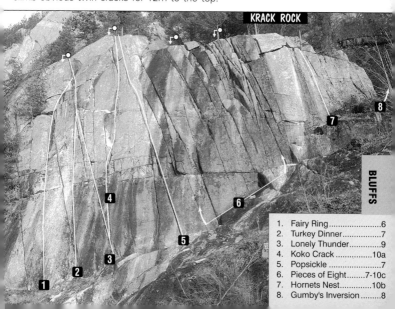

KRACK ROCK

BLUFFS

1. Fairy Ring.....................6
2. Turkey Dinner................7
3. Lonely Thunder.............9
4. Koko Krack 10a
5. Popsickle 7
6. Pieces of Eight........7-10c
7. Hornets Nest.............10b
8. Gumby's Inversion 8

The Smoke Bluff Wall

This high, tiered cliff provides the longest and some of the best climbs in the Smoke Bluffs. Hugely popular. It is divided into several areas to ease describing how to find the climbs.

The Pixie Corner area gives access to the top or bottom of *Jabberwocky*. It is also possible to walk in from the ledge below *Repeat When Necessary* at the left side of Neat and Cool, accessing the climbs right of *Phlegmish Dance*.

▰▰▰ SMOKE BLUFF WALL — LAUGHING CRACK AREA ▰▰▰

Walk in to Zombie Roof, then take a well-worn trail leftward (north). Walk 40m north below the wall, then go up right into a cave-like tunnel beside a huge boulder. Scramble steeply up a corner using fixed rope and continue 30m south to *Laughing Crack*.

So *	11c	**376**	12m

Jeff Thomson June 1998
A short face climb below *Laughing Crack*. Start 10m left of *Black and Decker*.

Laughing Crack ***	.7	**376**	25m

Glenn Payan March 12 1995
A superb finger and handcrack and a great gear lead for novices. There is often a line-up here of anxious first-time leaders, so please avoid unnecessary top-roping. You'll be laughing all the way...

Resoler *	11d	#7	**376**	**SPORT+**	24m

Jeff Thomson Glenn Payan June 1998
The open, slabby corner just right of *Laughing Crack*. Start just right of that route, and go for it. A ½"-1" CD will help the start. Finish into *Laughing Crack*.

Sweet Pea *	11c	**376**	32m

Jeff Thomson Glenn Payan June 1998
A face and crack climb that starts 10m right of *Laughing...* Bolts and gear. *Black And Decker* (11a) makes a good first pitch approach for this climb.

▎ *There are two short cracks off the treed ledge above Laughing Crack. To reach them, climb the short corner above (10a). Kraft (.7) is on the left, Dinner (.7) on the right (Jeff Thomson Katie Thomson Glenn Payan Aug 1998).*

▎ *The next two climbs start off the ramp left of the top of Laughing Crack, and can be gained from that route, or by scrambling up to the right of Krack Rock.*

Condo Bimbos	11c	**376**	15m

K.Langlett D.Parker Oct 1989
An obvious, vicious looking thin seam with 3 bolts.

Yuppie-I-O *	.8	**376**	12m

K.Langlett D.Parker Oct 1989
A much easier line to the right.

■■■ SMOKE BLUFF WALL — ZOMBIE ROOF AREA ■■■

At the base of the Smoke Bluff Wall is a wide, square alcove split by the redoubtable *Zombie Roof*. Climbs are described from right to left.

Killer Fridge ●   .9   *376*   30m
Bob Milward Dean Hart March 1983
Climbs the wall on the right. Overgrown.

Old Age ● ☺   .9   *376*   30m
R.Milward P.Shackleton R.Barley April 1984
The big left-facing corner at the right side of the wall which gains the *Jabberwocky* ledge. Much better than it looks—an exciting climb.

Outrage *   10d   *376*   2p.
R.Barley C.Austrom (Alts) D.Jones April 1983
Start up *Old Age*. Move up a corner, then go left to twin face cracks leading to the ledge left of *Jabberwocky* (10a). Continue through overlaps.

Through The Never 13c #6 *376* **SPORT** 15m
Jim Sandford July 14 1992
Start as for *Old Age*, then go straight up through the roofs.

Jacob's Ladder 12b #4 *376* **SPORT** 15m
Jim Sandford July 20 1992
Start 5m right of *Zombie*, and climb the roof past bolts. Station above.

Zombie Roof * 12d-13a   *376*   22m
P.Croft 1982 (believed to have never received a true red-point ascent)
This famous roof finger crack is a Squamish legend. The crux is met at the lip and is solved by all manner of gymnastic contortions. Never redpointed.

Black And Decker * 11a   *376*   15m
D.Hart S.Young R.Milward March 1983 RECLEANED: Jeff Thomson Sept 1998
The obvious corner with 2 bolts on the left side of the crag, above a thin crack.

Savage Amusement * 13b #6 *376* **SPORT**+ 20m
Jim Sandford June 26 1993
On the far left side of the *Zombie* alcove, climb a short crack to a horizontal fault (CD) which leads out to the lip of the roof. Traverse along the lip of the roof, and finish up the wall to a station.

Niagara Falls A3+   *376*   18m
Kris Holm Scott Jeffrey April 20 1992   (possibly climbed earlier)
Start on the left side of the Zombie alcove and follow the outer of two parallel cracks traversing the underside of the roof. A few hard moves lead diagonally to the lip at *Zombie*.

Three short aid climbs, all A3 from Andrew Boyd May 1997 start left of Zombie Roof and head out on three roughly parallel seams to lower-off bolts on Savage Amusement. Stuck Here Again is the farthest left and goes straight out to the lip and the 3rd bolt of Savage Amusement. Velvet Onion Lounge starts in the corner just left of Zombie and follows the left trending 'stair-like' seam to the 4th bolt. Wet Head goes close to and parallel to Zombie and lowers off the 5th bolt.

THE SMOKE BLUFF WALL

PIXIE CORNE

KRACK ROCK

fixed rope

SMOKE BLUFF WALL

NEAT & COOL

MOSQUITO

BATTERED BALLS

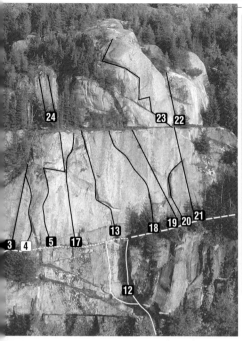

Mosquito, 5.8
Climbers Barry McLane, Bob Wilson
Photo: Angela Muellers

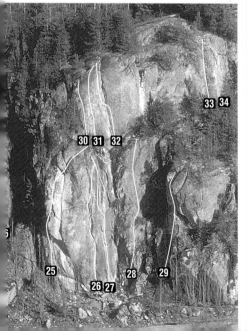

1. Black and Decker.............11a
2. So...................................11c
3. Laughing Crack 7
4. Resoler............................11d
5. Sweet Pea 11c
6. Condo Bimbos 11c
7. Yuppie-I-O 8
8. Savage Amusement 13b
9. Aid Climbs
10. Zombie Roof 12d-13a
11. Jacobs Ladder.................12b
12. Old Age 9
13. Outrage...........................10d
14. Through The Never..........13c
15. Killer Fridge 9
16. Alice 8
17. Senile Saunter.................10c
18. Long Distance Feeling......11a
19. Sparkys Crack 8
20. Gobbledegook 8
21. Jabberwocky....................10a
22. White Rabbit 10b
23. Wonderland 9
24. Kraft - Dinner 7
25. Pinball Machine 10b
26. S-M's Delight....................10b
27. Mosquito 8
28. Sphinxter Quits 8
29. Rock and Roll 10b
30. Curry The Dog 8
31. Alien Sex Fiends 11a
32. Phlegmish Dance...............8
33. Rolling Stones....................8
34. Rubber Soul 9

▬ SMOKE BLUFF WALL — UPPER LEVELS ▬▬▬

These climbs are approached by routes on the lower levels, or by walking around from Pixie Corner. It is poor style to drop a rope for top-roping down *Jabberwocky* if there are climbers below.

Jabberwocky ** 10a *376* 22m
T.Knight P.Croft 1978
A fine fingercrack. A bouldery start with a long reach gives way to easier climbing above. Good protection throughout. Try a shoulder stand if you're too short.

Gobbledegook .8 *376* 22m
R.Barley P.Shackleton 1980
A easier alternative to *Jabberwocky*, but not as well protected.

Sparky's Crack ● ☺ .8 *376* 25m
J.Turley 1982
A dirty crack, which would likely be popular if it was clean.

Long Distance Feeling 11a *376* 25m
R.Barley J.Turley (1pa) 1981   FFA: P.Croft T.Knight 1981
A better climb than it appears. A minor scrub would help a lot.

> *The upper pitch of Outrage can be reached by traversing left 15m beyond the Jabberwocky ledge. Likewise the next route.*

Senile Saunter ● ☺ 10c *376* 30m
R.Barley C.Mullard May 1989
A thin seam up a white wall, 15m left of *Outrage*, which is probably best accessed by traversing right from *Laughing Crack*.

> *The highest level on the Smoke Bluff Wall offers two good climbs starting at the top of Jabberwocky. It is also possible to get here by walking around from Pixie Corner*

White Rabbit * 10b *376* 10m
Unknown
The short pumpy lieback corner above the *Jabberwocky* belay.

Wonderland ** .9 *376* 30m
R.Barley P.Shackleton C.Murrell 1981
A fine exposed pitch across the headwall above and left of *Jabberwocky*.

> *The Smoke Bluff Connection *** (10a) is a popular series of pitches up the Smoke Bluff Wall on successively higher tiers, via Mosquito, Phlegmish Dance, Jabberwocky, Wonderland.*

A major fire in the Bluffs in 1970 levelled all but the largest trees.

■■■ *Smoke Bluff Wall — Mosquito Area* ■■■■

The following climbs are all grouped around the ever-popular crack of *Mosquito*, the first obvious feature close to the trail south of the Zombie Roof area, and north of the smooth wall of Battered Balls.

Alice .8 <u>376</u> 35m
J.Campbell R.Milward June 1983
A stepped corner with little protection, but nice climbing, 30m up left of *Mosquito*. It ends at the base of *Jabberwocky*.

Pinball Machine * 10b <u>377</u> 22m
Will Dorling Colin Moorhead March 1995
A well-protected pitch up corners and crackline starting 8m left of *SM's Delight*. From here, it is possible to continue up the bulge on the right (10a) to join *Curry The Dog* or *Phlegmish Dance*.

Curry The Dog .8 <u>377</u> 15m
Will Dorling Richard Dorling April 13 1995
Start from the top of *Mosquito* and go out left and up onto a ledge. Continue up a broken crackline. A range of gear is required, mostly CDs.

S-M's Delight * 10b <u>377</u> 25m
J.Campbell P.Kubik July 1980
A testing crackline just left of *Mosquito*. Harder than it looks.

Mosquito ** .8 <u>377</u> 25m
J.Campbell A.Hughes Feb 1980
A Smoke Bluff classic. Handjamming and liebacking to a good ledge. Delightful climbing and exceedingly popular, but suffers death by top-rope most days.

Sphinx'ter Quits ** .8 <u>377</u> 25m
Glenn Payan Jeff Thomson Feb 1996
A face climb immediately right of *Mosquito* starting off a large boulder.

■ *The next 5 climbs all start from the ledge system at the top of Mosquito.*

Rock And Roll ● 10b <u>377</u> 18m
I.Christiansen 1985
10m right of *Mosquito, a* deep corner leads up to a big block.

Phlegmish Dance ** .8 <u>377</u> 18m
P.Croft (solo) 1978
Immediately above the top of *Mosquito*, this little gem offers nice, well protected climbing up the square groove.

Alien Sex Fiends 11a <u>377</u> 18m
D.Hart B.McDonald K.McLane March 1983
Face climbing and mantelshelves up the wall beside *Phlegmish....*

Rolling Stones ● .8 <u>377</u> 12m
I.Christiansen R.Rybak Nov 3 1986
A crack 15m right of *Phlegmish Dance*.

Rubber Soul ● .9 <u>377</u> 12m
R.Rybak I.Christiansen Nov 2 1986
Another short crack 25m right of *Phlegmish Dance*.

BLUFFS

Battered Balls

Between the Mosquito area and Neat and Cool is a smooth wall beside the trail with a few generally desperate thin face climbs. Climbs are described from left to right.

Hummingbird ● 11d 12m
P.Croft T.Knight 1979
A face climb at the left edge, buried under a wall of moss.

Battered Balls 10d 12m
P.Croft D.Hatten T.Knight 1978
A thin seam with a desperate start. A shoulder stand is cool.

Roadside Distraction 12c 12m
Andrew Boyd July 1997
A thin seam above a mantleshelf to a vicious slab.

Finger Rippin' Good 10b 20m
Dave Sarkany Maria Cundy Sept 1972 FFA Doug Woods
Start just left of the wide crack up the centre of the cliff, and climb 2 discontinuous thin cracks, continuing up the headwall.

Thin Wall Special 11b 15m
A.Hughes S.Heliwell March 1980
Another thin seam, gained by a hard mantel and face climbing.

Too Desperate Men .9 (10m)
Jeff Thompson Glenn Payan June 1997
Climb the discontinuous cracks above *Thin Wall Special*. A right-hand finish is possible.

Dog Face 12b #4 10m
P.Beckham Jan 1989
A steep bouldery problem past bolts. Being eight feet tall helps.

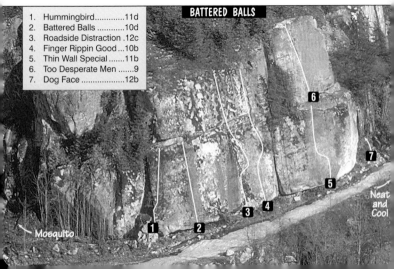

1. Hummingbird.............11d
2. Battered Balls 10d
3. Roadside Distraction .12c
4. Finger Rippin Good ...10b
5. Thin Wall Special 11b
6. Too Desperate Men 9
7. Dog Face 12b

Alaska Highway, pitch 1, 5.11c
Climber: Perry Beckham

St Vitus Dance, pitch 2, 5.9
Climbers: Robin Barley, Chris Murrell

The name of the Smoke Bluffs evolved in the 1970s from climbers'
affection for Carlos Castanada, although it was then referred to as The
Little Smoke Bluffs. Previously, Squamish residents had called the area
Bughouse Heights.

Neat And Cool

An immensely popular crag with a good variety of climbs. It is a sunny, pleasant area, but suffers badly from overcrowding and death by top-rope. Routes are described from the left, the first two of which begin at the lowest level, close to the main trail. It is one of the fastest-drying crags in Squamish. All of the more popular and better routes have anchors at the top. Climbs are described from left to right.

The name of the crag came from the words sprayed on the rock by a Squamish youth in the 1970s, "I am neat and cool". No self-esteem problems there. It is now a Smoke Bluff heritage site, and is still visible - just.

Strawberry Jam *   10b   x   8m
Chris Cooper Keith Rajala 1975   FFA Simon Tooley Jorg Beekman 1979
A short gem of a finger crack on a wall at the far left side.

The next two climbs start at the base on the far left side.

Raging Duck   10b   **384**   18m
I.Christiansen 1985

Pink Flamingo *   10b   **384**   18m
T.Ryan P.Kubik 1980

At the far left, stiff scrambling leads to a large ledge from which the next 12 climbs begin.

A Necessary Evil   10b   **384**   12m
S.Young J.Campbell April 1984

Chalk Up Another One   .8   **384**   10m
J.Campbell S.Young April 1984

Repeat When Necessary * .9   **384**   10m
K.Kraft J.Manuel D.Schildt 1979

Coffee Break   .8   **384**   12m
S.Ilcisin J.Manuel 1979

Fresh Start   .7   **384**   12m
S.Ilcisin J.Manuel 1979

Wasted Days And Wasted Nights .6   **384**   18m
K.Kraft D.Schildt 1979

Stumps   .8   **384**   18m
Unknown

Sally Five Fingers *   .8   **384**   18m
K.Kraft J.Manuel 1979

The Jigsaw Flow   .9   **384**   21m
Glenn Payan John Thompson April 15 1995

Cat Crack **   .6   **384**   20m
T.Knight P.Croft 1978

1000 Pardons .8 _384_ 28m
Glenn Payan John Thompson Oct 1995
You'll need them if you climb this on a busy day. Start at the base of _The Edge_, follow the narrow dyke traversing up left across _Cat Crack_, _Jigsaw Flow_, _Sally Five Fingers_ and _Stumps_.

The Edge 10a _385_ 15m
J.Turley G.Smith 1980

■ _The next 6 climbs are on the main wall._

Corner Crack * .7 _385_ 20m
C.Austrom 1977

Flying Circus ** 10a _385_ 20m
D.Mitten D.Lane 1977
A fine crack, but is becoming badly polished from heavy top-rope use.

Fear Of Flying 11a _385_ 22m
P.Hilltner P.Post July 1983

Lieback Flake .9 _385_ 22m
D.Mitten C.Austrom 1977

Corn Flakes * .6 _385_ 22m
N.Didlick M.Goetz 1976
A pleasant climb over a tottering pile of blocks and pedestals.

Neat And Cool ** 10a _385_ 30m
D.Lane P.Beckham 1979   Direct finish: J.Howe P.Kindree Y.Kamori Aug 1981
A classic Smoke Bluff route. A direct finish takes the steep slab on the left.

■ _The next 6 climbs are face routes on the wall that rises straight off the Smoke Bluffs Trail. Please avoid spreading your gear over the trail, or don't complain if it gets squashed by mountainbikes. Could be me._

Gross Incompetence * .8 _385_ 25m
R.Barley C.Murrell H.Richardson 1981

Geritol ** 10c _385_ 25m
D.Serl J.Campbell D.Harris 1979
A longstanding Smoke Bluffs classic.

House Music * 10c _385_ 25m
D.Hart R.Atkinson 1988

Where Ancients Fear To Tread ** 10c _385_ 35m
R.Suddaby R.Barley 1981
An excellent climb

Toasted Tits * 10d +1pa _385_ 20m
Robin Barley July 1997
Start up the shot holes and use the third bolt for aid.

Hans Groper 10c _385_ 30m
R.Barley (1pa) 1982 FFA: J.Howe Sept 1982
This climb existed before the rock was blasted away in 1985, so grope up through the shot holes to reach the arete.

BLUFFS

NEAT AND COOL

▬▬ NEAT AND COOL — RIGHT-HAND END ▬▬▬

These eight climbs are around the corner to the right of the main cliff, and look south across toward the Chief. A newly constructed residence is very close, so please keep the noise down.

Kangaroo Corner * 11a x 15m
P.Croft T.Knight 1978
Hard moves up a nice steep corner.

There You Go Andy! 12c x 12m
D.Caldwell Jan 31 1988
Just right of *Kangaroo...* , a thin crack and flake undercling.

King Of Rock 12c x 10m
W.Kraus July 20 1987
A fine thin crack that has suffered abuse from nailed ascents. **No hammers!**

Psychopath * 11c 12m
P.Croft P.Fodchuck T.Knight 1978
A good problem up a shallow scoop and arete.

Ali Butto 11a 18m
T.Knight P.Croft 1979
Face climbing past bolts above the pine tree, to the top of *Twisted*.

Neat And Clean * .7 20m
Anders Ourom Randy Atkinson 1978
A prominent corner flake which starts at a ledge 8m up, and curves its way leftward to the top of the cliff.

Twisted * 10c 18m
R.Clements J.Buszowski Sept 1983
Start up *Neat And Clean*, then step left and face climb to the top.

Clean Starts .7 8m
Unknown c.1981
A short corner, leading up to the ledge below *Neat And Clean*.

NEAT AND COOL FAR RIGHT

1. Psychopath 11c
2. Ali Bhutto 11a
3. Clean Starts 7
4. Neat and Clean..............7
5. Twisted 10c

The first ascent of Northwest Passage
Photo: Beckey collection.

INDOOR ROCK CLIMBING CENTRE LTD.

CLIFFHANGER

VANCOUVER
CANADA

CLIFFHANGER... VANCOUVER'S ROCK CLIMBING GYM OFFERS:

- INTRODUCTORY CLIMBING COURSES
- TECHNIQUE COURSES
- OUTDOOR GUIDING & INSTRUCTION
- CORPORATE TEAM BUILDING PROGRAMS
- "KIDROCK" CLIMBING PROGRAMS
- GROUP DISCOUNTS

OUR FANTASTIC CLIMBING FACILITY
IS LOCATED IN VANCOUVER
BETWEEN SCIENCE WORLD AND
MOUNTAIN EQUIPMENT CO-OP AT

106 WEST 1ST AVENUE

874-2400

CLIFFHANGER.BC.CA

Penny Lane

This is the long, open south facing cliff overlooking Hospital Hill. The climbs in general are stiffer than those at Neat and Cool and Burgers and Fries. There is considerable variety to choose from, although thin cracks and face climbs predominate. A short path leads straight up the front from the Smoke Bluff Trail. Access is also possible from the Loop trail at the west end of the cliff by climbing an easy groove and at the east end of the cliff via a gully which gains the trail that links Pixie Corner with Ronins Corner—a quick access to Ronins Corner. Descents are usually by rappel, although walking off is no problem. Climbs are described from the left (west) end.

Mirage   11a   ✗   2p.
B.Beard R.Parker 1980
A short crack leads to a tree. Face climb up the crest of the prow.

Short Walk   .8   _392_   35m
R.Barley P.Shackleton 1981
Traverse around the buttress, then up left of _Mirage_.

Whorehorse ●   10c+2pa   _392_   18m
R.Barley Sept 1989
Face climb, using two bolts for aid.

Drain Surgeon ●   .9   _392_   25m
Robin Barley Joe Turley April 1983
The gully-like cleft. Could use a good drain surgeon to clean it up.

> _The next six climbs all start from a small bay at the foot of the wide open corner of Quarryman._

Clandestine Affair **   .9   _392_   25m
R.Barley P.Shackleton 1981
A good climb, a lower jamcrack followed by a cruxy traverse.

The Yorkshire Gripper ** 11b   _392_   20m
P.Croft R.Barley 1981
Two thin cracks linked by face moves. A tricky mantel at the top.

Knob Hopping *   11a   _392_   25m
John Howe Jim Hegan Aug 29 1992
Good climbing between _Yorkshire Gripper_ and _Popeye And The Raven_. Start as for _Popeye..._ then up past 2 bolts. Small wires and CDs.

Popeye And The Raven ** 10c   _392_   22m
J.Turley G.Smith 1981
A very popular face climb up a steep ramp. The difficulties increase steadily to a nice technical crux.

Quarryman **   .8   _392_   25m
R.Barley P.Shackleton 1981
An excellent, varied corner climb. Good protection is available. The direct finish takes a thin crack above the flakes (10b).

Health Hazard   *   10a   *392*   30m
R.Barley D.Cody 1981
Good face climbing on the unsteep edge right of *Quarryman*.

The Last Post   *   11d   *392*   30m
K.McLane B.Protsch J.Turley May 10 1986
Bold face climbing above a stiff roof. Finish left of *Health Hazard*.

Weenie   *   11c   *392*   30m
S.Flavelle J.Howe July 1884
Face climbing to hard moves below a bulge. Pull up left to exit.

Short People   *   11a   *392*   30m
P.Croft M.Fish P.Kindree 1980
The curving crack. A long step at its top leads to a steep finish.

Jangling Ball Wall   *   11b   *392*   30m
S.Flavelle R.Barley Aug 1984
Cracks lead to a delicate bulge and good face climbing above.

Foot In Mouth Disease   11a   *392*   2p.
R.Barley B.Protsch (1pa) 1981   FFA: P.Croft R.Barley 1981
Climb a short dyke and belay on the slab. Then up the wall left of the prow.

Teenage Girls Won't Blow Gorbies   * 11c   *392*   2p.
E.Hoogstraten D.Caldwell 1988
Start as for *Foot In Mouth...*, but continue up the exposed dyke on the prow.

Up Up And Away   **   .9   *392*   30m
T.Knight P.Croft 1978
Easily up a corner to a fine lieback crack.

Air Time   11c   *392*   30m
D.Hutchinson R.Miller Sept 1 1990
The thin seam just right of the *Up Up...* lieback corner.

Just For Howie   .8   *392*   27m
R.Barley J.Campbell March 1981
Take the corner of *Up Up...*, then climb the wall on the right.

Exsanguinator   *   10b   *393*   27m
R.Barley J.Turley 1981
Start up *Witch Doctor's...*, then go left into a hanging corner.

Witch Doctor's Apprentice   * .9   *393*   27m
D.Jones D.Serl May 1986
The corner. Jamming, liebacking, stemming etc.

Power Windows   **   11a   *393*   33m
J.Sandford Nov 10 1985
Good face climbing from the top of a thin crack over to the arete.

Crime Of The Century   ** 11b   *393*   20m
P.Croft T.Knight 1978
A classic Smoke Bluff fingercrack. Bouldery start then good finishing moves.

Shakey The Moyle   11c   #3   *393*   **SPORT**   (10m)
R.Lutje K.Mortensen Dale Caldwell May 9th 1994
A long overdue continuation above *Crime of the Century..*

Penny Lane ★★★   .9   *393*   35m
K.Rajala C.McCafferty (aid) 1975   FFA: A.Ourom J.Arts 1978
The classic Smoke Bluff crack. A bouldery start leads to stemming in a shallow corner. The fine crack above gets easier.

Noname   .9   *393*   30m
J.Brodie M.Campbell c.1994
Start 10m right of *Penny Lane*, and go up left onto a long ledge below a narrow face. Climb past a bolt and move left into *Penny Lane*. A much harder continuation is possible, following a direct line to the top (11b).

Satan's Slit   .6   *393*   30m
A.Ourom L.Soet Feb 1974
A deep back and foot chimney.

Sunny Days In December ★ 12b   *393*   35m
K.Rajala C.Cooper Dec 1976   FFA: P.Croft 1988
A longstanding problem. Face climbing leads to a steep corner.

Climb And Punishment ★★ 10d   *393*   30m
P.Croft T.Knight R.Barley 1981
A steep flake and face moves above lead to an easier crack.

Partners In Crime ★★   11a   *393*   35m
C.Cooper K.Rajala 1976   FFA: R.Atkinson A.Ourom 1978
Classic stuff up a thin crack. The crux is a bulge at 10m, jam it or lieback it. Equally hard. Sustained above, but a little easier.

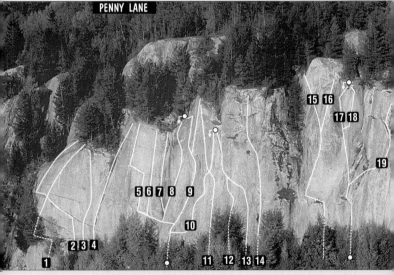

PENNY LANE

The Ugly American   10a   *393*   35m
Anders Ourom Kevin Wallace Sept 1998
A crack climb two metres right of and parallel to *Partners in Crime*.

Piggy's Perversions   .8   *393*   20m
R.Barley C.Murrell 1980
Best forgotten.

Werewolves Of London   11c   *393*   35m
P.Croft T.Knight 1979
A good but much neglected climb up the last buttress on the cliff. Start on the left, and step right into a thin crack up the crest.

Stiff Upper Lip   10d   x   25m
Joe Turley Sept 1992
On the east side of the *Werewolves Of London* buttress. Start 12m above the trail and climb a short dyke to an obvious undercling. Follow it leftwards and up a lieback flake to join *Werewolves*. Gear to 4".

Mr Bad Example   10d   x   22m
Stewart Wozny 1993
Start as for *Stiff Upper Lip* up to the dyke. Avoid the undercling: go straight up the wall past a bolt to join *Werewolves*.. Gear to 3".

There is a face hidden behind a big fir tree on the south-facing wall between Werewolves... and the gully. Nothing is known about it, except that it is believed to be 5.11+ with 6 bolts .

BLUFFS

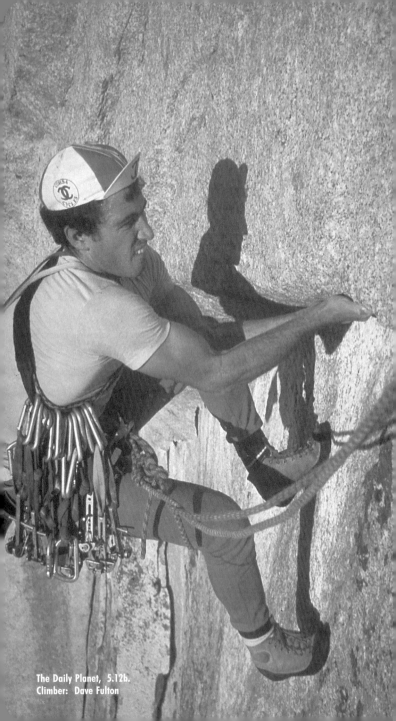

The Daily Planet, 5.12b.
Climber: Dave Fulton

Bughouse Heights

This is the line of west-facing buttresses and walls between Penny Lane and Pixie Corner, parallel to the Loop Trail and heavily screened by trees. This crag has many decent routes, and is a good alternative to the crowded wastelands of Neat and Cool and Burgers and Fries. Slow to dry out, but it can offer no-lineup freedom on busy days. Go look. Climbs are described from right to left.

> *There is a climb lost on a short, damp wall facing west, about 10m from the start of the main Smoke Bluff Loop Trail. It is buried under the moss. Pregnant Paws 11c (Tim Ryan and others, about 1989) The next three climbs are at the far right (south) end of Bughouse Heights, at the foot of the short groove that leads up to Penny Lane.*

Fata Morgana ** .8   2p.
Ray Parker Bryan Beard 1980
A worthwhile climb on the wide arete that divides Penny Lane from Bughouse Heights. Above is a lieback corner to a ledge (.8). Climb the crack above (.8).

Too Brown To Frown *11a
P.McKernin J.Black Sept 2 1993
Face climb past 2 bolts, 2–3m right of *Too Pink to Think* until possible to move right and cross the roof just left of *Fata Morgana* (.8). Keep left to easier terrain.

Too Pink To Think   11b
P.Croft T.Knight 1981
Climbs through a roof at the left edge of the white rock.

BUGHOUSE HEIGHTS — SOUTH

Penny Lane

Mirage

Too Pink to Think

Too Brown to Frown

Fata Morgana

foreshortened view from the Loop Trail

> *The next obvious feature on the wall (often wet) is the wide crack of Skullduggery. There are two climbs between it and Too Pink... One is okay, the other not.*

Squamish Logger ● ☺   .9   x   22m
J.Turley C.Zozikyan G.Smith Sept 1981
A thin crack crossing two faults about 15m up the trail from *Too Pink*.... Belay at a third fault and a birch tree.

Jade ●   .9   x   18m
I.Christiansen R.Rybak 1985
30m left of *Too Pink*... a left-slanting crack line [pin] to a big fir stump. Mossy.

The next four climbs are around an open wall, becoming a bit mossy, but well worth checking out.

Skullduggery *   10a   30m
S.Tooley J.Beekman 1981
An obvious wide crack on the upper tier. Harder than it looks.

Sting In The Tail *   10c   30m
D.Jones R.Miller D.Hutchinson March 1990
Good face climbing up the middle of the face left of *Skullduggery*.

Tail Wind **   10a   30m
D.Hart D.Jones R.Atkinson March 25 1990
Just left of *Sting...* face climbing up the left edge of the wall.

Salamander   .4   25m
Glenn Payan John Thompson Aug 19 1992
This climb is just left of *Tailwind*. Climb the chimney to reach the low-angle arete on the huge block left of *Tailwind* (10a).

The next 8 climbs are packed in close together on a series of aretes, walls and grooves. Some are so close you could take a chalk dip from each other. Described right to left.

Fat Legs   .7   12m
R.Rybak J.Sandford Oct 6 1986
Climb the groove, moving out right along cracks to finish.

Twin Peaks Of Kilimanjaro * 10c   #6   **SPORT**   16m
Glenn Payan Jeff Thomson Aug 1996
Start in *Fat Legs*, then go left onto the face. Good.

Sudden Impact **   11a   #7   **SPORT**   18m
J.Sandford R.Rybak Oct 6 1986 REBOLTED Jeff Thomson Dec 1998
A clean high-angle wall. Nice climbing.

Pancakes On A Wall ● .7   15m
D.Jones K.Neubauer March 11 1990
Left of *Sudden...* is a corner/gully. Climb the flakes on the left wall.

A number of variations to the following climbs have been done, to further confuse everyone. So this is a simplified version.

Tantric Exercise   11c   15m
J.Sandford April 16 1990
A short roof problem. Easy cracks above.

Multiple Choice *   .9   15m
D.Jones T.Ryan April 1990
Straight up the main corner, or exit out right.

Power Scrub   .9   15m
D.Jones J.Sandford April 16 1990
Definitely! Start as for *Multiple Choice,* then exit out to the left.

Golden Parachute   10a   15m
D.Jones T.Ryan April 1990
If only. Pull through a short flake roof on the left to join *Power Scrub*.

BUGHOUSE HEIGHTS — TAILWIND WALL

BUGHOUSE HEIGHTS — SUDDEN IMPACT AREA

1. Skullduggery.............10a
2. Sting in the Tail..........10c
3. Tailwind 10a
4. Salamander 4
5. Fat Legs 7
6. Twin Peaks of Kiliman 10c
7. Sudden Impact 11a
8. Tantric Exercise..........11c
9. Multiple Choice 9
10. Power Scrub 9
11. Golden Parachute......10a

BLUFFS

clear-cut by mouse

▬▬ BUGHOUSE HEIGHTS — LOOP TRAIL STAIRS ▬▬

Climbs on the mossy wall immediately right of the foot of the Pixie Corner stairs on the Loop Trail. Described right to left.

Mudday Afternoon ●   .7   *x*   10m
D.Boekwyt Becky Bates Sept 1991
A line on the right—a few moves up to an easy flake. Heavily mossed over.

Passing Stranger ● ☺   10a   *x*   10m
Dave Jones , The unknown American
Snag a passing belayer with a few RPs for the central crackline. Mossed over.

Oozeday Afternoon ● ☺   10b   *x*   10m
Joe Turley 1992
The thin seams on the left, close to the stairs and sporting a pin.

It Fir Fun   .8   *x*   8m
J. Simms M.Buck K.Holm September 1998
An obvious short crack on the left (west) side of the stairs.

▬▬ BUGHOUSE HEIGHTS — CUTICLE DEATH ▬▬

Nice climbs with a view on small craglets directly above *Squamish Logger* on Bughouse Heights. Easiest access is from Split Beaver.

Cuticle Death   10c   *x*   12m
Bob Milward Scott Young May 1984
A left-leaning diagonal crackline.

Kinda Kute   10a   *x*   10m
Simon Tooley Jorg Beekman 1979
Just right of *Cuticle Death*.

Throbbing For Love   .6   *x*   10m
Kon Kraft 1982
A crack on a higher craglet, right of *Kinda Kute*.

PIXIE CORNER

view from Smoke Bluffs Loop Trail

foreshortened view

1.	Digital Dexterity	12c	5.	Trixie	10b	9.	Captain Hornblower	11a
2.	Little Feat	10c	6.	Pixie Corner	8	10.	Davy Jones Locker	6
3.	Stink Foot	10d	7.	Diddly Squat	12b	11.	Joe's Crack	9
4.	Big Foot	10b	8.	Weiner in the Bun	11a			

Pixie Corner

This is a group of large, south facing aretes separated by deep corners hidden in the trees at the top of the Smoke Bluff Wall, left of the stairs on the Smoke Bluff Loop trail. Hugely popular. Climbs are described right to left. Descend by walking down to the right.

Digital Dexterity   12c   #±5   **SPORT**+   18m
Unknown FFA: Jola Sandford July 13 1990
The vicious looking seam splitting the wall left of the stairs.

Little Feat   ● ☺   10c   12m
P.Beckham J.Daly 1982
The blunt prow left of *Digital...* Finish direct, nice climbing.

Stink Foot   ● ☺   10d   12m
J.Howe D.Lane K.McLane K.Flavelle May 20 1984
The wall on the left. Cross *Little Feat* and finish on the right.

Big Foot   ● ☺   10b   *x*   12m
R.Milward May 1984
Just left of *Stink Foot*, a short wall on a rounded prow.

Trixie   10b   8m
Don Serl Dave Jones 1982
Cracks just right of *Pixie Corner*.

Pixie Corner   **   .8   15m
J.Buszowski P.Fodchuck 1978
An inviting corner with twin parallel cracks. Good jamming and stemming.

Diddly Squat   12b   20m
K.Reid 1988
The thin seam to the left. A short problem, despite the length.

Weiner In The Bun   11a   20m
T.Knight P.Croft 1980
The largest arete. Start on the left side.

Captain Hornblower   11a   8m
Dave Jones Don Serl 1982
The wall between *Weiner in the Bun* and the corner. 3 bolts.

Davy Jones' Locker   *   .7   22m
Don Serl Dave Jones 1982
A moderate and pleasant climb up a large corner.

Joe's Crack   *   .9   18m
Joe Buszowski Simon Tooley 1979
The diagonal jamcrack to the left, harder than it looks. Mantel to finish.

Turley's Terror   ●   .7   *x*   10m
Robin Barley Joe Turley 1981
Cracks that start off a ledge 4m left of *Joe's Crack*.

Mad Hatter   ●   10b   *x*   10m
Jim Campbell Corina Atcheson 1982
A left-leaning line that starts same place as *Turley's Terror*, then heads toward the top of *White Rabbit*.

Lumberland

A west-facing crag north and downhill from the top of the Pixie Corner stairs. Walk over from the stairs, up from the Crystal Wall / Black Zawn area, or down from One Toque Wall.

The GMB .9   20m
Glenn Payan John Thompson March 29 '95
From the top of the Pixie Corner stairs, head north then downhill for 60m to an open glade (or walk up from Crystal Wall). The cliff is obvious, facing west. This stiff, well-scrubbed face climb is at the left side of the cliff.

Lumberland 10b   x   20m
R.Barley P.Shackleton 1981 RECLEANED
Sam Turley Stacy Morrison 1994
A crack in a convex wall right of *GMB*.

THE GMB
The GMB
One Toque Wall
Lumberland
Loop Trail
foreshortened view

Nubile Woman

As the trail to Octopus Garden starts to climb after the top of the Pixie Corner stairs, there is a rambling, parallel crag hidden on the left which meets the trail after about 60m. At this point the appealing crack of *Nubile Woman* can be seen splitting the wall.

Batter Up!   .9   x   20m
Glenn Payan June 1995
Start at *Nubile Woman*, step right and climb a clean streak.

Nubile Woman *   10a *   x   22m
T.Holwill S.Holwill July 1983
An obvious, good fingercrack.

Old Maid *   10a   #4   x   **SPORT** 20m
John Thompson Glenn Payan March 29 1995
A bolted face climb immediately left of *Nubile Woman*.

Missing Chris ●   10b   x   20m
Glenn Payan John Thompson July 3 1994
15m left of *Nubile Woman*, climb a 4 metre face to a right-slanting crack, gain the ledge above and continue up a right-facing corner to top.

Split Beaver

This is a clean buttress split by a series of fine cracks. Follow the Loop trail to the top of the stairs beside Pixie Corner. Turn south along the trail to Ronins Corner, then go 50m up to the crag.

Heavenly Ladder ** .9 20m
R.Barley P.Shackleton 1981
The deep square alcove on the left. Good stemming, nice moves.

Orifice Fish ** .9 20m
R.Barley P.Shackleton 1981
This steep crackline just left of *Split Beaver*, gives beautiful strenuous hand jamming. Continue up the corner above.

Split Beaver ** 10b 30m
N.Taylor P.Peart 1975
A hallowed Squamish classic up a striking crack splitting the middle of the wall. Handjamming leads to fist to rattly fist. The short corner above gives an easier finish.

Organ Failure ● ☺ 11c 15m
R.Barley P.Shackleton K.McComber (1pa) '81 FFA: P.Croft T.Knight '81
Very scruffy, although it looks good underneath the choss.

30m right of Split Beaver a long, unsteep prow reaches down to the trail. The next route takes the long jamcrack left of this prow.

Asleep At The Wheel ● .8 x 30m
D.Jones K.Neubauer March 11 1989
Climb the corner crack to greater difficulties higher up.

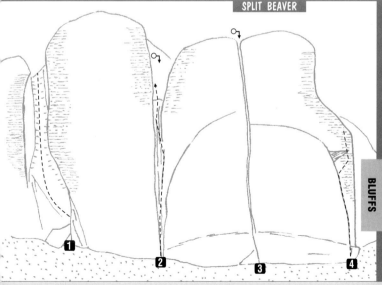

SPLIT BEAVER

BLUFFS

1. Heavenly Ladder............9
2. Orifice Fish.....................9
3. Split Beaver 10b
4. Organ Failure 11c

One Toque Wall

A collection of short but pleasant climbs on a crag near Octopus Garden. Take the Loop Trail above the Pixie Corner stairs. After a few minutes it levels off and a good trail heads out left to the crag. Or hike directly up from the Climbers Parking Lot via Crystal Wall and Lumberland. (See map page 342). All climbs except *Scorpion* have stations. Walk down on the right.

Sparkletoast * .7 10m
Glenn Payan John Thompson July 18 1994
A short appealing finger crack, the first route encountered on the cliff.

Red Kangaroo 10c x 12m
Glenn Payan John Thompson July 24 1994
A vague crackline about 15m left of *Sparkletoast*. Tricky moves low down then easier climbing above. Go up right to finish.

Tomasskicks 10b 10m
Glenn Payan John Thompson July 24 1994
From the main corner, climb a flake rightward to an awkward finish.

One Toque Over The Line * 10a 12m
Glenn Payan John Thompson July 24 1994
Climb a double crackline in the corner, then exit into another crack on the right over a lip. An easier finish takes the corner on the left.

Finger, Fist And Hand * .9 14m
Glenn Payan John Thompson July 18 1994
The fine crack on the left. A hard start, thereafter easier.

Scorpion ● 10a x 12m
Glenn Payan Graham Rowbotham Sept 18 1994
Start about 10m down and left of *Finger, Fist...*

Finger, Fist

ONE TOQUE WALL

One Toque

Tomasskicks

Sparkletoa

Silver Surfer, 5.11b
Climbers: Graeme Taylor, Sheila Sovereign

Octopus' Garden

One of the most remote cliffs in the Smoke Bluffs, it can be reached from either end of the Loop trail but has a long approach of about 10 minutes from the Neat and Cool area, a little less from Elephants Arse. Nothing but cracks here, so be prepared. Excellent stuff in moderate grades. Some descents are possible by rappel, otherwise walk down a narrow gully left of the cliff. Fastest approach from the parking lot is up via Crystal Wall and One Toque.

This crag offers what is probably the best collection of moderate grade quality cracks at Squamish, so don't have high expectations of picking your preferred route. If you gotta top-rope, this is one place to really give your karma bank a boost by being expeditious about movin' on promptly, or letting those who want to lead step through.

Electric Ball *   11b   18m
S.Young J.Campbell R.Milward 4/83 FFA: S.Young D.Martin 5/83
A sustained thin crack past an overlap. Belay at a second overlap.

Unearthly Delights **   .9   20m
R.Parker C.Guest June 1982
Climb the right hand of the twin cracks left of *Electric Ball*. Good hand jamming and liebacking through bulges above.

Root Canal   .8   20m
D.Jones C.Austrom March 1983
Start as for *Unearthly...* then follow the very direct fist sized crack.

Monkey Quotient **   .9   20m
D.Jones D.Serl Nov 1982
Start up *Root Canal*, then take the crack to the top of *Pipe Dream*.

Pipe Dream *   .8   20m
D.Jones R.Parker July 1982
The hand and fist crack which sports the cliff's only tree.

Octopus' Garden In The Shade *** .8   20m
R.Parker D.Hart May 1982
Super hand jamming left of *Pipe Dream*.

Edible Panties **   .7   20m
D.Jones R.Parker July 1982
The shallow corner crack on the left of the main cliff.

Call Any Vegetable *   .8   x   20m
R.Parker E.Cage July 1982
A diagonal hand crack, 7m left of *Edible Panties*.

Two overgrown, left slanting pairs of cracks lie 30m to the left of Call Any Vegetable.

Solstice Crack .8 x 18m
Ray Parker Chris Guest June 1982
Twin cracks, after a 10a start.

Crab Cracks .8 x 18m
Don McPherson Phil Severy March 1984
A short, left-leaning crack.

Just For Elise * 10d x 21m
Will Dorling Elise Hunt Damien Kelly June 1995
About 70m left of *Edible Panties*, and left of the descent gully.

When Mulhern Was Young 10a x 10m
Will Dorling Nick Watts June 1995
6m right of *Just For Elise* in the descent gully. Climb a thin crack beside a small dihedral.

OCTOPUS GARDEN

1. Edible Panties 7
2. Octopus Garden 7
3. Pipe Dream 8
4. Monkey Quotient 9
5. Root Canal 8
6. Unearthly Delights 9
7. Electric Ball 11b

BLUFFS

Respiration Rock

About 80m right of Octopus Garden is a small south-facing outcrop, nondescript except for a roof which is split by two cracks.

Coronary Bypass ●   10a   x   12m
C.Austrom D.Jones March 1983
The left hand crack through the roof.

Thorax Complaint ●   10c   x   12m
Jim Campbel Bob Milward April 1983
The right hand crack crosses the wider roof above a corner.

▮ *The next three climbs are in cracks to the right, described from the left.*

Hernia ●   .6   x   6m
Bob Milward April 1983
The right-hand of two cracks that join near the top.

Thrombosis ●   .8   x   6m
Bob Milward Jim Campbell April 1983
The left-hand of two cracks that join near the top.

Arthritis ●   .9   x   6m
Jim Campbel Bob Milward April 1983
Another left-leaning crack, right of the roofs.

Funarama

This usually quiet crag lies behind Octopus Garden, 5 mins walk up the Loop Trail from Elephants Arse and Ronins Corner. It is worth a visit. A bit scruffy at present, but more ascents would change that.

First Class *   .8   20m
D.Jones D.Harris April 1983
An attractive face crack, easy to spot from the Loop Trail.

Squatters Rights   .6   20m
D.Jones C.Austrom March 1983
Another face crack, just left of *First Class*.

September Song   10c   30m
Joe Turley Ted Marks Sept 6th 1992
30m uphill from *Squatters*, climb an easy left trending crack, then over a cruxy wave in the rock [bolt] to a horizontal crack. Traverse right, hands or feet in the fault to an easy crack and onward to the top of the crag.

Point Blank   .9   20m
R.Rybak K.Rybak Nov 1982
Just left of *September Song*, climb a zig-zag crack to gain left-trending cracks. Finish on the right.

Funarama   .9   15m
R.Rybak K.Rybak Nov 1982
A face crack just uphill from *Point Blank*.

Penny Lane — East End Gully

This covers the area between Penny Lane and Ronin's Corner. As the trail climbs up from the foot of *Werewolves Of London,* (the last buttress at the east end of Penny Lane) into the steep narrow gully which leads up to the cliff of Fern Gully and the west end of Ronin's Corner, these climbs are on the left above the trail.

Hangover   10d   x   12m
R.Suddaby P.Croft 1978
A nondescript, steep crackline on the left as the gully narrows.

Roving Band Of Quails   10c   x   12m
D.Mack D.Sarkany July 1985
The south arete of the wall opposite *Hangover*.

Slightly Overhung Corner   10a   x   10m
Joe Turley SamTurley June 1992
This short climb faces east at the top of the narrow gully between Penny Lane East and Ronin's Corner. 1 bolt and a #2 rock.

Spiderfly

This is a small, long-forgotten cliff hidden in the trees below Ronin's Corner, identified by 3 wooden hydro poles on top.

Spiderfly ●   12b   x   8m
Peter Croft Tami Knight 1979x
A wicked thin crack.

Something Short ●   11a   x   8m
Randy Atkinson Peter Croft 1979
To the right. Well, it's easier than *Spiderfly*.

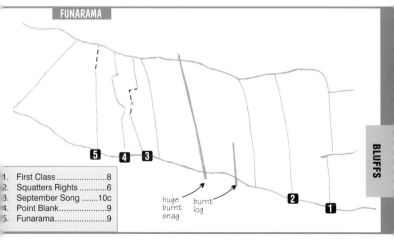

FUNARAMA

1. First Class 8
2. Squatters Rights 6
3. September Song 10c
4. Point Blank.....................9
5. Funarama.......................9

huge burnt snag   burnt log

BLUFFS

Pink Cliff

This is the prominent knoll sticking up behind Penny Lane, a clean little cliff also known as Politically INcorrect Kliff. Descend by walking off right. Climbs are described from left to right.

These two short clean climbs are on the west facing left-hand side of the cliff. Scramble up the trail to the base which also gives quick access to the top of the cliff. Belay well back on bolts.

Fidget With Your Digits   10b   #2   15m
John Simms Dave Vocadlo Nov 7 1993
On the west face of the cliff up an obvious slim groove.

Bolt It And They Will Come 10c #5   *SPORT*   18m
Ron Goldstone John Ohler 1994
Maybe. The sharp arete at the right side of the west face. Chains above.

The following climbs are on the main south-facing wall.

People Of Size   .6   18m
M.Desjardins J.Firstbrook Oct 1991
Low in the grade, even for a midget. Layback the left side of a thin flake, and follow the leaning corner above.

Vertically Challenged * .9   20m
M.Desjardins J.Firstbrook Oct 1991
Jam the right side of the lieback flake of *People*... to a small stunted tree. Face climbing above leads past 3 bolts on the headwall to the top.

Gender Neutral *   10d   22m
M.Desjardins J.Firstbrook Oct 1991
Start up a short corner, then follow bolts up the steepening headwall to join *Vertically Challenged*.

Pat On The Back   10a   25m
Jeff Thomson, Glenn Payan; November 1996
Start just left of the seam of *Environmentally Friendly*, then bolts to the top.

Environmentally Friendly * .7   18m
M.Desjardins J.Firstbrook Oct 1991
Climb the cracked scoop right of *Gender Neutral* to a steeper finish.

Free Range Turkey   .8   8m
M.Desjardins J.Firstbrook Oct 1991
5m to the right, a steepish groove leading to a tree.

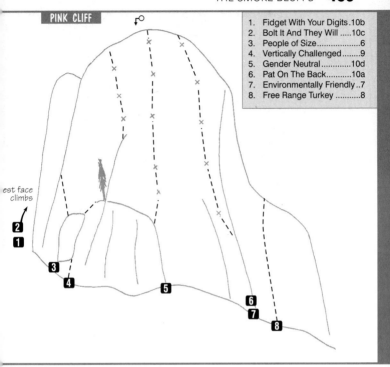

PINK CLIFF

1. Fidget With Your Digits .10b
2. Bolt It And They Will 10c
3. People of Size...................6
4. Vertically Challenged.......9
5. Gender Neutral 10d
6. Pat On The Back...........10a
7. Environmentally Friendly ..7
8. Free Range Turkey 8

est face climbs

■ *The next 2 climbs are on a pinkish wall 20m right. Scramble up.*

Wankulator   *   10d   x   12m
P.Beckham T.Holwill K.McLane March 1983
An excellent right facing corner. Start from a small ledge. A hard start leads to a difficult struggle. Small gear.

Deception   ● ☺   10a   x   10m
A.Ourom R.Atkinson 1978
The crack on the right.

> ***A Squamish story...*** *So what's the longest "I walked away"*
> *groundfall at Squamish? Nothing else even comes close to this*
> *one. In 1979, Paul Kindree soloed Diedre up to the last pitch,*
> *and finished off by a traverse to the right onto Sparrow. He*
> *slipped, and fell the height of almost three entire pitches before he*
> *landed on the treed ledge of Sparrow. Friends top-roped him out.*

BLUFFS

Fern Gully

A busy crag with several good moderate crack climbs and one heinous low-angle face route. Descent trail on the left of the cliff.

Dog-Legging .8 25m
Sean Williams Mike Pascoe Rosaria Mandaione Aug 1998
This is the slanting hand-size crack at the left side of the cliff.

Fern Gully * .4 25m
Neil Kirk James Molesworth Sept 1992
The prominent crackline on the lefthand side of the cliff: very appealing.

Tools of Moss Destruction 11b #5 **SPORT**+ 22m
Jeff Thompson Glenn Payan Aug 1996
The thin crack 2m right of *Fern Gully*, to face climbing. Finish left up a crack.

Rampage ** .8 35m
Neil Kirk Ernie Nomeland Oct 1993
A few tricky 5.9 moves lead to an easier crack system above then go left along a smooth ramp past a bolt and several scoops to the top.

Christa's Revenge * .7 30m
Neil Kirk Ernie Nomeland Oct 1993
Start on the far right of the cliff, then move left along a narrow ledge into the crack system of *Rampage*. Follow the cracks to the highest point of the cliff.

Hexxus's Red X's .7 30m
Neil Kirk Ernie Nomeland Oct 1994
Start as for *Christa's...* and climb directly up past a tree to exit right.

FERN GULLY

1. Dog-Legging 8
2. Fern Gully 4
3. Tools of Moss Destruction 11b
4. Rampage 8
5. Christa's Revenge 7
6. Hexxus' Red Xs 7

Up From The Skies A4
Climber: Luc Mailloux,   solo
Photo: Jia Condon

Ronins Corner — Left Side

Ronin's Corner is an eclectic group of routes on a series of cliffs along the Lower Loop Trail, in the southeast corner of the Bluffs. A Ronin is one who lives beyond the norms of conventional society, well suited to many climbers I know. The lefthand cliff, described here, is a complex puzzle of short grooves, blocks and twisting corners. Climbs are described from the left, starting at an obvious, clean, scooped gully 20m right of the gully at the east end of Penny Lane.

Free Spirit   10a   30m
D.Jones B.Kandiko March 14 1992
Cracks up the wall left of *Astral Travels* and a hard clip at the crux. Small gear.

Astral Travels *   .8   30m
D.Jones B.Kandiko March 14 1992
Step up into the gully, then cracks on the right wall lead to an obvious cracked groove left of the arete. Mostly 2-2½" gear.

Father and Son **   11a   #6   **SPORT+**   30m
Joe Turley Sam Turley July 1992
Start up *Astral Travels*, then traverse out to the right and gain the arete, which is followed to the top. Take a few nuts for the bottom crack.

Eggrolls Dude!   12a   #8   **SPORT**   30m
Greg McBob Drew McBob May 28 1993
Climb the obvious steep, smooth wall above the trail just past the gully of *Astral Travels*. Continue up the arete of *Father and Son* to the top.

Opening The Kimono * .8   x   28m
D.Jones G.Korba R.Korba March 29 1992
8m right of the vee gully is a steep corner with a cedar tree on the right. Climb it, and on to a good exit left of the summit block. A righthand finish to a small tree is easier.

Skyhook Logging   .8   x   28m
D.Jones R.Korba G.Korba April 11 1992
3m right of *Opening The...* climb a steep shallow groove to easier ground. Keep left above, climbing directly up to the tree belay.

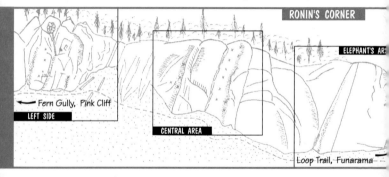

RONIN'S CORNER

ELEPHANT'S AR

Fern Gully, Pink Cliff

LEFT SIDE

CENTRAL AREA

Loop Trail, Funarama

Different Doorways   *   10b   x   25m
D.Jones G.Korba April 11 1992
Climb a shallow crack 5m right of *Skyhook...* to a delicate mantel, trend up left about 8m until below a prominent nose of rock. Turn it on the right, then straight up to the tree belay.

Daydream Believer   *   10b   25m
D.Jones G.Korba April 11 1992
Stem and lieback the right leaning corner. Keep left to another right leaning corner. Up it, then right again to a good ledge (Davey's Landing). Finish on the left or the right to bolt belays.

OAM - Open Air Mission   10d   25m
D.Jones G.Korba April 11 1992
Cracks 2m right of *Daydream...* to a stem rightwards across an over-hanging corner. Follow a ramp up left, finishing up a narrow chimney. Small RPs!

Prisoner Of Gravity   11c   25m
D.Jones G.Korba (2pa) April 18 '92   FFA: J.Bahnuk D.Paul April 25 1992
A tricky crux, much harder than the remainder of the route. Just right of *OAM* step up into a scoop. Climb with difficulty up a thin crack in the wall on the right. Continue up to a small left leaning groove and the headwall above.

Attitude Adjustment   10a   25m
D.Jones R.Crider April 19 1992
Climb a series of small stepped ledges for 8m, then exit left into a groove. Follow the line of weakness above to a bolt belay.

RONINS LEFT SIDE

BLUFFS

1	Free Spirit	10a	
2	Astral Travels	8.	
3	Father and Son	11a	
4	Eggrolls	12a	
5	Daydream Believer	10b	
6	OAM	10d	
7	Prisoner of Gravity	11c	
8	Attitude Adjustment	10a	

Ronin's Corner — Elephant's Arse Area

Just to the east of Ronins Central area is an impressively steep cliff facing across to the Squaw, split by a classic crack.

Elephants Arse Crack * 10c   30m
R.Barley C.Murrell 1980
Start at the lowest point of the arete at a really greasy corner. Climb it, and the diagonal jamcrack above.

Elephants Arse Arete * 10b   30m
R.Barley C.Murrell 1980
Start up *Elephants Arse Crack*, step left onto the arete and up.

Elephantiasis ** 10c   30m
R.Barley P.Shackleton April 1990
The hand and fist crack, starting out of another greasy corner.

Senate Seat * 12a   20m
Hamish Fraser Peder Ourom January 1993
This climb is at the far right side of the cliff, close to the Loop Trail. Start up *Terminator Two* then go out left to a bolt and up a thin crack.

Terminator Two * 10a   25m
D.Jones G.Korba March 28 1992
At the righthand side of the cliff, a right leaning crack leads to an arete with lots of variety and unlikely but easy moves.

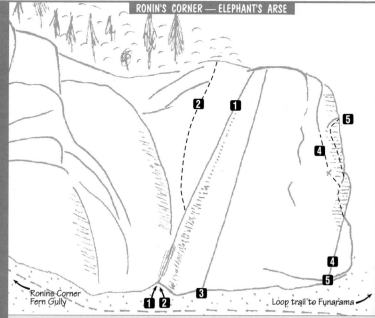

RONIN'S CORNER — ELEPHANT'S ARSE

Ronins Corner
Fern Gully

Loop trail to Funarama

1. Elephants Arse Crack 10c
2. Elephants Arse Arete .10b
3. Elephantiasis..............10c
4. Senate Seat 12a
5. Terminator Two 10a

Ronin's Corner — Central

The central area of Ronin's hosts an obvious series of deep corners and large aretes facing toward the Chief, and around the corner to the east is a large Elephant's Arse. Described left to right.

Deep Breakfast *   10a   15m
D.Jones K.Neubauer March 14 1992
An undercling arch. Step right above it to face climbing.

Ridge Runner **   .9   25m
D.Jones T.Ryan March 8 1992
The striking arete, a tad on the bold side. Excellent climbing.

Wobbler *   10b   28m
R.Barley C.Murrell 1980
Face cracks just right of the arete leading into a prominent groove.

Desperado   10c   28m
R.Barley C.Murrell 1980
Climb the arch out of *Magical Child*, then a slim groove above on the right.

Magical Child **   .8   22m
D.Jones K.Neubauer March 14 1992
The prominent cracked corner. A beginner's delight.

Dreams Of Passion **   11b   #6   **SPORT**   22m
D.Jones G.Korba April 18 1992
Directly up the centre of the impressive wall to the right.

Sky Dancing **   10c   22m
D.Jones K.Neubauer March 14 1992
Another fine arete. Dance up the edge as closely as possible.

MCM *   .6   22m
D.Jones T.Ryan C.Ryan March 8 1992
An excellent corner crack for the young, the old or the new.

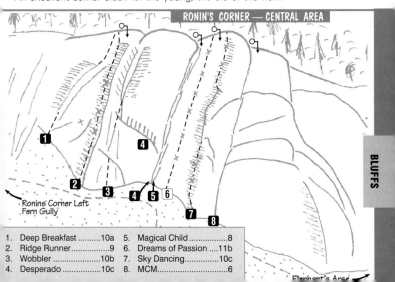

RONIN'S CORNER — CENTRAL AREA

Ronins Corner Left
Fern Gully

BLUFFS

Elephant's Arse

Cockburns

This crag offers some short climbs above and to the east of Call It A Day, and is reached from either the top of that cliff or directly from the Loop Trail. On the Loop Trail, the trail to the crag starts 70m up from Elephants Arse, beside a big snag. It is made up of a series of Pixie Corner-like prows and recesses.

Dancing In The Dragon's Jaws   10c   #3   x   15m
Glenn Payan Graham Rowbotham Oct 2 1994
The arete at the far left of the cliff. Begin in a short corner beside a big stump, then continue up the arete.

Fascist Architecture   10c   #2   10m
Graham Rowbotham Glenn Payan   Oct 2 1994
A short, awkward wall with a short, awkward crux on the right side of the gully that runs to the top of the cliff. Begin on a block.

Rhythm Of Circumstance * 10b   #4   15m
Graham Rowbotham   Glenn Payan Oct 2 1994
The central arete. Sustained and quite good after a tense start.

Primitive Cunning   10b   15m
Graham Rowbotham   Glenn Payan Sept 18 1994
Start just right of *Rhythm...* in the small right-facing corner, FP (crux) then follow cracks right of the arete.

Quest For The Perpetual Stiff Bamboo * .8   15m
Glenn Payan Graham Rowbotham Oct 2 1994
The fine arete on the right. Easy at first, with increasing difficulties. There is one bolt and one or two small nut and CD placements.

COCKBURNS

1. Fascist Architecture 10c
2. Rhythm of Circumstance 10b
3. Primitive Cunning 10b
4. Quest for the Perpetual......8

Call It A Day

A moderate-angled cliff with convenient top-rope belays, well suited to novices and teaching beginners in the far southeast corner of the Smoke Bluffs. Walk up the Loop Trail from Ronins Corner for a couple of minutes and you're there. A trail on the left leads to the top. The routes indicated are the most obvious leadable lines at a moderate grade, but many other variations are possible for the adventurous. The routes were established in May 1992 by Pam Cook, Lynn Gillespie, Chris Lawrence, Steve Smaridge and Graeme Taylor, who cleaned and climbed the lines while working for the Federation of Mountain Clubs of BC under Federal government funding for the Summer Guides Development Project. *Clean Streak* is so named for the lack of clothing with which the first ascent was conducted.

Chopper Malone .6 22m
A respectably pleasant climb. Worth a visit.

Clean Streak .6 22m

Buster .7 22m

CALL IT A DAY WALL

Chopper Malone

Clean Streak

Buster

BLUFFS

Cheap Mango Wall

A nondescript wall at the side of the Loop Trail, halfway between Funarama and Call It A Day. Much of this cliff is mossy and of no appeal, but at the right side it makes a better show where a 10m smooth wall sits above a mess of low angle terrain. These two climbs are positioned each side of this wall, described from the left.

Redug ● .9 x 15m
Dave Sarkany Maria Cundy Teri Pashuk July 1992
Follow cracks to a small roof level with the base of the smooth wall, pull over it and on up a broken crackline.

Salal Sodomy ● .7 x 15m
Dave Sarkany Maria Cundy Teri Pashuk July 1992
Head up right to a clean corner-flake at the right edge of the smooth wall.

Tunnel Rock

This cliff is close to the end of Plateau Drive in Valleycliffe at the point where the water supply for the District of Squamish emerges in underground pipes from a subterranean storage area. Walk down from Ronin's Corner until the cliff can be seen over to the left. There is a short road leading to it.

Go For Broke ● ☺ 10b x 35m
Ted Marks Joe Turley Oct 1992
The most obvious crackline 8m left of the road. Start up the hand size crack, which zigs right, then zags back left to the top.

**Jack Habrich the trapper, at his log cabin
in what is now Valleycliffe, behind the Cliffside pub. c1935**   Squamish Public Library

MOUNT HABRICH

Mount Habrich (pronounced Haybrick) is a striking 1700m alpine peak, 7km southeast of the Chief, easily seen from Highway 99 south of Alice Lake Park as a conical tower. It appears as the left-hand of a group of three summits; with Ledge Mountain (centre) and Sky Pilot (right). The climbs are in two groups; the southwest face in Shannon Creek; and the northeast face in the Stawamus River valley. Each has climbs of up to seven pitches, following crack systems of one kind or another with flaring cracks being the Habrich west-side specialty. *Solar System* is the only climb to spark much popularity prior to the magnificent *Life On Earth* (10c) in 1994.

The Southwest face on the Shannon Creek side of Habrich is a long-established climbing area with 9 routes. In fine summer weather, this face seems like a big crag, but in changeable weather its mountain character is quickly evident. By early May the climbs should be in condition, although there will be plenty of snow on the approach. Note that it can get surprisingly hot in mid-summer. A fast party could climb both *Life On Earth* and *Solar System* the same day. Most of the climbs take crack systems of one kind or another, many of which are decomposed in places.

Fluffy Kitten Wall on the northern Stawamus River side is at an elevation of 1000m −1200m and is damp or worse until mid-summer, so the season is short: July to mid-September. It is a place of long corner systems and cracks, at a lower angle than the photo may suggest. The primo route is the 7 pitch *The Wonderful Thing About Tiggers* (11a or 10c+1pa). From the top of the crag, it is quite practical to continue to the summit of Habrich up the Northeast ridge, which should make for a good day on the hill. A rough trail existed to Fluffy Kitten Wall prior to 1997, built by unknown climbers.

The north-eastern side of Habrich has seen occasional forays for many years, but little has come forth in the way of established routes. The first known attempt at climbing was in late summer 1976 by Corina Atcheson, David Harris and Dick Mitten. They attempted to reach the prominent dihedral (now *The Wonderful Thing About Tiggers*) at the right side of the face, reaching the Scratching Post ledge a couple of pitches up. The following year, Don Serl and John Wittmayer climbed to Scratching Post ledge via the chimney left of the present *Tiggers*, and attempted the dihedral above, but retreated off a pin and went out right to an easier line *Beggars* (.9). In September 1992 Serl, now with with Greg Foweraker, returned to the dihedral and they completed one more pitch, but were turned back by wet rock on what is now pitch 5.

Life On Earth, 5.10c
Climber: Julian Somers

Solar System, 5.10a
Climber: Robin Barley

Habrich — West Face

The climbs can be thought of as being in two groups: *Life On Earth*, and *Solar System;* and the rest which are long-established, adventurous climbs which see little traffic due to generally mediocre rock and often bushy climbing. But they offer remote character and enjoyable route-finding. The best of them is probably *Gambit Grooves*.

On a historical note, for many years climbers went up to try Dick Culbert's legendary climb of 1969 *The Nose*. Few succeeded, as that climb is not on the 'nose' proper, it is actually the south face, and many were taken aback by the 5.10 difficulty, climbed originally in big boots. *Life On Earth* is in fact, 'The Nose'. Its establishment is a testament to the tenacity of Robin Barley, who persuaded me to climb *Solar System* with him on a 35° day in the summer of 1994, hauling along drill and batteries and water, to rappel the true 'nose', to see what lay in store. We discovered that every long rappel down the great arete deposited us, just in time, on a small ledge.

Gear and Descent... The via normale on Habrich is the *Northwest Ridge*, an easy scramble except for its lower section, which sports a pitch or two of 5.7 - 5.8. It can be used as a descent, but most people choose to rappel down *Life On Earth* (five raps). Take double 50m ropes for all climbs.

Getting there... Until recently a 4wd truck allowed driving to within 2km of the trailhead, but since a bizarre Forest Service decision to blockade the Shannon Creek FSR, the approach is now considerably longer, so allow 3hrs for hiking, less by mountainbike. From the Apron, take the Mamquam FSR below the north walls of the Chief and turn right after 3.9km onto the Stawamus-Indian FSR. Follow this winding road uphill for a further 1½km, and turn right (400m past the bridge over the river) onto the Shannon Creek road. This leads up steeply behind the Chief (great views) and eventually reaches the Forest Service blockade 13km from the Apron parking lot.

Park here and continue for 5km on the road to the entrance of Shannon Creek Valley. The road up the valley is badly overgrown at present, but is passable on foot. At the large, obvious open area (from past logging) near the end of the road, head into the slash on the left and up into the heavy timber below the peak. Keep left of the gully dropping from the col northwest of the peak, but cross it eventually into open timber, then regain it immediately to avoid more cliffs above and continue, eventually diagonalling rightward to reach the centre of the south-west face. *Life On Earth* is a short walk over to the right.

West Ridge ** .7 ±5p.
B.Hagen G.Woodsworth 1965
This climb rises above the col west of the peak. Scramble up over small cliffs and ledge systems. Route finding may require some thought, especially in the lower part. The climbing is mostly easy, but most parties will rope up.

Cooper-Shellborn Chimney .8 7-9p.
C.Cooper R.Shellborn Oct 15 1980
Climb an obvious chimney system, followed by a gully, linking up to *Initial Route* after 4-5 pitches.

Initial Route .8 7-9p.
B.Hagen S.Pilkington A.Purdey D.Tate 1965
A nebulous route which climbs the broken, bushy area left of centre on the southwest face. Be adventurous and get lost.

Drug Stabbin' Time .9 7-9p.
W.Robinson C.Thomson 1983
Hazy details. Climb cracks above the lower, easy ledges for three pitches, followed by an overhanging block and a 5.9 off-width. Tension or climb left to a system which leads to easier terrain.

Diachronous Variation * .9+aid 7-9p.
R.Driscoll B.Fairley K.Legg A.Ourom 1984
A good variation on the previous route. Start just to the right and climb three good pitches, rejoining just past the overhanging block.

Gambit Grooves * 10b 7-9p.
R.Culbert R.Cuthbert T.Hall 1968   FFA: W.Robinson C.Thomson 7/82
Another nebulous route, although it is quite popular. Start about one ropelength left of *The Nose*. Climb 2 pitches up chimneys, and continue up slabs and cracks. A cruxy overhanging corner leads to a gully, beyond which is another groove and slab system.

Solar System ** 10b+3pa 7p.
R.Barley D.Serl Aug 1976
One of the two best climbs on the wall. Start just left of *Life On Earth Direct* and gain a series of flakes. 3 bolts for aid lead to an obvious ramp, beyond which are slabs leading to a large dihedral. The final pitch is difficult, an overhanging flake crack followed by a scruffy chimney.

The Nose * 10b 5-6p.
Dick Culbert Fred Douglas Alice Purdey Paul Starr 1969
This climb starts about 50m uphill to the right from the toe, and roughly parallels *Life On Earth* for about 3 long pitches before scooting way over to the right.

Have you joined the Climbers Access Society yet?

MOUNT HABRICH — SOUTHWEST FACE

HABRICH

Life On Earth ***½   10c   6p.

Robin Barley Nick Barley (Kevin McLane) Sept –Oct 1994
More direct variations: Robin Barley Don Serl August 1995

This is a superb climb, one of the best in the guide. The position is quite unbeatable on the huge, blunt arete overlooking the south and southwest faces, with the glaciers of Sky Pilot behind, good belay ledges and very sustained, exposed face climbing in long, long pitches. In the summer after the first ascent, the original line was straightened out, and a more direct line with better climbing resulted. All pitches as described are 45m or 50m in length. The climb starts at the right side of the face at the lowest point of the wide arete which defines the southwest and south faces.

From the toe of the buttress at a small swamp, scramble easily up on the right for 20m or so to a belay stance on a pedestal (4th). Above, make a few tricky face moves to gain the main dihedral. Climb it a few metres, then move left onto the face, past 2 bolts to the belay (10c). Climb the crack through a bulge above and continue up the decomposed groove a few metres until possible to move out left onto the face. Continue up and left past 3 bolts to reach moderate cracks near the crest of the arete. Where these cracks steepen, stem up into a left-trending groove past 2 bolts to gain a fine belay on the crest (10c). Face climb just right of the crest and continue directly up cracks on the steepening arete (10c). Continue straight up the arete, past a cute wire to a shallow groove. Tricky moves lead out left towards a groove. Up it a short distance, then step back right into a face crack. Belay above (10c). Go up left over a flake, then directly up a shallow crack to the headwall and the top of the climb (10b). The summit is a scramble of a few minutes.

Life On Earth Direct Start *** 11b (10c+1pa)   2p.

Don Serl Robin Barley September 1995

This fine variation lies to the left of the normal route, which it joins at the end of pitch 2. Start by the small swamp of boggy grass at the toe of the buttress, and move up on the face to a thin crack on the left. Undercling the roof above out right and step down to a good ledge. Belay to avoid rope drag (10c). Climb the dihedral on the left for a few metres and pull back right above the belay onto smooth water runnels to the first of 4 bolts, using one for aid [obvious]. Big knobs on the dyke above lead directly to the regular route (11b or 10c+1pa).

Pipeline, the long, 10d offwidth corner-crack on the Squaw is rarely climbed, but those who get on it can see through inside to Right Wing—the entire 100m high tower of granite is detached.

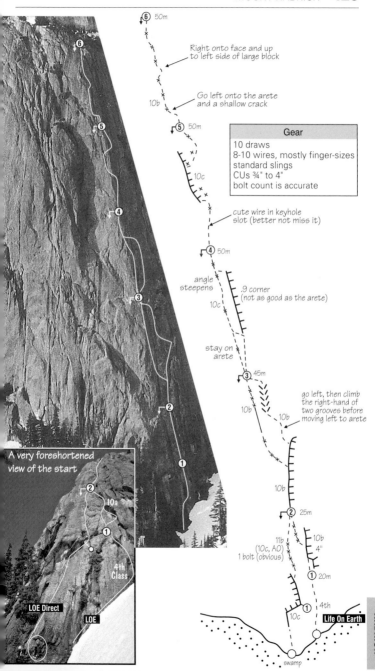

↓⑥ 50m

Right onto face and up
to left side of large block

10b

Go left onto the arete
and a shallow crack

⑤ 50m

10c

Gear
10 draws
8-10 wires, mostly finger-sizes
standard slings
CUs ¾" to 4"
bolt count is accurate

cute wire in keyhole
slot (better not miss it)

④ 50m

angle
steepens

.9 corner
(not as good as the arete)

10c

stay on
arete

③ 45m

go left, then climb
the right-hand of
two grooves before
moving left to arete

10b   10b

10b

② 25m

11b
(10c, AO)
1 bolt (obvious)

10b
4"

① 20m

10c

① 4th

A very foreshortened
view of the start

② ↓

10a

①

4th
Class

LOE Direct

LOE

Life On Earth

swamp

HABRICH

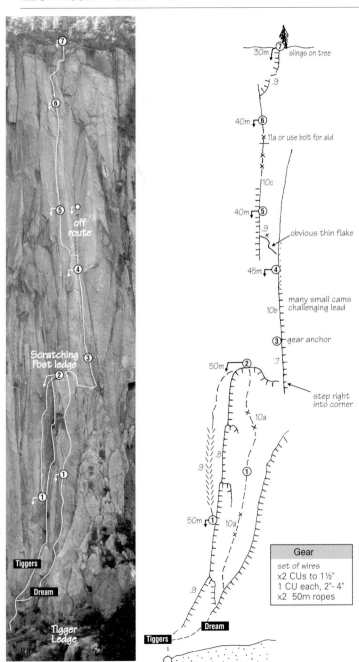

30m ⑦ slings on tree
.9
40m ⑥
× 11a or use bolt for aid
×
×
10c
40m ⑤
.9 — obvious thin flake
×
45m ④
many small cams
challenging lead
10b
③ gear anchor
.7
step right into corner

50m ②
10a
.8
.9
①
50m ①
10a
×
.9

Off route

Scratching Post ledge

Tiggers

Dream

Tigger Ledge

Dream

Tiggers

Gear
set of wires
x2 CUs to 1½"
1 CU each, 2"- 4"
x2 50m ropes

Habrich — Fluffy Kitten Wall

The northeast side of Habrich is a vast wall of steep old-growth forest rising to the alpine, featured with numerous big crags, virtually all of which offer difficult access. That, combined with the northern aspect and often damp conditions has been a major disincentive to climbing. Nonetheless, climbers have been occasionally active in this area for over 20 years, but few routes were established and an air of mystery has shrouded the area until recently. Quality climbs now exist, with potential for many more. In the summer of 1997, a small group of climbers, principally Brian Pegg, Robin Pegg, Andy Durie, Bob Yorke, and John Ford took aim at what was known as Stawamus Buttress, now Fluffy Kitten Wall, and developed several good climbs. Please see page 419 for more information.

*Please be aware that if you visit this crag,
you are entering a watershed.*

Fluffy Kitten falls within the watershed of the Municipality of Squamish, which has not yet developed guidelines for recreation use in local watersheds. But as is common in such areas within other jurisdictions, such as Whistler, please pay very careful attention to proper sanitation.

Always ensure human waste is buried at least 100m from a water source, 10–15cm deep, where biologically active top soil will speed decomposition. Burn or pack out toilet paper.

Getting there... It's about a one hour drive and hike, on a 2 wheel drive road with a few shallow waterbars. From the Apron parking lot, head up the Mamquam FSR below the north walls of the Chief for 3.7km to an open area. Ignore the road on the left (which goes to Crumpit Woods) and turn right 200m further, onto the Stawamus-Indian FSR. Pass the turn-off for Shannon Creek (Habrich West side) at 1½km. The first view of the crag is at 7km. Park near a prominent washed-out slide area 9½km from Highway 99. The trail begins about 60m before (north of) this wash-out. Walk down and cross the creek, (difficult in high water). A good trail on the other side leads up to the crag in about 30–40 stiff minutes. A rough trail exists to the top of the crag, around on the left side of the wall.

Don't forget the bug dope.

Gear and Descent... Rappelling off is best, although a rough and steep trail exists around the southeast side of the crag (rightside, looking down). Take two 50m ropes and a full rack of crack gear to 4".

Unknown   .8   4p.
Climb easily up ledges and a short chimney to a large bushy ledge (.6). Climb grooves and cracks up rightward to another ledge (.8). Up the corner above to bolts at the base of a dihedral (.7). Climb the dihedral to belay bolts (.8).

> *The following 3 climbs and several projects all start off Tigger Ledge, the large open terrace some 100m up and right of the trailhead.*

This Ain't No Pussy Crack   **   10a   45m
John Ford Robin Pegg August 1998
Start at the left side of Tigger Ledge and go up and left across an easy face to the bottom of a perfect arching finger and hand-crack. Climb it a bolt station. This is the first pitch of an incomplete project.

Pussy Galore   *   10b   4p.
p1, p2 Jay Foley Andy Durie September 1997
p3, p4 Jason Methot Jason Robinson and friend.
Climb up easy ledges left of centre off Tigger Ledge, then trend right to a clean finger crack. Climb it (10a). [A line of bolts going out left is an incomplete project]. Climb the dihedral above to a bolt by a bush (.9). Continue, moving left then up cracks to belay by a chockstone (.7). Traverse left then up a dirty finger-crack to a large tree ledge (10b). Rappel.

> *Two top-rope routes lie left of the first pitch of Pussy Galore. One takes the chimney at 5.9 (Michael Kosaka, Brian Pegg) and the other takes the face left of the chimney at 5.10c (Brian Pegg, Andy Durie).*

The Wonderful Thing About Tiggers   ***   11a   (10c+1pa)   7p.
Brian Pegg Andy Durie (1pa on p6) September 1997 FFA John Ford Andy Durie August 1998
p2 variation: Don Serl Greg Foweraker September 1992
p3, p4: Don Serl Greg Foweraker September 1992
This is the route of the cliff: long pitches and mostly natural gear. Climb easy ledges and a chimney left of centre off Tigger Ledge, to reach the base of a large left-facing dihedral. Climb it to a belay (.9). Move left from the belay to another, smaller dihedral, then move right to a belay station on a ledge at the top of a pillar—the Scratching Post (.9) [the direct line up the main dihedral is 5.8, *Serl-Wittmayer 1977*]. Traverse right off the ledge and down for 7m, then up a clean dihedral with a handcrack for 20m to a gear belay (.7). Climb the bottoming hand-crack above to a hanging belay at bolts. This is a challenging lead (10b). Continue up the crack for 5m, then swing out left and lieback a thin flake past a bolt. Traverse left from the top of the flake for 5m to another crack system. Climb it to a bolt station (.9). Climb the corner above to where the crack disappears and stemming leads past bolts to a ledge (11a or 10c+1pa). Climb the hand-crack above until an undercling out right leads to another. Climb it to a large ledge, and go up the dirty corner at the back (.9).

MOUNT HABRICH — FLUFFY KITTEN WALL

Scratching Post ledge

4   **6**

4

3

projects

top-ropes

5

6   **7**

2   **3** **4** **5**

Tigger Ledge

1. Unknown 8
2. This Ain't No Pussy Crack .10a
3. Pussy Galore 10a
4. Wonderful Thing 11a (10b,A0)
5. A Dream of White Kittens ..10a
6. Beggars 9
7. Lost World 7

A Dream Of White Kittens   **   10a   *429*   2p.
Brian Pegg Ian Sylvester August 1998
Start as for *Wonderful Thing...* , but move right to gain the left arete of the
Scratching Post pillar. Climb on past 2 bolts to a hanging belay (.9). Continue
face-climbing, traversing right past 2 bolts to finish in a finger crack and the
ledge at the top of pitch 2 of *Wonderful Thing...*

Beggars   .9   *429*   5-6p.
Don Serl John Wittmayer June 177
The right-hand route on the face. The original ascent was via the Scratching
Post ledge on *Tiggers...*, but a more logical approach is up the *Acheson-Harris*
route. Start as for that climb, then just below the main dihedral of *Tiggers...*,
move out right (see topo) and climb 3-4 pitches up to 5.9 to the rim.

Lost World   .7   *429*   2p.
Cornia Acheson David Harris Dick Mitten September 1976
This is a direct start to the long dihedral system on *Tiggers.* From Tigger Ledge,
scramble right up to a higher ledge system and climb in two pitches to join
Tiggers on pitch 3, or move left to end on the Scratching Post ledge.

MOUNT HABRICH — EAST SIDE

Fluffy Kitten Wall

Tigger Ledge

The fastest known time for a woman to run the Backside trail to
the top of the South Summit is 23 minutes 15 seconds, by
Genevieve Leger in 1998. She is a climber.

OTHER CLIMBING AREAS

Included here are a selection of other crags in the region where routes are known to exist.

Shannon Creek FSR

Getting there... The approach is as for Mt. Habrich (see page 421), up steep rough roads behind the Chief into the Shannon Creek valley.

High Country   A3   45m
Joe Turley Gene Smith Carlos Zozikyan July 1980
A steep north-facing aid pitch at the roadside, a few hundred metres uphill from the second of two very prominent large switchbacks above the clearcuts.

■■■ **WHITE ROCK**   ▬▬▬

A small outcrop of white granite is at the roadside near the entrance to Shannon Creek and sports a few climbs. The crag prominent displays a painted "15km" sign. The climbs are all cracks.

> *Dead Bernardo's Crack is an 11a top-rope crack on the left-hand wall*
> (*R.Barley June 1987*).

Fifteen Kilometre Crack   10b+1pa   12m
R.Barley B.Protsch June 1987

Nancy's   10a   10m
R.Barley N.Henderson B.Protsch June 1987

Emerald Frond   10c   10m
R.Barley B.Protsch June 1987

Easy Day For A Lady   A3   25m
Dan Canton Lisa Barrett July 1983
An aid crack on the west face, just right of a roof.

Crumpit Woods — Fern Hill

This is a small but interesting crag in Crumpit Woods, an extensive area of small summits and mountainbike trails east of the Smoke Bluffs. Take the Crumpit Woods road (see page 427), park near the yellow gate and walk in on the left along The Far Side–part of the famous Test of Mettle race course. At the top of the hill, after 10 minutes or less, a rough trail heads out left to the crag, about 100m.

Solitary Confinement   11a   #12   ***SPORT***   30m
Chris Atkinson Sept 1996
Look for the bolts—it's the only route completed so far, mostly 10a with bouldery-long reach crux in middle. There is a harder project to the left. 60m rope okay.

The Art Gallery

This is a unique west-facing crag about 2km north of the Smoke Bluffs with some unusual rock and a pleasant ambience. The rock, which is granitic in origin has been heavily metamorphosed and by quirk of geological fate is endowed with numerous small and large pockets, from single-digit dimples to two-handed holes, giving one-of-a-kind face climbing for Squamish. It is the best sport crag in the area for steep, moderate face routes. The first routes were climbed in 1991, but not included in the 1992 guide. Recent additions at a moderate grade, and potential for one or two dozen more short climbs make this crag a place of appeal and could ease some of the pressure on the ever more crowded Smoke Bluffs.

However, the area was closed in 1995 without any public debate by the Ministry of Transportation and Highways, who lease land in the area, so it is closed to climbing at present. The reason cited for the closure is public safety, as the nearby Gun Club use the crag and the entire hillside bordering the trails in Crumpit Woods as a back stop for their activities. This, to say the least, is a highly questionable designation of a public resource by a government agency, effectively enabling the Gun Club to expropriate a large area of prime recreation land for their exclusive use–at no cost–up to a kilometre beyond their authorised base area.

Alice Lake — De Beck's Hill

This is a sizable crag on the south-east side of DeBecks Hill north of Squamish. Drive north from Squamish Town Centre for 10km to Alice Lake Provincial Park and turn right up the Park road. After 1½km take the second turn on the right to the south end of the lake, about 2km from the highway, and park. Walk south on a dirt road and follow it uphill to the right, passing two obvious switchbacks to a crag. You'll know when you're there. 15 minute approach.

Escape Is At Hand For The Travelling Man   11a   #6   *SPORT*   15m
Jack Fieldhouse Remi Bilodeau August 1998
A short bolted climb behind a huge fir tree.

Unencumbered   10a   15m
Jack Fieldhouse (solo) August 1998
The corner immediately left of *Escape*, finishing at the same place.

Price Is Right   10a   #4   *SPORT*   12m
Jack Fieldhouse Sara Price August 1998
Continue leftward up along the tangled base of the cliff for 50m. Then head down below more rock, for 50m to a cascade-like wall. If this short face-climb looks to you a bit like a dried-up waterfall, you're right.

Porteau Cove

Some climbing was done in the 1970s on the smooth slabs that lie opposite the Provincial Park entrance. Very slick granite indeed, and no record of an ascent exists. Best to stay away, the highway is a bit too close! A climb was done in the mid 1980s that lies just east off the wide parking area north of the Park entrance.

Gymnastic Sisters   11c   (10d)   2p.
p1 Dean Hart Bruce McDonald, p2 Dean Hart Jim Brennan 1985
Scramble in from the right to reach a 6m corner with a hard start and a station at its top (10d). Continue up a naturally protected 11b/c to a bolt station on a big ledge—"easily the hardest stem problem I've done" says Dean .

Furry Creek Sign   .8
A climb has been reported a few hundred metres north of Porteau Cove on the small crag at the side of the road by the railway tracks. Pity it's fake rock.

Olesen Bluffs

For many years, climbers starting up the Backside trail have looked over to the rambling mass of unclimbed rock on the south side of Olesen Creek. Finally there is a route to look at. Walk up the stairs on the Backside trail, cross the creek on the footbridge, then immediately turn left up an open slope to an area of large talus boulders below a big rambling wall. Scramble up a right-slanting bush ramp for 15m or so, then go right to the base of a short climb, which in time may go the full height of the cliff.

Candle In The Rain   .9   10m
David Harris Helen Habgood September 1998
Start at the base of a shallow, right-facing groove, noted by pink rock and a veneer of bright yellow-green lichen. Bolts at the top.

Squamish River West Side

There is a vast amount of rock, with perhaps a half-dozen existing climbs, on the west side of the Squamish River–easily more rock than the Apron and Smoke Bluffs combined–stretching up to the sub-alpine slopes of Mount McFarlane. Unfortunately, there is no way of accessing it, short of a canoe or kayak. The District of Squamish conducted a feasibility study in 1998 to construct a pedestrian crossing near the Town Centre to what is a vast area of alpine peaks south of the Tantalus range, and the result looked promising, but at this time, appears uninterested in proceeding. Politics. Tell them what you think - their fax number is 604-892-1083.

About this guide

This guide was produced on a Pentium computer running Windows NT, using Adobe PageMaker, Adobe Photoshop, CorelDraw and Corel Photo Paint, and a 21″ monitor. In all, the final output of the guide amounted to 900 megabytes, and over 1,000 files were required for development.

It is now May 1999, and the guide was developed over eight months through the previous winter and fall, in my office between the Chief and the Smoke Bluffs. It was an unusually long and wet winter. The rain would hammer down for days on end, with a determination as if it would never stop. But it always did eventually, and the Chief would emerge again from the clouds, covered in snow.

The crags are dry now and the sun warm. Time to go climbing...

Special Supplement

March 2001

READ THIS

Beware: these are new climbs which are presented here as they were reported by the first ascentionists. Very few have had more than one, if any, repeat ascents and this information is by no means assured of accuracy, nor is it for the faint of heart.

This Special Supplement to the *The Climbers Guide To Squamish* covers new rockclimbs and first free ascents established since publication of this edition in June 1999, climbs that have been cleaned up and rebolted, and some grading corrections. Within the original 1999 pages, twenty-four have been selectively changed to update and clarify text and topos.

Information about new climbs and events on the crags have been taken from postings in the new route books at Mountain Equipment Coop (Vancouver) and Climb On (Squamish), numerous emails and faxes to the author, and many conversations. All comments and suggestions are much appreciated to help reduce errors and upgrade future revisions of the guide.

Of more than 140 new and now-free climbs listed here, about 21 are at Murrin Park, 8 at the Malamute, 58 are on the Chief, and the Smoke Bluffs has yielded, incredibly, 32 more. The Grand Wall is now all free, and with *69*, Squamish has one of the hardest gear pitches in North America. There are 8 new aid routes, three of which are major lines, and 19 climbs scattered around in other places.

Kevin McLane

Squamish, March 2001

CHANGES TO THE 1999 PAGES

MURRIN PARK

Valley of Shaddai (63)

Report All Poachers   10b   (65)
Tyler Freed, Kai Hirvonen; July 11, 1999
Climbs the obvious crack system 3m right of *Entrance Exam*.

Zap Crack   12+   (72)
Andreas Tayler Jeremy Blumel June 2000
Now free.

Em   11b   (72)
Jeff Thomson: 2000
Now free.

The Bog Wall (77)

Beyond the Bog   11-   **SPORT**
John Howe, Jim Hegan; August 2000
A sport route up the short, undercut arete up right of the crag.

Brunser Area (81)

Seams Easy   12d/13a
Andrew Boyd June 1999
Climbs the thin seam between *Psyched For Life* and *Fist*. Follow *Fist* to the small roof, clip a bolt on the wall above and pull roof with difficulty (brutal). Sustained above in thin cracks with good pro to a gear belay.

The Bro   10c
Peter Hiltner Jack Lewis 1983
A variation left of *Washington Bullets* which was not recognised in previous guides. Mantel into the shallow corner left of *Washington Bullets* and either climb the arete above, or move left to join *Sunny Boy*. A bolt was added above the shallow corner in 1999 by a party unaware of the prior ascent.

Milkman's Wall (85)

The Weak Link   10c
Colin Moorhead, Kai Hivonen; June 2000
The easiest climb on the wall, a rising traverse from right to left. Clip the first bolt of *The Pass* then go out left to the second bolt of *Horrors Of Ivan*. Continue on *Horrors*, then go left past the niche to finish on the final hand traverse of *Mr. O'Clock*.

Zoe Area (87)

These climbs are on a small cliff; Just For Fun Wall, barely 10m high, about 20m behind the top of Zoe Wall. Described right to left.

Little Monkies .7
Jeff Thomson, Glenn Payan; 1999 Possibly climbed before.
The parallel cracks at the right side of the cliff, the first route encountered.

Lost And Found 10c
Jeff Thomson, Glenn Payan; 1999. Possibly climbed before.
A thin crack right of centre on the crag. Pulling in from the left is easier.

Just For Fun 10d **SPORT**
Jeff Thomson; 1999
A pleasantly contrived route up the slightly overhung face..

Jugs And Jams 10-
Jeff Thomson, Glenn Payan; 1999
The lefthand line up jugs and jams.

Petrifying Wall (100)

Resist 12c
Jim Sandford, Kevin McLane; spring 2000
A good direct route up the cliff, a combo providing a new and better start to *Dead On Arrival*. Start just right of *DOA,* and climb the smooth wall past a bolt. At the base of the *DOA* corner, pull out right onto *No Surrender.* Climb it to a junction with DOA, and continue up *The Ghost.* A lefthand finish was also done near the top.

Above-The-Lake (108)

All Chalk And No Action 11b
Jeff Thomson Jack Fieldhouse (Glenn Payan) 1999
Immediately right of *Surveillance*, climb an undercling, jam and layback to a small roof. Take a thin crack above to a mantel. Finish straight up.

Don't Give Up 11c
Jeff Thomson Jack Fieldhouse (Glenn Payan) 1999
Start as for *All Chalk...* but make a hard move right above the 4th bolt to a finger jug. Follow the left-trending ramp to the same anchors as *All Chalk...*

The bracketed numbers ie (p78) refer to the relevant page in the guide.

Leviticus (110)

This steep, bulging crag opposite the entrance to Murrin Park and its clutch of one-pitch aid climbs up thin seams was largely ignored for thirty years. All things change, and over the last couple years, Andrew Boyd freed many of the lines, of which *Sixty-Nine* is now one of the hardest gear routes in North America, and *Leviticus* fast earning a reputation as a three-star 5.13a testpiece.

Sixty-Nine 13c/d
FFA: Andrew Boyd, Mike Mott; August 2000
Now all free and quite hard.
The route takes the thin seam of the old aid line on good but widely spaced protection, and was worked by toprope before its redpoint ascent. All gear was placed on lead, and early attempts resulted in a few 15m falls. It received a second ascent from Mike Mott. As an aid line, it can be climbed all clean.

Walk On The Wild Side 11, A2
Andrew Boyd, Dave McGhee; 2000
Climb to the initial seam of *Sixty-Nine* from the start of *Leviticus*. It has been top-roped at *13c*. Like *Sixty-Nine*, it can also be climbed on clean aid.

Hide The Hampster 13a/b
Andrew Boyd; October 2000
Another start to *Leviticus*, via *Walk On The Wild Side*. Gain *Sixty-Nine*, then traverse left into *Leviticus*. Good edges, long reaches: serious.

Nightmare Rock (116)

The first three climbs listed are on an impressive little wall about 30m from Highway 99 on the trail into *Hypertension,* all within 10m of each other. Some of them may have been nailed in the past, but no record was made. Described left to right, easy to find.

Road Runner 12b
Matt Maddaloni, Scott Cosgrove; July 26 2000.
A thin crack at the smooth left side of the wall. 3 bolts.

Uncomfortably Numb 11b
Eric Hamel, Luc Mailloux; April 20, 2000
A right-facing, stepped corner leading to a roof finish.

Final Cut 12a/b
Ben De Menech, Matt Maddaloni; July 24 2000
A steep, dynamic climb through overlaps and bulges.

Big Daddy's Ramp .9 (118)
Jim Baldwin, Jim Sinclair; July 1962
The initial ramp to the roof provides a good 5.9 climb, to a bolt rap station.

THE MALAMUTE

Lower Malamute   (139)

The Dregs   12a (11a,1pa)   *SPORT*   (141)
FFA: Andrew Boyd 1999
Now free.

The Real Dregs   10d (1pa)   *SPORT*   (141)
Robin Barley; 2000
Start as for *Invertigo*, then undercling right below the roof. Climb the wall up
its centre, using a bolt for aid halfway. Chains above.

Just Barley Adequate   10+   *SPORT*   (144)
John Howe, Jim Hegan; September 2000
A fun route at the right side of the long wall between *Chasing Rainbows* and
Fungus Razor.

Froggie Style   10c   (146)
Eric Hamel, Celine Gelinas; July 20, 1999.
Start as for *Id* then then follow a ramp out right, or go straight up the slab—
easier but more runout—to reach the base of a large, parallel right-facing corner
(.7). Climb it to an anchor with rap rings (10c).

Bust Her Berry   11d   (150)
Andrew Boyd July 1999
A linkup of *Berrycup* and *Dogberry*, as one 40m pitch.

Agonal Pitch 1   10b   (151)
Robin Barley; 2000
A new start from *Old Style* up a dyke to *Cling Peaches–Agonal*.

Underly Hanging Out   10c   (152)
John Howe, Jim Hegan; August 1999
A fine easier version of *Overly Hanging Out*. Start off Meares Island, (or make
a 50m rap-in from chains to this point) and climb to the crux overlap. Stay
low, and undercling right to a hanging belay. A long pitch (10c). Clip a high
bolt, step back down and traverse right until possible to climb the face (the
crux of *Survival Of The Flatus)*, on positive edges to reach a horizontal crack
and an easier slabby finish at the *OHO* chains (10b).

A new bridge constructed across the tidal pool at the south end now
gives easy access to the base of *Old Style*, and a host of superb climbs.

Upper Malamute   (153)

Science Friction   11d   *SPORT*   (157)
Jeff Thomson Jack Fieldhouse April 1999
Climbs near the edge of the steep face left of View Ledge, between *Slap And
Tickle* and pitch 2 of *Stephanie's Tears*; 18m.

Olesen Creek Wall (433)

Return Of The Grim Warrior   11c (A0)
John Fantini Robin Barley Oct 1999.
This is the wall above Olesen Creek, facing the Bulletheads. Reported as good.
Start just 50m from the Shannon Falls trail footbridge and climb a slanting
crack and hard face to a sloping ledge 35m (11c). Continue up a vague
groove system and bombay chimney, 40m, (11a). Take the easier face above,
15m, (10b). Up a big yellow corner and a 4 bolt ladder on the face. Follow
the overhanging crack to the top, 45m (11b).

The Bulletheads (172)

There has been a considerable amount of new route activity at the
south end of the Bulletheads, resulting in many bolted face climbs
in the area of the Slot Machine and Manāna Walls. For short crag
routes, this area is well worth a visit as an alternative to climbing in
the Smoke Bluffs; many of the climbs are quick-drying and sunny.

—— Slot Machine Area ——

Wanhella   10b   (176)
Steve Wickham Chris Joseph   October 1, 2000
On the right side of the 2nd pitch of *Slot Machine*. Rap in from the top of *Slot
Machine* or scramble up the faint trail on the right hand side of the wall. A
thin crack to slab, finishing at the top of the wall. 35m, small gear, bolts.

Dora's Delight   .8   (176)
Jeff Thomson, Kevin McLane; spring 2000
Takes the low angle face directly behind the top of *Slot Machine*. It passes
over the top of *Nuclear Arms*. 30m. Bolts and gear to 2".

Exfoliator   11b (1pa)   **SPORT**   (176)
Jeff Thomson; July 2000
From the top of *Slot Machine* this dark stained wall is visible just slightly down
and to your right (look for the bolts). Climb the face until you reach the last
bolt, which is used to pendulum over onto an arete. Follow it to the top. 30m.

Women in Comfortable Shoes   .9   **SPORT**   (176)
Jeff Thomson, Josh Lepawsky; July 2000
This almost horizontal climb takes a superb fat dyke across the left side of
the *Slot Machine* Wall. Start by a tree directly above *Coogee Crack*. 30m.

Stiff Upper Lip   11a   **SPORT**   (176)
Jeff Thomson; June 2000
Climb either *Arnold Grundlewimp* (gear) or *Women in Shoes* (sport) to the
Arnold belay in a wide, shallow scoop. Then follow the bolts up and left on
the thin dyke. 25m.

—— Manãna Wall ——

This long-forgotten cliff has undergone a refurbishment with the advent of Jeff Thomson and a drill. *Manãna* is the long crackline at the left side of the face. The climbs listed are all on the high-angle slab to the right, and share the same start. To get there, either climb a route on the *Slot Machine* wall and walk down a short ways to the left, or from the base of *Slot Machine*, go left and then up.

Xenolith Dance   10b/c   **SPORT**   (176)
Jeff Thomson, Glenn Payan, Jack Fieldhouse; July 2000
Clip the first bolt, and head out left to a station. Climb to a dyke above and continue to the top. 2 pitches.

Chassé Right   10a (10b/c)   **SPORT**   (176)
Jeff Thomson, Glen Payan, Jack Fieldhouse; July 2000
Climbs the first pitch of *Xenolith*. Continue to the dyke above, traverse it to the right edge of the wall, and climb directly up to the anchors. 2 pitches.

Shannon's Dancing   11a   **SPORT**   (176)
Jack Fieldhouse, Shannon Price, Jeff Thomson; July 2000
Clip the first 2 bolts of *Xenolith,* and then go right up the sustained thin face to a station. Continue straight up, crossing the *Chassé Right* and climb the wall until the bolts merge with *Xenolith Dance.* Follow it to the top. 2 pitches.

—— A Cream of White Mice Area ——

Several significant variations and alternatives have been established in this area, resulting in a fair bit of good climbing. *COWM* itself has been cleaned up significantly, and especially with the new lefthand start up the cedar groove, this sunny climb is often in dry condition. The cedar groove is 20m down and left of the original gully start (yes, the deep wet, slimy gully. Really, that's it. 5.9 dry or wet).

Eliminating Mice   10+ (1pa)   (178)
John Fantini, Robin Barley; 1999.
A excellent start and finish to *Cream Of White Mice*. Start 10m left of the cedar groove, and pull a fixed rope to a balcony. Climb a fin thin dyke, trending left to a wider one, then up to join the middle easy pitch of *COWM*. Climb the left side of the headwall above with one bolt for aid.

The Cat's Pyjamas   10a   (178)
James Friesen Nathan Loewen September 1999
Takes the arete just south of the last pitch of *Cream of White Mice*. Approach as for *Manana* then keep left up into a high recess. Follow a line of bolts up the initial wall and onto arete. 55m, 9 bolts and a couple of medium pieces.

Alegria   11b   **SPORT**   (178)
Jeff Thomson, Glenn Payan; June 2000
A bolted face/arete on the cedar groove's right wall, 20m left of the original gully start of *Cream of White Mice*, sustained slabby face. 38m.

—— Corazón Face ——

This is the highest-tiered face in the Bulletheads, dry and south-facing immediately above the top of *Bullethead East* (page 179). Interesting and occasionally exposed climbing. Climb any route to the area above *Cream Of White Mice* and then follow an inobvious, flagged trail up left to the base of the wall. Alternatively, grovel up the steep gully at the right side of the *Manāna* Wall, haul a fixed line, then go up and to the left. The climbs all start at the same bolted belay.

Ride the Bullet	10+	**SPORT**	(179)

Jeff Thomson, Glenn Payan; July 2000

The lefthand climb. Go up and left, and at the 4th bolt move out to a huge pocket at the edge of the face. Then go straight up, staying as close to the edge as possible. 40m.

Corazón	10+	**SPORT**	(179)

Jeff Thomson, Glenn Payan; June 2000

Start as for *Ride The Bullet*, but branch right at the 4th bolt, go up and right. Rap at 30m, or continue by scrambling up the low angle slab to the top. 30m.

Tonatiuh	10d	**SPORT**	(179)

Jeff Thomson, Glenn Payan; July 2000

Head out right, and then back left up a dyke a short way, before branching right up to the anchors. Rap, or continue scrambling up the low angle slab.

Dyke Link	10d/11a	**SPORT**	(179)

Jeff Thomson, Glenn Payan; July 2000

Climb *Tonatiuh* to the dyke and traverse it leftwards, to either *Ride the Bullet* or Corazón, and follow one of them to the top. 40 or 50m.

Tantalus Wall Area	(185)

Brain Damage	12c	(186)

Andrew Boyd Mike Stewart June 1999

This climb takes the spectacular big arete bordering the right edge of the main corner of *Milk Run*. From the base of the corner of *Milk Run*, head out right to the arete to a bolt. Use the arete until possible to gain the thin arching crack on the right. Sustained and strenuous all the way to the mid-height ledge in the corner. Mostly small gear. The 50m arete above is current project, believed to be harder.

Mouse In A Bottle	11d	(186)

Andrew Boyd June 1999

A face climb right of *Cannabis Wall*. Start 15m right of that route up a 4m flake/corner to crisscrossing dykes. Climb on to a chain anchor near the top of the 2nd pitch of *Cannabis Wall*.

Rock Loggers	11+	(186)

Myles Holt, Tyler Freed, Scott Links; June 2000   FFA: Tyler Freed, June 26, 2000

An alternative start to *Milk Run*. Start below the main corner and climb a zig-zagging, bolted line for 2 pitches to join *Milk Run*.

Freeway (190)

Freeway variations: High Octane 11b

Colin Moorhead   Kai Hirvonen   Sept 1999

This climb is at the right side of Crescent Tower, right of *Diesel Overhang*. After climbing the pitch above the Truck Stop roof, (pitch 8 in the guide), head out right on easy terrain to a hidden alcove and belay (.6). Stem a short corner and climb a roof crack to gain a hand crack on the south side of Crescent Tower, leading to the final chimney of *Cresent Ramp*. Take 2 #3 Camalots.

Freeway variations: Another significant variation was established by John Rosholt and Val Fraser. After the crux roof of Cab Overhang, avoid the hanging belay on the left and pass the next roof on the right (00TCU) to join the Autobahn pitch before the 2 final bolts. This makes it possible to climb *Freeway* in 7 long pitches if the first pitch in the guide is avoided, pitches 4 and 5 are rolled into one 50m pitch, and the *Express Lane* finish is taken.

Western Dihedrals (194)

Warriors Of The Wasteland 12b

FCA: Matt Maddaloni, Ben De Mench; September 2000
pitch 4: (Crackis-Mackis) Harry van Oort, Scott Jeffery, Mandy Kellner, Peter Holloway;Sept '99
pitch 7: (Pork Linker)   Harry van Oort, Mandy Kellner; Sept 1999

A new, 8-pitch route just left of *Western Dihedral*. Climb *Western Dihedral* for two long pitches (10c), (11a), to the base of the main corner. Head out left over cruxy face climbing to reach a crack heading up the the base of the long left-leaning corner of *Sea of Tranquillity* (11a). Below the corner, move out right onto the face past a couple bolts to reach a long, thin finger crack splitting the wall. Climb it into the top of the *WDihedral* corner (12a). Go out left across difficult face climbing past bolts to reach a belay in the first horizontal fault (12b). Climb up left to the spotted dihedral, and layback/jam to a belay out right of its top (11b). Climb up, then right across bulges and ledges, heading for the start of *Cloudburst* (10c). Climb it to finish (10d).

The Grand Wall (213)

A major cleaning event on a 6-pitch route between *Cruel Shoes* and *Exasperator* is underway in the early spring of 2001, and should result in a good 5.10 climb combining *Peasant's Route*, *Hangup* and then finish near the start of the long roof on *Zorro's Last Ride*.

Mechanically Separated Chicken 11a/b (215)

Matt Maddaloni, Ben De Menech; 2000

A new pitch left of the final flake onto Bellygood Ledge. From the ledge belay, head out left to a station below a big, right-leaning arch. Climb the arch, passing a loose block near its top, and then a bolt, to reach the top of the flake. Climb the last short corner to Bellygood.

The Grand Wall, Baldwin–Cooper   13b   (214)
Scott Cosgrove, Annie Overlin; July 2000

Free at last. The last link of aid on the *Baldwin–Cooper* route was broken when Scott Cosgrove climbed free from the *Underfling* across to *Perry's Lieback*. Cosgrove and Overlin climbed the entire route, including the *Roman Chimneys*, without falls.

The Penthouse   (222)

Mr Ciechanowski   10a   **SPORT**
John Howe Jim Hegan August 1999

The easiest route on the cliff. Start 20m right of *The Trimark Years*. Pull the roof on jugs, then climb without difficulty to the chains above. 25m, 6 draws.

The Upper Black Dyke   10c   (220, 223)
Kevin McLane, Sean Easton, Conny Ameluxen, Adam Diamond; Summer 1999

This 4-pitch climb has been sustantially cleaned up, all the old bolts replaced and it is now well worth doing as a finish to the Grand Wall, or as a route in its own right. It is harder than the grade in the guide, and a new 45m second pitch (Easton, McLane) has been added via a curving line up the wall to the right, past 6 bolts, regaining the Dyke at its second pitch belay. The pitches now go; 10a; 10b-c; 10b; 10b. The condition of the route may vary depending on rainfall, which will bring more stones down, and it is unlikely that all of the lichen will ever be removed. Be aware that the presence of climbers on this route raises stonefall issues for all climbers at the base of the Grand.

The Apron   (233)

Cha Cha Crack   13a   (235)
FFA: Andrew Boyd   June 1999

Now free: take several TCUs and small nuts: 3 fixed pins.

A Troll's Sonnet   10b   (237)
Brian Kuchinka, Brenda Lomax, Anders Ourom; August 2000

A direct, mostly bolted line that crosses the wandering central pitches of *Banana Peel*. Start just left of the belay for *BP's* 3rd (crux) pitch. Climb a cleaned streak, through a corner in a bulge left of the crux pitch on *BP* to the tree ledge; 4 bolts, some gear (.9). Continue with a mantel straight off the ledge, now to the right of *Banana Peel,* in a zig zag line up the slab past 6 bolts (10b).

The Passing Lane   10b/c   (238)
Kris Drozdzynski, Jola Drozdzynski; June 24, 2000. (Ed Fisher, Helen Habgood).

This climb is also known as *Last Exit*. Start just right of *Diedre Direct* and climb to the main corner (.9). Move right onto the slab and climb to a belay below the overlap. Cross the overlap and climb the slab just right of the corner to a station close to *White Lightning* (10b/c). Climb the narrowing slab above, and the direct finish to *White Lightning* (.9). Finish up the wall right of *Diedre*. Much of the lower section and the narrowing slab between *Diedre* and *White Lightning* were almost certainly climbed (without the bolts) in past years.

The Crossing   11b/c   (246)
Jeff Thomson, Jeremy Blumel, (Patch Hammond, Glenn Payan) March 2001
A fine, independent 8-pitch climb, right of the *Climbers Must Be Crazy* in its lower part, then treading a good line between *The Grim Reaper* and *Teetering On The Brink.* Remarkably sustained.

    Climb directly up a scrubbed line just left of *Critical Path* to a large treed ledge (11b/c, 10b). Continue up the open slab between *Climbers Must Be Crazy* and *Grim Reaper,* and belay below the left side of the *Snake* traverse (11a). Cross *Snake* then go up right in a rising line toward *Teetering* and a station (11a). Go directly up, crossing the traverse pitch of *Grim Reaper,* and on up the slab between *GR* and *Teetering* (11b/c). Pass the gentle bulge above at its right side, to a belay between *Anxiety State* and *Teetering* (11a). Climb up in a direct line to the headwall (11a, 11a). Finish right on *Jake The Snake* (.9).

Calculus Crack   .9   (249)
Recleaned: Kris Wild; 2000
This old climb at the left edge of the Apron has now been fully resurrected, gear belays and excellent climbing. After climbing to the forested ledge of *St Vitus Dance,* go out left to a bolted belay below a long crack system. Three long pitches; 5.6, 5.8, 5.7, lead to 4th class below Broadway.

Start From Scratch   10b/c   (249)
Kris Wild, Jen Reilly; May 17 2000
A 2 pitch direct start to *Calculus Crack.* Start off the trail to *Rock On,* and climb a groove to a ledge (10b/c). Climb a left-facing corner, finishing through a bulge to join *St Vitus Dance* at the start of the long crack (10b).

Karen's Math   10a   (249)
Bruce Stover, Kris Wild; November 18, 2000
Start at the far end of Broadway below Memorial Ledge and climb a flake, followed by a leftward traverse to reach the left side of Memorial Ledge.

Charlie Don't Surf   .9+   (250)
Brad Buck, Justin Peterman; July 1999
This climb is a direct start to *Pig Dogs On Parade.*

Blasphemy   12b   (251)
Andrew Boyd, Ken Sharpe, Kris Wild; 1999
A steep climb off Memorial Ledge to chains. 30m, 7 bolts and a small cam.

The best camping value in Squamish is at the

Chief campground, operated by the

Squamish Rockclimbers Association.

Squamish Buttress (253)

Both of the following climbs are to the right of *Heatwave,* which is just right of the crux 10c pitch of the regular *Squamish Buttress* route.

Progress Can't Wait 12a
John Rosholt   Hamish Fraser   Colin Taylor   August 1999
Climb the next crack to the right of *Heatwave.* A long pitch.

Gemini 12b
John Rosholt, Hamish Fraser, Val Fraser; August 1999
This is the most righthand crack on the wall. Jog left after 30m into a parallel crack right of *Progress Can't Wait,* and finish up there.

Sheriff's Badge (271)

A Fine Line 12b (272)
Jesse Brown   Brent Matheson   Colin Blenkinsop   David Sulina   1999
Takes the spectacular arete left of the *Blazing Saddles* corner. Take *Borderline* to the top of the 11c 2nd pitch. Climb the obvious crack above to a small roof. Surmount it and trend past bolts toward the arete which is climbed to the *Blazing Saddles* belay. Save a 1½" cam for the *BS* roof; 12 bolts, 45m.

Borderline 10d (272)
Susan Bolton   David Harris   Eric Hirst (alts)   July 1999
This climb has now been completed to join with *Angel's Crest.* Four pitches were shown in the 1999 edition of the guide. On the 5th pitch, climb an off-width crack past bolts, then move right and up the right side of a huge detached block and a possible gear belay on top (.9+). Continue up face climbing and several bolts to a station. 45m, (10d or .9+2pa). Go left along scruffy ledges for 2 pitches, and join *Angel's Crest,* with a touch of 5.8.

Posi-Traction 10c (273)
FFA: Matt Maddaloni   Ben Demenech; 2000
A pitch that climbs the slabby apron from the start of the big corner on the *Daily Planet* up right along the base of the wall to a junction with *Skull Fuck.*

Fortress of Solitude 12a (273, 336)
Peter Croft, Hamish Fraser; September 2000 (Dave Humphries, Greg Foweraker, Jeremy Blumel)
This is the long-awaited first free route up the front of the Sheriffs Badge, linking the *Daily Planet* with the upper corners of the 1976 aid route. Over a period of a few weeks, a new pitch was added above the *Planet,* moving left at the top of the big corner before the undercling traverse, up to the big roof; mostly bolts (11d). This now offers a fine alternative finish to the *Planet.* The 6 metre roof was crossed by a spectacular flake, and steep corners above gave access to the upper corners of the 1976 aid route. Of the nine pitches, four are 5.12, and the final 5.11 lead was climbed in mud and rain.

North-North Gully (286)

North-North Gully Approach

There is now a better, more direct approach from the Mamquam Forest Service Road to the *North North Arete* and the climbs off Astro Ledge. It is faster than traversing below the Zodiac as described in the guide, an approach that was devasted by windfall in 1991, and a huge rockfall in January 1999.

For the trail, park 1.2km from Highway 99, 300m before the Squaw parking area. Look for flagging, and follow the steep trail up the side of the North-North gully outwash, negotiating a few 3rd class bits before emerging into the upper gully. The long right-facing corner of *The Promised Land* can be seen above. A rough, exposed trail now heads out right (this is the last possible exit out of the gully), rising up to a high point overlooking Squamish, before dropping down to Astro Ledge. *North-North Arete* begins at the highest point.

The Holy Ghost Talk Show Hosts   10c, A1
Dave Ferguson Kevin Higgins Sept 1999
This climb appears to take the right side of the steep, southeast-facing wall not far to the left of the start of *North-North Arete*. The first pitch takes a "beautiful" corner with good rests and good pro to a tree ledge belay; 42m (10c). Climb a harder finger crack above to a dirty ledge; 15m (some A1, 5.11 free?). Climb the corner handcrack above, and go out left to gain a chockstoned chimney-slot; 30m (10+, A1).

The Squaw (289)

XTC Crack   11b   (291)
Andrew Boyd   Ken Sharpe 1999
This is a handcrack through the impressive 3m roof right of the start of *Godforsaken Land*. "Easier than it looks" they say.

God Forsaken Land   11+   (291)
FFA: Andrew Boyd, Mike Mott; July 29, 2000
Now all free. At the A0 bolt ladder on pitch 3, climb past the first 3 bolts, make a hard, scary mantle, then go up and left to an arete on runout 5.10, skipping the next 3 bolts. At the short A0 bolt ladder on pitch 4, climb straight over the bulge at the bolts: also serious (5.11+).

Skyline Arete   10d (A0)   (291)
Andre Ike, Jim Martenello; September 26, 2000
A fine couple pitches offering a continuation of *The Great Game*. From the bolt belay at the top of *The Great Game,* go out left to reach an arete. Climb it to a possible gear belay at its top. Continue up the wall above (3-bolt ladder for aid), trending left to finish (10d, A0).

Heliopolis

About 13 new climbs, totalling 19 pitches of bolted, low-angle face routes, mostly in the 5.10 grades, are currently under development on the steep southeast-facing slabs at the side of the Backside Trail, about halfway up to the Chief's south summit: all the work of Robin Barley. Development is expected to be completed in April 2001, and crag topos will be available at Climb On Equipment in Squamish and at the Mountain Equipment Coop in Vancouver.

Brew Pub Direct 11a
Joe Turley, George Hanzal; Sept 1999
About halfway up the trail to the South Peak, on the steep east-facing slabs about 100m past the arched boulder under which the trail passes. 9 bolts.

Raven's Castle (224)

Whatever 10c/d **SPORT**
John Howe, Jim Hegan; March 2000
Climb straight up from the start of *Joe's Dyke* pitch 2. Good.

Ladies First 10a **SPORT**
John Howe, Jim Hegan; March 2000
Move left from the start of *Joe's Dyke* pitch 2, then up a fault. Good.

BC Parks Rockclimbing Strategy
Cleaning Guidelines

All climbers should be aware of the guidelines listed below for new route and recleaning activities. They were developed in early 1999 by BC Parks and a group of long-time new route activists.

Number 4 is especially significant.

1. Minimise the impact of cleaning at all times.

2. Remove only the minimum amount of material, to ensure that the climb is safe and offers an appropriate climbing experience.

3. Remove no trees unless authorised by BC Parks.

4. Think carefully about the importance and quality of the route. Will this route continue to be used and does it justify the amount of cleaning proposed? How significant will it be to climbers for its length and difficulty?

5. During any cleaning activities, climbers must ensure the safety of any other users in the area. This is especially important when developing longer routes.

THE SMOKE BLUFFS

Fatty Bolger (346)

Where Is Roxie? 10d/11a
Jeff Thomson, Jack Fieldhouse; May 1999
A bolted line between *Rumours* and *Bumper*; 20m.

Ferrets Folly (347)

Rite On Jennejohn 10a
Kris Wild, Ed Spat, Jen Reilly; July 16, 2000
A 3-bolt climb at the right side of the cliff.

Beached Whale 10c
Glenn Payan, Jeff Thomson; March 2001
A short face climb, 15m left and downhill from *Ferret's Folly*. Glenn?

Island Crag (350)

Wall Of Nutrition .7
Robin Beech Fern Webb Eva Cameron August 1999
This route is described as being "about halfway between *Fissureman's Friend* and *The Anty Crest*." Climb handcracks and blocks to a good ledge, then up a slabby buttress to the base of *University Wallet*.

The following 4 climbs are centred on the *Fissureman's Friend* area, and described from right to left as they are encountered when approaching from the south.

Thirty-Something 12a
Jesse Brown, Dave Sulina, Brent Matheson; 2000
Start at the foot of *Fissureman's Friend* and climb the wall on the right, finishing into *Mossy Tongue*. Hard at first, then 11c above the ledge; 5 bolts, 28m.

This 11b
unknown
Climb *Gang of Foreplay*, step right and continue up the wall above past 5 bolts to the top. Sustained at first; 27m.

And That 11b
unknown
Follow *This*, then move left at the horizontal fault before continuing parallel to *This*; 30m.

And The Other Thing 11b
Jeff Thomson
This is the left-most climb at the crag. Climb *Gang of Foreplay*, step right and continue up the wall to the horizontal fault. Traverse left below *And That*, to reach bolts that lead to the top.

The Zip (249)

Five Year Plan .8
Robin Beech, Fern Webb, Eric Hamel; May 20, 2000
This is the corner at the back of the ledge left of Gaia. Harder to get there than to climb. Either: rap in, climb *Outside Edge*, or pull up a fixed rope.

Burgers And Fries (354)

One Bolt Wonder 12a
Jeff Thomson; 2000
It really is: on the west side of the large boulder behind a hydro tower, just north of Burgers and Fries.

All climbs south of *Lybia Sucks* have been closed by the landowner.

Boulder Gully (362)

Super-Baked 11c
Scott Likens Jordan Struthers; FFA Jordan Struthers. Both June 1999.
Start off boulders 5m right of *Supervalue* and climb the shallow corner above. Move left and finish as for *Supervalue*. 4 bolts and cams.

Smoke Bluff Wall (374)

Wet Dream 10a
Kris Wild Celine Gelinas June 1999
A deep corner above and left of *Laughing Crack*. At the fixed rope that leads up to that climb, tunnel under the big boulder then go up to the base of the cliff. Look up and right to see the corner. "Stunning", they say." Gear to 2".

In recent years , the short dirty corner above Laughing Crack *has been claimed by several climbers as a first ascent. It was done long ago by Kevin McLane, and that was highly unlikely to have been the first ascent.*

Alien Sex Fiend 11a
Jeff Thomson; 2000
Now has a direct, 2-bolt start, and the 2 upper bolts have been replaced.

Zombie Roof 13a (375)
This famous Squamish roof was redpointed by Andrew Boyd in September 1999, correcting almost 20 years of being never-really-free. All previous "successful" ascents had been yo-yo'ed.

Battered Balls (380)

Tattered Testicles 12c
Andrew Boyd   June 1999
A direct finish to *Battered Balls*. Gets cruxy at the last bolt. Use the station (replaced) as protection.

More of the Same 11-
Jeff Thomson Glen Payan
The thin slabby face above *Thin Wall Special*, a righthand alternative to *Two Desperate Men* (.9)

Neat and Cool (382)

Where Ancients Fear to Tread - Direct Finish 11+ (383)
Pat Delaney; July 2000 May have been climbed earlier.
Go straight up before the traverse, past a bolt. Maybe its time to let the ancients rest in peace, there is hardly a square inch of rock left that has not seen the hand of a top-roping climber, and various claimed leads.

Toasted Tits 11a-b (383)
FFA: Kai Hirvonen June 1999
Now free. The topo on page 385 is wrong, the climb goes straight up off the *Ancients* traverse.

Flaming Kangaroo 11a (386)
Andrew Boyd (solo)   1999
Climb *Kangaroo Corner* until possible to exit right on flakes and edges to the top of *There You Go Andy*. Bold.

Penny Lane (390)

Whorehorse 11+
Jeff Thomson 1999
Cleaned up, freed and now worth doing.

No Shit 11+ (391)
Pat Delaney (solo) August 2000
Left of the lower part of *Foot in Mouth Disease*, up a to a bulge. Short.

Another Bad Habit 11+ (393)
Rolf Ryback, B. Thompson; 2000
A harder version of *Popeye And The Raven*, between *Werewolves* and *Partners in Crime*.

Grumpy Old Men 11c
Rolf Ryback, B. Thompson; 2000
Right of *Partners In Crime*. Crux at the 3rd of 7 bolts. Trend left at the top, then traverse right past last bolt..

Octopus' Garden (404)

Electric Ball Direct Finish   10b
A couple bolts were added to the direct finish of this old Smoke Bluffs legend, in unawareness that it had been climbed sans bolts or gear by Guy Edwards in the early 90s.

McPherson's Fancy   11b-c
This climb, 300m left of the main part of the crag was abandoned long ago by Don McPherson; 4 bolts.

Funarama (406)

Unknown   10b/c, A0
unknown
A steep slab right of *First Class*. Low crux, bolt for aid and join FC higher up.

Futurama   10c/d
Drew Brayshaw, Robin McKillop; April 1999
This is up the obvious cleaned streak in the middle of the crag, next to a huge log leaning against the cliff. Try the direct start up a crack or mantel on the left, to gain the lefthand of the thin cracks. Cruxy moves near the top.

Funa-ramp-a   .9
unknown
Start 10m left of *Funarama* at an obvious left-right ramp. Climb it to the top of *Funarama*.

Ramapithecus   10b
Drew Brayshaw, Cam Campbell, John Ford; October 2, 1999
Start as for *Funa-ramp-a* until possible to pull out left onto flakes and up to the top. Small gear.

Ronins Corner (412)

French Toast   10b
Pat Delaney; August 3, 2000
Climb *Deep Breakfast* to the end of the undercling. Then go straight up.

Tunnel Rock (418)

Queasy Crankin'   10
Robin Beech, Eva Cameron; July 6, 2000
A bolted direct start to *Easy Skankin'*.

Easy Skankin'   .8
N. Lussier, R. Laverdiere; February 12, 2000
The obvious fist crack right of *Go For Broke*. Climb it, traverse right then finish up an arete.

OTHER CRAGS

Copper Cove (52)

Eleven new climbs have been packed in here by Robin Barley, and one by Drew Brayshaw, on the three small zawns which are passed enroute to the main cliff. There are 10 climbs on Tidal Zawn, the first one encountered, most of which are 5.10s with one 5.11, and 3 climbs at 5.7–5.8. Arid Zawn, holds one 5.11- climb, then finally Drizzle Zawn holds one 5.11-. They are reportedly interesting climbs, well worth an evening or two.

Shannon Falls (131)

A new trail has been established to the crag, directly from Highway 99 along the south bank of the creek. Dry and pleasant. BC Parks intend to close off the upper crossing over Shannon Creek.

Dirty Dicky .8 (134)
Jen Wasylyk, Bryce Bateman, Paul McSorley; September 24, 2000
Start as for *Cardhu Crack*, then go left up cracks, to a flaring hand-fist crack.

Papoose (123)

Ten metres from Highway 99 on the trail is a 20m cliff with two scrubbed cracks. Listed below, left to right.

Purple and Gold .7
Jen Reilly, Kris Wild; 2000
Unnamed 10a
unknown

Seal Cove (58)

Navy Seals 10a
Luc Mailloux Drew Brayshaw July 1999
Takes a chimney in a south-facing, overhanging wall at the north end of the rocky beach below the crag. Take a wide cam, and pray for low tide.

Fluffy Kitten Wall (427)

Several excellent multi-pitch climbs have been added to this cliff to the left of the *Wonderful Thing About Tiggers*. The climb marked as a dashed line on the far left of the page 429 topo has become *Cat O'Nine Tails,* to the rim, and *Cougar, Fee-Line,* and *Kitty Porn* all climb to the top station of *Pussy Galore*. This crag now holds a lot of good climbing, cracks and face. Descents are by rappel, on two 50m ropes.

Descriptions (edited) were provided by Brian Pegg.

Cougar 10a 3p.

Andie Durie, Brian Pegg; September 1999

Begin on the far left side of the Tigger Ledge, just above the last approach dihedral. Climb up and left across an easy face to the base of a blocky dihedral and up it to a ledge. Face climb above and right, pass a bolt, and climb thin cracks (crux) to the left side of a roof which is climbed on big holds to a crack. Belay 3m above the roof; 50m (10a). Climb slightly down, then make a committing step right across a face to a hard-to-see bolt. Go right past this and climb a long, superb hand-fist crack; 50m, (.9). Climb easy blocks and ledges to a sloping tree ledge belay; 30m (.7). Rap to the the the top of *This Ain't No Pussy Crack*, then down to Tigger Ledge.

Fee–Line 10a 3p.

John Ford Andy Durie; September 1999   pitch 1: Robin Pegg, Greg White; 1998

Start at the left of Tigger Ledge, same as for *Cougar*. Climb left across an easy face for 5m, then trend right into a dihedral to a station at the top of *This Ain't No Pussy Crack*; 45m (10a). Climb up and left, over a small roof and left into a series of splitter finger cracks which are followed to the top of pitch 2 of *Cougar;* 45m (10a). Continue up *Cougar* (.7) and descend as for that route.

Kitty Porn 11a 2p.

Brian Pegg, John Ford, Andy Durie; August 1998

From *Tigger Ledge*, just left of *Wonderful Thing About Tiggers*, climb easy ledges, angling for a bushy dihedral on the left edge of a large slab. Avoid the bushes and move up and right onto the slab and follow 7 bolts to a finger crack, and on to a hanging belay; 45m (11a). Follow the fine finger and hand crack to its end at a bushy ledge and a bolt; 45m. (10a). Rap the route.

Cat O'Nine Tails 10d, A0 6p.

Brian Pegg, Andy Durie, Robin Pegg, Geoff Williams, Cheryl Takahashi; August 2000

Start in a mostly dry gully 50m right of where the trail meets the cliff. Climb an easy chimney and ledges, then trend right and up across a sloping bushy ledge to belay at the base of a huge dihedral (.6). Climb up a little rock ladder in the big dihedral and step left to a belay ledge (.7). Lieback a flake, then move left up a steep corner-crack to escape from the big dihedral to a sloping belay stance (10a). Climb left-slanting dihedrals to bolts at the bottom of an oval face (.9). Climb directly right on fins to a bolt, past another bolt, then stretch left to a right-facing flake. Up past 2 bolts over thin moves with overlaps and thin flakes to a small ledge (10d). Climb the blocky right-facing flake, then step left to a thinner flake. Up this almost to the end, then right across thin moves to climb a hand crack to a belay (10b). Climb a left-leaning ramp then thin flakes, right onto a sloping ledge. Move left to a 6-bolt ladder, over a roof, then right to a hanging corner (.9 A0). Climb to a semi-detached flake with a bolt then up to a sloping ledge. Traverse up and right to a hanging corner above a vast exposed pit. Up the corner, then blueberry bushes to a tree belay (.9). It is possible to link the last two pitches.

Rap the route. When you reach the big sloping ledge at the top of pitch 1, scramble down and right (facing out) through jungle to find slings on a tree.

AID CLIMBS

Snow White   A4   (114)
Dean Lister; Spring 1999
Completed to the fault at the top.

The Seventh Dwarf   A4+   (114)
Matt Maddaloni (solo) Spring 1999
This thin route has now had a significantly harder finish added to it. Heads 0-2, short blades and LAs, cams to #3 Camalot and hooks. 25m.

Thunderbolts And Lightning   A2+   (142)
Derrick Horne (solo); Oct 1998
Missed from the guide: climb *Big Eave* then go directly out the roof crack.

Expect Minor Falcon Delays   A3   (194)
Adam Diamond, Conny Amelunxen; December 2000
Climbs *Deadend Dihedral*, and then breaks out right to climb a seam leading to a prominent eyebrow roof. Finish a pitch and a half above it. "Some of the best aid pitches I have done in Squamish" says Conny. *Deadend Dihedral* is A1/A1+ on small wires and cams. Part of this route is on *Slow Dyke*.

Bald Egos   A4   (324)
Conny Amelunxen, Adam Diamond; spring 2000
A major 12-pitch aid line that goes from *The Non Wall*, into *UWall*, then breaks out above the tree across *Drifters Escape*, into *Northwest Passage* and then finishes up high on the right side of the Pan Granitic Wall.

Bladerunner   A2+   (253)
John Furneaux, Patrick Delaney; October 2000
Takes a thin seam up the right side of the Kashmir wall. Two pitches have been completed so far, finishing just below the top of the wall.

Twice Fallen, None The Wiser   A3, .7   (278)
Andrew Boyd Mike Stewart June 1999
Start up *Well Hung Roof*, then takes the thin seam 2m to the right.

Something About Misery   A3-   (286)
Conny Ameluxen Brad Robinson June 1999
This a major aid route hidden from view on the southeast facing wall of the *Promised Land* in the North-North Gully. A topo will be posted in due course. 5 pitches, of which the 4th is the crack of *The Promised Land*.

I Shot The Sheriff   A4, .6   (337)
Andrew Boyd and company 1999
A full-featured aid route on the right side of the Badge up the first 2 pitches of *Cowboys and Indians*, then out right to cross the big roof, before heading up to finish as for *CI*. A topo will be posted in due course. 8 pitches.

Recleaning and Refitting

FROM: Kai Hirvonen, John Howe, Andrew Boyd, Kris Wild, Jeff Thomson, Scott Likens, Anders Ourom, Matt Maddaloni, Conny Amelunxen, Adam Diamond, Sean Easton, Kevin McLane, Ben De Menche, Drew Brayshaw, Steve Leader, Bruce Stover, Robin Beech, Colin Moorhead, Doug Woods . . . . . .and many other climbers.

CORRECTIONS AND WHOOPSIES

Elastic Man and ***Pleasant Pheasant*** **at Pet Wall have independent finishes, not
merged together as on the topo on page 98.**